ALSO BY ROB NEYER

Baseball Dynasties: The Greatest Teams of All Time
(with Eddie Epstein)

Feeding the Green Monster

Rob Neyer's Big Book of Baseball Lineups

The Neyer/James Guide to Pitchers
(with Bill James)

Rob Neyer's Big Book of Baseball Blunders

ROB NEYER'S

BIG BOOK OF

BASEBALL

LEGENDS

THE TRUTH, THE LIES, AND EVERYTHING ELSE

ROB NEYER

A FIRESIDE BOOK
PUBLISHED BY SIMON & SCHUSTER
NEW YORK   LONDON   TORONTO   SYDNEY

Fireside
A Division of Simon & Schuster, Inc.
1230 Avenue of the Americas
New York, NY 10020

Copyright © 2008 by Rob Neyer

All rights reserved, including the right to reproduce this book or portions
thereof in any form whatsoever. For information address Fireside Subsidiary
Rights Department, 1230 Avenue of the Americas, New York, NY 10020

First Fireside trade paperback edition April 2008

FIRESIDE and colophon are registered trademarks of Simon & Schuster, Inc.

For information about special discounts for bulk purchases,
please contact Simon & Schuster Special Sales at 1-800-456-6798 or
business@simonandschuster.com.

Designed by Ruth Lee Mui

Manufactured in the United States of America

1   3   5   7   9   10   8   6   4   2

Library of Congress Cataloging-in-Publication Data

Neyer, Rob.
Rob Neyer's big book of baseball legends : the truth, the lies, and
everything else / Rob Neyer.—1st Fireside Trade pbk. ed.
p.   cm.
1. Baseball—Anecdotes   I. Title.   II. Title: Big book of baseball legends.
GV873.N493   2008
796.357—dc22   2007049973
ISBN-13: 978-0-7432-8490-5
ISBN-10:   0-7432-8490-9

This book is for my grandparents, Connie Ivester and Gene Neyer.

I've never doubted a single word of your stories.

CONTENTS

Foreword   xi

Preface   xv

1903   Rube Waddell & Beans   1
1914   Bill Brennan & Grover Land   4
1923   Clarence "Climax" Blethen   7
1960   Tommy Lasorda & God   9
1977–1988   Ron Guidry & Willie Wilson   12
1991–2005   Greg Maddux & Jeff Bagwell   14
1933   Mel Ott, Ed Brandt &
                Walter Stewart   16
1915–1923   Ty Cobb & Carl Mays   19

SHOULDERS OF GIANTS
Taken from the Pages of SABR Journals   23

1952   Johnny Sain & Satchel Paige   32
1953   Browns Finish . . . Barely   35
1922   Browns & Yankees   39
1922–1927   Fred Haney & Babe Ruth   43
1918   Babe Ruth & Lee Fohl   45
1962   John Felske & Hal Jeffcoat   50
1986   Steve Boros & Steve Garvey   52
1944–1948   Harry Reid & Bud Beazley (sp?)   55
1969–1974   Mike Cuellar & Earl Weaver   59
1977–1986   Dave Kingman & Steve Palermo   62
1946   Danny Litwhiler & Suits   64
1973   Johnny Callison &
                George Steinbrenner   67

1977   Reggie Jackson & Billy Martin   69
1965   Billy Martin & the '65 Twins   72
1965   Maury Wills & 150 Steals   76
1975–1988   Fred Lynn   79
1952–1956   Billy Martin & Jackie Robinson   82
1977–1979   Thurman Munson & Carlton Fisk   85
1936   Dick Bartell & Cy Pfirman   89
1985   Ron Oester & .300   92
1929   Doc Cramer & Joe Vosmik   95
1918   Edd Roush & Zack Wheat   99
1952   Harvey Haddix & Hank Sauer   105
1958   Feller's Lost His Fastball   108
1946   Gene Benson & Johnny Berardino   113
1936–1938   Lou Gehrig & the Impostor   118
1947   The Death of Bob Feller's Fastball   121
1940   Bob Feller & Birdie Tebbetts   123
1956–1957   Ted Williams & Tommy Byrne   126
1961   Don Drysdale & Frank Robinson   131
1956–1957   Willie Mays & Sal Maglie   135
1970–1972   Willie McCovey & Willie Mays   139
1971   J. R. Richard & Willie Mays   141
1971–1972   Mazeroski & Clemente   143

THE GLORY OF HIS EDITING
The Hidden Genius of Lawrence S. Ritter   146

1913–1917   Honus Wagner & the Youngster   153
1906–1933   Cy Rigler & John McGraw   158
1916–1918   Hal Chase Tries to Throw One . . .   161

1928	John McGraw & "Buck Lai"	164
1930–1932	Jimmie Reese & Jewish Yankees	170
1965	Don Drysdale & Walt Alston	173
1959	Joe Taylor & Charlie Metro	175
1970	Joe Foy & Gil Hodges	178
1947–1948	Rex Barney & Burt Shotton	181
1939	Leo Durocher & Red Evans	185
1930	Leo Durocher & Ed Barrow (& Babe Ruth's Watch?)	189
1926	Pete Alexander & Joe McCarthy	195
1943–1953	Gerry Priddy & the Yankees	198
1932–1941	Joe McCarthy & Rookies	200
1940	Johnny Babich & the Yankees	204
1947	Vic Raschi & Jim Turner	208
1958	Casey Stengel & Virgil Trucks	211
1985–1990	Whitey Herzog & Roger Craig	215
1906	Frank Chance & Jack Harper	219
1967–1969	Johnny Bench & Gerry Arrigo	222
1965–1973	Sonny Siebert & Danny Cater	224
1926	George Uhle & Babe Ruth	226

1932 WORLD SERIES

When the Babe Did . . . Something	230
1934–1941	Bobo Newsom & Lefty Grove	241
1923–1924	Walter Mails & Jim Poole	246
1934	Dizzy Dean & Cincinnati	249
1932	Dizzy Dean & John McGraw	253
1960	Lou Boudreau & Ron Santo	257
1954	Alvin Dark & the Giants	260
1949	Yogi Berra	263
1960–1972	Bob Gibson & Tommy Davis	267
1924	Dazzy Vance & Rogers Hornsby	270
1970–1971	Denny Riddleberger & Boog Powell	273
1957–1965	Steve Dalkowski & Ted Williams	275
1946	Joe Tepsic & the Dodgers	278
1939	Pie Traynor & Cy Blanton	284
1967	Hawk Harrelson & the Orioles	286
1930	Al Simmons	289
1940	Luke Appling & Red Ruffing	291
1936	Babe Phelps & Van Lingle Mungo	293
1957–1959	Juan Pizarro & Fred Haney	295
1986	Dwight Gooden & George Foster	299
1928–1934	Paul Waner & Pat Malone	302
1966	Jimmy Wynn & Willie Stargell	306
Notes	309
Thank You Thank You Thank You	317
Index	319

ROB NEYER'S

BIG BOOK OF

BASEBALL
LEGENDS

FOREWORD

by Bill James

I have always been fascinated by the notion that for thousands of years humans had absolutely no knowledge that there had ever been such a thing as a dinosaur. Even when I was a kid in the middle of the twentieth century, dinosaurs were kind of a remote concept. We were taught in grade school that they had all killed each other off in gun battles and then miraculously liquefied into gasoline, which at that time was like twenty-nine cents a gallon because dinosaurs were huge. Nowadays, though, your average four-year-old has 208 little plastic replicas of different kinds of dinosaurs and knows the names of nineteen different species before he goes to kindergarten.

"Mommy, have you seen my stegosaurus?"

"Which one is that, dear?"

"You know, the stegosaurus. It's green, it has these things that stick up off its back. Looks kinda like a centrosaurus."

"Is that the one in the bathroom?"

"*Mom!* That's a *triceratops*. It doesn't look anything *like* a stegosaurus."

To the people who first realized that these overgrown armadillos had once roamed the earth and downtown Cleveland, the extent to which this knowledge has grown and spread throughout our culture would be beyond comprehension. It is such a strange idea, that knowledge of the past can be created—and yet it can be and is every day.

We used to call these Tracers . . . I don't know what Rob is calling them now. We'd pick up a story in an old book or out of an old newspaper, occasionally by interviewing an old ballplayer, and we'd try to backtrack on it, find out what had really happened, back when dinosaurs roamed the box scores. This was before Retrosheet, before you could search through 10 million old newspapers on the Internet. This was before the Internet, really, before the Internet had escaped from Al Gore's dungeon and invaded our living rooms, waving pictures of naked college girls. It was hard work, in those days, to figure out whether something had really happened. A lot of times you could narrow a story down to three or four seasons, figure that it had to have happened when the Browns were playing the Tigers, make up a list of seventy or eighty games, and head for the microfilm library. You'd be there for several days.

Organized knowledge about baseball's past has exploded so phenomenally, in the last twenty years, that to backtrack on most anecdotes no longer qualifies as research. I work in baseball now. Occasionally I run into some old ballplayer who has no idea how easy it is to check these things out, and he tells me about the time he threw out three runners at third base in the same game, or the time he hit a grand slam off of Mickey Lolich in Shea Stadium just before a cloudburst would have sent everybody home drenched but still tied. By "occasionally" I mean about three times a week. Pricking their bubbles would be rude. Any-one who owns a computer can now find out in seconds things about Bob Gibson in 1968 that Bob Gibson himself didn't know at the time, couldn't have dreamed of knowing.

This explosion of knowledge about the past, roaring up from behind us, exposes every exaggeration, every fictionalization, every enhancement, every substitution. It's a little sad. Paper-thin lies, once protected by layers of darkness, are now transparent in the glare. We know now that it wasn't Mickey Mantle in the batter's box, it was Roger Repoz, and it wasn't the ninth inning, it was the fourth, and the bases weren't loaded, and the score wasn't tied, and the frog did not become a prince.

Accuracy is a prickly concept for the modern quasi-journalist. Every-body is certain that he is more accurate than the other guy is. God forbid that anyone should think that I am speaking against accuracy in journalism, but something is happening here that borders on being unnatural. Journal-ism is mushrooming, enveloping things that for decades were more along the lines of gossip and reminiscence. "Journalists" a hundred years ago . . . and did the concept of a "journalist" even exist then? . . . journalists put things in the newspaper that were never quite meant to be taken as entirely true. Everybody understood that this was just supposed to be a good story.

My first memories are set in a small-town cream station where old men entertained one another for hours with retold yarns about absent and long-dead neighbors. The concept of an entertaining yarn—in print, no less—is almost incomprehensible now, as incomprehensible as the Internet would have been to those old, ash-gray men who remembered Teddy Roosevelt and still had strong opinions about him and didn't have working radios. The academics have won. The standards of accuracy that began in academia have been embraced by paid reporters and have now spread to the limitless legions of dignified researchers, pounding out accurate if boring biogra-phies about absent and long-dead heroes.

And I'm not saying that that's a bad thing, you know? Dinosaurs are more interesting than unicorns. I don't even read fiction; history is always more interesting. I am just saying . . . something humanizing and indefinable has been lost in the search for the truth—lost or, worse yet, thrown away. For thousands of years men made slightly heroic fiction out of their own petty lives. You can't get away with that anymore.

At a certain level, the pursuit of accuracy can be a very destructive process. I have spent most of my life trying to learn as much as I can about baseball history. I've gotten a little bit of this down on paper, but I'm getting old, and when I die, all of the rest will be lost. It's frustrating. I wish I could get more down on paper, but it takes so long to be sure you've got the facts right.

A lot of the old guys, they didn't worry about that . . . they just wrote down what they remembered and called it right, and who's going to argue. In a certain sense I envy them, and in a certain sense, they had it right. Accuracy is a nasty concept, a bristle-wire toothbrush that strips off the plaque and the enamel and cuts right into the tooth.

There's an ongoing effort now to accumulate "biographies" about everybody who has played in the major leagues. I'm all for it, and not for all the tea in Chinatown would I speak ill of the effort. It's just that . . . well, there is a problem with the entries, and the problem is accuracy. The problem is not that they're inaccurate; the problem is that they are compulsively accurate. You're reading the biography of a man, you want to get at his essence. What was it that made him tick? How was he different from other men? What made him the way he was? What did he truly love, and what was he afraid of?

These are not questions that are amenable to accuracy. They require speculation, conjecture, whatever you want to call it. They require that you look at a variety of events involving the man and draw some conclusion. This requires a certain audacity—even a certain amount of arrogance. It requires that you say what you think is true, even though there is no way for anyone to prove that it is true.

I don't mean to make excuses for the old writers, who sometimes told stories about players without worrying about veracity or even verisimilitude. I don't want to make excuses for them; I want to go beyond that, and to actually defend them.

Telling stories about players is, sometimes, a way of trying to get the essence of the man. Anecdotes are snapshots of a personality. We don't carry around every detail of the past in our minds. We don't always remember whether it was Tuesday or Saturday, whether it was the seventh inning or the twelfth, whether it was Bill Lee on the mound or some other goofball.

But we do remember *personalities*. We remember the people that we have worked with and lived with and loved a little bit, and we want to share those personalities with those who haven't had the opportunity. This is natural and human—just as it is natural and human to forget the details. That a story is misplaced in time and space does not make it untrue on a certain level.

In the movie *Shattered Glass*—I think that's the one; you'll have to forgive me if I've mixed it up with some other movie—a scene at the end gets at the same point. The movie is about the meteoric career of a young reporter who shot to the top of his profession in a few years by just making shit up. When he is finally exposed as a fraud (in the movie), one of his old colleagues has to interview him about his own story.

"Is that true?" asks the colleague.

"No," says Stephen Glass. "But it's accurate."

A little research reveals that James did indeed mix up the movies in his head. That scene is actually from Absence of Malice, *but this is an understandable mistake because Stephen Glass looks so much like Sally Field.*

PREFACE

Pay Heed, All Ye Who Enter . . .

Every year they die. You see an old fellow at the All-Star Game, or at the World Series, or in the South, or hanging at the winter meetings, and they lie to you, and the next thing you read in the paper where they are dead, old fellows not so many years before slim and fast, with a quick eye and great power, and all of a sudden they are dead and you are glad you did not wreck their story for them with the straight facts.

—Henry Wiggen in *Bang the Drum Slowly* (1956)

This book isn't for everybody.

Seriously.

Most of my other books have been intended for just about anyone who cares enough about baseball to want to read a book on the subject. Granted, some might find my usual approach too analytical. Egg-headed, even. But there were things in those books for even the most traditional, the most conservative, even the most reactionary of baseball lovers.

This book, though? Some poor guy is going to get this book, probably as a Father's Day gift, and despise every word before giving up in disgust. Because I've done something in this book that some will find sacrilegious.

I've checked.

I've checked the stories.

Oh, not all of them. There are so many thousands of baseball stories in the literature that I couldn't check all of them if I'd started when I was eighteen and lived to be one hundred. But I'm checking some of my favorites, and probably some of your favorites, too.

Why would I want to do this? Why would I want to take the chance—and as I've discovered, usually it's a real good chance—of discovering a story's not accurate, and perhaps shattering the long- and affectionately held illusions of a credulous public?

Because I think the truth is just as interesting as the myth. Actually, I think the myth is plenty interesting by itself, because of course every myth contains a kernel of truth (or so we've been told). But when you pile some literal truth on top of the truthiness? Delicious as frosting on a sugar cookie.

There's another reason to check.

Three years ago Jose Canseco published his memoirs to some fanfare. In his book, Canseco offered a great number of accusations. As we read them, though, should we have attached any credibility at all to an author who came up with whoppers like this one?

But I remember as a Cuban kid in the A's farm system . . . I was very aware that baseball was closed to a young Latino like me. That was only twenty-three years ago, but for baseball it was a completely different era. There were no Cuban players at the major-league level at that time.

Closed to a young Latino? Canseco joined the Oakland organization in 1982. At that time, Cuban-born Tony Perez was still five years from retirement. Cubans Bert Campaneris, Jose Cardenal, and Luis Tiant all were stalwarts in the 1970s. And that's only a few of the Cubans, to say nothing of all the Venezuelans and Dominicans who began invigorating the game in the 1950s and haven't stopped since. Baseball, closed to a young Latino in the 1980s? Please.

Here's Canseco on the trade that sent him from the Devil Rays to the Yankees in 2000:

> It was the first time in my career that I was completely, 100 percent healthy. I could have helped out the organization with my bat and carried the team—but I wasn't getting to play . . . The few times they did get me some at-bats, the Yankees put me in the outfield, even though I hadn't played out there in I don't know how long.

Not exactly. In his seven weeks with the Yankees, Canseco played in thirty-seven games—that is, most of the Yankees' games—and in most of them as the DH. He appeared in the outfield only five times. As I wrote in a review of *Juiced*, "Basically, whenever Mr. Canseco strays into charted territory, he gets lost."

In any event, of course, it seems that Canseco's headline-grabbing accusations of steroid use—his forays into *uncharted* territory—really weren't so misguided after all. But just imagine how seriously Canseco would have been taken in 2005, nearly two years *before* the Mitchell Report, if he'd just gotten the *easy stuff right*. But he didn't get the easy stuff right, so we had to wonder about the hard stuff.

So that's one reason to check: the things we can check may tell us a great deal about the things we cannot check. Another reason: it's a lot of fun. At least for me.

Here's my advice. If you received this book as a gift and aren't interested in what *really* happened, then skip those parts. It's pretty obvious where the stories stop and the objective truth starts, and there should be enough stories to keep you going for a while, all by themselves.

Within these pages, you'll find an amazing story about Bill Mazeroski's faith in Roberto Clemente's powerful throwing arm. Whether or not the

yelled: "The end of the world is coming and we will all be destroyed."

An ambulance summoned to the supposed fire conveyed the demented man to his home. The ton of beans proved a total loss.

That was Charlie Dryden's story, and Harry Davis stuck to it for many a year.

—Ira L. Smith, *Baseball's Famous First Basemen* (1956)

Before you ask, let me tell you: that clipping from the *Philadelphia North American* is absolutely legitimate. Still, doesn't it seem just a bit outlandish?

But Harry Davis sure enjoyed telling it, and Ira L. Smith obviously enjoyed repeating it (though with a small wink, at the end). In *The National Pastime* #25, a SABR (Society for American Baseball Research) annual, Tim Wiles—for many years the director of research at the Hall of Fame—recounted the story (apparently without a wink). Wiles had found the story in Michael Gershman's book *Diamonds* (1993), a highly regarded history of ballparks.

I'm not going to fisk this story. My friend—and Red Sox author-publisher extraordinaire—Bill Nowlin already has. As Bill wrote in *The Baseball Research Journal* a few years ago:

> What a great story! Naturally, I wanted to learn more. I was surprised I hadn't come across such a dramatic event while reading 1903's daily game stories in the *Boston Herald*. I'd read all the usual books about the Red Sox and hadn't heard this one before. I couldn't find anything on ProQuest, which made me wonder even more. So I took myself off to the Microtext Reading Room at the Boston Public Library. Surely Dryden would not have been the only sportswriter to have noticed 2,000 pounds of boiling baked beans splattering the bleachers at the ballpark, or the dozen factory whistles shrieking alarm.[1]

There were a lot of newspapers in Boston in 1903. Nowlin read all of them. Nothing about beans.

Photo courtesy of National Baseball Hall of Fame, Cooperstown, New York

GEORGE EDWARD ("RUBE") WADDELL, Pitcher,
PITTSBURG, 1900.

Rube Waddell

RUBE WADDELL & BEANS

"Freakiest thing I ever saw happen at a ballpark," Harry Davis used to say, "was when fans in the bleachers at Boston were showered with hot beans after a foul ball was hit over the fence.

"I know that doesn't make much sense," he'd continue, "but it actually happened, late in the 1903 season. And I've got a newspaper clipping to prove it."

Harry's clipping was from the front page of the August 12, 1903, issue of the *Philadelphia North American*. It showed a story written by Charles Dryden, famed sportswriter of those days. Here's the heading:

PRODIGAL WADDELL
PITCHED AND LOST

◆ ◆ ◆

AS A SIDE ISSUE, "RUBE" CAUSED
A BEAN FACTORY TO BLOW UP

Dryden, after reporting that the league-leading Red Sox had defeated the Athletics, 5-1, presented his readers with these rather amazing paragraphs:

> In the seventh inning, Rube Waddell hoisted a long foul over the right field bleachers that landed on the roof of the biggest bean cannery in Boston. In descending, the ball fell on the roof of the engine room and jammed itself between the steam whistle and the stem of the valve that operates it. The pressure set the whistle blowing. It lacked a few minutes of five o'clock, yet the workmen started to leave the building. They thought quitting time had come.
>
> The incessant screeching of the bean-factory whistle led engineers in neighboring factories to think fire had broken out and they turned on their whistles. With a dozen whistles going full blast, a policeman sent in an alarm of fire. Just as the engines arrived, a steam cauldron in the first factory, containing a ton of beans, blew up.
>
> The explosion dislodged Waddell's foul fly and the whistle stopped blowing, but that was not the end of the trouble.
>
> A shower of scalding beans descended on the bleachers and caused a small panic. One man went insane. When he saw the beans dropping out of a cloud of steam, the unfortunate rooter

story is completely true—and I'll let you find out in due course—is, if not beside the point of this book, certainly just one point. The stories tell us something about their subjects and they tell us something about those who tell the stories. It is neither unfair nor disrespectful to *check* these stories, and in fact I will argue that publishing—and yes, checking—these old stories is a sign of great respect. Because only a good story well told is worth all this effort.

His suspicions aroused, Nowlin decided to learn more about Charles Dryden, and the first thing he found is that Dryden's in the Hall of Fame. Well, not really. But Dryden did receive the J. G. Taylor Spink Award in 1965, which is as close to the Hall of Fame as a writer can get. His name's on a plaque in Cooperstown, and for most people that's close enough. The Hall of Fame's website includes a short biography of Dryden and says, "The humorist was often regarded as the master baseball writer of his time."

Humorist? Is that a clue?

You better believe it.

From the same page, Nowlin learned that Ring Lardner, upon receiving compliments for his own brilliant wit, replied, "Me, a humorist? Have you guys read any of Charley Dryden's stuff lately? He makes me look like a novice."

The whole thing was a joke. Dryden once wrote, with a completely straight face, that Waddell had once been found taking a bite out of the Washington Monument, but it was okay because he had rubber teeth. Dryden once wrote that left-handed pitchers are called southpaws because a left-hander who once tried out for the Cubs hailed from Southpaw, Illinois. Dryden was a comic at heart. In those days you could get away with mixing comedy and journalism, and according to one source, Dryden was "at one time called the Mark Twain of Baseball."[2]

This was one hell of a story, and what made it brilliant was that Dryden dropped it into the middle of an otherwise literal account of a real baseball game. And so he fooled a bunch of people, for the better part of a century, who should have known better.

BILL BRENNAN & GROVER LAND

When the second umpire failed to appear for a Federal League game between the Brooklyn Feds and the Chicago Whales, Bill Brennan was forced to work the game alone and stationed himself behind the pitcher's mound. This meant that Brennan had to make frequent long treks on a sweltering day to replenish his supply of baseballs. In the fifth inning a Brooklyn batter fouled away 20 baseballs, forcing the frazzled umpire to keep going for more horsehides. Desperately, Brennan decided to get a goodly supply, which he brought behind the pitcher's mound and stacked in a neat pyramid. The next batter was Brooklyn catcher Grover Land, who smacked a line drive straight at Brennan's prize pyramid of balls and sent the horsehides flying in all directions. In the mad scramble, each Chicago infielder came up with a ball. The first baseman stepped on his bag, but batter Land kept on running. The second baseman tagged him out, as did the shortstop and the third baseman. When Land reached the plate, the Chicago catcher also nailed him.

Land had been tagged out five times, but Umpire Brennan was not satisfied. He ruled that there was no putout since there was absolutely no way of telling if any of the Whales had used the batted ball. Chicago Manager Joe Tinker protested the game and took his argument to league President James A. Gilmore. Gilmore ruled he would not throw out the game unless the result affected the pennant race at the end of the season. It did not, so Grover Land went into the record books for clubbing the only inside-the-infield home run!

—Carl Sifakis, *Three Men on Third: And Other Wacky Events from the World of Sports* (1994)

There really was a Federal League, in 1914 and '15, and James A. Gilmore really did run the show. This Federal League did feature, among its eight teams, the Brooklyn Feds (or Tip-Tops) and Chicago Whales. Grover Land caught for Brooklyn in both seasons. Joe Tinker managed Chicago in both seasons. Bill Brennan did work as a Federal League umpire in both seasons.

So all the names check out. We've got that going for us.

One small problem with this story, though: a quick look at Grover Land's career reveals that he never hit a home run. Not in his two-year Federal League career, nor in his five seasons (or parts of seasons) with Cleveland in the American League. Like most catchers of his era, Land couldn't hit. In 293 games, he batted .243 with twenty-seven walks, twenty-one doubles, six triples and not a single homer in the record books.

Which blows a small hole in the story, obviously.

According to one source, this actually happened in a Dodgers-Cubs game. Same cities, same Bill

Brennan, same Grover Land, but different teams. As Jimmy Evans wrote in the 1952 baseball issue of *Sports Review*, "Every infielder came up with a ball and Land was tagged at every base but continued past home plate. Brennan solved the puzzler by ruling that no infielder could tell if he had the right ball. He therefore called it a home run, probably the only infield homer ever hit in the major leagues. . . . It's Odd but True!"

Bill Brennan, in addition to his two seasons as a Federal League arbiter, also worked in the National League from 1909 through 1913 (and then again in 1921, though that's not really germane to the issue at hand). But in that range of seasons, Joe Tinker managed the Cubs only in 1916, and Grover Land didn't play for the Dodgers at all; from 1908 through '13, when he played in the majors he played in the American League. What's likely is that Jimmy Evans simply ran across this story involving Chicago and Brooklyn and assumed the story was about a National League game.

So have we run into a dead end? Not necessarily. The possibility remains that Land's hit went for a double or triple, rather than a home run. Or perhaps the incident occurred in some sort of exhibition game. I did search *The New York Times* archives for references to Federal League President James Gilmore and found this note of interest, from May 23, 1914:

> CHICAGO, May 22.—James A. Gilmore, President of the Federal League, has decided in favor of the Chicago Club, in the game of May 14 with the Buffalo Club, which Manager Joe Tinker protested because of a decision by Umpire Goeckel. Another game will have to be played, Buffalo won the original game, 5 to 4.[1]

However, that protest had absolutely nothing to do with Grover Land . . .

> CHICAGO, May 18.—Manager Tinker's protest of the game at Buffalo last Thursday, when the Chicago Federals were defeated by the home team, 4 to 3, was received by President Gilmore of the Federal League to-day, but action was deferred pending the collection of evidence. Tinker claimed that a Buffalo batter ran back to the players' bench after hitting a ball, and later, seeing that the Chicago players did not make a play at first base on the hit, ran out to the base again. The rules, argued Tinker, require the base runner to stay on the base lines while running to first base. Had the Buffalo man been declared out, the Chicago manager claims, the winning run would not have been scored.[2]

The *Times* from 1914 and '15 has many scores of references to Gilmore, as the Federal League was a big story, mostly because of its collective attempts

---

🖎 *Ernie Lombardi once caught for the Dodgers, which I mention only as an excuse to recount this story . . .*

Lombardi graduated from the Pacific Coast League to the Brooklyn Dodgers in 1931, and he fitted right into the fantastic Flatbush follies. Manager Wilbert Robinson, whose abilities at remembering names were akin to Sam Goldwyn's struggles with rhetoric, called the giant catcher Joe Schnapps, which was apparently the closest he could come to saying Ernie Lombardi. Lom caught the opening game for Brooklyn and appropriately made three hits, but for some mysterious reason he was put on the bench.

After six weeks of inactivity, Lombardi went to Robbie and said, "When are you going to let me catch again?"

Robinson looked at Lom and said, "Why, Joe Schnapps! I'd forgotten you were on our club." That winter came the deal that sent Lombardi to the Reds, and he was to stay for a decade.

—Lee Allen, The Cincinnati Reds (G.P. Putnam's Sons, 1948)

The Dodgers opened their 1931 campaign on the 14th of April. Lombardi did not play. In the Dodgers' second game, young Al Lopez—even younger than Lombardi, but with more experience—started behind the plate, but left the game early and was replaced by Lombardi, who picked up two hits (not three). Did

🖎

Robinson forget Lombardi after that game? Brooklyn played eleven more games in April. Lombardi started three of those games behind the plate, and pinch hit in four others. Lopez had played well as a rookie and almost certainly was far better than Lombardi, defensively. Reasonably enough, Lombardi opened the season as the Dodgers' No. 2 catcher. Reasonably enough, that's apparently how he ended it. And reasonably enough, after the season the Dodgers traded him.

to raid the talent of the established major leagues. But that's the only mention of a protest that I found in either season.

Nevertheless, there must be *something* to this story, right? One version appeared as early as 1952, and the version that opened this chapter, though published in 1994, probably relied on an early book of baseball anecdotes—though if that's the case, it's one of the few books of anecdotes I haven't seen—or a newspaper column. Without some other hint, though, I just don't know when or where this, or something vaguely like this, actually happened.

CLARENCE "CLIMAX" BLETHEN

"Climax" Blethen, a 30-year-old pitcher for the Boston Braves, had lost all his teeth and had false teeth that he carried in his back pocket whenever he played. Getting on first base one day with a single, he steamed hard for second when the next batter hit a likely double-play ball to short. The shortstop tossed to the second baseman, and Blethen tried desperately to take the infielder out with a hard slide to prevent a good relay to first. Unfortunately, the hard-running Blethen forgot all about his teeth in his back pocket. He was out at second and out of the game as well, a bloody mess. He had managed to painfully bite himself in his backside with his false teeth.

—Carl Sifakis, *Three Men on Third: And Other Wacky Events from the World of Sports* (1994)

Blethen pitched in two major-league seasons: in 1923 with the Red Sox, and in 1929 with the Brooklyn Dodgers. So we've already got one issue; according to the story he pitched for the Braves, but he never did. Easy mistake to make, though, as the Red Sox and Braves both played in Boston, within a few blocks of each other, and both were terrible throughout the 1920s. So we'll assume this story refers to his time with the Sox, particularly because Blethen did turn thirty in 1923.

It's not at all difficult to check Blethen's '23 season, because he didn't debut until September 17 and pitched in only five games (always in relief). So we're looking for games in which Blethen singled (or reached base otherwise) and was knocked out of the game by a rough slide into second base. Sounds easy enough . . . and is, thanks to a friend in Boston and the recently digitized *Boston Globe*.

In his first game with the Red Sox, Blethen pitched the ninth inning and didn't bat. He pitched again the next day, three hitless innings, but again didn't bat. Blethen's next outing, against Ty Cobb's Tigers on the 21st, didn't go so well. Red Sox starter Curt Fullerton got kayoed in the second—he wound up 2-15 that season—and Blethen took over. He finished the game, but gave up twelve hits and eight runs. He also batted four times, but there's no indication in the box score or in the newspaper story that Blethen ever reached base or was forced from the action by a baserunning injury.

Blethen pitched twice more that season. On the 25th, he worked four innings and did bat, but again he didn't pick up any hits, and nothing in the gamer suggests that he got hurt while running the bases. He did leave the game, but was bumped for a pinch hitter after pitching a scoreless seventh.

Blethen's final appearance in a Red Sox uniform came in what you might call an interesting game. Especially if you're a Yankees fan. On the 28th at Fenway Park, Blethen gave up nine hits and seven runs in three innings . . . and he was the *good* Boston pitcher, as Sox starter Howard Ehmke, in six innings, gave up twenty-one hits and seventeen runs in the Yankees' 24-4 win (they didn't score more than seventeen runs in another game all season). Ruth doubled twice and homered. Lou Gehrig, starting for just the second time in his career—he'd homered the day before, in his first start—hammered three doubles and knocked in five runs.* Blethen batted once, but no hits and no hint of injury. Coincidentally—at least I think it's coincidentally—there *was* a notable baserunning injury. In the second inning, Yankee third baseman Mike McNally hurt himself while sliding home and was forced to retire from the contest.

Blethen gave up more than a run per inning with the Red Sox and spent the next five (nearly six) seasons in the minors, before returning to the majors with Brooklyn late in the '29 season. On September 25 he pitched to one batter in a game against the Phillies, then was bumped for a pinch hitter. The next day against the Phillies, he gave up a couple of runs and again didn't bat. That was the last time Blethen pitched in the majors.

A slightly different version of this story also appears in Nash and Zullo's *Baseball Hall of Shame* 3 (Pocket Books, 1987). The relevant portion:

> Although he pitched like a rookie, he didn't look like one. Climax wore a set of false teeth that he stuck in his back pocket whenever he played. Without his choppers, Blethen appeared much older and more menacing than he really was.
>
> Climax pitched briefly in relief in only five games, but his claim to shame came as a "pinched" runner.
>
> In a game against the Detroit Tigers, Blethen was a runner on first when the next batter slapped a grounder to short. Climax went sliding into second to break up the double play. But he forgot that his false teeth were still in his back pocket.
>
> When he slid into the base, his chompers clamped down on his butt. In every way imaginable, Climax was nipped at second.

In the heading for this story, Nash/Zullo provide an actual date, September 21, and we've seen that Blethen did pitch that afternoon. I'd love to know who first told this story, and I'd love to know how Nash/Zullo nailed down the exact game. But their version, which doesn't result in a "bloody mess" with Blethen forced from the game, seems plausible enough.

---

* The next day, the *Globe* ran a wonderful photo with an unintentionally hilarious caption: "Manager Miller Huggins, at right, showing Gehrig, promising first baseman, how to hold a bat."

TOMMY LASORDA & GOD

The following Friday night I pitched against Buffalo. Because of the problems with Bryant I desperately wanted to win this game. Late in the game Buffalo loaded the bases with no outs. Bryant was on the top step of the dugout, ready to pull me. In my entire career, I had never prayed on the pitcher's mound, but this time, I turned my back to the hitter, looked up, and thought, Lord, I've never asked you to help me win a game. All I've ever asked was the strength to do the best I could at all times. Lord, I'm in a jam here, and any help you can give me would be greatly appreciated.

Suddenly, I heard my name being called. "Lasorda? Lasorda?" It was incredible. I turned around.

It was the umpire, Billy Williams. "Come on, Lasorda," he said. "You gotta throw it sometime."

"Wait a minute," I told him, "I'm talking to God."

"Who?"

"God."

"Oh," Billy said, as if he understood, then turned around and walked back to home plate. He probably figured I was crazy, but on the one chance I had a direct line . . .

My first pitch was an inside fastball, neither inside enough nor fast enough. The batter jerked it down the left-field line. Our third baseman, George Risley, leaped as high as he could and deflected the ball. It bounced off his glove toward the outfield grass. A base hit, I thought as I ran to back up third base, two runs'll score at least. But our shortstop, Jerry Snyder, dived and backhanded the ball on the fly. Lying on his back, he flipped to second base for the second out, and the second baseman fired to first to complete the triple play. I'd played thirteen summers and eleven winters of professional baseball and had never before been involved in a triple play. As I walked nonchalantly off the field, I looked at Billy Williams, who was staring at me with his mouth open. Then I looked into the sky and said, "Thank you, Lord, but was it really necessary to scare me like that?"

That turned out to be the last game I ever pitched . . .

—Tommy Lasorda in *The Artful Dodger* (Lasorda & David Fisher, 1985)

Lasorda's last season as a professional player was 1960, when he pitched for the Montreal Royals, his team in eight different seasons. It didn't take long to find this supposed triple play; it happened on the 4th of July. From the next day's *Montreal Gazette* . . .

Speaking of the Big
Guy Upstairs . . .

Special pitches have had special names down through the years, and one is worth noting in particular. Back around 1915 the St. Louis Browns drafted a pitcher named Perryman from the Atlanta club. Perryman was described as a young man who entered professional baseball for the sole purpose of accumulating enough money to put himself through a theological seminary so that he might become a clergyman. He had a fast ball with a peculiar hop. It was called by those who had trouble hitting it "Perryman's halo ball."

—*Ira L. Smith and H. Allen Smith,* Low and Inside *(Doubleday, 1949)*

Emmett "Parson" Perryman pitched in just that one season, going 2-4 with a poor ERA in fifty innings.

A few years earlier, the Reach Base Ball Guide had published an item about Maxwell G. Carnarius. Better known as Max Carey, he was then attending the St. Louis Theological Seminary during the off-seasons, "but whether he will take up that profession upon his graduation remains to be seen . . . If his prowess as a ball player is a criterion of his ability as a minister he should be a power in the religious world."

It doesn't appear that Carey ever applied himself to ministering. After his playing career, he managed the Dodgers for a few years, then managed in the minors and did some scouting for the

In the second inning of the first game with runners on first and second, infielder Ron Kabbes lined a drive that bounced into the air off the glove of third baseman George Risley. Shortstop Jerry Snyder went back to the grass to catch the ball for the first out, and easily got the runners off second and first, Risley to Snyder to Joe Tanner to Alto-belli.[1]

Regrettably, the box score I've got does not list the umpires, so I can't confirm the presence of arbiter Billy Williams (which is a shame because he does have a bit of dialogue in our little drama). Looking at Lasorda's other offered details:

- Lasorda well-remembers his infielders, as Risley and Snyder were responsible for starting the tri-killing.
- It wasn't a Friday night, and it wasn't against Buffalo; it was a Monday night in Rochester.
- It wasn't late in the game; it was just the second inning. And the bases were not loaded; only the first and second sacks were filled.

Lasorda would finish the game, going all seven innings and allowing just two runs as the Royals won, thanks in large part to first baseman Joe Alto-belli's grand slam in the third inning. And, yes, it was the last game Lasorda ever pitched. In the July 20 issue of *The Sporting News*, this small item appeared:

ROYALS RELEASE TOM LASORDA, WINNINGEST MONTREAL PITCHER

MONTREAL, Que.—Tom Lasorda, pitcher-coach-road secretary of the Montreal Royals, was released July 9, after a long, illustrious I. L. career.

Lasorda was with the Royals seven full seasons and parts of two others, registering 128 victories, more than any other Montreal pitcher. Lasorda was 2-5 this season.

He said his release was due to a "falling out" with Manager Clay Bryant, with whom he had been associated four seasons. The parent Los Angeles Dodgers assigned him immediately to his new scouting duties in the Philadelphia area.

Lloyd McGowan

I don't know where McGowan came up with 128 victories for Lasorda in Montreal, as he fell roughly twenty shy of that number. Here's Lasorda again, in his book: "So in July 1960, I finally hung up my spikes. I had had a long and relatively successful career. I always said I was going to play in the major leagues and I had; I never said how long I was going to play in the major leagues. And I'd set the all-time International League record for career victories with 107. But the real evidence that my career had been successful was easy to measure: The spikes I hung up had cost me $35."

Lasorda did play in the major leagues. From 1954 through '56, he pitched in twenty-six games—eight with his beloved Dodgers, eighteen with the Kansas City Athletics—and went 0-4 with a 6.48 ERA. He *did* win 107 games in the International League (all while pitching for Montreal).

He did *not* set the all-time International League record for career victories.

I don't know who does have the record, but I know it's not Lasorda. In the early 1920s, the Baltimore Orioles' staff, all by itself, featured three pitchers who would win more than 107 games in the International League: Lefty Grove (108), Jim "Rube" Parnham (141), and (most notably) Jack Ogden, with 213 wins.

You don't want to mess with God. But *nobody* messes with Curly Ogden.

Orioles. He left baseball after the '57 season, according to his 1976 obituary in The Sporting News, *and later was involved with dog-racing tracks.*

RON GUIDRY & WILLIE WILSON

Michael Kay: Yankee pitching coach Ron Guidry celebrating a birthday today. Now, hold on to your hats, I'm starting to feel old . . . Ron is fifty-seven today.

Ken Singleton: I was talking to him earlier, around the batting cage. You were talking about throwing change-ups? He said he didn't throw his first change-up until about nine years in the big leagues. Struck out Willie Wilson to end a ball game on a three-two change-up. First one he ever threw in the big leagues.

Kay: That really must have pleased Wilson.

Singleton: He said Wilson actually called him gutless for throwing it. It was the third time he struck out, so [Guidry] said, "You couldn't hit anything else, either."

—WWOR telecast of Yankees–Red Sox game, August 28, 2007

Two of Willie Wilson's forty-one career homers came against Guidry, but otherwise he struggled terribly against him, going 11 for 58 in his career, with fourteen strikeouts. Guidry reached the majors in 1975, Wilson in '76. Wilson played his last game in 1994, Guidry in 1988. But Guidry hardly pitched in '76, and not at all against the Royals. So we're looking at a dozen seasons, '77 through '88, during which time both players were in the American League.

Did Guidry ever fan Wilson three times in one game?

He did not. There were nine games in which Guidry struck out Wilson at least once, and in five of those games he struck out Wilson twice. But *only* twice.

Did Guidry ever strike out Wilson to end a game?

Of those nine games, only two—July 23, 1983, and May 4, 1985—were complete games for Guidry. In the first of those, Wilson struck out once, in the sixth inning. Guidry retired Amos Otis on a fly ball to end the game. In the other complete game Wilson struck out twice, in the first inning and the eighth. Guidry finished his four-hitter by striking out Steve Balboni.

Let's see, what else might we check . . . Oh, here's something. Did Guidry ever strike out Wilson to end an inning late in a game?

Just once. In fact, it's the only *interesting* strikeout among the fourteen strikeouts. On the 11th of August in 1987, Guidry struck out Wilson for the last time (they would meet just once more, nearly a year later). In the bottom of the first inning, Wilson led off with a strikeout, looking. Then came three straight hits—Lonnie Smith, Kevin Seitzer, George Brett—followed by an out, and then another hit, an intentional walk, and two more hits. Which brought Wilson to the plate again, with six runs in and a runner on second base. He struck out again, looking. This really is nothing like the story Guidry supposedly told Singleton. But if there was a strikeout-related incident involving Wilson that did stick in Guidry's head for twenty years, this one looks like the best candidate.

Just moments after telling the story about Guidry and Wilson, Singleton told this one . . .

> Luis Tiant, of course, was a great pitcher for the Red Sox, pitched for the Yankees as well. When Luis was with Boston, Lee May was on our team, and he couldn't hit Luis Tiant, and Earl Weaver knew it. So when we would go into Boston, say on a weekend series, on Friday Lee would ask Luis on the field, "Which day are you pitching?" Luis would say, "I'm pitching on Sunday." So Lee said, "Saturday night I'm gonna have a good time because I'm not playing on Sunday."
>
> I think he was something like one for thirty-five against Luis.

When Singleton says "our team," he means the Orioles; he and May were teammates with Baltimore from 1975 through '80. In those six seasons, Tiant pitched (and started) against the Orioles in twenty-three games. Twelve of those starts came in '75 and '76, and May was in the lineup for eight of them. But from '77 through '80, Tiant started eleven times against the Orioles, and May started only two of those games. These six seasons comprised May's entire history against Tiant, and he went 4 for 31 (.129) with one walk, one double, and one home run. Among the thirteen Tiant starts that May skipped were three Sunday afternoons.

Singleton must have a million stories. The very next night he told this one:

> Ron Guidry . . . told me of a funny story, years ago, when Thurman Munson was catching him. In the first inning the visiting team came out and got three straight solid hits. The bases were loaded, and Thurman comes out to the mound and says to Guidry, "Do you want me to stop telling 'em what's coming?" And Guidry got upset and struck out the next three guys.

I couldn't track down that one, either.

Some stories just refuse to die a natural death . . .

"Do you know I got Stan Musial out forty-nine times in a row? Somebody counted and told me. I'd curve him and jam him with the sinker. Then there was Henry Aaron. I never got him out."
—Clem Labine in The Boys of Summer (Roger Kahn, 1972)

This claim also was published in obituaries of Labine after he died in 2007, notwithstanding the fact that it's absolutely not true.

Labine did not face Musial forty-nine times, not during the regular season anyway. Labine matched up with Musial forty-eight times, and Musial batted .238 (10 for 42) with six walks, one double, one triple, and one home run. Considering Musial's greatness, it was a brilliant performance by Labine. But forty-nine times in row? No. Just . . . no.

Nevertheless, well after corrections to the obituary had appeared all over the InterWebs, Sports Illustrated ran the following letter: "As a loyal Brooklyn Dodgers fan, I mourn the loss of Clem Labine, a clutch pitcher who was underappreciated. One of his more unbelievable stats: he retired Stan Musial—the greatest NL hitter of all time and a man who made a career of killing Dodgers pitching—49 consecutive times.—Bob Kurtzer, Denver, N.Y."

And so the legend endures . . .

GREG MADDUX & JEFF BAGWELL

Leading 8-0 in a regular-season game against the Astros, Maddux threw what he had said he would never throw to Jeff Bagwell—a fastball in. Bagwell did what Maddux wanted him to do: he homered. So two weeks later, when Maddux was facing Bagwell in a close game, Bagwell was looking for a fastball in, and Maddux fanned him on a change-up away.

—George Will in *Newsweek* (April 25, 2006)

Bagwell played in fifteen seasons, which is a long career but doesn't come close to that of Maddux (who has five seasons on Bagwell at the beginning of their careers and, at this writing, two seasons and counting at the end). In all fifteen of Bagwell's seasons he faced Maddux at least once, so we might as well start at the beginning, which was 1991.

One may, with the help of the SABR Baseball Encyclopedia, quickly look up not only the dates of Bagwell's 449 homers, but various other details. But of course he hit a lot more homers than Maddux gave up, so it's easier to check Maddux's log instead. Which I will now do, looking specifically for Bagwell as the hitter and leaving the other details for later.

Bagwell did not homer against Maddux in 1991, 1992, 1993, or 1994. But in 1995, when Maddux gave up only eight home runs all season, Bagwell hit two of them within a week, on May 28 and June 3. Next came single homers in 1996, 1998 (one of three Maddux gave up in one game), 1999, 2004, and 2005. That last bomb is particularly notable; on April 29, Bagwell played his last game until September, and hit his last home run. Maddux gave it up and pitched six otherwise solid innings to beat Roger Clemens.

So we've got (or rather, I've got) the specific dates of each home run, and the play-by-play accounts are just a few clicks away. Remember, we're looking for a game that's in the late innings, with Maddux's team—the Braves, until 2004—comfortably ahead of Bagwell's Astros. Did one of these home runs come in a situation like that? Let's check each of them. First I'll list the date, then the inning, then the score (with Maddux's team listed first), then the number of runners on base . . .

28 May 1995	8th	2-0	0
3 Jun 1995	5th	0-0	0
18 Sep 1996	6th	6-1	0
2 Sep 1998	2nd	1-0	0
11 Aug 1999	3rd	5-1	1
26 May 2004	3rd	0-1	1
29 Apr 2005	3rd	2-1	0

I enjoy tables. You might not. So let me sum up. In his career, Greg Maddux gave up seven home runs to Jeff Bagwell. None of them came when the score was 8-0, or 7-0. Five of those seven homers came in close games, the two teams within two runs of one another. Leaving aside the specifics of the story, would a competitor like Maddux groove a fastball in a close game? You sure wouldn't think so.

Which leaves two games: September 18, 1996, when the Braves were up 6-1 in the sixth inning; and August 11, 1999, when the Braves were up 5-1 in the third. Neither situation makes a lot of sense, but we'll start with those games and look for the last specific: it's two weeks later—okay, it's any point later in the season—and Maddux slips a third strike past Bagwell in a key spot.

Except—and by now you're probably way ahead of me—both of these games were relatively late in the season, which means few (if any) chances for Maddux to have struck out Bagwell. In 1996, after September 18 Maddux made only two starts, both against Montreal. In 1999, after August 11 Maddux made eight starts . . . but none against Bagwell's Astros.

But wait! (And if you're ahead of me here, kudos to you, sir.) What about postseason games? Might Maddux have struck out Bagwell in October? Not in '96; the Astros didn't qualify for the derby that year. But in 1999, the Braves and Astros faced off in a Division Series, and Maddux started the opener.

In the first inning, Bagwell struck out with nobody on base. In the third inning, he flied to center field. In the fifth, he singled. In the top of the seventh, he flied to center. And in the bottom of the seventh, Maddux got bumped for a pinch hitter. Maybe that first-inning strikeout is what we're looking for, though. The game was close; it was zero-zero.

But that's all, folks. There's nothing else to see here. I don't doubt that Greg Maddux, in some fashion or another, set up Jeff Bagwell at some point during their long careers. Or rather, I don't doubt that Maddux believes he did that. And maybe he did. Pitchers have been telling stories like this one for nearly as long as there have been pitchers. But believing you did something and actually doing it are sometimes different things.

🖎 Warren Spahn tells this one about being set up by Ted Williams . . .

It amazed me that he knew every pitch I threw, and he said, "That fastball that you threw to me is pretty effective. You ought to use it more often." So now, we're playing the All-Star Game in Washington, D.C., and I remembered what Ted had said. And I had two strikes on him, and I threw him a fastball right here. And he hit it into the bleachers for a home run. And if you ever watched the pitcher during a ball game, when a guy hits a home run, he has nothing to do. He would pick up the rosin back and throw it and whatever. Well, I happened to think about Ted, and I looked around at second base and I said, "You conned me, didn't you?"

And he did. You know, he used to spend the time that he wasn't hitting in a ball game looking through the hole in his cap, the little air hole, and watch the pitcher. He never watched anything else other than the pitcher, so that either they tipped pitches off, or he had a good idea about what they were going to throw him. So he was great, but he wasn't that great. He had some inside information.
—*Fay Vincent*, The Only Game in Town *(2006)*

As Spahn tells the story, Williams complimented his fastball in 1947, in the annual series between the two Boston teams. The All-Star Game was played in 1956. Did Spahn really throw a fastball in a key spot because of something Williams had told him nearly nine years earlier? I guess we'll never know.

MEL OTT, ED BRANDT & WALTER STEWART

Mel Ott, now a front office executive for the New York Giants, tells an amusing story of the 1933 World Series between the Washington Senators and the Giants. It seems that the Senator pitchers went over to scout the Giants one day before the Series began.

"I was facing a pitcher named Ed Brandt," Mel recalls, "and he could have gotten me out by throwing basketballs up there. I never could hit him. Well, on this day, the Washington pitchers saw Brandt strike me out twice on inside curves—each time on three pitches, too. Then I popped up twice and grounded out another time. I never did get that ball out of the infield. So the first game of the World Series comes and Walter Stewart, a left-hander, was pitching for Washington. I told myself: 'I'll bet Washington thinks I can't hit an inside curve. I'll take one to see.' Sure enough, the first pitch was an immediate curve for a strike. On the next one, I slammed the ball into the seats for a homer. Nobody threw me an inside curve after that."

—Bob Addie in the *Washington Times-Herald*
(reprinted in *Baseball Digest*, September 1950)

You've probably never heard of Ed Brandt, but he won 121 games in the majors, and if he hadn't spent most of his career pitching for lousy teams—the Boston Braves, mostly—his 121–146 record might have been reversed. Well, probably not reversed. But evened out, because his 3.86 career ERA was right in line with the league average during his career (1928–1938). According to the 1933 *Who's Who in Major League Baseball*, "He is a powerful left-hander with blinding speed and a curve that is far better than the average."

In '33, Brandt was in his sixth season with the Boston Braves. Which brings up one problem with Ott's story: Ott's Giants did not play the Braves one day before the World Series began. The Series began on October 3. The Giants did not play on October 2. They did play on October 1, but that was against the Dodgers. To find a game against the Braves, you have to go back to September 26, the concluding game of a three-game series. And, yes, on the 24th Ed Brandt did start against the Giants.

Did he strike out Mel Ott twice? He did not. According to the box score published in the *Times*, Brandt struck out only one batter. What's more, we know Ott did not go 0 for 5, as he recounts: "Then I popped up twice and grounded out another time. I never did get that ball out of the infield."

According to the box score, Ott went 1 for 4 and

Photo courtesy of TSN/Icon SMI

Mel Ott

the hit was a double. What's more, he began the Giants' game-winning rally by getting hit by a Brandt pitch (inside curveball, perhaps?).

Did Brandt strike out Mel Ott once? I don't know. For that information, I'll have to send off to the Hall of Fame for Ott's daily logs. If he did strike out in that game, it must have been against Brandt, who pitched a complete game (but lost in the bottom of the tenth).

While "we" are waiting for the package from Cooperstown, we can cursorily address this question: Is it *likely* that the "Washington pitchers" (as Ott described them) were scouting the Giants on the 24th?

On the morning of the 24th, the Giants owned a six-game lead with roughly a week to play, so if you were going to scout a National League team, they'd have been the one. Likewise, the Senators had essentially clinched the American League pennant. So, yes, it would have made sense for the Senators to scout the Giants (and vice versa). Where *were* the Senators on the 24th? Most of them were in Washington, playing the Athletics. In those days, though, it was not uncommon for a manager to send a player, and perhaps even multiple players, off on a scouting mission. And of course

---

Another running theme in baseball history: outfielders giving lousy advice to pitchers . . .

I have a Joe DiMaggio and Hank Greenberg story. Johnny Murphy is in, pitching in relief already. It's about the eighth inning, ninth inning. It's the ninth inning. At that time, you walk through center field, exit, to get, the bullpen was beyond. You walk past the center fielder. Murphy is passing Joe DiMaggio.

And DiMaggio says to Murphy, "Why don't we fast-ball this once? You know, everyone is curving the son of a gun; don't curve him." Well, Murphy's curving, because that's the kind of a pitcher he was. So, from center field to the mound, Murphy says, that might be a good idea.

So, he fast-balled Greenberg. Home run. The game's over. Now, in the clubhouse. No sound. We're in there. We got beat. DiMaggio's over there, Murphy is here, and I'm over on this side. And about less than five minutes, DiMaggio stands up, and goes over to Murphy and says, "Don't you ever listen to another word I say."

—Tommy Henrich in Fay Vincent's The Only Game in Town *(Simon & Schuster, 2006)*

Murphy surrendered four homers to Greenberg, but two of them came before DiMaggio joined the Yankeees in 1936. Which leaves only two: one in 1937 and one in 1946. The one in 1937 came in the second inning, in one of Murphy's rare starts. Which leaves only the

23rd of June in '46. The game was in Detroit. With the Yankees holding a 7–5 lead in the bottom of the eighth, the Tigers had two runners on base when Murphy was summoned from the bull pen, "only to see Greenberg belt the ball high into the left field tier . . . "

But it wasn't the ninth (as Henrich recalled). And the Yankees didn't get beat. In the top of the ninth, DiMaggio hit a game-tying homer (his second of the game). And in the eleventh, Henrich himself hit a two-run shot—his second homer of the game—and the Yankees wound up winning, 10–8. Gaining credit for the victory? Fireman Johnny Murphy, who pitched three innings and allowed just that one run.

there probably was a train leaving Washington for New York every half hour.

About that supposed strikeout, though? Okay, I now have Ott's daily sheets for 1933. And, yes, Brandt *did* get him on strikes once in that game.

So what about Ott's home run? He couldn't have got that wrong, could he?

Hardly. With two outs in the first inning of Game 1, Ott homered against lefty Walter Stewart, into the lower right-field stands at the Polo Grounds. The Giants won that game, 4–2. Four days later in Game 5—they didn't take any days off that year—Ott homered against right-hander Jack Russell. It was the top of the tenth inning, made the score 4–3, and a few moments later the Giants clinched the World Championship. Ott hit the Series' first homer and its last, and both provided the margins of victory. We should probably forgive him a bit of poetic license.

TY COBB & CARL MAYS

Our club got to where we could beat Carl Mays, the great underhand pitcher, most any time he started, and fans often wondered why. We did it because we had studied his way of thinking, and crossed him.

It is well known among batters that May's great point of strength was in his low ball. He keeps it just about the knees and worries a batter to death. But he always manages to keep it high enough for the umpire to call it a strike.

We discovered one day that if Mays couldn't control his low ball he lost his poise and was easy to beat. His mind was in such habit of having that low one—his strength—work successfully that when it didn't his grip was gone.

After watching him closely I found that he sized up batters according to where they stood in the batter's box. As you may know, I usually stand well forward and meet the ball out in front. By pitching to me in that position Mays's low ball would come just above my knees. The next time up I stood far back in the box, which put me a yard farther away from him. His low ball came over as usual, but when it reached the back end of the box it was an inch or two below my knees.

The umpire called two balls and Mays was surprised. Something was wrong, but he couldn't understand. I knew, of course, he would have to steady himself and get the next one up. Instead of waiting, I swung on that one and got a hit.

One after another of our batters tried the scheme and we drove Mays from the box. After that we could beat him most any time we wanted to by standing in the back of the box. That shifting completely upset him.

—Ty Cobb in *Memoirs of Twenty Years in Baseball* (ed. William R. Cobb, 2006)

One thing you have to love about the Peach: he never let a chance to establish his own brilliance pass without taking a vicious cut. What's not clear is how brilliant Cobb actually was. He's often regarded as a self-made player who thought his way into stardom. I don't know about that, though. At nineteen, he was one of the dozen or so best hitters in the American League. At twenty, he was *the* best. Cobb did apparently have a powerful intellect, but it wouldn't have done him much good if he'd not been blessed with all that physical talent.

Anyway, Mays pitched in the American League from 1915 through '23, and Cobb was active throughout those seasons, all of them with the Tigers. And those Tigers could really hit. In addition to Cobb—the greatest hitter in the American League before Babe Ruth hit his stride—the Detroit lineup featured stars Bobby Veach and Harry Heil-

In 1972, Exposition Press published *Baseball's Great Tragedy: The Story of Carl Mays—Submarine Pitcher*. Authored by Boston newspaperman Bob McGarigle and little-known today, the book was assembled with a great deal of help from Mays, whom McGarigle interviewed at some length.

The story Cobb tells about Mays does not appear in the book, but Cobb does play a key role. According to McGarigle, one afternoon in Fenway Park, Mays "decked the Georgia Peach in a tight situation and Ty had responded by throwing his bat at him. Cobb had needed police protection to get off the field that day."

That was in 1915, Mays's rookie season. Which apparently set the tone for their professional relationship.

Before another game Cobb challenged Mays, who recalled, "The first time he came to bat I decked him but good."

Cobb wasn't going to let that go. On the next pitch (again, according to Mays) Cobb "dragged a bunt down the first base line." Mays fielded the ball, but before he could throw to first, Cobb slammed into him, spikes first.

"I lay there stunned for a moment and then rolled over onto the infield grass and sat up. When I got courage enough to look at my leg, it was just a bloody mess. I remember wondering if I would ever run again. . . .

"The mistake I made was in getting in his way on the baseline. The baseline was his—according

mann. From 1915 through '23, the Tigers finished 1st, 1st, 2nd, 3rd, 3rd, 6th, 3rd, 2nd, and 2nd in the American League in runs scored. Over those nine seasons the Tigers scored more runs than anybody else in the league.

So how did Carl Mays fare against these hard-hitting Tigers? Using Mays's daily sheets from the Hall of Fame, we find that in fifty-two games he went 23-12 with a 2.72 earned run average against Detroit. Over those same nine seasons, his ERA against everybody else was—coincidentally enough—also 2.72. So considering the Tigers' propensity for scoring, Mays actually pitched *better* against the Tigers than against other teams. Which should at the very least result in some skepticism about Cobb's story.

But of course it's possible that Mays dominated the Tigers for some years, only to have the tables turned by Cobb's brainstorm. So let's look at those nine seasons individually. If Cobb's tale is true, we would expect to see some obvious point at which the Tigers went from patsies to powerhouses . . .

	Games	Innings	Batting Avg	W-L	ERA
1915	4	11	.210	0-1	4.22
1916	5	36	.234	3-2	1.77
1917	5	40	.145	4-1	0.90
1918	7	59	.234	4-3	2.12
1919	5	29	.319	1-1	2.48
1920	8	55	.311	6-1	3.13
1921	8	38	.237	3-0	2.84
1922	7	43	.332	1-3	5.23
1923	3	17	.299	1-0	3.63
Totals	52	328	.263	23-12	2.72

Well, if we're looking for a line, we can place it between 1921 and 1922, right?

Unfortunately, that "analysis" has two big problems. The first, and the more obvious, is that if we were guessing when that line would be drawn, we would have guessed much earlier. If Cobb and his Tigers did figure out how to beat Mays, why did it take them seven years?

The other, less obvious problem is that interesting things don't really care what year the calendar says it is. When you see the results broken down by year, you might assume there really *was* a dividing line. On May 14 in 1922, Mays got hammered by the Tigers: twelve hits and seven runs in seven innings. *Ah, dividing line.* Or not. In his next three starts against Detroit, Mays pitched twenty-three innings and didn't allow more than two runs in a game.

There's another possibility for a dividing line, which can be seen by looking at the column for batting average. Granted, batting averages were generally trending upward in the late teens and early '20s. But the Tigers' batting average against Mays seemed to take a great leap forward in 1919, and we can in fact trace the surge back to 1918.

That season, Mays beat the Tigers with complete games on July 19 and then again three days later, giving up seven hits in eighteen innings. But in their next meeting, on the 6th of August, the Tigers touched Mays for fourteen hits in ten innings, and three weeks later they got him for eleven hits in nine innings.

Now, it should be said that in neither of those games did the Tigers "drive Mays from the box"; he started and completed both games. Still, the first nineteen times Mays pitched against the Tigers, from May 11, 1915, through July 22, 1918, he posted a 1.56 ERA and limited them to a .189 batting average. Afterward, in thirty-three games and 201 innings, his ERA was 3.49 and the Tigers batted .305 against him.

So maybe that is the game—if there is one—and the dividing line: August 6, 1918. Beginning with that game, the Tigers *did* hit Mays harder than they had before. But to what end? Remember Cobb's other claim? "After that we could beat him most any time we wanted to by standing in the back of the box. That shifting completely upset him."

Here's a simple graphical representation of Mays's twenty-three wins and twelve losses against the Tigers, with 8/6/18 highlighted:

```
LL  L    L LL   LL L            L LL
WW WWWWW W  WWW  W WWWWWWWWWWW W  W
```

Now, I make no pretense of being a mathematician, or even a statistician. But does that look to you as if the Tigers could beat Mays "most any time we wanted," as Cobb claimed? If anything, it looks as if Mays could, as they used to say, just throw his glove on the mound and expect to beat the Tigers. Mays *beat* the Tigers on August 6, 1918. He did get roughed up in his next couple of starts—one more in 1918, the next in 1919—but then he pitched six shutout innings against the Tigers. And after a loss—a well-pitched loss, but still a loss—in May 1920, Mays won nine straight decisions against Cobb's Tigers (they really were *his* Tigers, as Cobb took over as manager in 1921).

So, did they not beat Mays because they didn't want to beat him? Or did they not beat Mays because he was, regardless of whatever adjustment

to him—and he just ran right over me after knocking me to the ground. I carry the scar of that spiking to this day. It is more than six inches long. The doctor, incidentally, did a wonderful repair job and I only missed a couple of pitching turns."

The book includes a wonderful full-page photo of Mays's scar, which resembles the head of an elephant with an extraordinarily long trunk. One can imagine how much blood was shed that afternoon. One quibble, though: from 1915 through '22, Mays went more than five days without pitching after an appearance against the Tigers just once. After starting against them on August 8, 1922, he didn't pitch again until the 16th (coincidentally enough, against the Tigers again). But Mays pitched a complete game on the 8th, and the newspapers don't mention any spiking.

In 1923, he went nearly three weeks without pitching after a start against the Tigers, but again the papers didn't mention any incident involving Cobb. Mays did go for long stretches without pitching in 1923—his last season in the American League—but he attributed this to Miller Huggins's not liking him (and the *Times* mentioned Mays leaving the club to tend to his ill wife, during one of those stretches). So I don't know what to make of Mays's scar, except that he must have gotten it somewhere.

That's not the end of the Cobb-Mays story (as told by Mays). On August 16, 1920, Mays beaned Ray

Chapman. The next day, Chapman died. Mays's next start was on the 23rd, against the Tigers. According to Mays, before the game a note was delivered to him from Cobb. It read:

If it was within my power, I would have inscribed on Chapman's tombstone these words: Here lies the victim of arrogance, viciousness and greed.

Mays gave up ten hits that afternoon, but beat the Tigers 10–0. He recalled, half a century later, "After reading that note from Cobb I wouldn't have let them score a run if I had to pitch twenty-seven innings to beat them. . . . The Yankees played great ball behind me, didn't make an error. And if my memory is as keen as I think it is, Del Pratt staked me to a good lead in the first inning by hitting a three-run homer. Or maybe it was the Babe. The Babe was always rising to occasions like that."

Mays's memory was keen. The Yankees did play errorless ball, and the Babe racked up two assists. In the first inning, Del Pratt did hit a three-run homer (and knocked in four more runs later in the game).

Cobb and his mates might (or might not) have made, a great pitcher perfectly capable of making his own adjustments?

I will suggest that most of the evidence points to the latter. The Tigers did get in their lumps in 1922, knocking Mays around pretty good in four of his seven starts against them. But if Cobb really was smart enough to figure out how to hit one of the top pitchers of that era, it wouldn't have taken him seven years.

SHOULDERS OF GIANTS

Taken from the Pages of SABR Journals

No, this section isn't about Mel Ott, Willie Mays, and Barry Bonds. My fellow members of the Society for American Baseball Research have been doing incredible research, for no reason but the love of the thing, for something like thirty-five years now. Everything in this book is in the spirit of their best work, and below are some of my favorites from the last decade or so.

When Cobb Killed a Guy

When Ty Cobb composed his memoirs during his last years, the man taking notes was Al Stump. Cobb's book: *My Life in Baseball: The True Record* (Doubleday, 1961). Just before *he* died, Stump published *Cobb: A Biography* (Algonquin, 1994), which gave Stump a chance to write about having worked with Cobb, not to mention all the stories Cobb told him that weren't considered fit for publication in 1961.

In *Cobb*, Stump wrote this chilling passage:

In August of that 1912 season, Cobb was on another of his heavy-hitting streaks when he drove his Chalmers auto to Detroit's train station. His habit when roadward bound was to have his wife Charlie accompany him to the train, then drive herself home. . . . This time the Tigers were leaving for an exhibition game in Syracuse, New York. It was late on a Sunday with streets deserted, when Cobb found himself never so happy to be armed with a gun.

On Trumbull Avenue, three men stood in the street, waving their arms. As soon as he stopped his car one of the trio demanded his money. To protect his wife, he slid out, to be met by punches from all three. Cobb knocked down one of them, while the others circled. He dropped another. But the third man climbed onto Cobb's back and stuck a knife into him. Cobb pulled out his pistol, which would not fire. He kept on swinging

Writer Allen Barra witnessed the events described below, and ranks this as his all-time favorite baseball story . . .

In 1993, Ron Shelton was shooting the baseball scenes for his movie *Cobb* at Birmingham's Rickwood Field. One of the producers knew Roger Clemens and asked him to play Big Ed Walsh, opposite Tommy Lee Jones as Ty Cobb.

In a tense scene, the two were shouting insults at each other. (Walsh: "Cobb, I hear you're from Georgia, where men are men and sheep are nervous." Cobb: "Your wife left her panties with me. Got 'em in my pocket.")

Clemens was instructed to throw a pitch fairly up and in, not too fast, not too close. He did, but it was a little too fast and a little too close. Jones glared and shouted more insults, and Clemens threw another one just a little faster and closer.

Shelton and his assistants began to squirm; it looked as if Jones and Clemens were a couple of Method actors caught up in their roles. Someone whispered to Shelton, "What are we gonna do if that next pitch is about six inches closer to his head?" Shelton shook his head and mumbled, "Then we're shooting the Ray Chapman story."

Barra adds, "By the way, to my knowledge, this is the only known confrontation between Academy Award and Cy Young winners."

and at one point had two muggers on the ground. When the gang split and ran, he chased them. "I caught up with one and left him in sorry condition," he declared. "I ran down the other. He'd ducked into a dead-end alley between two houses." Using his gun's sight like a blade and the butt end as well, he slashed away until the man's face was faceless. "Left him there, not breathing, in his own blood," he went on with satisfaction. Cobb believed he killed this mugger. A few days later a press report told of an unidentified body found off Trumbull in an alley.

T.C. was bleeding badly, and a hysterical Charlie begged him to go directly to a doctor. The knife used on him had inflicted a six-inch wound in his lower left back. Instead, he drove on to the train station with a kerchief stuck in the cut.

Actually, Stump first told this story in a magazine article about the last few months of Cobb's life and placed the incident in early June rather than August. For his later book, though, Stump did some research. He did not do nearly enough research to verify Cobb's claim to have killed one of his attackers. Doug Roberts did a *great deal of research* and presented his findings in *The National Pastime* in 1996.

Cobb was assaulted and stabbed on August 11, 1912. It seems that Cobb's assailants were not a complete mystery to him. It seems that several days before the ambush, Cobb had attacked a newsboy in the Tigers' locker room, perhaps in a dispute over a craps game. According to the *Detroit Journal*, police were tipped that Cobb had "got in wrong" with a gang member "when he trounced a young fellow in the club house."

And did Cobb really kill somebody? For one thing, from the first time I read this story some years ago, I wondered, would Cobb really have left his wife alone in the car and taken off after a group of thugs? For another, Doug Roberts checked the coroner's files and autopsy records for August and September 1912 and found "no victim even remotely resembling a man dying as a result of blunt trauma to the skull. The only trauma victims during those months were those who had been struck by streetcars, a fairly common occurrence in those days."

What's more, while Stump wrote that "a press report told of an unidentified body found off Trumbull in an alley," Roberts spent two days looking at microfilm of the Detroit newspapers for the days following the assault and found no such report.

Cobb's wound was not particularly serious. He took the train to Syracuse, where a doctor judged the wound, between the shoulder blades, to be "half an inch in diameter and a quarter of an inch deep." The wound was cauterized, and the next afternoon Cobb collected two singles in an exhibition game.

Not long before he died, in a haze of drugs and alcohol and terminal illness, Cobb told Stump, "In 1912—and you can write this down—I killed a man in Detroit."

Stump did write it down. And then he wrote it down again, some three decades later. But it wasn't any more true in 1994 than it had been in 1961.

Cobb and Cochrane

Speaking of Ty Cobb, it's been written more than once that Cobb, late in his life, provided financial support for his fellow Hall of Famer (and ex-Tiger) Mickey Cochrane. Cobb could certainly afford it; by the 1950s he was a multimillionaire, thanks to both his keen mind and any number of advantageous stock tips over the years. In Charles C. Alexander's outstanding biography of Cobb, he writes:

> Besides his organized and public philanthropies, Cobb also did more than his share of individual, mostly private charitable deeds. After leading Detroit to two pennants and a world's championship, Mickey Cochrane had suffered a frightful beaning in 1937. He never fully recovered from his head injury and was thoroughly down on his luck by the 1950s, when Cobb began sending him regular checks.[1]

Alexander, an academic who's not generally shy with the source notes, does not offer a source for this information. But it comes up again, and more vividly, in Al Stump's book:

> The elderly Cobb became expert at tax loopholes, while also aiding hard-up ballplayers. Each month he mailed support checks to some three dozen men who had once faced his spikes and not backed away. Johnny _____ had been admired in the American League for planting a ball in Cobb's face in a sliding situation, loosening some of his teeth. Johnny was one of "my boys" who received support checks. Their names were kept confidential. Another beneficiary was Mickey "Black Mike" Cochrane, a future Hall of Fame catcher. Near-fatally beaned by a pitch in 1937, Cochrane afterward could not function. The Cobb fund helped support him for the rest of his life.[2]

The version that got into the movie *Cobb*—written and directed by Ron Shelton, using Stump's book as a primary source—shows Cochrane in a sig-

If somebody can tell me how to check this one, I'll get right on it . . .

Casey Stengel was telling how Ty Cobb used to score a man from first base on a single to right field.

"It was a remarkable thing," said the Professor. "Cobb would put on the hit-and-run and he'd never stop at first base. He'd go right on to second—and where's the right fielder gonna throw the ball? There's only one place; he's got to throw it to second base with the shortstop covering.

"So, when the right fielder gets over his surprise, he throws to second base an' Cobb slides in on his backside an' wraps his legs around the fella. So how's he gonna throw the ball home now, which is where the other runner is because he didn't stop at third base, either. An' it's a run scored an' a great play.

"Tried it once myself. Know what happened? They got me at second base an' got the other fellow at the plate an' my manager said maybe I shouldn't try that play any more."

—Jerry Mitchell in the New York Post *(reprinted in* Baseball Digest, *June 1970)*

nificantly worse light. In the script (my source because I wasn't able to get a tape of the movie before press time), Cochrane shows up at Cobb's hotel room in Cooperstown, drunk as a skunk and dressed like an indigent. Cobb asks why Cochrane isn't wearing his tuxedo, as they're both scheduled to attend a dinner that evening, and Cobb had sent Cochrane the money to purchase one. Cochrane protests that the money never arrived, and Cobb accuses Cochrane of spending the money on booze. Cobb tears a stack of bills off the wad in his pocket, throws it at Cochrane, and screams, "How could you be so good behind the plate and so bad everywhere else!"[3]

Rough stuff.

And quite probably not true. Or even close to true. In the wake of Stump's book and Shelton's movie, Norman Macht related his conversations with Cochrane's youngest daughter, Sara, in *The National Pastime*. According to her, Mickey and Ty did have a relationship. In 1960, Cobb—who made a big chunk of his fortune investing in Coca-Cola—called Cochrane to tell him Coke would soon be sold in cans, and thus the

Photo courtesy of Transcendental Graphics

Ty Cobb

stock would be a good investment. And Sara did confirm the Cooperstown tuxedo story . . . sort of.

"In Cooperstown they had lunch with Mr. and Mrs. Tris Speaker," she told Macht. "They never intended to stay in Cooperstown long enough to attend the formal dinner that evening, and my father had not brought a tuxedo with him because he did not expect to do anything where he would need one."[4]

Indeed, in photos taken of Cochrane in the late 1950s, he doesn't look like a man down on his luck. A little beefy, sure, but always well turned out. According to Sara, her father not only had enough money to take advantage of Cobb's stock tip, but also enough to pay for her wedding that summer. Earlier, he had paid her tuition at the University of Colorado.

A few years later, SABR member Charlie Bevis's biography of Cochrane goes into more detail about Cochrane's later years (he died in 1962 of lymphatic cancer, only fifty-nine years old). As Bevis notes, the notion that Cochrane "could not function" after the beaning in 1937 is simply preposterous. After being fired as Tigers manager in 1938, Cochrane flew to Montana and bought a ranch, then returned to Detroit and took a job as a sales rep, hawking "steel, wire, and rubber goods."[5]

In 1942, Cochrane joined the navy and spent a few years running the baseball program at the Great Lakes Naval Training Center. At some point, when Cochrane's son Gordon was fighting in Europe, Cochrane "pushed to get into the action too" and wound up on a captured island for a few months. From the Pacific, Cochrane sent a letter to a writer at the *Philadelphia Public Ledger* that included this passage: "The boy has been in some heavy action in Belgium. So far he's come out all right. He went back from the lines for some rest, probably is going up there again by now and I have my fingers crossed."

When that was published in the newspaper, the boy was already dead, killed in action in a farmhouse in Holland.

After the war, Cochrane continued to run his 4K dude ranch in Montana, spending summers there while maintaining a residence in Grosse Pointe, Michigan. In 1950, he joined the Philadelphia Athletics as bullpen coach. Just a few weeks into the season he was promoted to general manager, but was let go in September. "Well, it's back to the ranch," he said.

The ranch wasn't particularly profitable, and a scouting position with the Yankees lasted for just one season. In 1958 he admitted, "I'm eating regular, but I'm not doing much of anything now and could use a baseball job."[6] In 1960 he got one, as the Tigers hired him in a scouting position that was, due to Cochrane's failing health, mostly a sinecure.

This reminds me of the story about Ty Cobb hitting .350 when he was 70 . . .

Who pitched the fastest fastball? Some people say Bob Feller, others say Sandy Koufax, and Nolan Ryan has his supporters, too. But ask an oldtimer for his opinion, and he'll invariably say Walter Johnson.

The Big Train was a gentle, exceedingly modest man, but he was not without pride. In 1939, more than a decade after Johnson had retired, he went to spring training with the Senators as a radio announcer. In camp, everyone was talking about Roberto Ortiz, a Cuban rookie with blinding speed.

Ortiz was a bit of a blusterer, and one day he decided to show the old master how it was done. He began warming up right in front of Johnson's seat in the stands. Johnson watched Ortiz rear back and fire about 15 minutes. Then the Big Train took off his coat and tie, climbed over the railing, and called over Walter Millies, a Washington catcher.

The 52-year-old Johnson began warming up alongside Ortiz, and soon started to time his pitches so they left his hand at the same moment Ortiz's were leaving *his* hand. Johnson's cannonballs were smacking into Millies' glove before Ortiz's pitches arrived in his catcher's mitt! Finally, the Cuban stopped throwing and just watched Johnson smoke away.

When asked about this contest later in the day, Johnson said, "I couldn't resist the temptation. May the good Lord forgive me."

—*John Thorn*, A Century of Baseball Lore *(1974)*

It's true that the 1950s were a relatively thin time, financially, for a man who had, not so long before, been one of the game's biggest stars. It is certainly conceivable that Ty Cobb sent the occasional check. But the notion that Cochrane spent the '50s as a drunken, brain-addled bum, stumbling along from handout to handout, is simply not supported by the facts at hand.

When Bill Veeck (Maybe) Almost Kicked Branch Rickey's Ass

In his (and Ed Linn's) classic book, *Veeck—As in Wreck*, Bill Veeck related the following . . .

> I have always had a strong feeling for minority groups. The pat curb-stone explanation would be that having lost a leg myself, I can very easily identify with the deprived. Right? Wrong. I had tried to buy the Philadelphia Phillies and stock it with Negro players well before I went into the service. . . .
>
> Let me make it plain that my Philadelphia adventure was no idle dream. I had made my offer to Gerry Nugent, the president of the fast-sinking club, and he had expressed a willingness to accept it. As far as I knew I was the only bidder. The players were going to be assembled for me by Abe Saperstein and Doc Young, the sports editor of the Chicago *Defender*, two of the most knowledgeable men in the country on the subject of Negro baseball. With Satchel Paige, Roy Campanella, Luke Easter, Monte Irvin, and countless others in action and available, I had not the slightest doubt that in 1944, a war year, the Phils would have leaped from seventh place to the pennant.[7]

In the 1998 edition of *The National Pastime*, co-authors David Jordan, Larry Gerlach, and John Rossi analyzed a huge number of sources—their eleven-page cover story included forty-one footnotes and source notes—and concluded, after giving Veeck his due as an open-minded iconoclast, with this: "Nevertheless, we must face the fact that Bill Veeck falsified the historical record. This is unfortunate. His actual role in advancing the integration of major league baseball is admirable and can stand on its own merit."[8]

Jordan et al.'s central argument was that while Veeck supposedly came close to purchasing the Phillies and stocking the roster with black players in 1942 or '43, not even a hint of the story surfaced until 1962, when Veeck was working on the first volume of his memoirs. Given the (naturally) self-serving nature of memoirs and Veeck's (well-known) tendency toward self-promotion, plus the cogent argument made by Jordan and his co-authors, it wasn't difficult to believe that Veeck's "plan" was, at best, just an ill-formed idea back in the early '40s or, at worst, purely an invention of his imagination many years after Jackie Robinson integrated the National League.

SABR member Jules Tygiel, perhaps best known for his wonderful book *Baseball's Great Experiment: Jackie Robinson and His Legacy,* wasn't nearly so sure. Nine years after the original article was featured on the cover of *The National Pastime,* Tygiel's rebuttal was shunted nearly to the back of *The Baseball Research Journal,* and one can only hope nobody missed it. Because if Jordan spectacularly debunked Veeck's story, Tygiel just as spectacularly debunked the debunking.

Not that Tygiel didn't have a vested interest in the story. Tygiel, along with other authors over the years, had interviewed Veeck and included the story in his book. "All of us took Veeck at his word," Tygiel wrote in the *BRJ,* "none of us sought to corroborate the tale."[9]

This time, though, Tygiel sought to do exactly that. First, though, he acknowledged the credentials of Jordan and his co-authors. Jordan had written three biographies and was widely considered a top historian of Philadelphia baseball (I have depended on his histories of the Athletics and the Phillies many times over the years). Gerlach and Rossi were both history professors of long standing; when their article was published, Gerlach was the president of SABR. One would have been hard-pressed in 1998 to find credentials less impeachable.

What's more, Tygiel noted, the authors had searched the mainstream newspapers of the era, plus *The Sporting News,* the African-American weeklies, and the *Communist Daily Worker* (which covered baseball and actively agitated for integration).

"Moreover," Tygiel writes, "the three authors found numerous inaccuracies, inconsistencies, and improbabilities in Veeck's version of events. . . . Veeck, they argue, might have thought about buying the Phillies and might have been influenced by 1942 articles in the *People's Voice* and *The Sporting News* that speculated about how successful an all-black team would be in the National League, but he had never seriously attempted to bring this scenario to fruition."

There's no question about the inaccuracies, inconsistencies, and improbabilities in the story Veeck told, though they're really no more than we might expect from a born storyteller telling a story roughly twenty years old. As Gerlach et al. originally noted, Red Smith wrote, in 1946, about Veeck's plan to purchase the Phillies. Granted, Smith's source probably was

Grantland Rice related that Cobb's fires did not abate in retirement. Many years after his career was over, Cobb found himself in reminiscent conversation with the old Cleveland catcher Nig Clarke. Clarke was boasting about his hand-speed and how he'd often appeared to make a tag when he actually hadn't, and how Cobb himself had probably been called out a dozen times on plays at Clarke's plate when he'd actually been safe.

Enraged, Cobb grabbed for Clarke's throat and, wrote Rice, "It took three men to pull him off."

—Dan Okrent and Steve Wulf, Baseball Anecdotes (1989)

Veeck, and Smith did not mention the part of the plan that involved the Negro Leaguers. But as Tygiel discovered, in 1949 Veeck *did* mention that part of the plan, in a speech to the Chicago Urban League. In a 1953 book, *Great Negro Baseball Stars*, author A. S. Doc Young wrote about Veeck's 1946 purchase of the Indians, "Negro writers soon recognized Veeck as a person likely to give an ear to the proposition of Negroes playing in the American League. Perhaps they had heard the unsubstantiated story that Veeck once shocked baseball's late commissioner Kenesaw Mountain Landis, with a proposal to buy a major league club and transform it into an all-colored aggregation." [10]

None of this proves that Veeck didn't make up the whole thing. But if so, he did it well before 1960. What I *think* is that Veeck really did make preliminary gestures, at least, toward buying the Phillies, and I *think* he also entertained the notion of stocking the roster with the best black players. Obviously, he wasn't able to do either of those things, for a variety of reasons. Tygiel's central point, though, is that while we don't have a great deal of evidence to suggest exactly what was on Veeck's mind in 1942, we don't have nearly enough evidence to know what was *not* on Veeck's mind.

Matty's Fadeaway

Christy Mathewson's best-known pitch was his fadeaway, the pitch that later became known as the screwball. But where did Matty pick up the pitch? As Dick Thompson wrote in the 1996 edition of *The Baseball Research Journal*, "Scanning the reference works on Mathewson for its origin will get you three different theories." The most intriguing is the theory propounded in various books by Negro Leagues researcher (and advocate) John Holway, who claimed that black pitcher Rube Foster taught Mathewson the pitch in 1902 or '03, shortly before Matty reached the majors. Actually, Holway did admit the Foster connection was essentially a legend. [11]

In Ken Burns's documentary *Baseball*, narrator John Chancellor says, "John McGraw himself quietly hired Foster to show the New York Giant pitching staff what he knew. Christy Mathewson is said to have learned to throw his celebrated fadeaway from Rube Foster."

There's room for doubt in there. But in their book *Shadow Ball* (intended for a young audience), Burns and his collaborators wrote that McGraw "knew there was no chance of slipping Foster into the big leagues. Instead, he paid Rube to teach Mathewson his fadeaway." [12]

As sure as the sun sets each evening, right? But as Dick Thompson demonstrates, "Foster's role is nothing more than a fable. Every author who has made the claim that Foster taught Matty the pitch has done so without offering original research. That's because no such link exists."

Thompson has instead traced Mathewson's fadeaway to 1898, when he pitched for a semi-pro team in Honesdale, Pennsylvania. There, one of his teammates was a pitcher named Dave Williams, who would later pitch briefly for the Boston team in the American League. As Mathewson said in a 1912 magazine article, "In Honesdale, there was a left-handed pitcher named Williams who could throw an out-curve to a right-handed batter. Williams exhibited this curve as a sort of 'freak delivery' in practice, over which he had no control. He showed the ball to me, and told me how to throw it."

That article was published in *St. Nicholas Magazine*, which might explain how it escaped the attention of so many researchers over the years. In 1898, when Matty discovered his signature delivery, Rube Foster was nineteen years old and had probably never traveled far from his native Texas.*

---

* Regrettably, in his 2001 biography of Foster, *The Best Pitcher in the Country*, author Robert Charles Cottrell lends credence to the notion that Foster's tutoring played a role in Mathewson's outstanding 1904 season, in which he won thirty-three games. Actually, even that's a year off, as Matty had won thirty games in 1903. If you're going to draw a dividing line, it's after 1902. Cottrell is a history professor at Chico State and should know better.

JOHNNY SAIN & SATCHEL PAIGE

One of my favorite pitchers was Satchel Paige. He was one of the few power pitchers who could also be a finesse pitcher. I pinch-hit for a pitcher against the Browns, and the St. Louis hurler got three straight balls on me. Then he was relieved by Paige. On the first pitch he spun a little curve over for strike one. I was taking. Then he threw a little-better breaking ball. I didn't swing. Strike two. Now, here's a guy who can do anything he wants to, so I didn't know what to expect. His third pitch was a great curveball that came in at throat level and dropped across the plate. I swung and missed. Strike three. That was one of only twenty times I struck out in my career in 774 at-bats, and the only one I didn't mind. I was a breaking-ball pitcher, yet he struck me out with breaking balls. Three *different* breaking balls. That meant a lot to me.

—Johnny Sain in *We Played the Game*, Danny Peary (Hyperion, 1994)

Sain is best known as a great pitching coach, really the first semi-famous pitching coach (though there were others of note before him, including Earle Brucker, Mel Harder, and Ray Berres). As a player, Sain is best known for his years with the Braves, as half of "Spahn and Sain and pray for rain." But he also put in three seasons (and parts of two others) with the Yankees, first as a swingman (in '52 and '53) and then as one of the league's top relief pitchers, later gaining credit for twenty-two saves in 1954.

But we're talking about hitting. For all the information that's now so readily available, I believe that if you're looking for pinch-hitting stats, your only source remains the old Macmillan *Baseball Encyclopedia* in its many editions, which gives me an excuse to crack open the *first* edition, published in 1969.

In nearly seven full seasons with the Braves, Sain had only six at-bats as a pinch hitter. Which is irrelevant, because Satchel Paige was in the other league. It's interesting, though, because in 1952, Sain's first full season with the Yankees, he got *twelve* pinch-hit at-bats. Oddly, he got only one in '53 and none in '54, though in both seasons he fared pretty well when he did hit. Of course, from this distance it's hard to understand a lot of things Casey Stengel did. We probably can just look at those numbers and wonder.

We don't have to wonder when Sain might have pinch-hit against Satchel Paige, though. We know it must have been in '52 or '53, because those are the only seasons in which Sain pinch-hit at all, and we know that Paige did pitch for the Browns both years.

From there, it's simple enough to search the *Times* archives, and there it is, on the first hit. It was the 25th of June in '52, and it was 102 degrees at Sportsman's Park in St. Louis. The Yankees grabbed a big lead early, but were down 10–9 in the ninth when Paige and Sain took center stage . . .

Photo courtesy of National Baseball Hall of Fame, Cooperstown, New York

Satchel Paige

The Yankees, who had forfeited a 7–3 lead in the third, thought they had a good chance in the ninth. Bearden could not locate the plate and his first three pitches to pinch-hitter Johnny Sain were wide. Here Manager Marty Marion left nothing to chance. He called for Paige, and Old Satch proved a wonderful choice. He fanned Sain on three pitches.[1]

The story, as Sain tells it, is exactly the sort of story that we would expect, even if essentially true, to have some of its details blurred by the years (or purposefully exaggerated by the teller). Not this one, though. The details provided by Sain all check out exactly. Or at least the ones we can check. One thing we simply can never know—unless someone was charting pitches, and that piece of paper still exists somewhere—is which pitches Paige threw to Sain. Was it really three straight curves?

The Browns' catcher that day was Les Moss. And on the same page in the same book that Sain tells his story, Moss says this about Paige:

In 1956, Bill Veeck was running the Miami Marlins in the Triple-A International League and signed Satchel Paige, who was nearly fifty years old. One of his teammates that season was outfielder Whitey Herzog, who tells this story about Satchel's legendary control . . .

We were on the road in Rochester one night, screwing around in the outfield. They had a hole in the outfield fence just barely big enough for a baseball to go through, and the deal was that any player who hit a ball through there on the fly would win $10,000. I started trying to throw a ball through the hole, just to see if I could. I bet I tried 150 or 200 times, but I couldn't do it, so I went back to the dugout.

When Satch got to the park, I said, "Satch, I bet you can't throw the ball through that hole out there."

He looked out at it and said, "Wild Child, do the ball fit in the hole?"

"Yeah, Satch," I said. "But not by much. I'll bet you a fifth of Old Forester that you can't throw it through there."

"Wild Child," he said, "I'll see you tomorrow night."

So the next night Satchel showed up early for batting practice—first time in his life he'd ever been that early. I took a few baseballs, went out to the outfield, and stepped off about sixty feet, six inches, the distance from the mound to home. Satch ambled out, took the ball, brought it up to his eye like he was aiming, and let fire.

I couldn't believe it. The ball hit the hole, rattled around, and dropped back out. He'd come that close, but I figured it was his best shot.

Satch took another ball and drilled the hole dead center. The ball went right through, and I haven't seen it since.

"Thank you, Wild Child," Satch said, and then went back into the clubhouse.

—*Whitey Herzog and Kevin Horrigan,* White Rat: A Life in Baseball *(Harper & Row, 1987)*

Nobody ever talks about this, but I would rank Paige's three seasons with Miami, in the strong International League, among the top sustained pitching performances of all time. Paige turned fifty in the middle of the '56 season and stayed with the Marlins through the '58 season. Overall, in 340 innings he went 31 and 22 with a 2.40 ERA.

Satch was all business on days he pitched, not showing any emotion on the mound and being very quiet in the dugout. He was about forty-six or forty-seven and no longer had much of a curve, but he could still throw his fastball in the high eighties and put it right where he wanted. He was easy to work with because he'd throw eight or nine fastballs out of every ten pitches and just one or two little curves or sliders. He didn't throw junk.[2]

Exactly one week after striking out Sain, Paige turned forty-six. While Sain claims to have been struck out on three curveballs, he also specifically describes Satchel Paige as a power pitcher (and, yes, if you threw in the high eighties in the 1950s, you were a power pitcher). And for all that's been said and written about Leroy Robert Paige, I don't know that anybody's marveled over the very existence of a forty-six-year-old power pitcher.

BROWNS FINISH . . . BARELY

Two days later, 3,174 fans sat in on the "Wake of the Browns" on the final Sunday of the season, September 27, the same Sunday that the American League rejected Bill Veeck's second request for permission to move his Browns to Baltimore. The Browns went down to their one hundredth 1953 defeat losing a 12-inning struggle to the White Sox, 2 to 1. It ended on an especially drab note. When the game ran into extra innings, and plate Umpire Art Passarella called for a fresh supply of baseballs, he was advised the supply was exhausted. It looked as though the game might have to be called "on account of lack of baseballs," but Passarella went over the scuffed balls that previously had been thrown out, and picked out the least damaged ones. When outfielder Bill Wilson of the White Sox caught the last ball of the game, it had a gash on it from seam to seam. Thus ended the proud 1902 dream of Ban Johnson when he moved his Milwaukee franchise to St. Louis, then the fourth city in the land, "to add strength and balance to the league."

—Fred Lieb, *The Baltimore Orioles: An Informal History of a Great Base Ball Club* (1955)

What a mess. By the early 1950s, it was clear that St. Louis could no longer support two major-league teams. In 1944 the Browns outdrew the Cardinals, but that October the Cards topped the Browns in the only all–St. Louis World Series, and after the war the Browns never came close to matching the Cards' attendance.

And it sure didn't have anything to do with the ballpark. Both teams played in Sportsman's Park, which was owned by the Browns; if not for the Cardinals paying rent, the Browns would have been in even worse shape than they were. As it was, almost every time the Browns came up with a good player, before long they sold him to the Red Sox or the Tigers.

When Bill Veeck bought controlling interest in the Browns in 1951, he had every intention of driving the Cardinals out of town. Through a variety of methods he did make some headway, if not nearly as much as he would later claim. In *Veeck—As in Wreck*, he wrote that in 1952, "We had lifted our attendance almost 300,000, and the Cardinals had dropped 300,000."

Well, no. The Browns' attendance jumped about 225,000, from (roughly) 295,000 to 520,000. The Cardinals' attendance did decline, but by just 100,000, to 913,000. The Browns had Bill Veeck and a seventh-place team. The Cardinals had Stan Musial and a third-place team. Still, Veeck was itching for a fight, and Cardinals owner Fred Saigh was not the sharpest of operators. But then Veeck got blindsided by a brewery magnate . . .

I would have run the Cardinals out of St. Louis, I'm sure of it, except for one thing. Saigh had gotten himself into income-tax trouble. He had already been indicted by mid-1952, and I had to the face the possibility that he might have to sell the team.

What a lousy thing for him to do to me.

As soon as I read the verdict, I began to talk to Milwaukee—and, to a much lesser extent, Los Angeles and Baltimore—about moving my franchise.

And yet, I was only going through the motions of protecting myself. We had done so well and had come up so far and were putting together, it seemed to me, such a good team that all the momentum was with us even if I lost Fred Saigh.

At one point, I almost did have it made. In negotiating to sell his club, Saigh went down to Houston to talk to some Texas millionaires. The Cardinals owned the Houston club in the Texas League, so the association was close. There was no question that the money was there, it was just a matter of making the Houston park acceptable. I came that close.

And then out of nowhere—*out of nowhere*—came Gussie Busch with his full-bodied and well-foamed bankroll. . . .

I wasn't going to run Gussie Busch out of town. And I certainly wasn't going to run Anheuser-Busch Inc. out of town. Busch wasn't buying the club himself, the brewery was buying it.

The brewery could run the club as part of its advertising budget, lose an unlimited amount of money and just write it off the company profits.

By the time I hung up the receiver, I knew I had been knocked out of the box.[1]

In 1953 the Boston Braves moved to Milwaukee. They were the first major-league franchise to relocate since 1903 and they promptly set a National League attendance record. Veeck had tried to get into Milwaukee—his old minor-league stomping grounds—before the Braves, but was blocked by his fellow owners. Next, in March of '53, Veeck tried to move the Browns to Baltimore but again he was blocked, with five of the seven other clubs voting against the transfer.

Veeck kept trying, with other possible new homes including Toronto, Montreal, and Kansas City. In a gesture of surrender, Veeck sold Sportsman's Park to the Cardinals.*

---

* Gussie Busch wanted to rename the ballpark Budweiser Stadium. Bowing to league pressure—it supposedly was considered poor form to name a ballpark after a beer—Busch named the ballpark after himself . . . and then created a beer named after himself. So if not for the tender sensitivities of the National League, we might never have been "blessed" with Busch and Busch Light.

While all this going on, attendance naturally tanked, with the Browns averaging fewer than 4,000 paying customers per game. And they didn't do even that well in the last game of the season, drawing only 3,174 for that Sunday afternoon contest against the White Sox.

> There was no official assumption on the part of the ball club that it was the last Brown's game in St. Louis.
>
> Bob Fishel, Browns' publicity director who handled the public address microphone during the game, gave no sign of the prospective change as he bid the fans goodbye. He coolly announced:
>
> "Thank you for attending the last game for the season—and good afternoon."
>
> A band played Auld Lang Syne, the shadows lengthened across the diamond and the fans quietly dispersed with a few gathering around the stairs to the Brownie dressing room to say goodbye to some of the players.[2]

That same weekend, the owners in both leagues were meeting in New York, separately. The National League reportedly was considering expanding from eight teams to ten, hoping to beat the Americans into California. Meanwhile, just a few hours after the Browns lost to the White Sox, 2–1 in eleven innings, the American League owners voted down Veeck's proposed move to Baltimore. As it was obvious the Browns could not survive in St. Louis, the vote essentially was designed to force Veeck to sell the franchise. Two days later, with Veeck agreeing to withdraw, the Browns were sold to a Baltimore syndicate. And so the Orioles were created.[3]

So what about the supposed shortage of baseballs in that last game? I cannot confirm that the last ball used in the last game "had a gash on it from seam to seam," but Harry Mitauer wrote this in the *St. Louis Globe-Democrat*:

> The Browns weren't hitting much in their final series. That probably was due to batting practice curtailment the last two days. They didn't warm up at all yesterday.
>
> With business bad and the resultant shortage of cash, the club's supply of baseballs dwindled. Balls were rationed the first two days with practice continuing as long as the balls lasted.[4]

🐦 *1950s outfielder Jim Dyck told this one . . .*

In 1953, when I was with the Browns we had a long losing streak, and we were playing the Yankees, who had won 18 straight. Milt Richman, who was later inducted into the Hall of Fame of sportswriters, was covering our games. He was a good friend of Marty Marion, and he asked Marty who was going to play today, so he could write the story.

Marty said, "It don't make any difference how I make out the lineup, we'd just lose. Why don't you make out the lineup?"

So Milt made out the lineup, and that's when we broke the streak.

—*Gene Fehler,* More Tales from Baseball's Golden Age *(2002)*

The date was June 16. The Yanks had won eighteen straight and the Browns had lost fourteen straight. Duane Pillette started for St. Louis at the Stadium, and he—with a fair amount of help from reliever Satchel Paige—whipped the Yanks 3–1 and handed Whitey Ford his first-ever loss as a starting pitcher. According to the Times, *the Yankees missed setting a new American League record and the Browns missed setting a new franchise record.*

So what did Richman's lineup look like? Not all that different from usual, with one gigantic exception: manager Marty Marion started for the first time all season and played third base for the first time in a career that stretched back to 1940. He went 0 for 5 and handled his one defensive chance cleanly.

Mitauer also wrote: "Brownie fans who hung Bill Veeck in effigy Friday night brought the dummy back out again yesterday. They had it swinging from the right field stands for several innings, then pitched it on to the field."

Veeck generally is remembered as a man of the people. But for six months in 1953, he was nobody's favorite in St. Louis.

BROWNS & YANKEES

Though the Browns lost their 1922 series to New York, they won one of the un-forgettable games in baseball, pulling out a late May victory in New York, 7 to 2, after umpire Ollie Chill had called the last Brownie out in the ninth with the Yanks ahead, 2 to 1. Truly, it was one of the "believe it or not" games of baseball. It was the first game played by the Yankees after Babe Ruth and Bob Meusel had fin-ished 70-day suspensions, and a crowd of 49,152 crammed into the Polo Grounds, where the Yankees still were tenants. As usual, it was the hard-working Shocker who handled this one for St. Louis and a two-run homer by Aaron Ward had given New York the one-run edge it enjoyed in the ninth. Sam Jones, Shocker's oppo-nent, got two out in the ninth, when two pinch-hitters, Chick Shorten and Pat Collins, stung him for singles. Fleet-footed Johnny Tobin tapped to first baseman Wallie Pipp, who tossed to Jones, covering first base, and the base umpire, Chill, waved Tobin out. The Yankee players ran to the clubhouse and the great crowd swarmed out on the field.

However, Fohl, coaching at first, had noticed that Jones had slightly juggled the ball before holding it securely, and at that moment the fast Tobin had crossed first base. Lee took it up with Brick Owens, the plate umpire, who told Chill in his opinion the Tobin was safe. In the meantime, the tying Brown run had scored. The umpires ordered play resumed; the crowd had to be shooed back into the stands, and some of the unbelieving Yanks had to be dragged from the showers and put back in their monkey suits. When the game was continued after a twenty minute delay, Jones had lost his stuff, as the Browns flogged him for five additional runs, four scoring on a grand slam homer by Bill Jacobson. Jones, who later was to pitch for the Browns, was so disturbed by this upheaval that he lost his next nine games.

—*The Baltimore Orioles: An Informal History of a Great Baseball Club!*
(Frederick G. Lieb, 1955)

This one's so loaded with specific details— burdened, really—that one might think it's point-less to check Lieb's veracity, because how could he have come up with all those details without solid sources? On the other hand, it's a pretty good story *and* Lieb is well-known for making stuff up. Anyway, between Retrosheet and the *Times* it's exceptionally easy to check most of the key facts.

Let's start with an easy one: Did the Browns ever beat the Yankees 7–2 that season?

They did not. But on May 20 in New York, the Browns did beat the Yankees 8–2. Urban Shocker was the winner, and Sad Sam Jones was the loser.

There is one apparent problem with May 20: Isn't May 20 too early for Ruth and Meusel to have served seventy-day suspensions? Actually, no. Those suspensions began in March, during spring training. So we've obviously found the game in question. Let's see what the *Times* had to say about it . . .

First, this *was* Ruth's (and Meusel's) first game of the season. Before the game, Ruth—though not exactly short of precious metals—was presented with a "handsome silver loving cup . . . a silver baseball bat and a nice floral wreath from admiring friends." The *Times* gave the attendance as 38,000—obviously an approximation—far short of Lieb's specific 49,152.

Of the attendance, the *Times* writer noted,

> There were 38,000 fans in the park when the game began, and only a handful were turned away at the gates. It was the biggest throng of the year at the Brush Stadium and within a few of the greatest crowd that has ever watched from grandstand and bleachers. But there was no confusion, inside or out. The fans came early in a steady stream. A half hour before game time there were still vacant seats for those who wanted them. Not until the field was cleared and the umpires took charge was the last bleacher seat filled. After that that the gates were closed on a few dozen who lingered outside.

According to Philip J. Lowry's *Green Cathedrals* (the only comprehensive history of major-league stadiums), the listed capacity of the Polo Grounds (née Brush Stadium) hovered right around 38,000 from 1917 through 1921, but jumped to 43,000 in 1922 (and 54,000 in 1923). My guess is that the *Times* writer saw a full house, and reverted to 38,000 (and considering the roundness of the number, we know he wasn't referring to an official turnstile count). If Lowry's figure for 1922—43,000 capacity—is correct, there might well have been more than 38,000 in the ballpark. But more than 49,000, as Lieb says? Given what little we know, that figure seems questionable. Which really is neither here nor there, except good storytellers know that particularly specific details, even if invented, lend credence to the whole enterprise.

The heart of this story is the ending. Was the game apparently over, with the Yankees back in their clubhouse, some of them showering already?

If that's what happened, the *Times* missed it. From the game story:

> Came the ninth and the Yankees' last stand. Severeid grounded out to Ward. One out. Ellberbe did the same. Two out. The crowd began to look around for the exits, and Lee Fohl rushed his reserves to the res-

cue. Shorten batted for McManus and singled to centre. Collins hit for Shocker and smashed a vicious single off Scott's glove, Shorten racing to third.

The crowd stopped its exiting and paused to watch the game, which apparently was not yet over. Tobin, the next batter, bounded to Pipp, and there was a great and widespread sigh of relief. But Wally juggled the ball for a second, then recovered and threw to Jones, who covered the bag. Sam caught the ball and Umpire Ollie Chill raised his hand in a gesture that meant "out." Then Sam dropped the pill and the runner was safe, while Shorten crossed the pan with the tying run.

And then came six more runs, capped by "Big Bill" Jacobson's grand slam (after which, "strong men wept and a fair St. Louis rooter in a field box fainted"). But no mention of plate umpire Brick Owens overruling Chill, nor of a twenty-minute delay while the Yankees were summoned from their clubhouse. I checked the *Daily News* and the *Herald-Tribune*, too, but again no mention of those odd happenings.

And finally, one last question: Was Sam Jones really "so disturbed by this upheaval that he lost his next nine games"?

Hardly. I made a list of Jones's next nine starts, which ran from May 24 through July 9. He pitched decently enough in the first two, but lost both. He got hit hard in his next three, and lost two of them (with a no-decision in the other, which the Yankees wound up losing 10–6). After his start on June 14, the gamer in the *Times* included this item:

> One of the mysteries that is puzzling Manager Huggins and causing him to spend many restless hours at night is Sam Jones. What is the matter with the pitcher is a deep mystery. His pitching arm is all right, and he seems to have everything that a pitcher needs to win, but he cannot get by. In a measure, no doubt, this is due to the fact that whenever he takes a turn in the box he is opposed by some pitcher the Yankees are unable to do very much with. On the other hand, he is unable to hold the opposition in check.

That game made Jones 0-4 with a 5.22 ERA in his five starts since May 20. So Miller Huggins sent him to the bullpen. Jones made four brief relief appearances, and gave up a run each time. He started again on June 24, didn't survive the fourth inning, and got hung with another loss. But Huggins sent Jones out there again five days later, and this time he pitched into the tenth inning and earned the victory. And in the second game of a July 4 doubleheader in Philadelphia, Jones completed his mini-comeback with a five-hitter to beat the Athletics 6-1.

That makes eight starts (remember, Lieb said Jones "lost his next nine games"). In his ninth start, on July 9, he got knocked out in the seventh inning, but didn't get a decision. In the nine starts, then, Jones went 2–5 with a 4.90 ERA. Even if Lieb literally meant "games" rather than starts, Jones didn't lose his next nine after May 20, because he didn't take the loss in any of his relief outings.

Like many of Lieb's stories, this one's true enough to give it a thick veneer of believability, but falls well short of literal truth when you check the specifics.

FRED HANEY & BABE RUTH

Fred Haney, who is not averse to telling stories on himself, tells one about the first time, as a busher just brought up by the Detroit Tigers late in 1922, he made his first appearance at the Polo Grounds, where the Yankees then were playing.

"In my first time at bat," he says, "I hit a home run. I'll admit it wasn't much of a blow. It just sneaked into the lower deck of the grandstand, a few feet inside the foul line. But it was a home run. When our half of the inning was over and we were changing sides, I passed Babe Ruth and said to him: 'Watch out, Big Boy. You're still in front, but I'm gaining on you.'

"The Babe didn't let on he heard me, but went on his way to the dugout. He was first up in the Yanks' half and he hit a real Ruth homer—a mile-high screamer that came down deep in the upper tier in right. As he trotted by me at third base, head down, as usual when he was rounding the bases, he said, without so much as looking at me: 'How do we stand now, kid?' "

—Frank Graham in the *New York Journal-American*
(reprinted in *Baseball Digest*, August 1956)

This is another story that I first ran across many years ago, when I was working for Bill James. This one never got into one of Bill's books, mostly because I ran out of time, because after many hours of scouring microfilm, looking for every single game Haney might have played against the Yankees, I still didn't have any definitive answers.

I do still have my notes, though, and now I've also got the SABR Home Run Log, which makes the sleuthing *so* much easier.

Haney played in the American League from 1922 through the first few months of the '27 season, first with the Tigers and then the Red Sox. We might start with '22, because that's when Haney places this incident, and anyway it's based on the notion that Haney was a brash rookie, willing to tease even the Great and Mighty Babe.

One problem, though: Haney did not hit a home run in 1922. He debuted with the Tigers early in the season, on the 18th of April, and wound up playing in eighty-one games. But he didn't homer. What's more, 1922 was the last season during which the Yankees played at the Polo Grounds; in '23 they moved into the Yankee Stadium.

But what about later seasons? Haney did hit eight home runs as an American Leaguer: four in 1923, one in '24, and three in '27 (before the Red Sox sold him to the Cubs). Did any of those homers come against the Yankees? Yes, three of them did.

Did any of those come in games in which Ruth also homered? Yes, two of them did.

On the 11th of August in 1923, in the second game of a doubleheader in the Bronx, Haney led off the top of the ninth with a home run off Bob

Photo courtesy of National Baseball Hall of Fame, Cooperstown, New York

The Babe in 1920 or '21

Shawkey. In the bottom of the inning, Ruth hit a home run of his own, help-ing fuel the Yankees' four-run, game-tying rally (they would win in the tenth). Funny thing, though: Haney's and Ruth's homers *both* failed to clear the fence; they both were inside-the-parkers, which doesn't exactly square with Haney's story.[1]

They both homered on May 29, 1927, too. Haney homered to lead off the third; in the *Times,* James R. Harrison called it "a long sock into the left field bleachers." Ruth homered to lead off the bottom of the eighth, begin-ning a seven-run rally.

So our candidate is that game in 1923. It *was* fairly late in the season, and Ruth *did* hit his twenty-eighth homer of the season just a few moments after Haney hit his fourth, and they *were* in the Yankees' home ballpark. Many of the details—okay, most of the details—don't match those in Haney's story. But then again, when he told the story, he probably wasn't all that con-cerned with the details. He was concerned with his and the Babe's verbal jousting. And of course that's the one thing we can't check.

BABE RUTH & LEE FOHL

Babe Ruth, greatest home run hitter of all time, rose solidly to the defense of Bucky Harris here, March 15, in the much-discussed controversial move made by the Yankee skipper in the 1947 World's Series when he walked Pete Reiser purposely with what proved to be the winning run in Floyd Bevens's near no-hitter.

"I would have done the same thing myself—and would do it every time under the same circumstances," said Ruth. "It is playing percentage to walk a home run hitter if he is the winning run.

"I remember on one occasion back in 1918. The failure of a manager to walk me not only lost the ball game but cost the manager his job.

"We were playing Cleveland and Lee Fohl was managing. Steve O'Neill was behind the bat. We went into the ninth inning trailing, 8 to 5, and loaded the bases.

"O'Neill wanted to walk me. Fohl, who was the manager, refused, and told O'Neill to let Fred Coumbe pitch to me. I socked the first pitch out of the park. The next day Fohl was fired.

"Tris Speaker often walked me with three men on base—if he was two or three runs ahead and a home run would beat him. 'Put the big lug on,' he would say. 'It only costs you one run. If you let him hit, it will cost you four.' "

—*The Sporting News* (Stan Baumgartner, March 24, 1948)

Well, just a rudimentary check of Ruth's specifics turns up one problem: Lee Fohl was not fired in 1918. In 1918, he managed the Indians for all 129 games (everybody played an abbreviated schedule that season because of the war). He did manage only seventy-eight games in 1919, though. So the Babe's a year off.

Officially at least, Fohl was not fired; officially he resigned on July 19. According to a report in the *Times*, Fohl tendered his resignation with the following explanation: "I feel that the fans are not for me, and as I have your interests at heart first and my own last, I think it best for all concerned for me to step down and out. The team has a chance to win the pennant and I don't want to appear in the light of being a hindrance to it. I hope Cleveland will win the pennant."

More from the *Times*:

The unfortunate ending of yesterday's game with Boston, when Ruth hit a home run with three on bases, giving Boston the game, 8–7, is said to have caused Fohl to resign. Fans who saw the game were bitter in their criticism of Fohl for picking Coumbe, who had not pitched a game in two months, to pitch to Ruth, instead of one of the first-string hurlers.[1]

This passage does cast some doubt on Ruth's story, as it suggests that Fohl's mistake was not in pitching to Ruth, but in choosing the wrong pitcher to pitch to Ruth.

Did this game mean anything? Here's what Franklin Lewis wrote in *The Cleveland Indians*, his franchise history published in 1949 . . .

> It is doubtful if any one game ever played in the major leagues surpassed the dramatic contest unfolded in League Park on July 18, 1919. The significance of the crushing outcome and the human equations that came to the fore will be permanent signposts on Cleveland's baseball boulevards.

Ruth had the wrong year, but Lewis nails the date: July 18, 1919. The Red Sox were defending World Series champs, but they weren't good in 1919 and they'd lost nine straight games to Cleveland. Hi Jasper started for the Indians that afternoon. Ruth hit a two-run shot off Jasper in the fourth, and the game was 3–3 heading into the eighth.[*]

The Indians scored four in the bottom of the eighth and took a 7–3 lead into the ninth. Myers was out of the game, but his relief let in a run. With two outs and the bases loaded, "the next batter"—as Lewis wrote—"had to be, as if in a plot, Babe Ruth!" Lewis tells what happened next (or what he believed happened next) so well that I'll stay out of his way for a moment.

> Three pitchers were warming up in the Cleveland bull pen in the right-field corner, in the shade of the big wall. Two were right-handers, the third Fritz Coumbe, a left-hander who threw a wide and bothersome curve.
>
> As Ruth dawdled outside the batter's box, wiping his hands across the letters of his uniform, Fohl yelled to the umpires to stop the game.[*] He looked to center field to pick up a secret signal flashed by Speaker. The signal was one of dozens employed by Fohl and Speaker.
>
> A right-hander should relieve Myers, read Speaker's signal.

Actually, I have to get in the way here, because two questions come to mind. One, why a right-hander to face the Babe? The standard choice would be a southpaw to face the lefty-hitting slugger. And two, why was

---

* According to Lewis, Hi Jasper was a rookie. He wasn't, having pitched 107 innings with the Cardinals in 1916.

Speaker flashing a signal? That one's easier to answer. In that era, many teams employed either a player-manager or a playing captain who made many of the decisions that today we associate with managing: infield defense, pitching changes, and the like. It's not surprising that Fohl would take cues from Speaker, a veteran superstar and perhaps the most admired player in the league. What's surprising is that Speaker's cue would include a right-handed reliever. Okay, back to Lewis.

> Fohl looked to the bull pen and made a motion with his left arm. Coumbe threw one last warm-up pitch and turned to walk to the mound.
>
> The Tribe infielders looked sharply at Speaker when they heard his voice in back of them.
>
> "No! No!" the Gray Eagle was shouting. "No, no, not Coumbe."
>
> But Fohl had sat down on the bench, and Coumbe was warming up by then. Speaker turned his back to the plate, and there was a slight droop to his shoulders. Bobtailed thoughts coursed through Speaker's mind. Had Fohl read the sign right? Should he run in and argue with Lee? Or had Fohl decided that a left-hander, even if he threw "slow stuff" such as Coumbe practiced, was a better bet against the left-handed Ruth than any right-hander?
>
> The fans noticed Speaker's confusion, and there was a murmur throughout the stands. There was a mass gasp a few seconds later when Coumbe wound up and delivered what was described by observers as a "perfect curve." The ball cut across the plate, waist high. Ruth swung with a vicious grunt, but the speed of the ball had fooled him. His bat had completed the arc before the sphere reached the plate.
>
> Steve O'Neill, the burly catcher, called time and trotted out to the mound.
>
> "Look, pitch this guy very low, in the dirt if you have to get it down that far," he told Coumbe. "But don't give him anything up high or inside. Put him on if you have to, but keep that ball out of the pocket."
>
> Again Coumbe wound up, and again he pitched. And again it was a beautiful slow curve. But again, alas, it was in the groove, and that time the mighty Ruth had followed the ball perfectly. Some say the ball was found later on top of a laundry building on the far side of Lexington Avenue. Some say it bounced and rolled to Euclid Avenue, a dozen blocks to the north.
>
> Three happy Red Sox crossed the plate in front of the grinning Bambino. The greatest slugger of all time was just getting the feel of home runs then. He had almost completed the transition from pitcher to outfielder, and home runs were nails useful in barricading himself against a return to the rubber.
>
> That particular home run was one of twenty-nine Ruth hit in 1919,

but it did the damage of a thousand. The Indians, their spirits crushed, couldn't score in the last of the ninth and soon they were taking the dreary walk through the passageway to their dressing room, losers by an 8-to-7 score. The game might be retrieved, they told themselves, but the implications were eternal.[2]

Eternal is a strong word, and Lewis attempts to earn it—if just implicitly—by tying this incident to Ruth's permanent switch from pitching to outfielding. That's a bit of a stretch. Ruth drew a starting mound assignment just three days later and pitched again four days after that. By that point he had little interest in mound duties, but was pressed into service because ace Carl Mays had jumped the club. Once Mays was traded in late July and reinforcements arrived, Ruth was off the hook and would start only three more games over the season's last two months.

That said, Fohl's resignation—or firing, depending on whom you believe—certainly did have long-term ramifications. Speaker took over as manager, and while the Indians couldn't catch the White Sox in 1919, they did play well enough down the stretch to finish second. And in 1920 they won their first pennant in franchise history (and wouldn't win another until 1948). Fohl, meanwhile, took over as manager of the St. Louis Browns in 1921. In his first season, the Browns finished above .500 for only the second time since 1908. In his second season, the Browns missed winning *their* first pennant by the barest of margins, finishing one game behind the first-place Yankees.*

Would the Indians have won in 1919 if Fohl had still been managing? Would the Browns have won in '22 if Fohl had *not* been managing? Obviously, we cannot know. And all because Fred Coumbe hung a curveball.

Postscript: There's something else about Ruth's story that intrigues me: "Tris Speaker often walked me with three men on base—if he was two or three runs ahead and a home run would beat him. 'Put the big lug on,' he would say. 'It only costs you one run. If you let him hit, it will cost you four.' "

That sounds an awful lot like an intentional walk, doesn't it? I first began researching the subject of bases-loaded intentional walks—BLIBBs, I called them—in 1997, and I was able to find only one verifiable case: on July 23, 1944, Giants manager Mel Ott ordered a BLIBB for Cubs outfielder Bill "Swish" Nicholson. Since then, researchers Bill Deane and Ev Parker have confirmed that Athletics manager Connie Mack ordered up a BLIBB to

---

* The Browns would win just one pennant, in 1944, before moving to Baltimore in 1954.

Cleveland's Nap Lajoie in 1901. Deane has also discovered an unlikely example: in 1928, John McGraw—perhaps overreacting a bit to the game's new power dynamic—ordered a bases-loaded intentional walk for Brooklyn's Del Bissonette . . . who was playing in just his sixteenth game in the majors (but already had five doubles, two triples, and four homers to his credit).

It's also been written that Mel Ott drew a BLIBB in 1929. The Phillies and Giants had a doubleheader on the next-to-last day of the season, and Ott—then only twenty years old—entered the day tied for the National League home-run lead with Philadelphia's Chuck Klein. In the first game, Klein went ahead with his forty-third homer of the season (thus breaking the National League record held by Rogers Hornsby).

In the second game, Ott singled his first time up.

> According to an account in the *New York American*, on Mel's next at-bat, Phillies pitcher Phil Collins threw the first three pitches "increasingly wide." The next pitch was described as "even wider," but the little slugger went after it, swinging and missing. The same thing happened on the following pitch. The next pitch was so far outside that "Ott couldn't have reached it with a pole." In a flagrant exhibition of poor sportsmanship by Phillies manager Burt Shotton . . . Ott was intentionally walked in his remaining five trips to the plate to protect Klein's lead. The last walk came with the bases loaded, forcing in a run, and Mel was so disgusted that, with the Giants having a lopsided lead, he deliberately stepped off first base and allowed himself to be tagged out.[3]

I know it wasn't official, but I would say that last one probably counts, wouldn't you? Anyway, less than a year after I first wrote about BLIBBs, Buck Showalter ordered one for Barry Bonds. And at this writing, it hasn't happened since, so there are three recorded (so far) instances since the nineteenth century. And yet Ruth suggests this happened to him with some frequency.

We can assume that Ruth drew many walks while the bases were full. We can assume that some of those walks were intentional, in the sense that the pitcher wasn't interested in throwing anything remotely hittable. Would any of them have passed muster as Intentional if an official scorer had been keeping track? I have no idea. But if you're interested in burying your nose in microfilm for a few weeks, here's your big chance. The truth is out there.

In the same Stan Baumgartner column, Ruth closes with this:

"Last year I saw the Giants play the Cardinals. The Cards led, 2 to 1, going into the ninth. The Giants had two men out and a run on base. Big Johnny Mize was at bat and a right-hander in the box. A left-hander was warming up in the bullpen. It would have been playing percentage to walk Mize, but he was allowed to hit. And instead of a southpaw going in to pitch against him, he hit the right-hander's second toss over the right field wall for a home run. That's why I say Bucky Harris was right. You can't take a chance with dynamite and Reiser was dynamite."

Oddly—or maybe not so oddly, given what we know about the memory of old men—Ruth's thirty-year-old memory was no more accurate than his year-old memory. Here, Ruth is recalling a game at the Polo Grounds on July 24, 1946. With the scored tied 1–1 (not 2–1 as Ruth says) in the bottom of the ninth, Mize hit a 420-foot homer into the "upper right-field stand" to beat right-hander Johnny Beazley and the Cardinals.[4]

JOHN FELSKE & HAL JEFFCOAT

Felske has a strong pragmatic intelligence, and through twelve years as a catcher, he has mentally recorded managerial excesses. Once he played under Pete Reiser, an outfielder of infinite talent who destroyed his career by running head first into walls. By the time Felske played for him, Reiser was a sour man who ragged at his players. After one particularly unpleasant session, Felske went out and got the hits that won a game.

"I only was on you," Reiser said later, "because it makes you a better ball player." Telling the story Felske smiled a hard smile. "Reiser got on me because he was a disappointed man. Both of us knew that, but I just walked away."

At Palatka, Florida, Felske played for Hal Jeffcoat, who spent twelve years in the major leagues. During that season, Jeffcoat was fired. He immediately called a team meeting.

"Before I go," Jeffcoat said, "there's just one thing I want you all to understand. None of you sons of bitches will ever make the major leagues."

—Roger Kahn, *A Season in the Sun* (1977)

This would have been in 1962. In those days, Organized Baseball ranged from the majors all the way down to Class D. There were seven Class D leagues in '62, and the Palatka Cubs were the worst team in the Class D Florida State League. Like many minor leagues at that time, the F.S.L. worked under Shaughnessy rules, with the season split into halves. At the close of the first half on June 24, the Cubs had the league's worst record. Jeffcoat was fired—officially, he resigned—on or about July 18.[1]

He was wrong about his sons of bitches, though. Wrong about a lot of them. True, most of the P-Cubs didn't enjoy long professional careers, and many of them did not advance beyond Class D. But among the twenty-nine men who played for the

Cubs that summer, five eventually played in the majors.

- Billy Connors went 3-4 with a 2.53 ERA. He pitched in only eleven games, and it's quite possible that he didn't arrive until after Jeffcoat was gone. Connors reached the majors in 1966, pitched in parts of three seasons for the Cubs and the Mets, and wound up with a 7.53 ERA. He later was a pitching coach in the majors for many years.

- Jake Jaeckel went 5-12 with a 4.94 ERA in a league that was extremely pitcher-friendly. So we might forgive Jeffcoat for his presumed skepticism. Nevertheless, in 1964 Jacckel got into four games with the major-league Cubs and pitched eight scoreless innings.

- Infielder Bob Pfiel, an everyday player for Jeffcoat (and his three successors), earned a World Series ring in 1969, when he batted .232 in sixty-two games with the Mets.
- Right-hander Steve Shea wasn't a P-Cub for long, throwing only twenty-one innings. He pitched briefly for the Astros in 1968, and more briefly for the Expos in '69, finishing with a solid 3.22 ERA in fifty major-league innings.

And then of course there's John Felske. He got into four games with the major-league Cubs in '68 and played some with the Brewers in '72 and '73. As things turned out, of course, Roger Kahn was wise to talk to Felske about managing, because Felske became a manager. He started managing in the minors in 1974 and took over as manager of the Phillies in 1985, presumably with memories of Reiser and Jeffcoat and all the managers he'd played for still fresh in his mind. Two years later he was fired, and afterward Mike Schmidt, his best player, said, "Communication with John was a problem. He was too sensitive. If somebody even made a suggestion, he'd blow his stack."[2]

In Mike Schmidt's book, *Clearing the Bases* (2006), he doesn't have a single word to spare for John Felske, his manager for two years and two months. On the other hand, he does find room for the following, related to the Phillies' trading Larry Bowa for Ivan DeJesus (and Ryne Sandberg), and five players, including Manny Trillo, for Von Hayes: "All this was a direct result of free agency. The Phillies traded guys who would soon become free agents rather than lose them for nothing. Manny Trillo, for example, wanted top dollar or he was going elsewhere, so we traded him. On the other hand, the organization signed Ed Farmer, the top reliever in the American League, as a free agent."

Wait a minute . . . *THE Ed Farmer?* The same Ed Farmer who entered the '82 season with a 4.14 ERA? Granted, in 1980 Farmer had been pretty good with the White Sox, saving thirty games and posting a 3.34 ERA. He'd been pretty good in '79, too. But the best reliever in the American League? In 1981, Farmer pitched fifty-three innings and got hung with a 4.61 ERA. Also in 1981: Milwaukee's Rollie Fingers *did* win the Cy Young Award, New York's Rich Gossage *did* finish sixth in the voting, and Kansas City's Dan Quisenberry *did* post a 1.73 ERA.

So how did this happen? Here's a clue: on page 60, Schmidt writes about 1987: "Glenn Wilson took over as my sidekick when Ed Farmer left." So that's probably it: when it came to his buddy, Schmidt simply couldn't remember straight.

STEVE BOROS & STEVE GARVEY

I've been around long enough now that I've played for quite a few managers. One thing I've noticed is that whenever teams change managers, they usually try to get somebody who's exactly the opposite of what they had before. Dick Williams was too tough, so they hired Steve Boros. He was too nice, so they hired Larry Bowa to make sure we wouldn't get away with anything. It's culture shock is what it is. . . .

Steve Boros lasted just that one year. And I never saw him get mad. He had the weirdest way of getting thrown out of a game I've ever seen. Steve Garvey, who was finishing his career with the Padres, got tossed one night, for the first time ever. The funny thing was, he didn't do anything; he was on deck when Bip Roberts was coming in to score, and they called him out. Bip threw his helmet and said some things. Garvey was walking to the plate to go to bat and the umpire thought he had said it, so they threw Garvey out of the game.

Next day they were at home plate exchanging the lineup cards, and Boros pulled a videotape out of his jacket pocket. He said, "Here, watch this. If you do you'll see Garvey didn't say anything." And they ran him right there.

—John Kruk in *"I Ain't an Athlete, Lady": My Well-Rounded Life and Times*
(Kruk with Paul Hagen, 1994)

Well, maybe. Kruk was a rookie with the Padres in 1986, and Boros was the manager, and Garvey was finishing up his career, and Bip Roberts did play in 101 games. My first impulse was to scour Garvey's game log in Retrosheet, looking for an ejection, but then my first impulse always seems designed to maximize the amount of time I waste. Fortunately, it occurred to me that if Boros was ejected, that would have been newsworthy. And doubly newsworthy if Garvey had been ejected for the first time in his long career. Sure enough, a quick search of the *New York Times* archives turned this up, from the June 7, 1986, edition:

Steve Boros, the San Diego Padres manager, was ejected before tonight's game against the Atlanta Braves for bringing to the plate during the exchange of lineups a videotape of a controversial triple play.

While presenting his lineup card at home plate, Boros also brought a tape of Thursday night's triple play, in which Umpire Charlie Williams called out Bip Roberts at home plate to complete the play.

Williams promptly ejected Boros for displaying the tape.

Steve Garvey, who was the on-deck hitter at the time of the third-inning play Thursday, objected to William's call and was ejected for the first time in his major league career.

"Look, you can see the skid mark where his hand came across the plate," Garvey said to Williams at the time. "Hey, we got to bear down."

For his remarks, Williams ejected Garvey. "He was trying to show me up," the umpire said.

It was also the first time in Boros's major league managing career that he was ejected.[1]

On the 5th, in the top of the third, Roberts had led off against Atlanta's Zane Smith with a single, and Tony Gwynn followed with a single that moved Roberts to second. Next up, Kevin McReynolds hit a ground ball to Smith, who started a routine 1-4-3 double play, which turned into a triple play when Roberts got nailed trying to score.

According to both Kruk and the UPI, that is. But since when does a runner have time to score—or even try to score—on an apparently routine double play in the infield? And indeed, Retrosheet's game account has Roberts being tagged out at third base, not home plate, with the throw going first to third. Now, this would of course be an odd play, too. Roberts could have walked to third base while the double play was being turned—unless he simply rounded the base too far and was caught trying to get back.

To resolve this apparent discrepancy—was he called out at home by plate-umpire Williams? or at third by somebody else?—I turned to the *San Diego Tribune*, which seems to have the story exactly right.

> For history's sake, the blow-by-blow: With his team trailing, 3–1, Padres rookie Bip Roberts, playing in his first game since suffering a groin injury on May 20, led off the third with his second hit of the night, a single to right field, and Tony Gwynn singled him to third.
>
> That brought up Kevin McReynolds. He hit a ground ball sharply, and Zane Smith, the Braves' left-handed pitcher, fielded it as he came off the mound. Smith whirled and threw to second baseman Glenn Hubbard, who stepped on the base and then relayed the ball to first baseman Bob Horner for a routine double play.
>
> But the play wasn't over. Roberts made a belated break from third to home as Hubbard threw to Horner, and Horner fired the ball to Atlanta catcher Ozzie Virgil Jr. Roberts head-faked and ducked under Virgil, his hand brushing across home plate—an apparent run to make the score 3–2.
>
> Williams didn't see it that way. Virgil noticed that the umpire had made no call, and he ran over to tag Roberts as he lay sprawled on the

🐟 *Longtime Phillies executive Bill Giles grew up around baseball, and his book is full of funny stories, most of which don't check out precisely. Take this one . . .*

Fun-loving players such as John Kruk always add to the joy of working in major league baseball. While some players feel they need to be intensely serious to be successful, Frank "Tug" McGraw did not have that problem. He was about having fun as well as being a terrific relief pitcher and tough competitor.

In the heat of the pennant race in 1980, he came into a game against the Cincinnati Reds in the bottom of the ninth. There were two outs, and the bases were loaded with slugger Tony Perez at the plate. McGraw struck him out and was asked after the game if he was nervous in that situation.

"I read the other day that 10,000 years from now the earth will be a big ball of ice," McGraw replied. "When that happens, no one is going to care what I did against Tony Perez."

—Bill Giles in *Pouring Six Beers at a Time: And Other Stories from a Lifetime in Baseball* (Giles with Doug Myers, 2007)

Sounds like a late-season save, doesn't it? Perhaps, but it couldn't have been real late, as the Phillies didn't play the Reds—they were in different divisions, by the way—after the 3rd of August. McGraw's last save (and last appearance) against the Reds in 1980 was on

But he retired the Reds in order, and Tony Perez didn't bat. He couldn't have. In 1980, Perez was a Red Sox, not a Red, and hadn't been one since 1976. McGraw did save a couple of wins against the Reds in '76, but in neither of them did he strike out Perez with runners on base. On April 28, with the Phillies clinging to a 7–6 lead in the ninth, McGraw did strike out Perez with one out and nobody on. Johnny Bench then tripled, but McGraw struck out Bob Bailey to end the game.

Whatever the vagaries of Giles's memory, it's a good line.

ground. Williams called Roberts out, though television replays indicated the player had indeed touched home safely.[2]

According to Mark Kreidler in the *Tribune*, "Garvey had played 2,201 major-league games—and all of his college and high-school days—without ever being told to take a hike."

" 'He showed me up there at home plate. He had no business doing that,' Williams said. 'That's the gist of it. The rest will be in the report (that he files with the league).' "

Again according to Kreidler, Garvey went to the plate and told Williams that if he just looked at the ground, he would see the marks in the dirt where Roberts's hand must have brushed the plate. And told Williams, "We've got to bear down," which probably is what got him kicked out.

A lot of people think the "magic words" when you're yelling at an umpire begin with an *m*, end with an *r*, and have an *f* in the middle, and those will usually do the trick. But umpires absolutely hate *bear down*, too, because it implies not that he made a mistake (which is bad enough) but that he just isn't trying hard enough. Combine *bear down* with actually suggesting to an umpire that he, you know, look at some actual evidence, and you're just asking to get dumped.

Oh, and about that videotape? I haven't seen it. But all the postgame accounts suggest that Garvey did say *something*, and that Boros brought out the videotape because it proved Roberts was safe.

HARRY REID & BUD BEAZLEY (SP?)

. . . Which reminds me of a story. We had a coach at Reno High School, was a coach for many, many years. Bud Beazley [sp?] was his name. He was a pitcher, for the Sacramento Bees, which was a triple-A baseball team. He was a left-handed pitcher, really quite good. But he did some unusual things. For example, when the manager came to take him out once, he lay down on the mound and wouldn't leave. One time the manager came out to get the ball from him, he threw it in the stands. The reason I mention this, he's the only person in professional baseball that was thrown out of a game before it started. And that's kind of how I look at President Bush on the appropriations bills: he's talking about vetoing things before we even get to them.

—Senator Harry Reid (D-Nev.) in press conference, July 10, 2007

I've never heard of Bud Beazley, and I don't even know if that's how to spell his name. I spelled it that way, when replaying the clip on my TV, because I'm familiar with Johnny Beazley, who won twenty-one games with the Cardinals in 1942. But "Bud" isn't Johnny, who never pitched west of the Texas League. The only other Beazley I can find, Dan Beazley, wasn't a "Bud" or a pitcher; he was a "Hoke" and an outfielder. There's also an Earl Beesley, and he did pitch, but not in the Pacific Coast League.

The popular spelling is B-E-A-S-L-E-Y. Hf there really is a Bud, he probably was a Beasley. So now it's just a matter of plowing through all the Beasleys— there are a bunch of them—who played during the years when the Sacramento Bees existed.

Except they didn't. Considering that Harry Reid's a Mormon, he must know that the Pacific Coast League's Bees played not in Sacramento, but rather in Salt Lake City from 1946 through 1957. And con-sidering that Reid was born in 1939, these must be the Bees to whom he's referring.*

Or not. Turns out Reid was right about Sacra-mento and wrong about the Bees. Only one Beasley pitched in the PCL during Reid's youth: the Beasley who pitched for the Sacramento Solons from 1944 through the middle of the '47 season, then joined the PCL's Seattle Rainiers.

I say "the" Beasley because I am not, at the moment, sure about his given name. The Professional Baseball Player Database, usually reliable and my go-to source for information about minor leaguers, says his name was Andrew. Dennis Snelling's *The Pacific Coast League: A Statistical History, 1903–1957*, also is usually reliable and says his name was Bud: Bud Louis Beasley. For the moment I'll simply call him Beasley, which seems to be true.

---

* There were earlier Bees, in the Pacific Coast League (1915–1925), the Utah-Idaho League (1926–1928), and the Pioneer League (1939–1942).

Yet another odd mixture of baseball and politics, this one from Jolly Charlie Grimm . . .

We had our own night club on Catalina, a spot called the White Cap . . .

The most spectacular incident in the White Cap occurred when the Cubs were getting ready for the 1939 season. A handsome young man bearing the credentials of radio station WHO, in the Cubs' shouting territory of Des Moines, in the old Western League, joined our jolly press group that spring. The press table, down on the field, wasn't more than twelve feet long, but this fellow, arriving early, grabbed at least half of the space. Des Moines was a Cub farm, and this lad had come prepared to make platters of the action during our practice sessions and send them back to Des Moines. The Chicago writers took a dim view. What was this guy doing there, crowding them out? In those days, the newspaper reporters looked on all radio announcers, even if they were nice people, as interlopers. Who did they think they were, barging in like this?

. . . The reporters were indignant. Warren Brown and Ed Burns gave him a baleful glance. And so did Jimmy Corcoran, a little red-thatched Irishman who was everybody's friend.

That night, in a gathering of the clan in the White Cap, this man from WHO showed up. There were words, and Jimmy Cork, who would have to eat a stalk of bananas to make the lightweight limit, went into action. He took a swing at the

Photo courtesy of David Eskenazi Collection

Bud Beasley

Also true: Beasley wasn't your garden-variety pitcher. Let's start with Snelling's short bio:

> Had played only semi-pro ball in Reno plus short stint with the House of David when signed to Sacramento contract. Developed elaborate routines on the mound both to disrupt the batter and to entertain fans. Taught high school until June each season; 1995 marked his 61st year in the classroom.[1]

No wonder Harry Reid knows a Bud Beasley story; the guy must have been a legend in Nevada. He was a legend wherever he pitched, too. He didn't pitch much—in parts of five PCL seasons, he won only twenty-three games—but he made a big impression. In *The Grand Minor League*, Dick Dobbins wrote of Beasley, "A school teacher from Reno, he joined the team late and left it early. But while he played he drove opposing batters crazy with a delivery that included windmill arms and multiple pumps before he ever threw the pitch. Beasley was a Pacific Coast League original."

I've not been able to track down an account of Beasley getting kicked out of a game before it started, but he just might have led the league in ejection percentage. In the Dobbins book, Beasley recalls two incidents in great detail . . .

> On one occasion in Los Angeles, I got kicked out of the game for rolling the ball to home plate. The ball was loaded, and the batter asked for the ball. The umpire asked me for the ball, and I rolled the ball to him. So of course, by the time it got to the plate, it was unloaded. So I got fined and kicked out of that one.
>
> I'm pitching a game for Emeryville in 1946 and I don't like the feel of the ball, so I ask for a new one. As I'm walking back to the mound with the new ball, I don't like the feel of that one either, so I ask for another. The umpire gives me the original ball, remarking to Lilio Marcucci, my catcher, "The dumb left-hander has the same ball."
>
> Well, the dumb left-hander winds up and throws the ball over the stands and out into the street. So I go up and ask, "Now may I have a new ball?" The umpire responds, "Yes, and you can have a bar of soap, too. Go take a shower."

So Harry Reid offers his story about Bud Beasley, and as he's turning to leave, one of the attending reporters—and if you're out there, canny reporter, please drop me a line—could be heard telling Reid that "Dave Bristol, manager of the Braves" also was once thrown out of a game before it started. To which Reid responded with a wry smile, "So Bud Beasley's not the only guy? Okay."

Not the only guy, indeed. Just a few examples:

- Bristol, who did manage the Braves in 1976 and '77, was actually ejected before a game in 1975, when he was the Expos' third-base coach. It was July 6 in St. Louis, and when Bristol went to the plate to exchange lineup cards, he continued a scrape with Cardinals outfielder Reggie Smith from the previous evening. In addition to getting kicked out of the game before it began, Bristol also drew a hefty $350 fine.
- June 7, 1986, before the game, Steve Boros brought his lineup card to the plate. Also brought videotape of triple play from the night before and was immediately ejected by Charlie Williams (see page 52).

man from Des Moines, who ducked. The Cork's punch landed in the expansive midriff of Ed Burns. The target he missed was the kid from Iowa, whose name was, and is, Ronald Reagan!

. . . I had come to like Reagan. A few days after this White Cap caper, Ron came around to say good-bye. He was leaving the Magic Isle to take a movie test. At first, I didn't think he was serious, but Bob Lewis took him over to the boat dock after practice. And that's the last I saw of Ronald Reagan.

—Charlie Grimm in Jolly Cholly's Story: Baseball, I Love You! (Charlie Grimm with Ed Prell, 1968)

Two things about this story bother me. One, if you take a swing at a guy and he ducks, how do you hit another guy in the midriff? And two, the timing here isn't right. The Cubs did train on Catalina Island in the spring of 1939—they trained there every spring from 1921 through '51, except during the war years—but this almost certainly couldn't have happened in 1939, because by then Reagan had already established himself in Hollywood. He starred (as a radio reporter) in 1937's Love is on the Air, *and has nine screen credits for 1938. So if this happened as Grimm recalls—and he was managing the Cubs at the time—it probably happened in 1937. In fact, that was the year in which Reagan got his Hollywood screen test. If the Cubs had not trained in California, Reagan wouldn't have been there for his screen test, and he might*

☞

have spent his entire professional career as a baseball broadcaster; in 1936, The Sporting News conducted a fan poll, asking its readers, "Who is your favorite baseball broadcaster?" and "Dutch" Reagan finished fourth among broadcasters not in major league cities.

Grimm lived to see his eighty-fifth birthday, and nearly three years of Reagan's Presidency.

- On July 16, 1989, Angels manager Doug Rader was ejected before a game against the Orioles, for arguing Mike Devereaux's disputed game-ending home run (fair vs. foul) from the night before.

- Earl Weaver accomplished this feat at least twice. On August 15, 1975, he got ejected during the first game of a doubleheader against the Rangers, and then again during the meeting at home plate prior to the nightcap. Just a bit more than ten years later, on September 29, 1985, he did it again. Ejected during the first game of a doubleheader against the Yankees, he got ejected before the second game, too (that daily double got him a three-game suspension from the league).

- And finally, my favorite, on July 30, 1996. Before the second game of a doubleheader, umpire Joe West got upset when Mets coach Bobby Wine was a little late bringing out the lineup card. West ejected Wine. Of course, that brought manager Dallas Green out of the dugout. West ran him, too.

I'm sure there are many more. I do wish I had the time to track down Beasley's pregame ejection, and let me say this in defense of the Honorable Senator from Nevada: among the examples I've been able to find, none of the offenders were players. So maybe what Reid *meant* to say was that Beasley was the only *player* thrown out of a game before it started. Perhaps the Senator did not get his facts wrong. He simply misspoke.

MIKE CUELLAR & EARL WEAVER

Yes, technological advancements are transforming the pitch counter, but that same technology can't do much for the pitchers themselves. Today's starting pitchers are not nearly as durable as the older models, who routinely finished what they started before rigid pitch counts helped the complete game to become an endangered species.

But even though it is utilized, referenced, and debated more than ever, keeping a pitch count isn't anything new. But let's just say it wasn't quite as important in baseball's past, as an anecdote from Hall of Famer Jim Palmer will demonstrate.

"The first time I ever kept a chart," the former Oriole great recalled recently, "Cuellar gave up a leadoff hit with a 5–2 lead with Carew, Oliva, and Killebrew coming up, and I said, 'Mr. Weaver, that's his 135th pitch.' "

And legendary manager Earl Weaver responded, "Get your rear end to the other end of the dugout. I'll let you know if he's tired."

Palmer said, "So I got the idea right then that pitch counts didn't mean much to Earl."

—J. P. Pelzman, NorthJersey.com (July 1, 2007)

Mike Cuellar joined the Orioles in 1969 and was an Oriole for eight years. Harmon Killebrew left the Twins after the 1974 season. In those six seasons, '69 through '74, all the other principals—Palmer, Weaver, Carew, and Oliva—were in their assigned places. According to Retrosheet, Cuellar pitched against the Twins twenty-one times in those six seasons.

I went through all twenty-one of Cuellar's starts, looking for games in which 1) Carew, Oliva, and Killebrew played, 2) Cuellar was pitching with a late-inning lead, 3) the Twins' leadoff hitter reached base, and 3) Carew, Oliva, and Killebrew were coming up.

You might be surprised by how few games came anywhere close to meeting all those qualifications. For one thing, it was *never* Carew-Oliva-Killebrew, in that order. In all six seasons when they were in the lineup together, it went Carew-Killebrew-Oliva, perhaps because their managers wanted Killebrew breaking up the left-handed hitters. That's a trifle, for our purposes.

What's not a trifle is that they weren't often in the lineup together at all. Because of injuries, Carew missed most of 1970, Oliva most of 1972, and Killebrew most of 1973. Of those twenty-one games, in only eight did all three start. In seven of those, Carew-Killebrew-Oliva batted two-three-four; in the other, Carew led off and Danny Thompson batted second, followed by the other guys.

🖎 Ken Kaiser (and his co-author David Fisher) tells good stories . . .

After a ball was fouled out of play, or if a ball got dirty, or even if a pitcher just didn't like the feel of a baseball, I'd put a new baseball in play. The pitcher would look at the new ball I'd given him and most of the time he'd keep it. But, every once in a while a pitcher would decide he didn't like the new ball and toss it to me to be exchanged for another new ball. I am now about to reveal, for the first time, my big secret. When that happened I'd put the first ball in my ball bag—and then I would take out the same ball and throw it back to the pitcher. The same ball! I did it a thousand times. Two thousand. Only once did a pitcher realize what I'd done. Jim Palmer. One afternoon in Baltimore I tossed him a new ball and he looked at it, rolled it over in his hand, walked a few steps toward the plate and flipped it back to me, telling me, "This is the same ball I just gave you."

—Ken Kaiser and David Fisher,
Planet of the Umps (2003)

So that's eight games. In only six of those were the Orioles ahead in the seventh inning or later. Remember, Palmer specifically recalled a 5–2 lead. There's just one match there: May 12, 1970. That was the score, heading into the bottom of the seventh.

The leadoff man did *not* single, though. George Mitterwald led off and grounded out. With the pitcher due next, thirty-six-year-old rookie Minnie Mendoza slapped a pinch-hit single into right-center field.* Which brought up leadoff man Cesar Tovar, who walked. And *then* came Carew-Killebrew-Oliva.

Carew singled, scoring Mendoza, and Weaver pulled Cuellar. The Twins scored another run, but the Orioles wound up winning 5–4.

So that one's reasonably close. But then there's *this* game, which in some ways is a better match: May 13, 1969. Heading into the bottom of the eighth, the Orioles led 2–1. Tovar led off with a single, with Carew and the others coming up next. Those last two details match Palmer's recollection exactly.

What's missing, though, is the rest of the story. After Tovar's single, Cuellar balked. Carew followed with an inside-the-park homer, and the lead was blown. *Then* Weaver yanked Cuellar, but it was too late; the Orioles wound up losing 4–2.

What's also missing are 135 pitches. After Tovar's single, Cuellar had pitched seven-plus innings and given up seven hits and one walk, with five strikeouts. Does that add up to 135 pitches, usually? Not usually. In the 1970 game, before giving up Carew's single, he'd pitched six and one-third innings, and given up six hits and three walks, with five strikeouts. Does that add up to 135, usually? Not usually.

Using a pitch-count estimator devised by Tom "Tangotiger" Tango, I come up with roughly 106 pitches in the 1969 game, and 106 in the '70 game. Could the estimator be off by more than thirty pitches in one of those games? It's highly unlikely. My guess is that Palmer, nearly forty years later, simply doesn't have his facts straight. Not nearly straight.

I ran the estimator for each of Cuellar's starts from 1969 through '74, and only three of his twenty-one starts against the Twins reach even 125 (estimated) pitches. Remember, if Palmer's memory is accurate, Cuellar would have to have thrown *more* than 135 pitches: the 135 before Carew, and however many he threw afterward.

Here are those three games (with estimated pitches in parentheses):

---

* This would be the last of Mendoza's three career hits.

- July 16, 1970 (137): Killebrew made the last out in the seventh, Oliva the first out in the eighth, and none of the estimable trio batted again in the game.
- June 9, 1971 (134): Carew and Killebrew made the second and third outs in the eighth, Oliva the first out in the ninth. None of them batted again while Cuellar was finishing his ten-inning, complete-game win.
- June 12, 1974 (136): Killebrew pinch-hit in the seventh and didn't play afterward. Carew led off the eighth and grounded out. In the bottom of the ninth, Danny Thompson led off with a homer, cutting the Orioles' lead to just one run, 4 to 3. Glenn Borgmann grounded out. Carew was up next. If the pitch estimator is right, Cuellar had thrown approximately 130 pitches.

Is *that* the game Palmer remembers? Perhaps. Or perhaps partly. It's certainly possible that his mind has somehow combined the events of May 12, 1970, with those of June 12, 1974. But you know, Jim Palmer was once famous for his memory. And those two games were separated by nearly four years. Oh, and there's also this: typically, the man who charts the pitches is the man who's slated to start the next game. After June 12, Ross Grimsley and Dave McNally started before Palmer. Palmer also started the Orioles' third game after that 1970 start.

Which means what, exactly? I don't know. I'm not going to suggest that Palmer's story doesn't contain some kernels of truth, somewhere in there. I'm just having trouble finding those little suckers.

DAVE KINGMAN & STEVE PALERMO

One time I saw Piniella get so angry after losing an argument that he went back into the dugout and tried to kick the water cooler—and he missed that, too—and fell down. As a lot of people have learned, arguing with an umpire can be dangerous. One time, Steve Palermo was working first base and he threw Dave Kingman out of a game when Kingman argued about a checked-swing strike. After the game Kingman wouldn't let it go. He told reporters, "Tell Palermo he's got the worst case of bad breath I've ever seen. He's got to cut down on his garlic." The next day Palermo was behind the plate. Kingman singled in his first at bat and, as he started running to first, he turned to yell something at Palermo—and stumbled and fell, straining a muscle. He was out for a week. The only thing that Palermo was upset about was that it was only a week.

—Ken Kaiser in *Planet of the Umps* (Ken Kaiser with David Fisher, 2003)

Steve Palermo worked in the American League from 1976 through 1991. Dave Kingman played in the American League for a month in 1977, and from 1984 through '86. In those days, umpires were hired by one league or the other and stayed there. And of course there weren't any interleague games. So our range here is September of '77 and '84 through '86.

In '77, Palermo did umpire four games in which Kingman played, but the slugger wasn't ejected from any of them. After which Kingman returned to the National League, and their (regular-season) paths didn't cross for six seasons. They finally met again in '84, when Kingman became Oakland's everyday designated hitter. The man couldn't hit for average to save his life and wasn't much on drawing walks, either. But he could still hit the long ball, and he was durable. Nobody in the American League hit more homers from '84 through '86, and he averaged 150 games per season.

So if Kingman missed significant time because of an injury, it'll be obvious. And so it is: in 1984, he played almost every game until late May. He played on May 29, and then not again until the 12th of June. According to the Retrosheet box score, Palermo *was* behind the plate on the 29th. Also according to Retrosheet, in the previous game, on the 28th, Palermo *was* working at first base, and in the second inning he *did* eject Palermo for arguing about a checked swing.

You'd almost think Palermo (or his co-author) checked this story before I did.

Almost. There's one problem. Or rather, two. The first you've probably noticed already. It was not "only a week" that Kingman missed. He missed nearly two weeks. The other isn't really a problem, I guess. One gets the impression that Kingman got hurt after his single, early in the game, and was forced to exit. He did single in the second inning, and it's certainly possible that he fell down and hurt himself (or hurt himself and fell down). But he stayed in the game, ran the bases, scored, and later would hit a double while going the distance.

Anyway, here's what Bruce Jenkins wrote about Kingman's injury in the *San Francisco Chronicle*:

> The A's have lost Dave Kingman for at least a week, and possibly much longer, because of a torn ligament in his left knee.
>
> Kingman was injured Tuesday night when he tripped and fell about 15 feet from home plate after singling to center field against Detroit. He played the remainder of the game as the designated hitter. . . .
>
> Kingman, who signed for the major-league minimum $40,000 as a free agent this spring, leads the American League in home runs (14) and ranks second to Baltimore's Eddie Murray with 44 RBIs. He had started 88 consecutive games before yesterday, often playing despite a painful pulled muscle in his left leg.[1]

There's no mention of Kingman turning around to shout something at Palermo, but that seems like a strange detail for someone—presumably Palermo, since Kaiser wasn't there—to have invented. If it's true, then Kingman's fit of pique probably cost him the RBI crown that season, as he finished the season with 118, only 5 behind leader Tony Armas. And just two years later, Kingman, thanks in part to his lovely personality, found himself out of baseball.

DANNY LITWHILER & SUITS

Before the Fourth of July in 1946, only three Braves had hit home runs. So Lou Perini offered to purchase a $100 suit of clothes for every round-tripper hit by a Braves player.

Perini's offer must have inspired me, because in the month of August I hit eight home runs and received $800 to purchase suits. Actually, I had all the suits I needed, and I used the money for family things. I was beaned on August 31, or I may have hit more homers in the month of September.

—Danny Litwhiler in *Danny Litwhiler: Living the Baseball Dream*
(Litwhiler with Jim Sargent, 2006)

Litwhiler opened that season with the Cardinals, but played in only six games with St. Louis before the Braves purchased his contract on the 9th of June. He did hit eight home runs after joining the Braves, and it's true that he didn't hit one before the 4th of July; in fact, he didn't get started at all until August, hitting his first on August 5 against Dodgers rookie Joe Hatten. However, Litwhiler didn't hit eight homers that month. He hit his sixth on the 25th, then didn't hit another until the 22nd of September. And his eighth and final home run came on the 28th, again off Hatten.

It's true that Litwhiler might have hit more homers if he hadn't been beaned, and his memory is solid: it happened on August 31. Specifically, it happened in the fourth inning of a doubleheader against the Phillies. Litwhiler was taken to the hospital after suffering what the Associated Press reported as a "fractured left cheek bone," courtesy of right-hander Dick Mauney. But it's not at all clear

how many *more* homers Litwhiler might have hit. He was out of the lineup for only a week, but on the other hand he did struggle for the next couple of weeks, going 8 for 31 with just one extra-base hit (a double). It wasn't until the last week of the season that Litwhiler really started hitting again, finishing up 7 for 20 with a couple of homers. So that beaning might have cost Litwhiler a couple of hundred bucks.

Actually, I can't confirm Perini's offer, though it doesn't seem like something that Litwhiler would just have imagined while writing his book. I will note, however, that the cited motivation for the offer—only three Braves with homers before the 4th of July—just wasn't the case. Granted, the Braves had hit *few* home runs: only nineteen of them. But they were hit by twelve different Braves. In fact, I think that's where Litwhiler got mixed up, as only one Brave—catcher Phil Masi—had hit as many as three homers. Litwhiler simply misplaced a three.

Masi didn't hit another homer the rest of the season. Litwhiler led the club with his eight, followed by Ray Sanders and Tommy Holmes with six apiece. The Braves were outhomered for the season, 76–44, but did enough other things well to finish 81-72, their best record since 1933.

Litwhiler didn't play particularly well for the Braves in 1947, and after a slow start in '48 he found himself traded to Cincinnati. Not long afterward, Litwhiler faced a young Philadelphia Phillie named Robin Roberts . . .

> I remember one game as a pinch-hitter in Philadelphia in 1948. Robin Roberts had just come up to the Phillies. I was sitting on the bench, and I noticed Robin's delivery was tipping his curve and fastball. If I saw white in his pitching hand, it was a curve. If I did not see white, it was a fastball. He was not covering the ball in his windup.
>
> I called to Hank Sauer, our hard-hitting right-handed batting left fielder. I told Hank I could call all of Roberts' pitches with nobody on base. I called every pitch correctly on one batter, and I asked him to call them for me on the next hitter. He did.
>
> Hank came up to bat and hit a home run to tie the game. As soon as he got back to the dugout, he came over and grabbed my hand and said, "Thank you!"
>
> I told Hank to keep the information to himself, because when too many people know about tipping signs, it usually gets back to the pitcher.
>
> Later in the game, Grady Hatton, our third baseman, got into an argument with an umpire—who threw Grady out of the game. I was sent in to play third. In the eleventh inning Roberts tipped off his fastball and I hit a home run to win the game.
>
> We didn't see Roberts again for about a month. Hank and I could hardly wait to face him again. Unfortunately, someone must have clued in Robby during the meantime, because he kept the ball well covered during his windup.

Litwhiler's memory is pretty good. He and Sauer both homered against Robin Roberts on June 23. Roberts was a rookie, and this was just his second start. Sauer homered in the sixth. Litwhiler's homer came not in the eleventh, but in the ninth. They didn't see Roberts "about a month" later; they saw him *exactly* one month later, on the 23rd of July in Cincinnati. Sauer went 0 for 4, and Litwhiler singled once in three at-bats but was quickly erased in a triple play. Roberts didn't give up any home runs and beat the Reds 6 to 1 for his fourth victory.

I'm not going to say Litwhiler was wrong about Roberts's tell, early in his career. Litwhiler was a good player, a fantastic college coach, and a real in-

---

🐟 *Joe Garagiola told this one . . .*

Bob Muncrief, a much-traveled pitcher, finally hooked up with the Chicago Cubs and Frankie Frisch. In a game against the Pittsburgh Pirates, Ralph Kiner hit a key home run against the back wall in Wrigley Field to tie the game. When Muncrief got back to the bench, Frisch asked him what it was. "A doggone good curve ball. He hit a pitch," Muncrief said.

"Well, just forget about it and throw him fast balls the next time, Rock, and he won't get a loud foul," advised Frisch.

The next time up, with two men on, Kiner hit a fast ball, not only for a home run but *over* the back wall. This shot made the first one look like a bunt.

When he got to the bench, Muncrief looked right at Frisch and said: "Well, brains, he hit yours a whole lot farther than he hit mine."

—Baseball Is a Funny Game
(Garagiola & Martin Quigley, 1960)

There is just a brief window during which this might have happened, as Muncrief spent just one season in the National League, and for a third of that season he was with the Pirates, and thus a teammate of Kiner's.

But Muncrief, having been waived by Pittsburgh, joined the Cubs on June 6. Four days later, Frisch signed to manage the Cubs, replacing Charlie Grimm (who got kicked upstairs). And on September 4, 1949, Muncrief surrendered two homers to Kiner at Wrigley Field, in

☞

the second and sixth innings. Garagiola's details are a little off, though. He says the first was "key" and tied the game. That's true. He says the second was a three-run shot. But the second was also a solo shot. And for what it's worth, Muncrief, despite lasting only five-plus innings in the rain-shortened game, did gain credit for the victory, the eightieth—and last—of his major-league career.

novator in the world of baseball equipment. But it's worth noting that Robin Roberts *always* gave up a lot of home runs. He relied on high fastballs and he threw a lot of strikes, so he gave up a lot of homers. It's also worth noting that all ten of the homers that Roberts gave up in '48 were solo shots. Which goes a long way toward explaining why he's in the Hall of Fame.

JOHNNY CALLISON & GEORGE STEINBRENNER

Ralph Houk: George didn't bother me much that year, but there was one time in Texas. We had a chance to win a game. I sent Johnny Callison up to pinch-hit and he struck out or popped up. It was a big pinch hit if he had made it. George called me that night and said get rid of Callison. I said we can't get rid of Callison. Besides, we've only got about a month to go and we're going to have to pay him anyway. And in a couple of days you could expand the roster, so there was no reason to get rid of him.

But George said, "You go tell him he's gone."

I decided I wouldn't do that, so I called Lee MacPhail and I said, "Lee, I'm not going to tell Callison he's gone. I'm just not going to do it." And Lee said, "Let me talk to him [Steinbrenner]."

A little while later, Lee called and said, "You better tell Callison."

—Phil Pepe, *Talkin' Baseball: An Oral History of Baseball in the 1970s* (1998)

For those of you who weren't around thirty-five years ago, let's run through our cast of characters.

Ralph Houk managed the Yankees from 1961 through '63, and then again from '66 through 1973. "George" was (and at this writing, still is) George Steinbrenner, who bought the Yankees for $10 million on January 3, 1973.* Johnny Callison was a three-time All-Star with the Phillies, one of the game's best-hitting rightfielders in the early and middle 1960s. Lee MacPhail was the Yankees' general manager in '73.

So we know that if this happened, it must have happened in '73, because that was the only year during which Houk worked for Steinbrenner.

Anyway, the specifics here are pretty close. On August 15, Callison pinch-hit for Felipe Alou and grounded out with a couple of runners on base, ending the eighth inning and leaving the Yankees on the short end of a 3–1 score (which was how it ended). The game was not in Texas; it was in New York, and the Yankees were playing the Angels. However, two nights later the Yankees *were* in Texas when Callison played his last game for the Yankees (and forever). His appearance consisted of one half-inning in right field, and Houk can hardly be blamed for not remembering that. The next day, Callison drew his release.

So, no, I don't have a problem with Houk's de-

---

* Amazingly, of the $10 million purchase price, only $833,333.33 was actually Steinbrenner's money; the rest came from ten of Steinbrenner's acquaintances, described somewhere as "a group of rich millionaires."

tails; he's close enough. I do have a problem with his characterization of Steinbrenner as a tyrannical asshole. Which isn't to say Steinbrenner wasn't a tyrannical asshole, because I've got a groaning shelf loaded with books full of evidence that he was. But this particular anecdote is, when looked at with some moderate amount of sophistication, really a love letter to Steinbrenner.

For one thing, the Yankees were not "a couple of days" away from expanding the roster; when they released Callison, they were still a couple of *weeks* short of September 1, which is when you expand the rosters. Maybe Steinbrenner was simply being petulant, but maybe he understood that roster spots are precious. And Callison was the waste of a good roster spot. At that point he couldn't hit, at all. In forty-five games, most of them as the Yankees' rightfielder, Callison batted .176 with *four* walks and *one* home run. He'd been a good hitter as recently as 1970, but by '73, though he was only thirty-four, Callison simply couldn't hit.

The Yankees were in a terrific pennant race, and if they'd won on August 15 they'd have been just one game behind the first-place Orioles (and a half-game behind the second-place Tigers). The Yanks played terribly in September and finished seventeen games out of first place . . . but on August 18, when they released Callison, no one could know that. Steinbrenner didn't give a damn about Callison or his sixteen years in the major leagues. Steinbrenner just wanted to win, and he knew—or believed, correctly— that it would be easier to win without Callison than with him.

Particularly if Callison's roster spot went to somebody who could actually play. Which it did. The same day the Yankees released Callison, they picked up Mike Hegan, who'd mostly been riding the bench in Oakland. Hegan was far from a *good* hitter, but after joining the Yanks he started thirty-five games and batted .275 with six home runs.

Steinbrenner might have been a jerk. But with Callison, the Boss's only mistake was waiting as long as he did.

REGGIE JACKSON & BILLY MARTIN

So here is how it all ended in 1977.

Billy Martin benched me in the fifth game of the playoffs against the Kansas City Royals. That was October 9.

On October 18, there was that business of me hitting three home runs on three swings in the sixth game of the Series against the Dodgers. It was called the greatest game a hitter ever had in a World Series. I can live with that. (Smile.)

But I almost didn't get the swings because we almost didn't get out of Kansas City because Mr. Martin had to slap me one last time, with the whole world watching.

The ending of 1977 wasn't any easier than anything else had been. I almost didn't get the chance to become Mr. October.

—Reggie Jackson in *Reggie* (Reggie Jackson with Mike Lupica, 1984)

Jackson continues, "I finished the regular season with thirty-two home runs, 110 RBI, a .286 batting average, ninety-three runs, thirty-nine doubles and—miraculously—my sanity. Then I promptly went one-for-fourteen in the first four games of the playoffs against the Royals and left myself wide open for Billy to get his last parting shot on a Sunday night in Kansas City with the American League Championship series tied 2-all and a pennant hanging in the balance . . .

"This, to me, was vindictive on Billy's part. He was actually willing to risk blowing a pennant just to show me and everyone else once and for all who was in charge. Unbelievable."

That's Reggie's side of the story. Billy Martin did a book of his own, of course, and he remembered things just a bit differently. According to Martin, with left-hander Paul Splittorff starting Game 5 for the Royals, he looked at the numbers and "knew it would be in the best interests of the team to play Paul Blair in right field and not Reggie Jackson."

Before he posted the lineup for Game 5, Martin told George Steinbrenner that he planned to sit Jackson. According to Martin, here's what happened next:

As we were talking, Catfish Hunter was walking by us. George said, "Hey, Cat, you played with Reggie at Oakland. Can Reggie hit Splittorff?" Without breaking stride, Cat looked back at George and said, "Not with a fucking paddle," and kept walking. George said, "You do it, but if it doesn't work, you're going to have to suffer the consequences." I said, "Fine, as long as if it works, I get the credit."[1]

Did it work? To the everlasting regret of my eleven-year-old self, it worked all too well. I was at

When Jim Bouton told stories like this, it got him banned from Old Timers' Day for twenty-five years. When Billy Martin told them, before long he'd get hired to manage the Yankees (again).

We didn't have much money that year. The other players did, and they'd rush off to go someplace, and Lois and I and Mickey and his wife Merlyn would go back to our apartments next to the Concourse Plaza. We were told the apartments had a nice breeze in the summer. Cross ventilation, we were told. Our apartments adjoined one another, and the cross ventilation turned out to be a window in my bedroom taking the air to a window in his apartment. It was so hot that we had to watch television in bathing suits. Because our bedroom windows were adjoining, it was possible for each of us to crawl outside and peek in and see what the other was doing in bed. Lois and I were always teasing Mickey and Merlyn about doing that, and they'd be teasing us, and one night I went outside, and it was absolutely pitch black, and I started crawling over to Mickey's bedroom window. I was down on my knees, and as I was making my way, bang, I hit heads with someone. It was Mickey. I said, "What are you doing?" He said, "What are you doing?" We caught each other.

—Number 1 *(Billy Martin & Peter Golenbock, 1980)*

Royals Stadium that night, and I thought I was watching a World Series team. Which I was. But it was the wrong team.

Splittorff pitched well. After seven innings, the Royals led 3–1. Willie Randolph led off the eighth with a single, though, and Royals manager Whitey Herzog summoned reliever Doug Bird—right-handed reliever Doug Bird—to face Thurman Munson. Bird struck out Munson. But Lou Piniella followed with a single, Randolph scooting to third base. Designated hitter Cliff Johnson was due next, but Johnson batted right-handed and had batted .167 against righties since joining the Yankees in June.

As Jackson recalled, "Billy just turned quickly and said, 'Reggie, hit for Cliff.' "

Reggie singled, and Randolph scored. The rally ended there, with the Yankees still down 3–2. In the top of the ninth, though, the Yankees scored three more runs. In the bottom of the ninth, Freddie Patek grounded into a double play to end the game and break my heart. And would you like to guess who started the Yankees' ninth-inning surge with a base hit? Paul Blair.

So, yeah, it worked. Damn it.

But what kind of numbers did Martin have, really? Jackson had been a Yankee for only one season. Granted, Splittorff was a real good pitcher—in '77 he went 16–6 with a 3.69 ERA—and he'd started against the Yankees four times that season. Jackson didn't play in one of those games and batted only eleven times against Splittorff all season. He walked once, doubled, and homered. Not exactly the largest of sample sizes.

In 1976, Jackson's one season as an Oriole, he didn't face Splittorff at all. Splittorff reached the majors in 1970, but they didn't face off during that season, either. So the sum of their history ran from 1971 through 1975, plus those eleven moments in 1977. Did Martin have all of those numbers? Did Catfish hunter remember them, as he was walking past his manager in the locker room?

Probably not. We have them, though, and it turns out that Jackson really wasn't so bad against Splittorff. From 1971 through '77, he batted 275/305/449 with three walks and fourteen strikeouts in seventy-two plate appearances. Not great, by any means. Against all pitchers over the same period, Jackson batted 277/361/513.

The difference between those numbers, though, looks to me like a fairly typical difference, especially for a left-swinging slugger like Jackson. In fact, from '71 through '77 he batted 258/321/467 against all left-handed pitchers. Which is roughly what he'd done against Splittorff.

So if you're going to sit Jackson because of his numbers against Splittorff, why not sit him against *all* left-handed starters? Answer: because if you wanted to platoon every player on the team with 258/321/467 against his same-sided pitcher, you'd need a thirty-man roster.

Managers tend to over-manage in October. You want unorthodox? In this same game, the biggest in Royals history, Whitey Herzog chose Cookie Rojas as his designated hitter. Maybe Herzog had a good reason, but thirty years later it's hard to imagine what that might have been. Oh, and just a few days earlier, Jackson had taken the collar against Splittorff in Game 1, going 0 for 4 with a strikeout.

Backs against the wall, season on the line, managers tend to do things they wouldn't do, *shouldn't* do from April through October. I don't believe it made a lot of sense to bench Reggie. But Billy Martin, for all his faults, didn't usually let his personal grudges get in the way of winning. Like most great managers, he didn't care if you were black, white, purple, or an egotistical jerk. If you could play, he'd play you.

Oh, and there's this: entering the American League Championship Series, Paul Blair had faced Paul Splittorff thirty-six times and batted .417 with power. Whatever was going through Billy Martin's head, consciously and subconsciously, it worked.

Damn it.

BILLY MARTIN & THE '65 TWINS

In 1965 Calvin and Sherry asked me to be the Twins third-base coach, and I agreed, and the day camp opened the rumors started that I was after manager Sam Mele's job, which I just couldn't believe. Sam and I worked very well together. He appreciated my ability to teach, and he let me coach at third the way I felt was right. In spring training, I told the players that I was going to make them more daring base runners, that I was going to get them thrown out at home deliberately just so they'd be more aggressive. The spring training games began, and I did just what I said I'd do, and I got three or four of our runners thrown out at home during exhibition games. Billy Robertson, Sherry's and Calvin Griffith's brother, didn't like what I was doing out there. Billy didn't understand what I was trying to do, and he went to Mele and tried to get me replaced as third-base coach.

At the end of the season we won the pennant, largely because the players had been more aggressive, and Calvin went to Sam and asked him who had taught the guys to steal and to run the bases. Sam told him the truth. He said, "Billy taught them."

—Number 1 (Billy Martin & Peter Golenbock, 1980)

They were playing a different game in the 1960s, and particularly in the American League. In 1964, the Twins stole forty-six bases all season long. The Red Sox stole *eighteen*. Not that anybody was stealing much. The Indians led the league with seventy-nine steals, and the pennant-winning Yankees stole fifty-four.

So it's not at all clear that the Twins were doing anything wrong in 1964, before Martin arrived. One inconvenient truth that Martin doesn't mention: in '64, before he worked his magic, *the Twins led the American League in scoring*.

That said, things *did* change in 1965, and for the better. In '64, the Twins scored 737 runs, seven more than the No. 2 Yankees; in '65 they scored 774 runs, *ninety-four* more than the No. 2 Tigers. The Twins' home-run output dropped from a league-leading 221 to just 150, fourth in the league. But they doubled their steals, from forty-six to ninety-two.

It's really pretty amazing that they lost seventy-one homers but somehow gained thirty-seven runs. And the new stolen bases can't nearly account for those numbers. Before we explore the Twins' other baserunning, let's look at some key stats from both seasons . . .

	1964	1965	Δ
Runs	737	774	+37
Hits	1413	1396	−17
Doubles	227	257	+30
Triples	46	42	−4
Homers	221	150	−71
Walks	553	554	+1
K's	1019	969	−50
Steals	46	92	+46
Caught	22	33	+11

Again, nothing here seems to balance the precipitous decline in home runs, and yet the Twins somehow upped their run production, in a season that saw the league-wide scoring drop slightly (from 4.06 runs per game to 3.94). It's not likely that Billy Martin ever looked up these stats, but it seems that he sensed *something* changed for the better. Or perhaps he just looked at the standings, as the Twins jumped from seventh place to first place, which must have ranked among the great one-season turnarounds to that time.

Of course, what we really want to know is, did the Twins run the bases better in '65 than they had in '64? Were they more aggressive, generally?

We'd like to know how many times the Twins took an extra base, but that's really not something we can measure precisely, even with the play-by-play accounts (and we do have those). We can look at some things, though:

- In 1964 the Twins hit 919 singles and were out trying for doubles nine times; in '65 they hit 947 singles and were out at second base eleven times. Not much difference there.
- In '64 the Twins hit 227 doubles, and nobody was out trying for a triple; in '65 they hit 257 doubles and were out at third base three times.

We would expect an increase in aggressiveness to result in more extra bases *and* at least a few more outs. But there's no clear pattern here. The Twins hit more doubles, but weren't thrown out (significantly) more often at second base. They were thrown out a few more times trying to stretch doubles into triples . . . but they actually hit slightly fewer triples in '65 than in '64.

🖋 Longtime baseball man Cal Ermer told this one sometime not long before the 1967 season . . .

One day in New York—this was 1962—there was a free-for-all. Boog Powell was hit on the helmet by Bud Daley's pitch and Robin Roberts retaliated by knocking down Roger Maris and the trouble was on. You know Billy Hitchcock, managing Baltimore then, is a quiet, gentlemanly type guy, but he was storming mad and went after Ralph Houk. Both managers were tough, but wisely restrained themselves, or we would have had a real donnybrook.

Naturally, both managers were bounced and that was when I, as a Baltimore coach, made my managerial debut in the majors.

Dick Williams was the first man up and tried to bunt for a hit and the ball came back up and hit him. I contended he was still in the box and not out, but he was called out by Umpire Charley Berry. I came in to dispute the call and was bounced before opening my mouth.

Thus my first big league managerial stint lasted exactly one pitch. I hope it was not the last.
　　　　　　—Wirt Gammon in the Chattanooga Times (reprinted in Baseball Digest)

Close. Very close. It was June 11, 1962, at Yankee Stadium. Boog Powell led off the fourth and was beaned by Daley (Powell, a rookie, would be out of the lineup for a week). In the bottom of the fourth, Maris led off. Robin Roberts did *buzz Maris with his first pitch, shortly after which the two clubs "produced one of the stormiest demonstrations in recent years at the staid old Bronx ball park." Hitchcock and Houk traded punches—none landing, though—and enough players were milling about that three cops "rushed onto the field to restore order."*

Both managers were ejected, leaving Ermer in charge of the Orioles. His career did last longer than one pitch, though. With Maris leading off, Ermer was in charge while Maris and four other Yankees batted (including Yogi Berra, who homered). And Johnny Temple led off the fifth for Baltimore. Then came Williams, and Ermer—at that moment, coaching third base—was ejected after arguing about the interference call. So he managed for seven batters: Williams (and we don't know if Williams saw just one pitch) and six others.

This would not be Ermer's last managerial stint. In 1967, he took over as manager in June, with the Twins in sixth place, but only six games out of first place. They finished in a rush, 66-46 the rest of the way, and wound up just one game behind the Impossible Dream Red Sox. The Twins dropped to seventh place in '68, and Ermer lost his job to coach Billy Martin (who'd been bypassed in '67 and would guide the club to a division title in his first season as manager).

If the Twins were more aggressive in '65, we would also expect to find their base runners were more often taking the extra base on hits and ground balls. So I counted, in '64 and '65, all the times the Twins 1) hit a single with a runner on second base, 2) hit a single with a runner on first base, 3) hit a double with a runner on first base, and 4) hit a ground ball to an infielder with a runner on third base (with fewer than two outs). We'll call those "opportunities" for an extra base.

In 1964 the Twins had 472 opportunities, and the runners went for the extra base 236 times. Exactly half. They were thrown out fifteen times.

In 1965 the Twins had 568 opportunities, and the runners went for the extra base 326 times; 57 percent. And they were thrown out only twenty times. They apparently *were* more aggressive in '65, with no additional cost. So they had that going for them. Which was nice.

Remember what Billy said, though? "At the end of the season we won the pennant, largely because the players had been more aggressive . . ."

Largely? I would submit three other reasons for the Twins' pennant in '65. One, they hit better in clutch situations. In '64 they batted .238 with runners in scoring position, and in '65 they batted .267 in that situation. The qualitative difference isn't actually that large, because their slugging percentage was actually lower in '65 (because of the drop in homers). Essentially, in '64 the Twins were 7 percent better than league average with runners in scoring position, and in '65 they were 11 percent better. So that's one thing.

Here's another thing . . .

The Twins were terribly unlucky in 1964. They scored 737 runs and allowed 678 runs, and those numbers typically would lead to an 87-75 record. Instead the Twins finished 79-83. Based purely on that difference, we would have expected the Twins to improve, perhaps significantly, in 1965.

Here's another, bigger thing . . .

In 1964 the Twins gave up 678 runs, which was tied for fifth most in the league. Their team ERA was 3.58; the American League ERA that season was 3.63. Offensively they were excellent, and defensively there were just average (in fact, their adjusted ERA—their team ERA, adjusted for park effects—was 100 on the nose, exactly average).

In 1965, Johnny Sain took over as the Twins' pitching coach. As would happen so many other times during Sain's coaching career, his pitching staff showed immediate and dramatic improvement. The Twins allowed only 600 runs and posted a 3.14 ERA, which was third lowest in the league. And if you consider park effects—the White Sox's ERA was lower, but they played in a pitcher's paradise—the Twins clearly had the second best pitching/defense in the league, just a bit behind the Orioles.

So again, we might ask, largely? Hardly. On a list of reasons for the Twins' winning their pennant, Billy Martin's beloved aggression certainly deserves a place. But that place is somewhere below the pitchers, the pitching coach, and a healthy measure of better luck.

MAURY WILLS & 150 STEALS

A good base stealer must be decisive and know all the pitchers and their moves. These are characteristics that can be learned. I studied the pitchers closely and knew their mannerisms thoroughly, so I could "read" them easily. I never hesitated. I started out at full speed.

Writers erred in thinking that I had what they called a light slide. It may have looked as if I were skimming across the infield dirt. But it didn't feel like a light slide to me. My right leg was always bruised. In 1965 I was 30 games ahead of my record-setting base-stealing pace of three years earlier, but my leg started bleeding internally. I had to stop stealing bases in August. I've always thought that if I had not been stopped by a recurrence of the hemorrhaging, I could have stolen 140 or even 150 bases that year.

—Maury Wills, *How to Steal a Pennant* (Maury Wills with Don Freeman, 1976)

Sniff test: Wills did steal ninety-four bases in 1965, which was by far the second most that he stole in a single season (more on that in a moment). However, he did not "stop stealing bases in August." He stole eleven bases in August and eleven more in September. Granted, this *was* well off his pace from earlier in the season.

Unfortunately, there's no particularly obvious dividing line in 1965 between stealing a lot and stealing not so much. After stealing a base on the 6th of August, though, Wills went six straight games without a steal. He hadn't done that all season, so that's probably as good a dividing line as any. That steal on the 6th was Wills's seventy-fifth of the season, and it came in the Dodgers' 111th game. In '62, Wills hadn't stolen his seventh-fifth base until the 2nd of September, in the Dodgers' 137th game. So Wills, in talking about his record-setting pace, really

wasn't so far off. In '65, he *was* roughly thirty games ahead of his '62 pace (that season he stole 104 bases to break Ty Cobb's single-season record).

Of course, the striking thing about Wills's record-setting season is what he did *after* the 2nd of September: in twenty-eight games, Wills stole twenty-eight bases. He probably figured if he did it once he could do it again, and again. But you probably don't need me to tell you that averaging a steal per day isn't easy. Anyway, for Wills to have finished with 140 steals in '65, he'd have to have stolen sixty-eight bases in the Dodgers' last forty-seven games, which I'm guessing is a pace that nobody has matched in major-league history.

So, no, I don't think a healthy Maury Wills in '65 would have stolen 140 bases, let alone 150.

He would probably have topped his old record, though. Entering August, Wills had stolen seventy-two bases in the Dodgers' 105 games. If he'd been able to maintain that pace through the end of the season—granted, "pace" can be problematic—he'd have finished with 111 steals.

But in the end, what of it? Lou Brock stole 118 bases in 1974, and Rickey Henderson stole 130 in 1982.

What's most interesting about Wills's base-stealing efforts isn't that he stole "only" ninety-four bases in 1965. What's most interesting is how few bases he stole in various other seasons. In 1962 he stole 104 bases. In 1960 he'd stolen fifty; in '61 he'd stolen thirty-five. In 1965, he stole ninety-four bases. In '66 he stole thirty-eight.

In addition to *How to Steal a Pennant*—which essentially was Wills's book-length argument for his worthiness as a major-league manager—he's listed as the coauthor of two other books, *It Pays to Steal* (1963) and *On the Run* (1991). The former was published too early to help explain Wills's relative paucity of steals after 1962 ('65 notwithstanding), but the other books do offer some clues.

In 1966 Wills had stolen thirty bases by the middle of July, but on the 15th he suffered a knee injury when Fat Jack Fisher fell on him during a run-down. Wills stayed in the lineup, but stole only eight more bases the rest of the season. That injury goes a long way toward explaining why Wills never was a truly great basestealer again. However, in *On the Run* he says that in 1967, "The Pirates were a hitting team"—he'd been traded to Pittsburgh after the '66 season—"and nobody took a pitch for me so I ended up with only 29 stolen bases. The next year I stole 52." He would never steal more than forty bases in a season again, but by then he was getting up there in years.

The funny thing about Wills is that he repeatedly, in his books, says he wasn't really that fast compared to the other prolific base stealers, that while they got by on speed he had to get by on his brains. And there's no doubt, in many ways, he was an incredibly bright guy. But when he wasn't healthy enough to run fast, he didn't steal nearly as many bases.

Wills was an everyday player for only twelve seasons. Nevertheless, it's not impossible to build a Hall of Fame case for him. I don't really buy the case, though, because it's partly predicated on the notion that Wills changed the game, which isn't really true (the stolen base was making a comeback before he arrived in the majors).

He believed it, writing in *On the Run*:

> If I had not stolen 104 bases in 1962, I do not believe there would have been a Lou Brock or a Rickey Henderson or a Vince Coleman as we

Maury Wills tells a baseball story . . .

There was this close game. Our starting pitcher was getting hit pretty good. The manager, Walter Alston, came out to the mound. He wanted to kill some time until our relief pitcher, Bob Miller, could get warmed up in the bullpen. But the umpires made him bring in Miller right away.

When Miller got to the mound, Alston says, "After Bob here has thrown his warm-up pitches, Maury, you call time and say there's something in your eye. While the trainer is fooling with it, Bob, you'll have more time to warm up."

Miller and I both say, "OK." He starts to throw his warm-up pitches. I go back to shortstop. When he's finished I suddenly throw up my hands. I holler at the umpires like I'm in terrible pain. I dance around, I grab at my eyes. I'm doing a great act.

All the players, the trainer, they gather around me. Suddenly I look up. There's Bob Miller. He's got a towel in his hands and he's saying, "I know a good way to get things out of people's eyes."

—Quoted in "Maury Wills: A Revealing Look at a Man on the Go" (Sport, May 1966)

The story above was drawn from Wills's night club act; in his heyday, he spent much of the off-season playing to crowds in Los Angeles and Las Vegas, among other places.

Later in the piece, he admits to

☞

author John Devaney, "Those baseball stories I tell, they really happened. But not to me. Charlie Dressen told them to me. Like that one about Bob Miller. Actually it was Dressen who was the manager, Pee Wee Reese the shortstop, and Clyde King the relief pitcher. I listen to stories and I remember the ones I can use, the kind of stories that fit me best."

Of course, one might ask how Wills knew they really happened. Dressen's say-so? There's really no way to check this one, but I will note that Clyde King doesn't mention the incident in his memoirs.

know them today because no one would have believed that a ballplayer could do it. They wouldn't have gotten the opportunity. They would be playing baseball in a different way.

I revolutionized the game . . . [1]

He wasn't the only one who believed it. Buzzie Bavasi, the Dodgers' general manager during Wills's first stint with the club, would later write the same thing in his memoirs.[2]

Which doesn't make it true. Players stole bases in the 1960s for the same reason they stole bases during the Dead Ball Era: because the conditions at that time favored the running game.

But what if Wills had broken Cobb's career record of 892 steals? Would that have been enough to get Wills into the Hall of Fame? Probably not, but anyway the record always was only a remote possibility, simply because Wills didn't reach the majors until 1959, when he was twenty-six. From 1960 through 1969, Wills's peak years as a base stealer, he averaged fifty-four steals per season. Even if he'd averaged eighty per season in the '60s, he would still have fallen roughly forty steals short of Cobb's record.

FRED LYNN

I always played my best baseball either against the best teams or in key games. I feel like I was always a prime-time player whenever we needed something. That's when I liked to play, with the game on the line or in All-Star competition against the best there is. I have always played to the level of my competition. I even do it now. If I'm playing someone who isn't as good as me, I don't play as well. But if you put me against somebody who is as good as me or better that makes my game go up.

—Fred Lynn in *The Pastime in the Seventies: Oral History of 16 Major Leaguers*
(Bill Ballew, 2002)

If I were Fred Lynn, this isn't exactly something I would brag about. Which isn't to say that he *is* bragging. But baseball's not like chess. When you're playing chess, you can pick your spots. In baseball, not so much. If you don't play your best against the lousy teams, you lose. And those games count in the standings just like the games against the good teams.

Lynn did play particularly well in All-Star Games (which is the easiest of his assertions to check). He was an All-Star for nine straight years, 1975–1983, and played in the game each year. Final tally: twenty at-bats, four homers, and ten RBIs.

Impressive? Sure. But how much can twenty at-bats tell us, really? Not much. Which is why I'd like to focus on Lynn's other claims, that he played his best "against the best teams or in key games."

To check those, we must first define our terms. There aren't standard definitions of *best teams* or *key games*, so the best we can do is come up with something reasonable. For the sake of this exercise, let's define *best teams* as those that won at least ninety games in that particular season (with prorated records in 1981, the strike season). And we'll define *key games* to include 1) all postseason games, and 2) all games after August in which Lynn's team was within five games of first place, on either side. And we'll consider only 1975 through 1988, as '88 was Lynn's last good season.

Over those fourteen seasons, overall Lynn hit 286/363/493. The breakdown? He hit 262/334/435 against the best teams (which averaged ninety-five wins) . . . and 294/372/512 against everybody else. Clearly, Lynn did *not* play his best baseball against the best teams. Like every other hitter in the history of the game, he fattened up against the crummy teams and took his hits against the good teams when he could get them.

In the same book as Lynn's quote, Bob Boone says, "I had some real good playoff games and All-Star Games. I always felt that when the team needed it, I could turn it on . . . Like I said, I always thought I was a pretty good offensive player. Plus, I always hit best when there was stress, when the game or the season was on the line."

Boone did exceptionally well in the 1980 World Series, and in the 1986 American League Championship Series. Overall, in eight postseason series, comprising thirty-six games, he batted .311 with two doubles and two homers. Over his long career he batted .254, so in postseason games he essentially was six singles better than expected. Or maybe eight, given the better quality of pitching in October.

Hey, those eight singles counted.

There's better evidence for Lynn's memory of key games. Prior to 1989, he played for five teams that were in serious pennant contention in September, and he did well in each of those Septembers.

- In 1975, when the Red Sox wound up four and a half games ahead of the second-place Orioles, Lynn batted .333 in September.
- In 1977, when the Red Sox finished two and a half games behind the Yankees, Lynn batted .270 with three homers in September (this was his worst stretch drive).
- In 1978—you know what happened in '78—he hit 297/403/455 and was particularly hot over the last couple of weeks when the Red Sox needed to win almost every game just to force the playoff with the Yankees.
- In 1982, by then playing for the Angels, Lynn missed most of early September with a rib injury, but got back into the lineup on September 18 and was brilliant the rest of the way—particularly the last weekend of the season, with the pennant still on the line—and the Angels beat out the Royals by three games.
- In 1984, the Royals beat out the Angels by three games, but don't blame Lynn, who hit seven homers and drove in twenty-two runs; it was his best month of the season.

Lynn played in only three postseason series—the AL Championship Series and World Series in 1975, the ALCS in '82—but he played *exceptionally* well in those series; in fifteen games he batted .407 and knocked in twelve runs.

So, yeah. You might not believe Lynn had some special *ability* to hit better when his teams particularly needed him—I don't believe he had that—but you certainly can understand why he might *think* he had that ability. He played well in pennant races, he played well in October, and he played well in All-Star Games. He did it, he knows he did it, and he believes, naturally enough, that he did it because of something inside him.

Something else that probably comes naturally to Lynn: the feeling that nobody realizes just how good he really was. In his *New Historical Baseball Abstract* (2001), Bill James ranked Lynn as the seventeenth-greatest center-fielder in major-league history. Since then, Lynn has perhaps been passed by Bernie Williams, but I think it's safe to say that today Lynn might comfortably be placed among the top twenty. Yet in 1996, his first year of Hall of Fame eligibility, Lynn drew only twenty-six votes. A year later, he drew twenty-two votes and fell off the ballot forever.

I wouldn't argue that he belongs in the Hall of Fame. There are a few Hall of Fame centerfielders who weren't as good as Lynn, but Lynn (and Vada Pinson) are just on the wrong side of the line. Still, it's a shame that when people think about Lynn, their thoughts typically begin and end with 1975. Because he was a damn good player for a damn long time.

BILLY MARTIN & JACKIE ROBINSON

> Another reason I enjoyed beating the Dodgers was the competition with Jackie Robinson. There was a black lawyer in Berkeley by the name of Walter Gordon, who helped my mother when I was a kid. He had also helped Jackie, so when we played in the Series, I always wanted to show Walter that I was a better second baseman. That was my real challenge. And always I outhit, and always I outplayed him. Every Series we played in.
>
> —Billy Martin in *Number 1* (Martin & Peter Golenbock, 1980)

Martin played for the Yankees from 1950 through the middle of the '57 season. In those years, the Yankees played the Dodgers in four World Series: 1952, 1953, 1955, and 1956. In '52, '53, and '56, Martin was the Yankees' top second baseman during the regular season, and the only Yankee second baseman during the World Series.

In 1954 he was drafted—for the second time—and spent all of that season and most of the next stationed in Fort Carson, Colorado, where he played for (and managed) both the base team and a semi-pro team in Goodland, Kansas.[1] The Yankees' five-year pennant streak got busted by the Indians in 1954. The Yanks won again in '55, but Martin wasn't supposed to be discharged until a few days after the World Series. According to an Associated Press story dated August 29:

> Billy Martin's chances of playing in the world series appear slim, even if the Yankees make the grade.
>
> The Army granted today a request by the 27-year-old second baseman for a thirty-day furlough, effective at once. This furlough, however, will expire at midnight Sept. 28—the day the world series is scheduled to open.
>
> Authorities at Fort Carson, where Martin is winding up his military duty, made it plain they would expect the baseball star back on time—world series or no world series.
>
> Martin, a corporal, is due for final training and processing for discharge. His separation date from the Army is Oct. 8, and the world series will end Oct. 4, even if it goes the full seven games.
>
> The fort's information officer, Capt. W.G. Newkirk, said that so far as he knew "There is no way to get out of" the final processing and completion of training.
>
> "I don't see much chance of Martin getting to play during that period," he said.[2]

Somehow, though, Martin eventually was excused from duty during the World Series (so were

Photo courtesy of Transcendental Graphics

Young Billy Martin

five of his buddies from Fort Carson, who attended the Series as guests of the Yankees). Running through each of the Martin-Robinson matchups . . .

In 1952, Martin's first Series as more than a bench player—he'd appeared just briefly in the '51 Series—he played in all seven games and batted .217. He did hit a three-run homer in the Yankees' 7–1 win in Game 2. Robinson also homered, but hit even worse than Martin, going just 4 for 23 (.174). But the most famous moment of the Series came in Game 7 and involved both men. In the bottom of the seventh inning, the Yankees led 4–2 with two outs, but the Dodgers had the bases loaded. Robinson lifted a soft pop between the mound and first base, and it looked as if the ball would drop when first baseman Joe Collins lost the ball in the sun. Martin, though, dashed over to make the catch, and the Dodgers never threatened again.

In '53, Martin was the big star of the Series. He tripled twice, homered twice, and batted .500. In the ninth inning of Game 6, his twelfth hit of the Series—which tied the all-time World Series record—drove in Hank Bauer

Ron Luciano told this one, which you can certainly believe if you like . . .

Ballplayers, as well as umpires and managers, get letters and phone calls warning them not to appear in a certain city. During one recent World Series an umpire was accompanied by armed guards every time he left his hotel room because of a serious threat. This is not a recent development. In 1950, for example, Yankee shortstop Phil Rizzuto received a letter warning him, Hank Bauer, Yogi Berra, and Johnny Mize that they would be shot if they showed up to play against the Red Sox. Casey Stengel thought about it. Under the circumstances, Stengel did the most prudent thing: He issued a uniform with another number on the back to Rizzuto and gave Rizzuto's old uniform to Billy Martin.

—_Ron Luciano & David Fisher,_
Strike Two _(1984)_

Just in case you're wondering, Martin doesn't mention this "incident" in his memoirs. Nor do his many biographers.

with the game- and Series-winning run. And Robinson? He played well, tying for the team lead with eight hits.

In '55, of course, the Dodgers finally broke their long jinx against the Yankees. Didn't have much to do with Jackie, though; he scored five runs, but his .182 batting average was the worst on the club. Meanwhile, Martin batted .320.

In '56, as usual, Martin and Robinson both started every game. And as usual, Martin outplayed Robinson. Robinson batted .250 with one home run; Martin batted .296 with two home runs.

So Martin undoubtedly was right: he did outplay Robinson every time they met.

Before Martin reached the majors, Robinson did play in two other World Series, both against the Yankees. In 1947, he batted .259 and scored three runs in seven games. In 1949, he batted .188 and scored two runs in five games. The Dodgers, of course, lost both Series.

In his career, Robinson played in thirty-eight World Series games. He batted .234, scored twenty-two runs, and drove in twelve. But Robinson's got a lot of good company. Willie Mays, for instance. Mays played in twenty-five postseason games and batted .247 with just one home run, scoring twelve runs and knocking in only ten. It happens.

THURMAN MUNSON & CARLTON FISK

In fact, they did have civil exchanges during their encounters at the plate, but—bottom line—they really didn't like one another. Though the two persistently denied any feud to the press, actions do speak louder than words. Thurman would frequently check his rival's statistics in the newspaper, while Fisk was infuriated at the mention of Munson's name. Fisk later remembered one instance in which Munson found out in the morning paper that he was losing to Fisk in the assist department during one year late in Thurm's career. With Ron Guidry on the mound sporting a masterful ten-strikeout game, Thurman purposely dropped about a half dozen balls and threw them to first to edge Fisk for the title.

—Christopher Devine, *Thurman Munson: A Baseball Biography* (2001)

This story has been one of my favorites for a long time. It's a hell of a good story. I don't know where I first came across it, though, which is why I turned to the most recent biography about Munson and hoped it would be there, with documentation, as McFarland's baseball books are generally well-sourced.

Indeed, Devine's book *is* well-sourced . . . but there's no source for this particular story. And that it's apparently based on Fisk's memory is obviously a waving red flag. Still, let's check out the particulars.

Guidry first pitched for the Yankees in 1975. He started one game that season and struck out two batters (two Red Sox batters, to be precise). He didn't start any games at all in 1976. He started twenty-five games in '77, thirty-five in '78, and nineteen in '79 before Munson's plane went down. Now, we could easily check—thanks to Retrosheet—Munson's fielding stats in each of Guidry's starts, and we could even more easily check Munson's stats in the relatively few games in which Guidry struck out ten hitters.

Believe it or not, though, it's even easier than that. Retrosheet, in addition to listing a batting log for each season in Munson's career, also lists a fielding log. So it's easier than easy to simply scan each season and look for games in which he racked up an unusual number of assists. Six—"Thurman purposely dropped about a half dozen balls"—does seem like a lot, doesn't it?

In those three seasons, Munson didn't collect more than four assists in any one game. He got exactly four assists in three games, and three assists in six games. Of those nine games, Guidry started twice and relieved once. Those three games:

- April 29, 1977: Munson got four assists, and two of them did come after Guidry strikeouts (he finished with eight in the game); the other two assists came on a caught stealing and a 2-3 groundout.

- ◆ August 21, 1977: Munson got three assists, but only one came after a Guidry strikeout; the other two were caught stealings.
- ◆ May 6, 1979: Munson got four assists, but none of them came after strikeouts; he caught two guys stealing, got another trying to advance from first to second (on a ball in the dirt?), and got an assist on a sacrifice bunt.

I suppose this is the point at which I could forget about Guidry and check the rest of those three- and four-assist games; not only in those three seasons, but all the seasons before those, too. I want another clue, though. And perhaps the single best source for good baseball stories is Dan Okrent and Steve Wulf's *Baseball Anecdotes*.

Bingo. Here's *their* version:

> Thurman Munson, who died in the crash of his private airplane in August of 1979, was a great catcher, a pretty good hitter, and a team leader. He was also something of a mule, as this story told by former Yankees PR man Marty Appel attests:
>
> Munson did not like being compared with Boston's handsomer, more stately catcher, Carlton Fisk. One day Appel quite innocently listed in his press notes, AL ASSIST LEADERS, CATCHERS: FISK, Boston 27; MUNSON, New York 25. Players rarely read the press notes, but on this day, Munson did. "What's the idea of showing me up like this?" he demanded of Appel. "You think for one minute he's got a better arm than me? What a stupid statistic!"
>
> Munson stormed off. Then, during the game, he dropped a third strike, recovered, and threw to first base to get the batter. The same thing happened in the next inning, and it began to dawn on Appel what Munson was doing. A short time later, Munson dropped another third strike, thereby passing Fisk as the league's leader in assists by catchers.[1]

This makes more sense, doesn't it? I didn't ask this question earlier because it didn't serve my purpose, but since when are catchers' defensive stats listed in the newspapers? And since when do catchers care who finishes with the assists "title"?

Thus armed, I turned to Marty Appel's memoir, which was published in 2001 (the same year as Devine's book about Munson) and is quite a fun read.

Bingo Bango. Here is Appel's *official* version:

Munson was cocky and confident and full of self-assurance, but he was not without his own insecurities. It aggravated him terribly that Carlton Fisk, who was always getting hurt, seemed to get more attention.

"It's that [Curt] Gowdy on NBC," Munson told me. "He's from Boston. He can't stop talking about Fisk on national telecasts."

I accidentally pushed a Munson button one day in June when I put some fielding stats in the daily press notes. In those days, fielding stats were only published monthly in *The Sporting News*. I would cull some interesting ones and make a small note of them.

So one day I showed "Catcher, Assist Leaders: Fisk 48, Munson 46, Sundberg 40."

Not a real big deal.

In the clubhouse before the game, Munson was in my face.

"What the hell is this?" he said. "This is a bullshit statistic. How could you print this?"

That evening, a batter struck out in the first inning and Munson dropped the ball. He had to throw to first to retire him. Joe Garagiola Jr. tapped me on the shoulder and told me to look down.

Munson was pointing a finger at me, as though to say, "That was for you."

Twice more in that game, he dropped third strikes and threw to first. Each time he looked up at me. Three assists. He had passed Fisk. And he was right, at least as far as that was concerned; it was a bullshit statistic.

"Did you drop those on purpose because of that press note?" I asked him after the game. He ignored me. He was strolling from the shower to his locker, toweling himself off and singing "America loves burgers, and we're America's Burger King!"[2]

Appel places this incident in 1976, when Munson first assumed the role as Yankee captain—the first since Lou Gehrig—and also won the American League's MVP Award. Not just 1976; *June* of '76. Checking Retrosheet again, we find two June games in which Munson was credited with at least three assists: the 4th and 5th in Oakland. He got three on the 4th; all three were caught stealings. He got four on the 5th; three caught stealings and one pickoff at third base.

So much for June of '76.

There's nothing else for it, then: I'm going to check every game during Munson's career in which he recorded at least three assists. This time I'll spare you the details, and so I'll be back in a moment—well, for me it'll be more like thirty moments—with some final words . . .

Over his entire career, 1969 through 1979, Munson totaled more than two assists in thirty-two games. In all those years and all those games, *not*

🖋 *You ever heard of a team having to use its fifth-string catcher because one through four are all hurt? It happened to the Phillies in 1970 . . .*

McCarver has another footnote attached to his name. During a game in 1970, his right hand was broken when it got in the way of a foul tip off the bat of Willie Mays. Mike Ryan entered the game as McCarver's replacement. A few minutes later while still in the same innings, Willie McCovey slides into the plate and into Ryan. The result? A broken hand for Iron Mike.

Two more catchers called up from the minors to replace McCarver and Ryan also suffered injuries. The Phils had to activate coach Doc Edwards, a former backstop.

—Rich Westcott, Tales from the Phillies Dugout *(Sports Publishing, 2006)*

McCarver and Ryan were injured on the 2nd of May in San Francisco, in the sixth inning. Mays got McCarver with the foul ball, and just two batters later, McCovey spiked Ryan while sliding home. McCovey was out. Ryan actually stayed in for the last two outs of the inning but didn't play again until July 6. Rookie Jim Hutto finished the game, but he was just an emergency fill-in; first base and left field were his usual positions.

Within a few days, the Phillies summoned catcher Mike Compton and Del Bates—Compton's backup—from their Triple-A farm

club in Eugene, Oregon. On May 23,
Compton went down with a pulled
muscle, and Bates took over. On the
5th of June, Bates took a foul tip off
his right hand (he would never play
another inning in the majors).
Compton was still on the active
roster, but he was the only real
catcher around. And that's when
the Phillies activated coach Doc
Edwards, who hadn't played since
1965. He was the regular for most
of June, then gave way in July to
Ryan, and played his last game in
late August, as McCarver returned
to action in September when the
rosters expanded. In thirty-five
games, Edwards batted .269,
significantly higher than his career
average, but managed just one
unintentional walk and zero extra-
base hits in seventy-eight at-bats.

There's an amusing sidebar to
this strange series of events.
Compton's injury was just one of
five players the Phillies lost in late
May, which spurred team executive
Bill Giles to try something unusual.
A fellow named Jacob Zook from
Lancaster County sold circular
"hex signs"—usually you would
see them mounted on barns in rural
areas—and Giles acquired three
and had them installed atop the
Phillies' dugout. Giles, a New
Yorker, said, "I'm new at this
Pennsylvania Dutch superstition,
but it's worth a try."

once did Munson record three putouts after strikeouts. In only two of those thirty-two games did Munson record two putouts after strikeouts, but even those can't be the source for this tale. One of those games was in 1971, when Fisk didn't play with the Red Sox until September. The other was in 1977, but by then Appel had left the Yankees for greener pastures.

Which brings us back to . . . where? Nineteen seventy-six, I guess. We know that Munson never dropped three third strikes and turned them into assists. Not in one game. Not according to Retrosheet. But maybe he did intentionally drop two third strikes, in a game in which those were his only assists? Because I love this story, and because Appel tells it with such gusto—*America loves burgers!*—I'm going to check each of Munson's two-assist games in 1976. But that's it. Really.

Munson got exactly two assists in seven games in '76. Of those fourteen assists, only one was of the K23 variety. Aside from '76, only two and a half other seasons fit the parameters as we know them. Why? Fisk's first full season with the Red Sox was 1972. He played regularly that season, and also in '73. In '74, he didn't play after June 28, which gives us half a season. In '75, he didn't play at all until late June. So his assists could never have matched Munson's that season. You know about '76. And after '76, Appel no longer worked for the Yankees. I checked those other seasons. Nada.

So I suppose I give up. Obviously, something happened. Somewhere. At some time. But I've got three versions of the same story, and none of the versions checks out. Here's one last stab, though. . . . On the 20th of May in 1976, the Yankees were playing the Red Sox. With two outs in the first inning, and nobody on base, Fred Lynn struck out. Munson didn't catch the ball cleanly and had to throw to first to record the out. Later in the game, Munson picked up two more assists, both on caught stealings. Before the game, he trailed Fisk in assists, 15–13. Fisk played in this game, but didn't get any assists. So after the game, Munson was on top, 16–15.

But that one doesn't make for a particularly good story, and I'm sorry for that. Truly.

DICK BARTELL & CY PFIRMAN

The Giants had won the pennant in 1936 and were playing the Dodgers in the last game of the season. Bartell needed two hits for a .300 average. The first time up he fouled out to Babe Phelps, Dodger catcher. Dick tried to break his bat, he was so mad. The second time up, Max Butcher pitched four balls so far from the plate it looked like an intentional walk, since two men were out and there was none on, and Brooklyn was leading 6 to 0. Some thought it was intentional because the Brooklyns didn't want him to get a hit. In the fifth inning, his third time up, he flied out to left field. Dick figured he'd have two more turns at bat before the game was over.

In the seventh inning, Jeffcoat was on the mound for Brooklyn. Cy Pfirman was umpiring behind the plate. The umpire called the first pitch a strike.

Bartell turned and said to him, "Watch those, Cy. I'm after a hit today as I've never been before."

Pfirman told him to stand up to the plate. The second ball was more off than the first. "Strike two," cried the umpire.

"Please, Cy," Dick pleaded. "Bear down."

The third pitch came over. "Strike three. You're out."

Dick, who thought it was a ball, threw his bat down. He raved and stamped his feet and crowded Pfirman away from the plate. The umpire tried to ignore him, in the time honored manner, by dusting off home plate. Finally, Bartell said too much and Pfirman waved him out of the game.

Bartell went mad. He rushed toward the umpire with mayhem in his heart. Jimmy Ripple tried to shove him away. Then Bill Terry and Adolfo Luque joined in trying to calm the raging shortstop. Still, Bartell tried to break away and only gave up when the huge Pancho Snyder came over. Snyder led him away toward the clubhouse.

—Jimmy Powers, *Baseball Personalities* (1949)

In Bartell's memoirs, he tells essentially the same story, except he doesn't strike out. Instead, the first two pitches nearly hit Bartell, and both of them are called strikes. He complains after the first. After the second, he says, "Bear down, Cy. I've got a lot at stake here. Be a little more careful."

Pfirman responds, "Quit complaining. Go back in there and hit."

Bartell looks at Pfirman.

Pfirman cusses at Bartell.

Bartell says, "Look, don't use profanity to me. I don't use it and you got no business using it to me."

Pfirman kicks Bartell out of the game.

And *then* he gets mad. According to Bartell, "That was the only time in my eighteen years as a player that I ever cussed out an umpire."[1]

Well, maybe that last bit is true, though it would be a surprise considering that Bartell's nickname—and the title of his book—was "Rowdy Richard."

But what really happened on September 27, 1936? I've got two contemporary accounts from the local newspapers. First, the *Daily News:*

> Bartell, trying desperately to land in the .300 hitters' circle, came to the plate in the seventh inning. With the count one ball and no strikes, Pfirman called a strike. Bartell blew up. Hot words were exchanged and suddenly Bartell screamed and rushed the arbiter. Jimmy Ripple pulled him away pleading with him to be calm. Terry galloped up, pointed a finger and shouted, "Don't hit him, Dick! Don't!"
>
> Bartell continued to rage and froth. He struggled so violently with Ripple, who held a half nelson wrestling hold, that Dick's shirttail came above his belt line and several buttons were missing. He finally cooled out and walked to the clubhouse with boos and cheers in his ears. Pfirman ordered him from the game. No other punishment will be given Bartell, and he will be in the World Series starting lineup Wednesday.[2]

Next, the *Herald Tribune:*

> Bartell really was brooding when he went into the ball game. He needed two hits to raise his batting average for the season over .300. When he popped a foul to Babe Phelps in the first inning against Van Lingle Mungo he tried to break his bat. The next time he appeared at the plate Max Butcher was pitching, the Dodgers were leading, 6 to 0, and there were two out. Somehow Butcher succeeded in throwing up four balls, outside or so far inside that they sent Bartell staggering back. One suspected it was an intentional pass, for there is no love lost between the Flatbush clan and Bartell.
>
> Things went from bad to worse for Bartell in the fifth when he flied to right. Still he figured to have two more chances before the game ended when the big blowoff occurred in the seventh inning. By this time George Jeffcoat was twirling curve balls for Brooklyn. When he broke one over which Bartell thought was a ball and Pfirman called a strike the hysteria began. Bartell raved, stamped his feet and crowded the umpire. The latter, in the best fashion of arbiters, dusted off the plate.
>
> Suddenly he had heard too much. Apparently Bartell didn't smile

when Pfirman said so. At any rate, Pfirman waved him out of the game. Batting averages and such mean nothing to umpires.

But to Bartell it was as if he had been stung by a hornet. In he rushed as if to commit mayhem. Ripple shoved him back, none too gently, then wrestled him away. By this time Luque and Terry had joined the party, but still Bartell tried to zigzag away from them. When he saw Frank Snyder's bulky form before him he finally gave up and was led away.[3]

You might have noticed that Powers, Bartell, and the newspapers have different ideas about the count when Bartell exploded. Powers says it happened after strike three, Bartell says it happened after strike two, and the newspapers say it happened after strike one. Newspaper writers make errors, obviously, but considering the elapsed time between the event and the various accounts being set to type, I think we should consider the *Daily News* and the *Herald Tribune* our more reliable sources.

In fact, Powers's inclusion of Ripple, Terry, Luque, and Snyder into the proceedings leads one to suspect that his source was the *Herald Tribune,* and that he turned the at-bat into a strikeout simply because it's a better story that way. And one that makes more sense, by the way. For all of Bartell's protestations otherwise, he comes across here as a lunatic, jumping all over Pfirman after just one questionable call.

Bartell entered the game with a .299 average. After those first two hitless at-bats, he'd dropped to .298, so he needed two hits in two (or three) remaining at-bats to top .300. His Giants had already clinched the National League pennant, so Bartell was freed to think of only himself . . . to the point that he looked as if he might punch an umpire and get himself suspended for some of the World Series. The next time somebody tries to tell you that the players in the good ol' days didn't care about statistics, don't you believe it.

Umpire Bill Klem is in the Hall of Fame because he umpired forever, but he was famous for always having the right answer . . .

During the middle '30s, before he became chief umpire of the National League, Klem was working home plate in St. Louis in a game between the Cardinals and the New York Giants. A fiercely magisterial man, he had lately returned to his position after haranguing the Cardinal bench in general and manager Frank Frisch in particular. Johnny Mize was at bat for the Cardinals and Hal Schumacher was pitching for the Giants. Klem suddenly discovered, like a burlesque comic doing a long take, that he had an afterthought for Frisch and left the plate to deliver it without bothering to call time.

Unable to check his windup, Schumacher pitched weakly to Mize, who hit a double. The Giants, led by Bill Terry, advanced noisily on Klem for redress, on the ground that since there had been no umpire around there had been no play.

Klem permitted the double to stand.

"Suppose, Bill," Terry said finally, "suppose the ball had gone through Mize? How would you have called it?"

"Why," replied Klem, "I would have called it what it *was.* Play ball!"

—Gilbert Millstein, "Why They Argue With the Ump," The New York Times, *July 29, 1956*

RON OESTER & .300

I learned a lot about playing the game the right way during my rookie year, and one of the best lesson came during the last series of the year.

We were finishing the season on a West Coast trip, and Ronnie Oester was batting exactly .300.

Ronnie didn't wear batting gloves, so he used to develop blisters on his hands—really deep ones that would turn into full-fledged holes in his palms by the end of the season.

We were out of the playoff picture, and Ronnie had busted his hump all year, so Pete told him he had no problem sitting him if he wanted to stay at .300 for the year.

"Are you kidding?" he asked Pete. "That doesn't mean anything to me. I just want to win some games."

That's what I liked about Ronnie. He was just a great teammate. He didn't have a selfish bone in his body.

He ended up playing the remaining games and didn't hit much of anything. His average dropped to .295 for the season, but I doubt if he even noticed.

—Tom Browning in *Tom Browning's Tales from the Reds Dugout*
(Browning and Don Stupp, 2006)

Oester, the Reds' second baseman, began the season with fifteen hitless at-bats, but pushed his batting average to .300 on May 15 and spent the rest of the season in the .285–.305 range. Browning's memory—or perhaps his co-author's ability to consult Retrosheet—is dead solid. The Reds ended their season with seven games on the West Coast: two each in San Francisco and San Diego, and three in Los Angeles. When the trip began, the Reds had not been mathematically eliminated from pennant contention, but they were dead after losing the first game against the Padres.

At that point they had four games left and Oester's average was .300 on the nose. He went 0 for his next 7, which dropped his average to .296 and obviated any motivation to stop playing. But he went just 2 for 9 in the last two games and finished, just as Browning recalls, at .295. Oester played for five more seasons, but never did hit .300 in a career that stretched from 1978 to 1990.*

I'm sure you know that many players have been benched—or have essentially benched themselves—to back into a batting title. Alex Johnson, Willie Wilson . . . even George Brett did it (in 1990, when he edged Rickey Henderson by four points). What you might not know is that many players have

---

* In his last season, Oester did bat .299 as a part-time player.

backed into far less prestigious accomplishments, like batting .300. Just a few examples . . .

In 1980, Reggie Jackson went into the final game of the season batting .298. His first time up, he tripled and scored a moment later when Eric Soderholm homered. That was in the bottom of the second. In the top of the third, with Jackson's average sitting on .300—well, .2996, but for some reason we round these things upward—his place in the lineup was taken by someone named Ted Wilborn. It was the first time in Reggie's career that he batted .300, and would be the last. In his memoirs he wrote, "It's funny but that was a big deal for me. Even with all the other accomplishments it meant something—it was another barrier I was able to jump over." Jump. Slither. Whatever.

In 1992, A's second baseman Mike Bordick was sitting right around .300 throughout September. On the last day of the month, he went 2 for 3 to reach .300 on the nose. The A's had already clinched the division title and had three games left against Milwaukee. Bordick *did* start the first game of that series and lost three points off his average after going 0 for 5. With nothing to lose in the second game, Bordick singled in his first at-bat and homered in his second, which got him back to .300. He came up again in the fifth, and a hitless at-bat would have dropped him back to .299. Instead he was intentionally walked, and manager Tony La Russa wasn't taking any chances afterward. La Russa pinch-hit for Bordick his next time up, and Bordick didn't bat at all in Oakland's last game.

In 1998, Yankees third baseman Scott Brosius began the last day of the season with ninety-eight RBIs and a .302 batting average. The game was meaningless, of course—that's the year the Yankees won 114 games—but Brosius apparently wanted to bat .300 (which he'd done before) *and* crack the 100 RBI mark (which he hadn't). Brosius started the game, but three hitless at-bats dropped his average to .300 exactly (that is, .3 with zeros into infinity). One more hitless at-bat would have dropped the average to .299435, so in the seventh inning Brosius was pulled in favor of rookie Mike Lowell.

There are various other examples, including (but not limited to) Gerald Perry (in 1988).

Not just hitters, either. In 1988, Minnesota's Allan Anderson tossed a shutout against the A's on the 27th of September. That gave him a 2.45 ERA, No. 2 in the league and just a hair more than Teddy Higuera's 2.41 mark. On the 1st of October, Higuera gave up three runs in six and two-thirds innings, lifting his ERA to 2.45. Or to be precise, 2.4545; Anderson's, precisely, was 2.4465. Both figures rounded to 2.45, but technically Anderson's ERA was lower. And so it would stay.

Anderson's next turn in the rotation would have been on the 2nd, the last day of the season. Instead Roy Smith made his fourth start of the season, the Twins beat the Angels 3 to 2, and Anderson had his ERA title. When asked about it, he said, "Some people will take it one way, and some will take it another way. I can't control what other people think. . . . It could be a once-in-a-lifetime thing. Look at Bert [Blyleven]. He's pitched nineteen years, and he finished second once."[1]

We've also seen players benched to avoid breaking Bobby Bonds's strike-out record, and we've seen pitchers benched to avoid losing twenty games.

Lest one think this is a modern phenomenon, consider the American League batting race in 1935. Entering the season's final day, Cleveland's Joe Vosmik held a four-point lead over Washington's Buddy Myer, .349 to .345. The Indians had a doubleheader scheduled, the Senators a single game against the A's. Vosmik did not start the first game. "And then," according to Shirley Povich in *The Washington Senators*, "the wires started telling of a batting rampage by Myer in Shibe Park." Vosmik went in as a pinch hitter in the ninth inning of the opener, then started the second game. But he went just 1 for 4 on the day while Myer went 4 for 5, with Myer finishing just one (rounded) point ahead, .3495 to .3489.

DOC CRAMER & JOE VOSMIK

ST. LOUIS, Mo.—Taking a leaf from the Blue Ridge League book, Stan Musial of the Cardinals pitched to his batting title rival, Frankie Baumholtz of the Cubs, in the final game. With third place clinched by the Redbirds, permission was obtained from Warren Giles, National League president, for Musial, who hurled for Daytona Beach in the Class D Florida State League in 1940, to go to the mound against Baumholtz.

A crowd of 17,422 saw Musial trot in from center field after Harvey Haddix had issued a game-opening walk to Tommy Brown. Baumholtz, already hopelessly out of the race because of a late slump, decided to bat righthanded as Haddix went to right field and Hal Rice moved to center.

Musial's mound career in the majors lasted for just one pitch. Baumholtz hit Stan's first delivery on the ground through Solly Hemus, the regular shortstop playing third base, for an error. Baumholtz reached base, Musial moved back to the outfield, and Haddix returned to the mound.

Years back, when Joe Vosmik and Doc Cramer were tied for the Blue Ridge swat crown on the last day of the season, Cramer moved in from the outfield and walked Vosmik four times to win the title, .404 to .399.

—*The Sporting News* October 8, 1952

The main story here is about Musial and Baumholtz, but it's a small story. It was just one pitch, the season and the batting race essentially over already (Musial finished the season at .336, Baumholtz in second place but eleven points behind). No, the interesting story here is the one about Joe Vosmik and Doc Cramer. Was a swat crown really so ill-gotten? It's hard to believe *The Sporting News*—for many years known as "The Bible of Baseball"—would have gotten a story like that wrong.

Cramer and Vosmik both got their professional starts in 1929, in the Class D Blue Ridge League; Cramer played for Martinsburg, Vosmik for Frederick, and neither ever played in that league again. So yes, this could have happened in the Blue Ridge League in 1929.

Not much else checks out, though. On page 291 of the 1930 Reach Guide, we find that Cramer did lead the league with a .404 batting average. And Vosmik did finish second. But it was a fairly distant second, as Vosmik batted .381.

Could they have been "tied . . . on the last day of the season"? Perhaps, if there was a doubleheader on the last day of the season. Cramer finished the season with 148 hits in 366 at-bats. If we assume he went 8 for 8 on the last day of the season, he'd have begun that day with a .391 average.

The story says Vosmik walked four times. Let's assume he did walk four times, and was out four times. He actually finished with 155 hits in 407 at-bats, so our hypothetical assumptions have him entering this hypothetical doubleheader with 155 hits in 403 at-bats . . . and a .385 batting average. So no, it's not all likely that the two were tied for the lead. But if we make a bunch of extreme assumptions, we can at least imagine that Vosmik was within striking distance.

He wasn't. It took me a few months, but I tracked down the coverage in one of the local newspapers. Frederick and Martinsburg *did* meet on the season's final day, and they *did* play a doubleheader. Vosmik went 1 for 6, and Cramer went 3 for 6. So they entered the twin bill like this:

	At-Bats	Hits	Avg
Cramer	360	145	.403
Vosmik	401	154	.384

In the first game Vosmik went 1 for 3, which left his average at .384. Cramer went 2 for 4, raising his average one point to .404. So in that last game, in which Cramer did pitch, he went in with a twenty-point lead in the batting race. It was all over, even the shouting. And Cramer didn't even pitch much. A young man named Henry Sherry started for Martinsburg. As the *Post* noted, "Sherry had little or nothing on the ball, but kept the locals hitting bad balls to get him out of bad situations. When he weakened in the sixth he was removed in favor of Cramer."

Oh, and they played only seven innings. Cramer pitched two innings, and didn't walk anybody.

Presumably, somebody at *The Sporting News* had access to the old Reach Guide. Somebody there *certainly* had access to the TSN archives. On December 12, 1929, the newspaper ran a wrap-up of the Blue Ridge League's season, and the headlines read like this:

ROGER CRAMER, ATHLETIC RECRUIT, WON BLUE RIDGE BATTING CROWN
Youngster Turned in Average of .404 to Finish Far in Front of Rivals; Vosmik Carried Off Second Place Honors with an Impressive .381

I'll admit, when I first read the story at the top of his chapter, I was ready to think the worst of ol' Doc Cramer. What kind of person wins a batting title like *that*? What kind of manager allows his player to win a batting title like that? But ol' Doc won this one on the square.

Vosmik had the better season, though. Vosmik played in eight more games than Cramer, scored six more runs, hit four more home runs, and drew thirty more walks. Vosmik also led the league in doubles, triples, and total bases.

Both Vosmik and Cramer wound up doing well in the majors, and they got there quickly. Vosmik was more or less an everyday player for ten years, and left the majors with a .307 career batting average; in 1935 he led the American League in doubles and triples and finished third in the MVP voting. Cramer lasted longer in the majors than Vosmik, though he wasn't quite the hitter that Vosmik was (he didn't have Vosmik's power or patience). He did make five All-Star teams (just one for Vosmik; they were teammates in '35) and finished his career with 2,705 hits (Bill James ranks Cramer as the "weakest" outfielder to play at least 2,000 games).

So where did our story get its start? I don't know. But that 1952 appearance in *The Sporting News* was not its first. The note below appeared in the October 1950 issue of *Baseball Digest*, right out of the Doc's mouth . . .

PASSED OUT OF THE PICTURE

Doc Cramer, Seattle Rainier coach, was tied with Joe Vosmik, another ex-American League outfielder, for the leadership of the Blue Ridge League, many seasons ago. The two were hitting .398 going into the final day and by previous arrangement with his manager, Cramer was allowed to pitch that day. History records that Cramer got four hits in four trips, and won the title with a mark of .404. Mr. Vosmik wound up owning the same average he started with—.398. And how did that happen?

"I guess I just kind of deliberately walked him four times," says Mr. Cramer, with a vacant smile. "As I recall it, Joe was pretty mad about the whole thing."

—Emmett Watson (*Seattle Post-Intelligencer*)

Of course, the two were certainly *not* both hitting .398 going into the season's final day. Cramer did *not* walk Vosmik four times, and Vosmik did *not* wind up with a .398 batting average. I will note, however, that Cramer did pitch in eleven games that season, and it's certainly possible that he

---

We do miss some things in the modern American League . . .

During a 1963 game against the Giants, Lindy McDaniel looked like Cy Young and Babe Ruth rolled into one. At Wrigley Field on June 6, 1963, the Cubs and Giants were tied at 2–2 in the top of the 12th. With one out, the Giants loaded the bases against Barney Schultz, and Chicago skipper Bob Kennedy summoned McDaniel from the bullpen.

The right-hander promptly picked off Willie Mays at second base, and then quashed the San Francisco rally by striking out Ed Bailey.

McDaniel wasn't done yet. In the bottom of the inning, he stepped up against southpaw Billy Pierce. On a 2–2 count, McDaniel slammed Pierce's next delivery into the left field stands for a 3–2 Cubs win.

—Pete Cava, Tales from the Cubs Dugout *(2002)*

I can't confirm the 2–2 count when McDaniel homered off Pierce, but otherwise it's all true, except McDaniel's heroics came in the tenth inning, not the twelfth. And one more detail makes the story even better: McDaniel led off the bottom of the tenth.

This was one of three homers in McDaniel's twenty-one-year career. The first came in 1957, when he went deep against Roger Craig, only to lose a few innings later on

☛

Charlie Neal's walkoff shot in the ninth. His third homer came in 1972. Pitching in long relief for the Yankees, McDaniel was allowed to bat for himself in the ninth inning of a 1–1 game and hit a solo shot off Mickey Lolich. It wasn't a game-winner, though, as the Tigers tied the game in the bottom of the ninth (the Yankees won in twelve).

did, earlier in the season, walk Vosmik four times in one game. And it's even possible that when (*if*) Cramer walked Vosmik, the two of them really were tied for the lead in the batting race. Whatever happened (or didn't), it had zero impact on anything that concerned anyone at the end of the season.

EDD ROUSH & ZACK WHEAT

Paul Green: Well, you hit .350 a few years in a row and led the league in hitting a couple of times so no one would complain.

Roush: I led it three times, but I got beat out of one. I hit .333 (in 1918) and Wheat hit .335. I had a ballgame in Cincinnati. It had rained and we were playing St. Louis, and there was a man on third with one out. I came in after a ball and my feet went out from under me. The ball hit my glove and bounced up and I caught it as it came back down while I was sitting on the ground. The fellow on third thought it was a hit and headed for home, so I threw it to third and the umpire called him out. So they protested the game.

Well, they threw the ballgame out, and in those days they threw out all the averages, too. I had three base hits in four times up, so I lost them all. You don't see anything about that; the writers won't write it. That's what beat me out of leading the league. It doesn't mean anything now. I was a good hitter, but so what? That was 1918. I won the title in 1917 and 1919, but in 1918 my dad got killed so I had to go home about three weeks before the season closed. Well, Wheat was leading, and they learned what happened in Brooklyn—that I was out of there—so they took him out while he was leading the league. You never heard that before, did you?

Green: No.

Roush: Of course not. See, they weren't about to write it, that's for sure.

—Forgotten Fields (Paul Green, 1984)

Edd J Roush (no middle name; just *J*) did win National League batting titles in 1917 and 1919, and in 1918 he did bat .333 and finish two points behind titlist Zachary D. Wheat.

A lot of other things are going on here. There's the protested game, and the lost hits. And there's Roush's dead father. And Wheat taking the coward's route to a batting title. Not to mention Roush's grudge against the writers, which apparently he nurtured for more than half a century. So let's take them one at a time, beginning with the protested game.

Actually, *two* protested games (supposedly) impacted the batting race.

On April 29, with the Cardinals visiting Cincinnati, things happened essentially as Roush remembered. Not exactly, but close. What really happened—at least according to contemporary accounts—was this: Roush actually had the ball in his glove, only to have it pop up in the air as he stumbled, after which he caught the ball again. The runner on third base headed home upon the initial touch and was called out when Roush threw to third. The Cardinals wound up losing 4–3, manager Jack Hendricks protested, and National League president John Heydler upheld the protest. According to the rule governing such games—which was changed in 1920—not only was the game thrown out, but so were all the statistics from the game. Including Roush's two hits in three at-bats.

So if you restore the April 29 game, Roush bats .336.

On June 3, it was Wheat involved, to his benefit, in a protested game the *Times* called "the most weird of the season." The contest went twelve innings and lasted three hours and twenty-six minutes.

> The deciding tally did not happen along until dusk was settling over the Flatbush diamond, and the few faithful fans who decided to stay to the end were beginning to wish they had elected to go home. To add to the joys of the protracted struggle is the fact that it may have been in vain, since Manager Robinson has announced that he would protest the contest to the National Commission, because of a decision by Umpire Charley Rigler on the bases in the sixth inning. This decision gave the Cardinals a run and made it easier for them to overtake the Dodgers, who were then leading.[1]

The Cardinals finished ahead, 15–12. And though the Dodgers picked up thirteen hits, Wheat didn't have even one; he went 0 for 5 in the game. The Dodgers' protest was upheld, as the Cardinals' Doug Baird was adjudged to have cut across the infield on his way to scoring a run, which of course is not exactly how you're supposed to do it.* Thus, Wheat's five hitless at-bats were duly thrown out of the records.

So if you restore the stats from the protested games—Roush's 2 for 3 and Wheat's 0 for 5—Roush wins the batting title by five points, .336 to Wheat's .331.†

---

* As the *Brooklyn Eagle*'s beat writer observed, "If that rule gives the runner the right to cut third base by 25 feet when he resumes his journey to the plate, merely because he had been to third once before, then the Kaiser is a perfect gentleman, the prohibitionists' statement that 600,000 people die in this country of alcoholism is perfectly true, and the shelling of coastwise passenger steamers outside of the war zone is a perfectly honorable proceeding."

† Researcher Joseph M. Wayman has written about the protested games and the batting title a number of times, most recently in SABR's *Baseball Research Journal Number* 22 (1993).

But you know what? Those were the rules at that time. Babe Ruth hit a walk-off homer in (coincidentally enough) 1918 that wasn't a homer, because in 1918 they didn't count those as homers unless the batter represented the winning run.* Otherwise Joe Friday would have worn badge number 715 instead of 714.

Anyway, all that stuff happened before anybody knew that Roush and Wheat would wind up battling for the title. Wheat was a spring-training holdout. The Dodgers opened their season on April 16, but Wheat didn't sign until two weeks later and didn't see his first action until May 7. After going 1 for 9 in a July 4 doubleheader, his batting average stood at .263 and his biggest fans in Flatbush couldn't have dared hope for a batting title.

But then Wheat started hitting and never really stopped. On July 11 he began a hitting streak that ran for twenty-six games. After an 0 for 3 on August 8, he ripped off a thirteen-game streak that upped his average to .344.

Roush's teammate Heinie Groh contended for the batting title for much of the summer, but by late August he'd fallen off the pace. Meanwhile, Roush was making his own run. Sitting at .300 on August 1, Roush had jumped all the way to .332 on August 24. That same day, Wheat went 0 for 7 in a doubleheader and dropped to .342.

So the battle was definitely joined.

But there was a bigger battle, in Europe. In April 1917, the United States declared war on Germany. In June, conscription began. But baseball continued as if nothing were amiss: schedules completed, the World Series played, nobody drafted. During the following winter and spring, with the war still raging and Pershing's American Expeditionary Force on the ground in Western Europe, there was a great deal of uncertainty regarding professional baseball. Owners took the opportunity to cut player salaries across the board (which led to Wheat's holdout; he refused to take the cut).

A shock wave went through the sport in late May, when Provost Marshal Enoch Crowder announced his "work or fight order," requiring all men of draft age—twenty-one through thirty-one—to either serve in the military or engage in war-related work. According to a report in the *Times*, "Strict enforcement of General Crowder's order would, it is said, wreck the two major league baseball clubs of Chicago. All the players of both teams except four are of draft age."

As the Spalding guide opined the next winter:

---

* In the 1960s, researchers discovered thirty-seven of these game-ending hits that could have been considered home runs, but were not; the rule was changed after the 1920 season. For more on this somewhat arcane subject, see Alan Schwarz's wonderful book *The Numbers Game: Baseball's Lifelong Fascination with Statistics* (St. Martin's Press, 2004).

The work or fight order of the Provost Marshal's office of the United States army was not dreamed of nor anticipated, and it was that order which really made Base Ball an impossibility. It gathered to the active forces of the United States all the available man power within the limit of the draft years. The law was not quite clearly understood at the beginning, the more so as there were those who believed that the national game was as essential as the theater and the moving picture industry. When a ruling was made, it was immediately apparent to all who knew professional Base Ball well that it would be impossible to go on. The major leagues, which were perfectly willing to abide by any desire of the Government, still wished to preserve intact a record for continuity that never had been broken since their organization, and asked for an extension. This was granted, but not in such a way that the major league seasons could be completed in toto.[2]

The National League's season was supposed to conclude on October 6, but the schedule was revised to end instead on September 2, Labor Day.

So when play opened on August 25, only nine days were left in the season, and Wheat had that ten-point lead over Roush. Here's what happened over the next *five* days, which included one doubleheader for Wheat and three twin bills for Roush.

	Wheat	Roush	Diff
August 25	.341	.335	+6
26	(no games)		+6
27	(no games)		+6
28	.340	.336	+4
29	.339	.333	+6

On August 30, at eight in the morning, Roush and his roommate, Groh, were in their hotel room in Chicago. There's a knock at the door: telegram for Roush.

WILL IN COMA STOP FELL OFF TELEPHONE
POLE STOP COME HOME STOP MOTHER

Home was Oakland City, Indiana, where Roush's father, Will, was the local manager of the Independent Telephone Company. Edd got home that night and, upon seeing his father, "knew then that he would never make it back to Cincinnati before the end of the season."[3]

He was still in Indiana on September 5, when his father died. The National League season had ended three days earlier. As you know, the season ended with Zack Wheat atop the batting list.

Photo courtesy of National Baseball Hall of Fame, Cooperstown, New York

Edd Roush

Remember what Roush said?

"I had to go home about three weeks before the season closed. Well, Wheat was leading, and they learned what happened in Brooklyn—that I was out of there—so they took him out while he was leading the league. You never heard that before, did you? . . . Of course not. See, they weren't about to write it, that's for sure."

There weren't about to write it because it wasn't true. As we've seen, Roush went home not three weeks before the season closed, but four days before. He missed six games. As for Wheat, his Dodgers had five games remaining: three against the Giants at the Polo Grounds, and two in Philadelphia (a doubleheader on September 2). On the 30th, he went 1 for 3 to maintain his .339 average. On the 31st, he went 1 for 8 in a doubleheader, his average dropping to .335. He did not make that final road trip for those last two games. Which apparently had little to do with batting averages, though. From the *Brooklyn Daily Eagle*:

Green apparently interviewed Roush in 1983, when he was ninety (he would almost reach ninety-five). Roush had been elected to the Hall of Fame, with somewhat shaky credentials, by the Veterans Committee in 1962. Here's how the interview concludes.

Green: Were you thrilled when you were told about Cooperstown?
Roush: Why, no. Why in the hell would I be? I should have been there ten years before. Good God almighty, they put guys in there who never even hit .300. When I went in in 1962, I told them, "This was the damndest thing I ever saw. What in the hell do writers have to do with it to start with? They don't know anything about baseball. All they know is whether you win or lose."
Green: I've heard players say that if they did the picking, things would be different.
Roush: That's right. After I got done talking, they changed the wait for the Veterans Committee from thirty years to twenty years. I told them, "What the hell good does it do if you're dead?" You play 'till you're forty, that plus thirty makes seventy years. How many ballplayers are alive who are seventy years old? I said, "I wouldn't give you a dime for it after I'm dead."
Green: I guess the game has really changed.
Roush: You're telling me.
Green: You had a good time?
Roush: It was a business. I had fun playing amateur baseball; professional baseball was a

business. I don't know what it is now.

Green: Big business.

Roush: Monkey . . . monkey business. Each club has a few who could have played in my day, but not many of them.

How many of the Brooklyn National League team will go to Philadelphia on Monday, September 2, for the morning and afternoon games of that Labor Day holiday, is not yet known, but Uncle Wilbert Robinson expects to put a team in the field. Besides his men over the present draft age of 31, several, such as Hi Myers and Jimmy Johnston, have received permission from their draft boards to finish the season. Rube Marquard and Burleigh Grimes, who enlisted in the Navy, have furloughs from active service until October 1.

One of those who will not go to Philadelphia is Zack Wheat, left fielder, now leading the National League batters. Zack will leave for the West on Sunday morning, September 1, and will be a full fledged farmer again on September 2.[4]

That ran in the *Eagle* the morning of the 29th . . . *before* anybody knew that Edd Roush was leaving for Oklahoma. Those last two games in Philadelphia would have no bearing on the pennant race, and Wheat—at thirty, he was of draft age—had work to do back in Missouri, where farm work might well have been considered war-related. There simply doesn't seem to be any truth in Roush's claim that Wheat ducked out early with the batting title in mind.

And what if Wheat had played those last two games?

If he'd gotten eight at-bats—his replacement in the No. 4 slot got four plate appearances in both games—and gone hitless or gotten just one hit, he'd have finished behind Roush. If he'd gotten three or more hits in eight at-bats, he'd have finished on top. And if he'd gotten two hits in eight at-bats? He and Roush would have finished at exactly .333 and stand today as the only players in major-league history to finish in a dead heat for the batting title.

HARVEY HADDIX & HANK SAUER

Remember the fuss last year when a number of National League pitchers hinted they might put a fat pitch down the middle to Henry Aaron?

Former major league pitcher Harvey Haddix remembers grooving one to Chicago Cubs slugger Hank Sauer. But it didn't help.

It was 1952 and Haddix was pitching for the St. Louis Cardinals.

Sauer and Ralph Kiner were locked in a late-season home run duel. Both had 37 home runs.

"Most of the players didn't like Kiner," remembers Haddix.

"We decided to groove one for Sauer. We told Sauer it was coming right down the pike, but he didn't believe it. He let the ball go by," said Haddix, now a farmer in South Vienna, Ohio.

"Well, I wasn't going to do it again. I said to myself, 'OK fella, you had your chance. This next one is going to be a real zinger.'

"I fired the ball right past him and struck him out."

Sauer and Kiner finished the season tied.

—Bob Broeg in the *St. Louis Post-Dispatch*
(reprinted in *Baseball Digest*, October 1974)

Sauer and Kiner did finish the season tied, with thirty-seven homers apiece.

Haddix started six games for the Cardinals, and just once against the Cubs. On the last day of the season.

In 1952, Haddix was a rookie but he wasn't just some raw-boned kid. When he debuted with the Cardinals on August 20, he was just a month shy of his twenty-seventh birthday and had been pitching professionally since 1947 and had spent most of 1951 and '52 in the service. Nevertheless, it's a little surprising that he'd have been confident enough, as a rookie, to groove a fastball and essentially throw a prestigious title to Sauer. On the other hand, why would he make up a story like this?

Everything checks out. Haddix did pitch to Sauer on the last day of the season, and Sauer and Kiner were tied with thirty-seven homers apiece.

I've not been able to find any extensive post-career interviews with Sauer, but a decent-sized reminiscence is in Danny Peary's *We Played the Game*—a massive volume of interviews with major leaguers regarding 1947 through 1964—and Sauer doesn't have much to say about '52. His son was born an hour after he learned he'd been named National League MVP—"It was quite a day!"—and his biggest thrill was hitting a decisive homer in the All-Star Game. But nothing about Haddix and the last day of the season.[1]

Purely out of curiosity, I wondered what Kiner

The players used to tell of Al Bridwell, toward the end of the season, being given the signs and failing to profit by it. Bridwell, who had been a Giant, was then on the Boston club. The pennant was already decided and Brid's old teammates wanted to see him hit .300. On the last day Bresnahan not only let him know what was coming, but asked Brid what he would like to hit. Then he would signal for it. With this great advantage Bridwell went to bat five times and didn't get a hit. He always said after that he would rather not know what was coming.

— *Ty Cobb in* Memoirs of Twenty Years in Baseball *(ed. William R. Cobb, 2002)*

Roger Bresnahan couldn't have let Bridwell know anything, because Bresnahan couldn't have been there in 1911. Not as a Giant, anyway; Bresnahan and Bridwell were teammates in 1908, but Bresnahan left the Giants after that season, never to return.

So if this did happen, Bresnahan wasn't involved. Which brings us to another obvious inaccuracy: this couldn't have happened—not really—while Bridwell was playing for the Boston Braves. In July of '11, the Giants traded him to Boston. But he finished that season with a .279 average, and even if he'd gone 5 for 5 (instead of 0 for 5, assuming he did go 0 for 5) on the last day of the season, he'd have fallen ten points

might have written about that chase for the home-run title. As it turns out, quite a bit.

> In 1952, as I went after a record seventh consecutive homer title, I found myself involved in yet another down-to-the-wire race. This time my competition was the Cubs' Hank Sauer, who would be voted the National League's MVP. I was one homer behind Sauer after 152 games, 37 to 36. Our last series was in Cincinnati, and we were sched-uled to play two games.
>
> Rather than taking the train with the rest of the team, I flew to Cincinnati at my own expense so I could get a good night's sleep. Be-fore the first game, I asked our young shortstop Dick Groat to pitch batting practice to me for about an hour and a half, which he was very happy to do. And it paid off. I hit my 37th home run to tie Sauer, who didn't homer that day. But on Sunday I didn't hit a homer, so that left him with an opening. We got on the train going back to Pittsburgh be-fore I was able to get any news about Hank's final game. I didn't know if he had homered and won the title outright. I was anxious, of course, because I wanted to break Babe Ruth's record, so when the train stopped in Indianapolis I jumped out and found the stationmaster. Through Western Union, I discovered that Sauer had *not* homered and we ended up tied. So I had broken a major league record held by my idol Babe Ruth! When I got back on the train I ordered champagne for all the players to celebrate.[2]

The above passage is taken from Kiner's most recent book, published in 2004. Oddly—considering the ease of checking such things these days—his earlier book, published in 1987, was a bit more accurate, at least when it comes to one detail we can check.

> Going into the final series of the season, against the Reds, I trailed Hank Sauer of the Cubs by one homer, 37–36. Although the Pirates were taking the train, I paid my own way to fly to Cincinnati. I never slept well on the train and I wanted to be rested.
>
> Despite taking extra batting practice against Groat the next after-noon, I didn't hit any homers on Friday night. But I did get one on Sat-urday to tie Sauer. I remember the Reds made a big production out of my going for another home-run title. Since they were well out of the pennant race, they geared their advertising toward me in hopes that I might draw a significant crowd. So, after all that buildup, Ken Raffens-berger walked me three or four times. I never got a chance to hit.
>
> I didn't know what Sauer had done. We took the train back to Pitts-burgh, and at every station I ran inside to the telegrapher to see if he could find out whether Sauer had hit a home run. It wasn't until about 2 A.M. at some cowtown, that I learned Sauer hadn't homered.[3]

The Pirates' last series was in Cincinnati, but it was a three-game series—Friday through Sunday—rather than a two-gamer (as Kiner claims in the recent autobiography). On the other hand, there's one detail here—not in the recent book—that's nowhere near accurate. Kiner says of the season's final game, "Raffensberger walked me three or four times. I never got a chance to hit." Pure fiction. Raffensberger issued only one walk while going the distance, and that was to pinch hitter Frank Thomas in the ninth. Kiner went 0 for 4.

So what did it all mean, in the end? Not much, probably. Kiner did break that record held by Ruth—most consecutive seasons leading one's league in home runs—but it's not at all clear if anybody noticed. On the other hand . . .

In 1960, Kiner's first year of Hall of Fame eligibility, he got three votes. At that time, the balloting was conducted every two years. In 1962, his count zoomed all the way to five votes. From there, he gained steadily and was, in the early 1970s, garnering roughly 60 percent of the vote each year. Finally, in 1975 his percentage jumped to 75.4; you need 75 percent, so he was in. Kiner needed 272 votes; he got 273.

Oh, and 1975 was Kiner's last year of eligibility. Sure, if the BBWAA hadn't elected him, the Veterans Committee might have; God knows that august body eventually put just about everybody else in. Still, what was the winning Hall of Fame argument for Kiner? For many years, I've heard only one: "Ralph Kiner led the National League in home runs in seven straight seasons." Which he did: 1946–1952.

But what if he'd instead led the National League in home runs in just six straight seasons? Would that have cost him at least two votes in 1975? I suspect it would have cost him more than two, perhaps quite a few more than two.

I know I'm engaging in rank speculation, but I believe that if Hank Sauer had taken Harvey Haddix seriously on the last day of the 1952 season, Ralph Kiner might today still be hoping for good news from Cooperstown.

short of .300. Bridwell did bat .291 during his stint that season with Boston, but would anybody have even been tracking that breakdown? I doubt it.

In 1912, his only other season with the Braves, Bridwell batted .236 and played sparingly. In 1913, his last season as a National Leaguer, he played quite a bit for the Cubs and batted .240.

So let's go back to 1911. Hey, maybe somebody really was interested in Bridwell's Boston-only batting average. Did the Braves play the Giants on the last day of the season? No, they didn't. The Braves finished their season with a Monday doubleheader in Philadelphia. Two days earlier, though, they had played a single game in New York, probably making up a game earlier lost to wet grounds or a shortage of baseballs or something.

In that game, on October 7, Bridwell went 1 for 4. Which leads one to wonder what on earth Cobb was talking about.

FELLER'S LOST HIS FASTBALL

Bob Feller, the retired pitcher, went out recently to make a TV commercial. He was to pitch a ball into a plastic backstop behind home plate. Some ad agency men gathered behind the backstop to watch.

"Stoop way down," Feller warned. "This pitcher's mound is high and from this angle I might hit someone."

One man didn't stoop low enough. Feller's pitch hit him in the forehead where a bump erupted.

"First time in 21 years that I hit a guy," said Feller. The last man was Hank Leiber, whose playing career ended soon after he was hit on the head. Feller told the prostrate ad man: "Now I know I've lost my fast ball because when you got hit you didn't even rub your head."

—Leonard Lyons in the *New York Post*,
reprinted in *Baseball Digest* (September, 1958)

Well, of course we know that wasn't really the first time in twenty-one years that Feller hit anybody with a pitch. Assuming this incident happened in 1958, twenty-one years would push us back to 1937. As a rookie in 1936, Feller hit four batters in sixty-two innings. From 1937 through 1956, his last season, he hit fifty-six more batters.

It should be said that Feller's sixty career hit batsmen is almost absurdly low, considering how hard he threw and how little control he had during most of his career. In 1938 he walked 208 batters and hit seven. In 1941 he walked 194 and hit five. In 1946 he walked 153 and hit three. Three! It's generally true that pitchers didn't hit nearly as many batters as they would later, when—and perhaps, at least in part, because—batting helmets were introduced. But Feller obviously was not working the inside part of the strike zone, and it's most likely because he was afraid—again, as many pitchers were—that he would mortally wound someone. Nobody'd been killed in the majors since 1920, of course, but serious concussions and actual fractures were not at all uncommon, and the story of Ray Chapman was well known. In May of '37, shortly into Feller's first full season, Mickey Cochrane's skull was broken in three places by a Bump Hadley fastball. Cochrane spent a week in the hospital and never played again.

So what Feller meant, perhaps, is that after hitting Hank Leiber he never hit another batter in the head. Here's an odd fact, though: Feller never beaned Leiber in an official game. He couldn't have. Feller spent his entire career with Cleveland, and Leiber spent his in the National League with the Giants and Cubs. Yes, it might have been some sort of exhibition game, during spring training or the actual season (teams would play exhibition games dur-

Photo courtesy of Sporting News/ZUMA Press/Icon SMI

Young Bobby Feller

ing the season, in those days). Those are hard to check. But what about an All-Star Game? That's exceptionally easy to check, and both Feller and Leiber were All-Stars: Feller multiple times, and Leiber in 1938, 1940, and '41. Oddly, Leiber was great in only two seasons—'35 and '39—but wasn't an All-Star in either season. More oddly, he was an All-Star in '41 and finished the season with a .216 batting average in fifty-three games. How in the hell did *that* happen?

I don't know if I can answer that question today, so many years removed from someone's strange decision. That .216 batting average does suggest a story, though. Leiber was great in '39, very good in '40, and never hit again. First came the .216 in '41, and then a .218 in '42 (in only fifty-eight games). After which he didn't play again, though my initial suspicion is that the war had something to do with that.

Anyway, let's check Leiber's All-Star Games. In '38, Feller was an All-Star but didn't pitch. In '40, Feller pitched but Leiber didn't play (he wasn't on the National League roster, actually, apparently because of an injury). And in '41, same thing; Feller started but Leiber was replaced on the roster.

Faced with the difficulty of checking exhibition games, I turned to John

Mike Norris is a member of the (unfortunately named) "Black Aces" club—American-born black pitchers who had won twenty games in one season—and last summer talked about using his status to promote baseball in inner cities . . .

Norris has accepted the challenge, and on Wednesday, he talked about how he became an Ace, and how it all fell apart. He talked about his old hero, Gibson.

"Mr. Gibson is a very direct-type person," Norris said. "[Meeting Gibson] didn't turn out like I thought. I was pitching in Baltimore and he was doing color commentary for ABC. I was leading the game 4–3 going into the bottom of the ninth."

Norris gave up back-to-back homers and lost. He was moping in the dugout when Gibson approached.

"He told me, 'Get your glove and go to the clubhouse, because you just embarrassed yourself.' I asked why. He said, 'You threw two pitches inside the whole night, and those were by mistake. You gotta have some guts.'

"When Mr. Gibson pitched, he'd pick out the biggest black guy on the team and nail him, and the other seven white guys were scared of him.

"I came back [the next season] and won twenty-two games," Norris said, "because of intimidation. That's what I got from Mr. Gibson."
—*Scott Ostler*, San Francisco Chronicle *(May 31, 2007)*

Sickels' biography, *Bob Feller: Ace of the Greatest Generation*, and quickly found this passage regarding spring training in 1937 . . .

> Still, [Feller] was wild more often than not, which was often to his advantage. No one dared dig in against him. The control problem had a serious consequence on April 4th, when the Giants and Indians met up again for a game in New Orleans. Feller and Hubbell started the game, attracting a large spring crowd of 13,000 fans. Both pitched well, and Feller tossed five scoreless innings, fanning five. But an out-of-control curveball clobbered Giants outfielder Hank Leiber in the head, damaging an optic nerve and causing a concussion. He returned to action within two weeks, but was bothered by dizziness for the rest of the season, spending a considerable portion of the first half on the disabled list.[1]

Feller does discuss this incident in both of his autobiographies, which were published forty-three years apart.

In the earlier book (1947), he wrote, "I have never forgotten Leiber lying there at the plate. I can honestly say that I have never tried to hit anyone with a pitch. If I was ever destined to have such an idea, that incident at New Orleans stopped it."[2]

In the later book (1990), he wrote,

> I had a scare in spring training. I hit a batter in the head—"beaned" him, something I never wanted to do in all the years I played baseball. I never hit a batter on purpose, and if any manager had ever ordered me to do it—and no one ever did—I would have disobeyed. There are some orders in life that you simply don't have to obey because they are so outrageously criminal or immoral. And deliberately hitting a man in the head with a baseball coming at 90 miles an hour or more, from only 60 feet, six inches away is one of those acts. If any manager had ordered me to stick a ball in a batter's ear, I would have told him to stick it in his own ear.
>
> The player I hit was Hank Leiber of the Giants. He was an outfielder who played in the National League for ten years. When I hit him, I prayed I hadn't hurt him or his career. I guess it was a little of both, because he was forced to miss the first half of the season—but when he came back he was able to pick right up and have a good season and an excellent World Series . . .[3]

Leiber played in only fifty-one games that season, and he managed only ninety-eight games in 1938, 112 in '39, and 117 in '40. Then came the quick descent into inadequacy. Do Leiber's strong post-beaning seasons mean the beaning didn't destroy his career? Not necessarily. If you're reading this, you probably know that Tony Conigliaro was terribly injured by a beanball in 1967. He missed the rest of that season, and all of the next. What you might not know, unless you're an old Red Sox fan, is that Conigliaro returned in 1969 and hit twenty homers, and in 1970 he hit thirty-six and drove in 116 runs. It wasn't until 1971—he was still only twenty-six—that things fell apart for Tony C. Aside from a brief comeback in 1975, his career was over.

But Conigliaro's case is the exception. Most of the time, once a player recovers from a beaning, he seems to recover for good.*

Perhaps Leiber did. At least until June 23, 1941, when he got beaned again, this time by Giants left-hander Cliff Melton, said to throw a "deceptive" fastball.[4] As John Drebinger wrote in the next day's *Times*,

> It was, in fact, a mighty trying day for the Chicagoans, for in addition to losing the ball game the Cubs also lost, temporarily at least, the services of their centerfielder, Hank Leiber.
>
> The big Arizonian and former Giant was laid low by one of Melton's stray pitches in the eighth inning, the ball striking Hank close to the base of the skull, approximately in the same region where Bob Feller cracked him in an exhibition between the Giants and Indians in New Orleans in the Spring of 1937.
>
> Although Hank never lost consciousness and was able to leave the field on his own power, he was taken immediately to the Illinois Masonic Hospital. The fact that he was wearing one of the new protective devices in his cap, similar to those worn by the Dodgers and Giants, added to the hope that this time he had escaped serious injury. Early reports from the hospital were that Hank was not badly hurt.[5]

The reports were wrong. Leiber didn't play again that season (which makes one wonder if his initial selection for the All-Star Game, played on July 9, was simply a kindly gesture extended by National League manager Bill McKechnie or someone in the league office). Still suffering in November, he visited the Mayo Clinic, "where special treatment worked a complete cure."[6]

Perhaps. But early in the '42 season, Leiber "suffered a wrenched muscle in his calf and was of little value thereafter." Nevertheless, the Giants wanted Leiber to play in 1943. He had a choice, though; with the war rag-

---

* Conigliaro was, unfortunately, exceptional in another way. Two days after his thirty-seventh birthday he suffered a heart attack and the resulting brain damage left him in terrible shape until he died eight years later. Leiber would outlive Conigliaro by nearly four years.

Oakland's Mike Norris won 22 games in 1980; it was the only season in which he won more than 12 games (and he won more than seven games only twice). So Norris is placing his conversation with Gibson in 1979, a season in which he went 5-8 with a 4.80 ERA.

Norris started only twice against the Orioles that season. Just one of those starts was in Baltimore: on the 9th of May he pitched a one-hitter and beat the O's 4–2. Two weeks earlier he'd faced the Orioles in Oakland and been knocked out in the sixth inning, but hadn't given up any home runs.

Did Norris ever give up two homers in the ninth inning and lose? No, he didn't. Not in 1979, anyway. In fact, just once did he give up two home runs in one game; on the 4th of May he gave up two to the Yankees: Jim Spencer hit a solo shot in the second inning, and then Spencer hit a three-run shot in the third. That put the Yankees ahead 5 to 2, and Norris was in trouble.

But he pitched into the seventh inning and picked up the win as the A's crushed the Yankees, 11–5. I do notice that this game was in New York, and was played between those two games against the Orioles. So, my guess is that Norris somehow conflated those three games into one career-changing experience.

I checked Norris's entire career, and there were only two games in which he gave up two ninth-inning homers. Neither of them explain Norris's fantastic 1980 season. One of the games was in 1981 and the other was his next-to-last '80 start.

ing, he could stay in Arizona and tend his chicken ranch, or he could be classified 1-A for the draft. Either way, he wasn't going to play baseball in 1943. Nor did he play afterward. Upon his death in Tucson, in 1993, the *Times* reported that Leiber had eventually become "a successful real-estate developer."

And while the two beanings were serious and certainly impacted his performance in both 1937 and 1941, there is little evidence suggesting that either beaning led directly to the end of Leiber's baseball career. It was the calf injury and the war, more than anything else.

GENE BENSON & JOHNNY BERARDINO

Johnny Berardino played second base on that Bob Feller tour in '46. He's a television star now. I'm the one put him in the soap operas. What happened: Dutch Leonard threw me a knuckle ball, and I hit it straight at Berardino. The ball ducked and hit him in the knee cap. The guy never played regular after that. He's been with "General Hospital" ever since. I made him a rich guy. So I think I should go see him. I think he owes me something for getting him out of baseball.

—Negro Leaguer Gene Benson in *Black Diamonds* (John Holway, 1989)

Bob Feller's 1946 barnstorming tour was a big event at the time, but few details have been documented since the original newspaper reports. When the tour *has* been mentioned in the literature, it's always distilled to "Bob Feller's All-Stars vs. Satchel Paige's All-Stars." That certainly was a chunk of Feller's cross-country enterprise, but only a chunk.

For the purposes of this story, though, Feller's vs. Paige's is mostly what matters, since Gene Benson played for Paige's team. That leg of Feller's month-long tour consisted of sixteen games, beginning in Pittsburgh on September 30 and ending in Kansas City on October 14. In researching the tour, I've found box scores for all but two of those sixteen games. But before going through those games one at a time, searching for Benson's blow that maimed Berardino, we should first make sure this tale passes a quick sniff test.

Gene Benson, Johnny Berardino, and knuckle-baller Dutch Leonard did participate in the 1946 barnstorming tour. Benson played in the outfield for Paige's team, Berardino played second base for Feller's team, and Leonard was one of the four pitchers available to relieve Feller (who started nearly every game).

So the names check out. It's true, too, that Berardino never again put in a full season, as a regular, after 1946. Quickly reviewing his career to that point . . .

In the spring of '39, Berardino broke camp with the Browns and was something like a regular from then through the '41 season.

According to *The Sporting News*, Berardino enlisted in the Army Air Corps *before* Pearl Harbor, with a stipulation that if he washed out of flight school, he'd be honorably discharged. He washed out the next summer and made his 1942 debut with the Browns on July 9, pinch-running in the first game after the All-Star break. But Don Gutteridge had got off to a good start at second base for the Browns, and Berardino played sparingly in the second half of the season.

By 1943 he was in the navy, where he spent the rest of the war. A free man in 1946, Berardino played in a career-high 144 games for the Browns. He was still only twenty-nine, he was one of Bob Feller's All-Stars, and he looked as if he still had a few good years left in him.

He didn't. Berardino played in only ninety games in 1947 and afterward played sparingly before his career petered out in 1952.

And Berardino did, of course, wind up making his fortune as an actor. As a child, he'd appeared as an extra in Our Gang comedies, and while still active as a player he picked up small roles in a horse-racing movie, *The Winner's Circle*, and a baseball movie, *The Kid from Cleveland*. Berardino was so well-known for his looks that when Cleveland acquired him in December 1948, his face was insured, as a publicity stunt, for a million dollars by Indians owner Bill Veeck.

Beginning in 1953, his baseball career over, Berardino began getting regular work as a bit player on TV shows like *The Cisco Kid*, *The Lone Ranger*, *Sea Hunt*, *The Untouchables*, and *Route 66*. He also appeared in a number of movies, including Hitchcock's *North by Northwest*.

On April 1, 1963, Berardino—who had, shortly after leaving baseball, changed his name to "Beradino" because it was easier to pronounce—first played the role of Steve Hardy in the premier episode of *General Hospital*, a new ABC soap opera. Beradino would play Dr. Hardy for nearly thirty-three years, until shortly before pancreatic cancer killed him in 1996.

But did Gene Benson really knock Berardino into a premature acting career?

As I mentioned earlier, Feller's All-Stars and Paige's All-Stars played each other sixteen times during the '46 tour. However, Dutch Leonard pitched only six times: in Cincinnati, Newark, Baltimore, Columbus, Richmond (Indiana), and Kansas City. Taking those in order . . .

- I've not been able to locate a box score for the Cincinnati game. I do know that Berardino hit a two-run homer in the fifth inning, and none of the three newspaper accounts I've found mention anything about an injury.
- There's no mention of Berardino in the accounts of the Newark game that I've found. Benson did collect three hits, and Berardino played all nine innings.
- In Baltimore, Benson singled and Berardino played nine innings. Again, no mention of any sort of ball-meets-kneecap incident.

- In Columbus, Benson went hitless and Berardino played nine error-free innings.
- In Richmond, Benson singled, Berardino played nine error-free innings, and Leonard pitched seven shutout innings to earn the victory after Feller got hammered for five runs in the first two frames. A local paper, the *Palladium-Item & Sun-Telegram*, covered the game in great detail but didn't mention an incident involving Benson and Berardino.
- In Kansas City, Benson singled twice, with at least one of those hits off Leonard. But there's no mention, in the extensive newspaper coverage, of a baseball caroming off Berardino, nor any mention at all of Berardino, who played all nine innings and was not charged with an error.

Which isn't to say a ground ball did not, at some point in one of those six games—or another in which Leonard *didn't* pitch—nail Berardino in the kneecap. But if Berardino did get hurt, it sure didn't show up anywhere you'd think it would. Following their two games in Kansas City against Paige's All-Stars, Feller's All-Stars headed west, for a couple of games in Denver and then thirteen (two of which were rained out) in California and the Pacific Northwest. I haven't found box scores for two of those games (Seattle; and El Centro, California), but Berardino definitely played in the rest of them. He played pretty well, too; in the eleven games after Denver, Berardino hit three home runs. Granted, by this point Feller's Stars weren't facing top competition—second-line black players and second-line white major leaguers, mostly—but the facts just don't support the notion that Berardino suffered a career-altering knee injury in the fall of 1946.

So what did happen to Berardino's career? Between the end of Feller's tour and Opening Day in 1947, Berardino was mentioned in *The Sporting News* nine times. No injury was mentioned, nor did anything suggest that Berardino would do anything but play every day at second base for the Browns in '47. In fact, the March 19 issue of *TSN* announced, "As was the case a year ago, another veteran of the infield was the first to be pronounced ready for battle. Johnny Berardino seems to be in his best stride."

So why did he play only ninety games in 1947? On June 17, *The Sporting News* reported, "Second Baseman Berardino of St. Louis suffered fracture of left forearm in second inning when hit by one of Ferriss' pitches."

Berardino returned to the lineup on July 25, which means he missed slightly more than five weeks (during which time the Browns played thirty-four games). It wasn't long before Berardino was shelved again, and

Ron Luciano (sort of) explains why Baltimore's Paul Blair was never much of a hitter after 1970 . . .

The brushback is a legitimate part of the game. It's the beanball I detest. In my football career I saw a lot of blood, much of it my own. It didn't bother me. I saw bones snapped so badly they actually lifted up thigh pads. That didn't bother me. I was working second base the day Bobby Valentine smashed into an outfield fence and fractured his leg so badly the bone was sticking through his pants and I thought he'd never walk again. But the worst thing I've ever seen was Paul Blair getting hit in the head with a baseball.

Ken Tatum was pitching for the Angels and Blair was the Orioles' star center field. I was behind the plate. Tatum was an overpowering fastballer with erratic control, and Blair was crowding the plate. I don't believe Tatum tried to hit him, but his fastball got away and sailed toward Blair's head.

It happened so quickly it was impossible to do anything about it except watch helplessly. There wasn't even time to shout a warning. But every fraction of that second is frozen in my memory. Blair was wearing a metal helmet without an earflap and the ball hit him solidly just below the helmet. It made a "splat" sound, like someone slapping jello. It was the worst sound I've ever heard. He went down hard. Blood started trickling out of his nose and mouth and ears into the dirt. I thought he was dead.

Freddy Frederico got to him quickly and handled the situation perfectly. He kept everyone away and took emergency measures. I wasn't any help at all—for the first and only time in my life I got sick on a playing field. Blair was rushed to the hospital. Tatum was never the same pitcher after that. Blair was never the same hitter. And I was never the same umpire—after seeing Blair lying unconscious in the dirt I couldn't tolerate pitchers trying to hit a batter in the head.

—Ron Luciano & David Fisher, The Umpire Strikes Back (1982)

This happened in Anaheim on May 31, 1970. It was the eighth inning, and Tatum had just hit Boog Powell with a pitch. The Angels were ahead 6 to 1. No Angel hitter had been plunked earlier in the game, so there's no obvious reason to think Tatum would have been head-hunting.

Of course, the most interesting thing about Luciano's story is the claim that neither Blair nor Tatum were ever the same afterward.

Blair was out of the lineup for three weeks. Initially, he showed no ill effects, then slumped in July. But Blair got hot in August, and by the end of the season his various percentages were almost exactly what they'd been on the day he got beaned. On the other hand, beginning in 1971 he was never again the player that he'd been from 1967 through '70. He put together decent seasons in '73 and '74, but his best seasons came in 1967 and '69, when he was twenty-three and twenty-five. Was his decline simply an uncommon

again the culprit was an errant pitch. Here's Fred Lieb in *The Sporting News,* August 20:

> When it rains, it pours. And bad luck has been raining on Johnny Berardino of the Browns for two seasons. It started in 1946 when he earned a place on the American League All-Star team—but wasn't picked. That was bad—but the things that have been happening to him this year have hurt more. His performance in 1947 did not parallel that of last season, but his slaps from Lady Luck have been coming with the same consistency.
>
> Johnny got off to a great start in 1946, hitting around .330 at the halfway post. This spring, however, the former University of Southern California star couldn't beg or steal a hit, and was batting .185 for 46 games when he suffered a broken bone in his left arm, June 17.
>
> Berardino was out for five weeks, until July 25, and while he was on the sidelines he apparently figured out what was wrong with his hitting. When he returned, he suddenly started blazing hits all over the landscape, and in no time worked his average up to .230. Then, when the Browns were in Cleveland recently, an inside pitch hurled by Allen Gettel struck Johnny on the back of the left hand, and put him on the shelf again.
>
> At first, it was believed another bone had been broken, but an X-Ray revealed only a bad bruise. However, the fact that the ball struck the same arm made the injury extremely painful and retarded healing.

When Berardino's arm got busted, he'd played in forty-six of the Browns' fifty-seven games.

That second plunking didn't really cost Berardino any time, and he continued to hit, finishing the season with a .261 batting average and (even better) a career-high .358 on-base percentage (though of course nobody was keeping track of that one). It wasn't until the *next* season, 1948, that Berardino simply stopped hitting; from '48 through '52, his batting averages were .190, .198, .213, .227, and .125. And in 1953, he began his second career.

So what happened? Those batting averages look like more than just the product of a natural decline.

There were, as it turns out, injuries. While editing *We Played the Game: 65 Players Remember Baseball's Greatest Era, 1947–1964,* Danny Peary interviewed (you guessed it) sixty-five players, and Johnny Berardino was among them. Asked about his return to baseball in 1946, Berardino told Peary, "I was concerned because I had suffered a back injury at Pearl Harbor for which I would need a lot of therapy." A few pages later he says, "Despite my troubled back, I had a fairly good year with the Browns in 1946."

And later in the book:

> I probably should have quit baseball in 1947, which was 10 years after I signed with Browns scout Jacques Fournier. Then I could have become a full-time actor five years before I did, resuming the career I began as a nine-year-old in Los Angeles. But then I wouldn't have had the distinction of playing for two of the worst teams of the postwar era, the St. Louis Browns and Pittsburgh Pirates. Twice!
>
> When I was in my twenties, it was exciting just being in the big leagues, no matter what the Browns did. But I had turned 30, and the constant losing became demoralizing. I waited for the season to end. . . .
>
> What made it even harder for me was my bad back and other ailments. The Browns had a team doctor but he didn't travel with us, so I had to wait to get back to St. Louis to get therapy. There wasn't much therapy in those days. When I tore ligaments in an exhibition game against the Boston Braves, they didn't send me to a doctor. They simply put on ice packs and had me walk around on crutches for a couple of weeks. Then they had me play again. It was amazing.

About ten years ago, Rich Westcott interviewed Berardino, who didn't mention anything about a knee injury hurting his career. He did say this (and please hang on for the unintended punch line): "If given a chance today, though, I wouldn't take baseball. It's a different game than when I played it. There's no grass. Everybody's so greedy. The way the pension situation for older players has gone just bums me out. And the game itself has been hurt in terms of quality. We had eight teams in each league. It was the cream of the crop. If you didn't hit two-fifty, you were gone."

response to aging? Various nagging injuries? Or was the beaning a significant factor?

According to Blair, the answer was none of the above. He told John Eisenberg, "The biggest factor why I didn't hit as high was Frank Robinson getting traded after the '71 season. With him behind me I knew at two and oh or three and one what they'd throw me. They're not going to walk Paul Blair to get to Frank Robinson, so they're going to throw me a fastball. After Frank was gone, they were throwing breaking balls, too. And the slider was a pitch I had problems with. I wasn't disciplined enough to take those pitches and walk. And that was my biggest downfall right there."

Sounds good. But not that good, you know?

As for Tatum, it's a fact that he seems to have peaked on the same day he beaned Blair. At the end of that game, his ERA in 113 major league innings was 1.27. In his next game he gave up a run, and from there through the end of his brief career he posted a 3.99 ERA in 169 innings.

LOU GEHRIG & THE IMPOSTOR

Next time you're falling all over yourself congratulating Mr. Lou Gehrig on his famous Iron Man streak, ponder this: one of those games was played by an impostor! The truth? Gehrig's streak nearly ended before 1939 and, if not for a last-minute fill-in, it would have.

How did this come about? As you know, Gehrig was devoted to his mother. On the morning of a late-season game one year, the Lou was helping her do the Saturday marketing. As they strolled down the boulevard, Gehrig stopped for some "window shopping," but Mom Gehrig did not notice and kept going. She turned the corner ahead and was set upon by three thugs. They went for her purse and her cries brought Gehrig running. He pulverized one of the mugs with a left to the jaw and was taking care of a second when the third laid a pipe across the back of his head, dropping him to the ground. They grabbed the purse and ran.

Thinking quickly, Mrs. Gehrig guided her Lou to a nearby doctor's office, then called the Yankees to tell them her son wouldn't be reporting for work that day. As was often the case, the pennant was well in hand, but there was the streak to consider. Gehrig had nearly lost it to a lumbago attack some years earlier, but this time he couldn't even stand up straight. Management told Mrs. Gehrig to take Lou home in a cab, keep him there until she heard otherwise, and—most important—swear the attending physician to secrecy and tell no one else about the incident.

As it happened, Ed Barrow's secretary was then dating an aspiring actor who was about Gehrig's height, and an excellent mimic. "Wouldn't it be funny if you put my beau in Lou's place?" she giggled.

With the game only a couple of hours away, her innocent joke suddenly made a lot of sense to the Yankee brass. The pennant was already in the bag, so what did anybody have to lose? "Does your young gentleman know baseball?" they asked her.

"Oh my, yes! My Danny's crazy about the Dodgers and can imitate everyone's batting stances and pitching motions."

Management quickly dispatched a car for the young fellow. Upon his arrival, he was quickly whisked into a back room and given the once-over. While not a dead ringer for Gehrig, he was not altogether dissimilar, either. Equipment manager Pete Sheehy, in on the gag, padded Gehrig's No. 4 uniform a bit and the kid looked okay from a distance. They swore him to secrecy, with the promise of a small sum to be paid upon completion of the assigned tasks.

The game began with Jack Saltzgaver at first base for the Yanks. Saltzgaver batted twice, but in the seventh inning "Gehrig" was sent in to pinch hit. The actor had been told to quickly take his place in the batter's box, take three big cuts and head straight to the locker room.

Instead he made a big show of swinging a bunch of bats in the on-deck circle and then walked slowly to the box, dropping a bat every few steps. When finally settled, he swung from the heels and missed the first pitch by a mile, twirling in the air and landing on his backside in very un-Gehrig-like fashion. He took the next pitch for a ball and then, on the third pitch, he shocked his new employers by pushing a bunt toward third base, which he beat out for a single! At that point, he was yanked for a pinch runner to a loud ovation. Jeep Heffner finished the game at first.

His noggin lumpy but intact, Gehrig came back the next day and played a doubleheader, keeping the streak alive on his own. For his part, the actor never played another inning of pro ball, but he did go on to a very successful career in Hollywood.

You know him as Danny Kaye.

—excerpt from a speech made by George Jessel at the
All-Star Game banquet in 1964

*T*he following investigation of this tale is conducted by long-time sportswriter Scribbly Tate, who over his eighty-year career has written more words than there are stars in the nighttime sky.

The first thing we'd like to do is figure out the year wherein lies this tale. We're told the Yanks had a big lead in the pennant race, so we may assume this was one of the years they grabbed the silk. The Yankees were winning pennants at two main points in Gehrig's career: the early part and the later part. Also consider that the lumbago incident is brought to the fore by the storyteller. That was in 1933. This leaves us with but three seasons in which this tale could have taken place: 1936, 1937, or 1938.

The mention of two other players helps pinpoint the year, too. Saltzgaver and Heffner (which sounds like the name of the law firm that handled my second divorce) were Yankee teammates for only two years, 1936 and '37. In both seasons, Saltzgaver played first base in four games. Heffner played just

one game there, though, that coming in 1937. We know Gehrig was coldcocked before a home game, and the tale also mentions that a doubleheader was scheduled for the next day. Since we know the game was late in the year and the Yankums had the bubbly on ice, I believe it's safe to confine our search to the time of year when the air is tempted by frost and the leaves are behooved to topple groundward by force of nature. By the middle of September of '37, New York had a ten-game bulge on the Tigers. On Tuesday, September 14, they hosted Cleveland and slugged 'em 17–5 and played a split zygote the next day. Trouble is, the box score shows Gehrig playing the whole game (and hitting his thirty-fourth circuit mash of the campaign).

In case that detail was a bit off, I looked at single games followed by a day off and then a double-header, but nothing there, either. In fact, Heffner's one stint at first didn't come in any of the games that Saltzgaver played there. Also, Gehrig played first base in all 154 decisioned Yankee games of 1937 and

Another of my favorite stories, this one from the pages of Bill James . . .

Hughie Jennings got a letter from a small town in Michigan, a letter from a pitcher who claimed he could strike out Ty Cobb anytime on three pitches. The guy said it would cost only $1.80—his train fare to Detroit—for Jennings to find out. Hughie figured well, you never know, and sent the dollar-eighty. The pitcher showed up—great, big, gangly kid, 6-foot-4 and all joints. They let him warm up and called out Cobb.

Cobb hit his first pitch against the right-field wall. His second pitch went over the right-field wall. The third pitch went over the center-field wall. Cobb was thinking they ought to keep this guy around to help him get in a groove.

"Well," said Jennings. "What have you got to say?"

The pitcher stared hard at the batter in the batter's box. "You know," he said, "I don't believe that's Ty Cobb in there."

—The New Bill James Historical Baseball Abstract
(Bill James, 2001)

their three no-decisions as well. Perhaps the story got the names of the replacements wrong and it all happened in 1938? Nope. Again the Yankees played 157 games, including suspended games, and Gehrig was credited at first base in all of them.

I suppose this never happened. The story did resurface in the 1990s when Junior Ripken was hot on Gehrig's trail. I myself heard it repeated on a couple of game telecasts and saw variations of it in a few of the less reputable newspapers. So there's still one question left . . . Where does this story come from? Did George Jessel (or one of his gag boys) just make up the tale?

I decided to do a bit more sleuthing. According to the archives at the Friars Club, Jessel bought the story from Phil Silvers, and he'd heard it from Humphrey Bogart in 1955. Bogie, I was told by someone who would know (hint: she's famous for giving a whistling lesson), had read the story in some men's magazine or other—one of those antecedents of *Maxim*—and there were a lot of them in those days, with titles like *Manly Monthly* and *True Testosterone Tales*.

These magazines, printed on the cheapest of paper stock, have not worn well in the decades since, most of them simply disappearing into dust. I finally found a collector of such things, though, and he allowed me to peruse his yellowed holdings. After donning protective gloves and a breathing mask, I dived in. On my third day of this, I was about to throw in the sweaty towel when I finally found it. My jaw dropped. There, on page 78 of the May 1951 issue of *Guy Illustrated* was this title and byline:

THE MAN WHO WOULD BE IRON HORSE
"TALENTED TONGUE TWISTER TAINTED TEUTON'S TENACIOUS TURN"
BY SCRIBBLY TATE

Suddenly the memories come flooding back: the overdue car payment, the toddler in need of shoes, the impatient (and well-connected) bookie, the frustrated (and well-lawyered) wife, the editor waving a $75 check for anything, *anything* baseball-related. It was I—me, Scribbly Tate—who had concocted this tallest of tales in a moment of extreme financial deprivation. And here, before your very eyes, I am once again being paid $75 to trace a tale whose origin lies in the most deceitful corner of my own forgetful mind.

THE DEATH OF BOB FELLER'S FASTBALL

If Feller was to replay his career, he would ask for only one opportunity that never came. "I wish," he said, "the Indians could have won the pennant when I was in my prime. I'd have liked to take my chances in a World Series when I had my good fast ball."

The blazing fast ball, Feller remembers, disappeared in 1947—in a game against the Athletics in Philadelphia. Ten of the first eleven Philadelphia outs had been strikeouts. Then Bob slipped off the mound and tore a muscle in his shoulder. "I never had a really good fast ball after that," he says.

—Hal Lebovitz, "Bob Feller's Disappointment," *Sport*, October 1959

Ah, the pernicious nature of injuries. They don't show up in the records, and if they're not serious enough to knock a player off the active roster, you might never guess he was hurt at all. And if you just looked at Feller's stats in 1947, in isolation, you'd have no reason to think anything was wrong. He led the league in wins, innings, and strikeouts and finished with the second-best ERA (behind Joe Haynes, one of the great one-year wonders).

Compare Feller's 1947 to his 1946, though, and something definitely looks wrong. Or at least different. In '47, Feller pitched 299 innings and struck out 196 hitters. But in '46 he'd pitched *371 innings* and struck out *348 hitters*. Granted, that was a season for the ages and wasn't likely to be repeated. But Feller's strikeout rate fell from the highest of his career in '46 to the lowest of his career in '47. Sure looks like something changed.

But did it change in that game against the A's?

I put together a log of Feller's starts in '47, and the "game against the Athletics in Philadelphia" must have been the game of June 13. It's the only game in which he struck out *more* than ten batters, and his other high-strikeout games—ten in each—were against the White Sox and the Red Sox early in the season.

Armed with that clue, I found the following in *The Sporting News*, in a discussion of things that Indians player-manager Lou Boudreau could expect to happen in the second half of the season.

Boudreau can expect Bob Feller—for all the publicity given his extra-curricular business deals—to challenge the 30-victory mark. Bob never performs so well as when he is under criticism. The night of June 13, in Philadelphia, he struck out nine of the first 11 batters to face him. Press box observers as well as his teammates agreed that never before in his career had he thrown the ball with such blinding speed. He looked good enough to break his own single-game record of 18 strikeouts, even to pitch his third no-hitter.

But when he threw a third-strike curve to Barney McCosky in the fourth, Feller's follow-through carried his right foot into a depression in the mound. He stumbled and fell hard to both knees. He would have landed on his face if he had not shot out his hands to break the fall. Bob said later that he hurt one knee and temporarily numbed the fingers of his pitching hand, but he insisted he could continue on the mound.

Obviously, though the mishap had affected his invincibility. He added only three more strikeouts, turned the job over to Klieman with the Athletics threatening in the eighth.

Feller came back, June 17, to defeat the Senators, 5 to 3, whiffing nine.[1]

Makes you wonder, doesn't it? Four days after he supposedly suffered a career-changing injury, Feller pitched a complete game and struck out nine Senators. But I've chopped his 1947 into parts: Opening Day through that June 13 game in Philadelphia, and everything that came afterward.

	IP	ERA	H/9	K/9
Before	109	2.80	6.0	7.2
After	190	2.61	7.4	5.2

Oddly, Feller's ERA was slightly lower after the injury, but the other stats suggest that he wasn't nearly as dominant after he hurt himself. And in 1948 he struck out 5.3 batters per nine innings . . . almost identical to his post-6/13 strikeout rate in '47. In '49 he struck out 4.6 per nine innings. In that strikeout-unfriendly time, 4.6 was still good enough for eighth best in the league. But Feller was not the same pitcher he had been. He was thirty.

In 1952, *Baseball Yearbook* said of Feller, "Today much of his steam on his sizzling fast ball is gone. But Bob's pitching skill has increased ten-fold and his curve is close to the best in the game."[2]

Perhaps. But Feller won only nine games that season and his 4.74 ERA was significantly worse than league average. He would pitch effectively as a spot starter and sometime reliever over the next few seasons, but Feller was never a great pitcher after he turned twenty-nine. Considering that he pitched more than a thousand innings in the majors before he turned twenty-two, perhaps Feller simply was not destined for dominance into his thirties. But that June afternoon in 1947 does seem to have marked a turning point in his career.

BOB FELLER & BIRDIE TEBBETTS

THE FASTEST PITCH EVER THROWN

Someone asked Birdie Tebbetts how often Bob Feller struck him out and Tebbetts said that reminded him of a story.

"In the winter of 1939 one of the New York writers called me at home," Birdie began. "He said he's been checking the records and he found that I was the only man in the league Feller hadn't struck out. He wanted to know if that was true.

"I told him it was, but I wouldn't want the word to get back to Feller.

"So then he called Feller and he said, 'Bob, I understand Tebbetts is the only man in the league you've never struck out.'

"Bob said, 'That's very interesting. Who told you?'

"The guy said, 'Tebbetts himself.'

"The next spring we played the Indians in an exhibition game in Florida and Feller was pitching. I batted against him twice. Both times he got two strikes on me and both times I got a hit. But that doesn't matter. It wouldn't have counted if he had struck me out in an exhibition game anyway.

"Well, the first time I batted against him after the league season opened there was a man on third and two out. The leadoff man tripled, then Bob struck out Rudy York and Pinky Higgins. I stepped into the box and the count went to two and two.

"I said to myself, 'If he throws me the curve ball I'm out, but I'm not going to let him throw the fast one by me.' Feller wound up and fired the ball and I swear I never saw it. The umpire must have seen it, though. He called me out.

"Rollie Hemsley was catching and he turned to me and said, 'Birdie, that was the fastest ball ever thrown in the history of baseball.' "

—Harry Jones in the *Cleveland Plain Dealer* (reprinted in *Baseball Digest*, May 1953)

At the time, Tebbetts—along with first baseman York and third baseman Higgins—would have been playing for the Tigers. Those three teamed up for only three seasons, 1939 through '41, before Feller enlisted in the United States Navy two days after the Japanese bombed Pearl Harbor. So we'll check 1940 first, and the other seasons if necessary.

First, though, there are the memoirs. Feller came out with his first autobiography in 1947 (*Strikeout Story*) and another in 1990 (*Now Pitching: Bob Feller*). Tebbetts's memoir, *Birdie: Confessions of a Baseball Nomad*, were published in 2002.

Feller doesn't say anything in either of his books about the strikeout in question, but Tebbetts *does* show up in the narrative. Feller, a seventeen-year-old rookie in 1936 (which also marked the debut of twenty-three-year-old George Tebbetts), tied Dizzy Dean's modern record with seventeen strikeouts in a nine-inning game. And two years later he broke the record by fanning eighteen Tigers. But not Tebbetts, who was one of only two Tigers in the lineup that afternoon who did *not* strike out (Roy Cullenbine was the other). That was on the last day of the 1938 season. On the first day of the 1940 season, Feller tossed a no-hitter, his first, against the White Sox in Chicago. His next start would be five days later in Cleveland, against Tebbetts and the Tigers.

"When the game started," Feller wrote, "there was some speculation and hope that I might equal Johnny Vander Meer's feat of pitching two no-hit games in succession. Barney McCosky, first Tiger to face me, ended that quickly. He smashed a double to right field."[1]

That was the beginning of a short afternoon for Feller, who lasted only three innings in a game the Indians eventually lost 12–2. According to the box score in the *Times*, Feller struck out only one batter . . . but was it Tebbetts (who *was* in the lineup)? And if not, did Feller strike out Tebbetts later that season? And was their pre-1940 relationship really strikeout-free? Before we try to answer those questions, let us turn (as promised) to Tebbetts's book . . .

> By the way, I always hit pretty well against Feller. That is, until I told that to a reporter during the off-season. The guy printed it and Feller must have read what I said because next time I came up against Feller, in our first game in Cleveland, he threw three straight strikes across the plate and I never once saw the ball.[2]

This memory was published nearly fifty years after our story appeared in *Baseball Digest*, and a few of the details are different—the strikeout takes only three pitches (rather than five), and Tebbetts simply says he'd fared well against Feller (rather than never striking out)—but the outline is the same. Whatever the truth of this story, Tebbetts obviously carried it with him for a long, long time.

Did Tebbetts hit well against Feller? And/or had he never struck out against Feller, through the 1939 season? Unfortunately, we don't have play-by-play information for those four seasons, 1936 through '39. But we do know when Feller started, and we do—or rather, I do—have Tebbetts's daily sheets for those seasons. So at the very least, I can compile Tebbetts's stats in the games Feller started.

And after doing that, I know this: Tebbetts most certainly did *not* "always hit pretty well against Feller" before 1940. From 1936 through '39, Feller started seventeen games against the Tigers. Tebbetts started eight of those games and pinch-hit in three others. In his eleven outings against Feller, he collected the grand total of three hits. In their first meeting ever, Tebbetts tripled in three at-bats. In the last game of 1938, when Feller got those eighteen strikeouts, Tebbetts went 2 for 2 and drove in two runs in Detroit's improbable 4–2 victory.

And that's it. In twenty-eight at-bats, three hits. Granted, a few of those at-bats came against relief pitchers, but Feller generally finished what he started. My educated guess is that between twenty and twenty-four of those twenty-eight at-bats came against Feller. Let's be charitable and say twenty; that would give Tebbetts a .150 batting average against Feller. When he recalls hitting "well," I think he's remembering that he didn't strike out every few at-bats like most of the other hitters in the league.

Because Feller was truly astonishing in his time. As Cyril Morong has pointed out, in 1936—remember, he was seventeen years old—Feller struck out eleven batters per nine innings when the league average was roughly three per nine innings. Nobody in the American League—except perhaps a few veterans who had faced Dazzy Vance in his prime—had ever seen anything remotely like Feller.

But I digress. On April 21, 1940, Feller made his second start of the season. He struck out only one batter in his three innings, and that one batter was . . . Birdie Tebbetts, who would strike out only fourteen times in 379 at-bats all season. So Feller did strike out Tebbetts in their first meeting of the season, just as Tebbetts remembered. And it would be somewhat impolite to point out that Feller did not strike out York and Higgins, or for that matter anyone else.

TED WILLIAMS & TOMMY BYRNE

I was on the Red Sox when Ted hit .388. That was in 1957, when he was thirty-eight years old. Was I surprised at what he was doing? Not in the least. I'd been watching him for more than fifteen years by that time, so I was never surprised at anything he did with the bat.

I was hitting right behind him that year. You know, if he was leading off an inning he couldn't wait to grab his bat and get up to the plate to watch the pitcher take his warm-up throws. Or if he was the hitter and they were changing pitchers he would move up to watch the new pitcher warm up, to see what the ball was doing. He was always studying. Well, one day we've got the bases loaded against the Yankees and they're making a pitching change, Ted's the hitter, and I'm on deck.

The Yankees bring in Tommy Byrne, a good left-hander. Tommy was something of a character; a well-educated guy, but he would do some quirky things now and then. When Tommy reaches the mound Ted turns around and calls me over. "Have a look at this guy," he says. "See what his ball is doing." So I walk over and we're standing together about seven or eight feet from the plate, watching Byrne get ready. Tommy didn't like that. He winds up, watching us out of the corner of his eye, and the first pitch is right at us, with something on it. We ducked under it, and Williams says, "Flaky left-handed bastard. If that ball had hit us I would have gone out there and pinched his head off." And then Ted stepped in and hit one right back through the middle for a base hit.

—Mickey Vernon in *Baseball Between the Lines* (Donald Honig, 1976)

We're blessed with box scores and play-by-play accounts for the great majority of the American League's 1957 campaign, so the details here are terribly easy to check.

It's funny, for some reason when I think of Byrne, I think of a guy who enjoyed a great deal of success as a young Yankee, but flamed out quickly. In fact, by 1957 he was thirty-seven years old, in his thirteenth season in the majors. He was, as Vernon says, (relatively) well-educated, having played ball at Wake Forest University for a few years. And Byrne later served as mayor of Wake Forest (the city).

Anyway, in '57 Byrne pitched against the Red Sox only three times: on April 26 (his first outing of the season), and on September 4 and September 21 (his last two outings of the season). He made only four starts that season, none of them against the Sox. So we've got three relief appearances to check, and of

Photo courtesy of Transcendental Graphics

Ted Williams on deck

course the first thing we want to know about each game is whether Vernon and Williams were in the lineup for Boston.

On April 26 they were not. Vernon did not play. Williams faced Byrne twice, with a walk and a fly-out.

On September 4 they were not. Williams did not play. Vernon pinch-hit for Sammy White in the ninth inning and walked, but it was Art Ditmar on the mound (Byrne didn't enter until the tenth).

On September 21 in New York, both Williams and Vernon *were* in the lineup. Williams batted third (as usual), Vernon cleanup. Bullet Bob Turley started for the Yankees, and in the second inning he got into a heap of trouble. With one out and the bases loaded, Williams came up and crashed one into the right-field stands for the fifteenth grand slam of his career. Next up, Vernon also homered, making the score 7–0.

At which point our story breaks down.

Byrne pinch-hit for Turley in the bottom of the inning and came out to pitch the top of the third. He retired all three batters he faced, and none of them were Williams or Vernon. Byrne did face both of them in the fourth inning, but a) it wasn't immediately after a pitching change, b) the bases were not loaded when he faced Williams, and c) Williams didn't hit a single. He drew a walk, as did Vernon.

Rich Westcott tells this one about Richie Ashburn and Sal Maglie . . .

If it helped his hitting, Ashburn was never one to let an opportunity pass. The Hall of Fame outfielder was constantly in search of ways to give him the edge.

In one game during the mid-1950s, Sal Maglie was pitching for the New York Giants against the Phillies. Maglie, who was nicknamed "The Barber" because he was never reluctant to deliver a pitch under a batter's chin, was about as mean as any pitcher around. He could wither a batter just with his scowl.

Ashburn waited in the on-deck circle as Maglie warmed up at the start of an inning. As each pitch came in, the two-time batting champion took a swing with his bat.

When Ashburn went to bat, Maglie's first pitch came straight for his head. As he sprawled in the dirt, Ashburn heard The Barber grumble, "Nobody times my pitches."

—*Rich Westcott*, Tales from the Phillies Dugout *(2006)*

The Boston Globe's *Hy Hurwitz told this one about the Splinter . . .*

It is customary for Ted Williams to get in the last word in any debate. This is something that baseball people have encountered on many an occasion in the past. During the recent World Series, Pedro Ramos of the Yankees was telling about his experiences with the former Red Sox slugger.

"When I first came into the American League with Washington," Ramos said, "my ambition was to strike out Ted. I went four or five years and never got him once. Finally, however, I struck him out.

"I got the ball and saved it. One day, I brought it over to Ted and asked him to autograph it. He did.

"The next time I pitched to Ted, he hit a home run that must have gone five miles. When Ted was going around the bases, he said to me, 'Get that one back and I'll autograph it for you, too.' "

Ramos debuted in the majors in 1955. We don't have play-by-play data for him until 1956. Beginning with that season, though, it's fairly easy to check the Ramos vs Williams matchups. From 1956 through 1959, Ramos pitched against Williams in twenty-two games, encompassing sixty-five plate appearances and exactly zero strikeouts.

In 1960, Williams's last season, they didn't meet until the 16th of August. Williams grounded out in the first inning, then walked a couple of times. But in the seventh inning, Ramos struck out Williams, finally (bonus: that K ended the seventh inning and preserved a 2–2 score).

Williams and Ramos next faced one another on September 17 in Washington. In the first inning, Williams grounded into a force play. In the fourth, Williams singled to left field. And in the sixth, with the score still 0–0 and Willie Tasby

Williams led off the sixth against Byrne, and again Williams walked. After which he was replaced by pinch runner Marty Keough.

So this simply didn't happen in 1957. Not close. Not with Tommy Byrne.

Two obvious avenues of inquiry remain. Vernon also teamed with Williams in 1956 and quite possibly spent a good deal of time in the cleanup slot. Byrne did pitch for the Yankees in '56. Maybe Vernon just got the year wrong.

In 1956, Byrne pitched against the Red Sox in eight games, and a careful check of the box scores and game stories suggests that Byrne did not give up a hit to Williams all season. Actually, it's possible, albeit unlikely, that Williams got a hit off him in the September 29 game. He went 1 for 6 that day, but the *Times'* box score and game story do not indicate who was pitching at the time. In this thirteen-inning game, the Yanks used six pitchers. Also, Williams did not drive in a run, and Vernon did not bat cleanup that day (he pinch-hit for the pitcher in the seventh and doubled).

Nevertheless, it's an incident in 1956 that Vernon is remembering here.

Incident? It was one of the more momentous days of Ted Williams's career, and what's somewhat surprising is that Vernon didn't remember it with perfect clarity. It was the 7th of August. Here's how the *Times'* John Drebinger began his story about the game:

> BOSTON, Aug. 7—Don Larsen who, according to Casey Stengel, can be one of the game's great pitchers any time he puts his mind to it, had his mind on his work today. The Yankee hurler blanked the Red Sox on four hits for ten innings.
>
> But in the last of the eleventh, luck went against Larsen. Two Yankee errors helped fill the bases with none out. With the struggle still scoreless and Ted Williams the batter, Stengel elected to call on Tommy Byrne to stave off the inevitable. It didn't work.
>
> Williams drew a base on balls and that won it for the Bosox, 1 to 0.[1]

But there was so much more to the story than that. In the top of the eleventh, Mickey Mantle lifted a high fly to short left field. Williams ran in and dropped the ball for a two-base error. According to Williams, "I was furious, because I'd dropped the ball, and because I felt I didn't get any help from the shortstop, and because the fans were booing like hell."[2]

Yogi Berra was up next, and he sent a drive to deep left field, where Williams made a nice running catch. The boos turned into cheers, which only made Williams more furious. On his way back to the dugout, he spit a couple of times (in which directions, it depends on whom you ask). Then, one more big one. As young infielder Billy Consolo would recall, nearly fifty years later:

> Oh, boy, now the Big One. I watched the whole thing, best seat in the house. Ted comes in from leftfield and spits a couple times, and everybody's booing and there's a fan, right on top of our dugout, standing on the dugout itself, just giving it to him. Ted stops and looks at the guy. Just then, someone threw a golf ball. Fenway doesn't have a second deck, but there's a roof and there's people up there. One of them threw a golf ball and it landed right on the plank that's the top step of the dugout. The ball bounced way high in the air, right in front of Ted. He watched it.
>
> That set him off. He reached back and got a big gobber and just let it go at that guy on the dugout.[3]

Just a few weeks earlier, there had been a couple of spitting incidents. On the 17th of July, Williams hit his 400th career home run and, upon crossing the plate, theatrically aimed a gob of spit in the general direction of the press box. A few nights later, he did it again. But this was the worst yet.

So what happened next? Among other things, the seed of a great story was planted inside Mickey Vernon. Here's Williams, from his memoirs:

> In our half of the eleventh, the Yankees brought in Tommy Byrne to relieve Don Larsen with the bases loaded. Byrne was a left-hander, and a pretty good one. I stood pretty close to the plate, watching him warm up, and he practically dusted me off just warming up.
>
> But after he got two strikes he got cute and on a 3-2 pitch he walked me. Walked in the winning run. Even *that* made me mad. I didn't want any walk. I wanted to hit the damn ball. I threw my bat in the air, and almost didn't go to first base. Del Baker, our first-base coach, had to remind me. I was just disgusted with the whole thing.[4]

Notice that Williams doesn't say Byrne *actually* dusted him off, but that he *practically* did. Which could mean a lot of things, but it doesn't sound as if Byrne threw the ball directly at Williams and Vernon (as Vernon suggests). But Vernon was batting cleanup that day, right behind Williams. We just don't know if Williams's game-winning walk became a line drive in the story because Vernon's memory failed him, or because it made for a better story.

Shortly after the game, the Red Sox announced that Williams would be fined $5,000, which was widely hailed as the largest fine since 1925, when Babe Ruth had been fined the same amount for general insubordination.

That night the writers tracked Williams down, and he answered their

on base, Williams hit a liner over the big wall in right field.

A couple of weeks later Williams, in the last at-bat of his career, hit his 521st home run. If not for that, the last man to surrender a homer to Williams would have been Ramos. And if Ramos had retrieved the ball and gotten Williams to sign that one, too, today he'd have himself one hell of a souvenir.

By the way, there's at least one other version of this story with the same punch line. From the famous comedy duo Nash & Zullo:

In a 1946 game, Detroit Tigers ace Dizzy Trout struck out Boston Red Sox slugger Ted Williams with the bases loaded in the bottom of the ninth to win 4–3.

Dizzy was understandably overjoyed. His catcher, Bob Swift, shook his hand and gave him the ball. After a quick shower, Trout went to the Boston clubhouse and asked Williams to autograph the ball. Williams obliged.

Two weeks later Williams blasted a tremendous three-run homer off Trout. As he rounded first base, Williams hollered to Dizzy, "If you can get the ball back, I'll sign that one for you, too."

Ted Williams hit six homers against Trout during their time together in the American League. None of those six was a "tremendous three-run homer." Four of them were solo shots, and the other two came with one runner aboard. Two of those six—both solo—did come in 1946.

Sonny Siebert told this one about his teammate Pedro Ramos . . .

"This happened in 1964, when Pedro and I were with the Cleveland Indians. Now, first of all, you have to know that Pedro loved to dress like a cowboy. He'd wear cowboy boots and a cowboy hat and a belt with holsters and guns on both sides. We called him the 'Cuban Cowboy.'

"The second thing you need to know is that Pedro had married a beautiful girl. In fact, she was a former Miss Cuba. Well, one day Pedro was lying on the bed watching TV, and he asked his wife to turn it off. She didn't move fast enough to suit him, so Pedro pulled out his pistols and started shooting the TV: Blam! Blam! Blam!

"He destroyed his TV set, lost his wife, who divorced him, and got evicted from his apartment . . . all in one motion. So after that, we started calling him 'Pistol Pete.' "
—*Sonny Siebert in* Tales from the Ballpark
(Mike Shannon, 1999)

questions through his hotel-room door. He blamed the writers for all his troubles, of course. And it worked! Letters to the editor were overwhelmingly in Williams's favor, and a "half-dozen funds were started to pay his fine." In the Red Sox's next game after the Big One, Williams was greeted by a huge ovation. In the sixth inning (not the ninth, as he would later recount in his memoirs) he homered: "When I crossed home plate I made a big display of clapping my hands over my mouth."[5]

The fans loved him for it, and Williams never spit again. In his outstanding biography of Williams, Leigh Montville wrote, "In the noisy court of public opinion, this was a showdown Williams pretty much figured he had won. And he pretty much had. The Red Sox and Yawkey never collected the $5,000 fine."[6]

DON DRYSDALE & FRANK ROBINSON

An incident that happened in a ball game in 1961 in which Don Drysdale was pitching may have caused the changes in his throwing habits that made him become one of the best pitchers of his day. His wife told Dusty of the change that came over Don after the game at the Los Angeles Coliseum involving the Cincinnati Reds and the Dodgers.

"Frank Robinson, right fielder for the Reds, was at bat," Dusty remembered. "Don threw the first pitch pretty close to Robby's head. I walked out to the mound and said, 'Son, you have better control than that. Now use it!' " The second pitch was very close, but Cincinnati Manager Fred Hutchinson came out of the dugout protesting vigorously. Dusty stood his ground. The third pitch was back of Robinson's head. Dusty took off his mask and walked quickly out to the mound.

"Son, you are through for the day!" Dusty told Drysdale. That was the first time a pitcher had been tossed out of a ball game for throwing at a batter. Both Walter Alston, Dodger manager, and Coach Leo Durocher came charging out of the dugout. Dusty looked at Leo and pointed to him, saying, "Leo, you're not running this club, even though you think you are. Let me talk to the boss, not you." With that, he turned to Alston and said, "Walter, get me another pitcher, because Don is through!"

The new pitcher came on. Drysdale was later suspended and fined. After his five-day involuntary lay-off, Drysdale came back to pitch almost perfect control ball.

"To the day I retired, Don's control was excellent," Dusty said. "I don't know if this incident had any effect on Don, but his control was certainly better from that day on."

—Dusty Boggess as told to Ernie Helm,
Kill the Ump! My Life in Baseball (1966)

The teller of this tale is Dusty Boggess, a National League umpire from 1944 through 1962. In Don Drysdale's autobiography, *he* remembered this outing a bit differently:

> I got suspended just once, after an incident involving Cincinnati's Frank Robinson in 1961 at the LA Coliseum. Frank was a great hitter, who actually changed his stance after his first year by moving up on the plate and closing his feet. On this particular day, I pitched him inside and he went down. Dusty Boggess, the plate umpire, came out to warn me.
>
> "Shit, Dusty," I said. "What do you want me to do? Lay the ball right down the middle so he can beat my brains in?"

I came right back in and threw another pitch inside, and down Frank went again. This time, the ball hit Robinson, and Boggess immediately threw me out of the game. I was suspended for five days by Warren Giles, the National League president, and fined $100. I wasn't too happy about it, and neither was Buzzie Bavasi, our general manager. But there was nothing we could do, except to try to point out how ridiculous it all was. I mean, pitchers all over baseball were hitting batters without being ejected or suspended, but I guess that might have been one case where my reputation hurt me instead of helped me.

You might have noticed a few differences in these stories. For one thing, Boggess suggests he kicked out Drysdale after a pitch *nearly* hit Robinson, while Drysdale says a pitch actually did hit Robinson. More substantively, Boggess suggests, in sort of a backhanded way, that his little lecture might have changed the course of Drysdale's career. Drysdale (as we'll see in a moment) explicitly denied that the incident changed anything at all.

Here's what the *L.A. Times* reported the next day.

> The only highlight, if you want to call it that, of a rather tedious afternoon was when Don Drysdale, the Dodgers' tempestuous twirler, was ejected from the game by umpire Dusty Boggess after Don hit Robinson on the right forearm with a pitch in the sixth inning.
>
> The third of five flingers employed by L.A., Drysdale opened the sixth round by buzzing the ball behind Don Blasingame's head before the Blazer popped up.
>
> Then the Dodger side-winder whipped two inside pitches past Vada Pinson before the latter doubled for the second of his three hits.
>
> After Drysdale's first serve made Robinson hit the dirt, Boggess approached the mound and warned Drysdale, which meant an automatic $50 fine.
>
> Robinson, who likes to crowd the plate, went down on the next pitch, too, although it wasn't as tight as the first one.
>
> Cincy skipper Fred Hutchinson charged out of the dugout and complained about Drysdale's low-bridging tactics to Boggess.
>
> On the next pitch Robinson became the 15th batsman plugged by Drysdale in 126 innings. Big D departed after Boggess told him he had "better control than that."

In case you're wondering why Drysdale was coming into the middle of a game, it was because 1) it was the last game before the All-Star break, and 2) Dodgers starter Roger Craig got knocked out in the third inning (Koufax pitched in this one, too, and got knocked around in his two innings). The Reds wound up winning, 14–3 (remember, this was the year the Reds won their only National League pennant between 1940 and 1970). Take-home information: Drysdale wasn't ejected after nearly hitting Robinson; he was ejected after nearly hitting him. Twice. *And* hitting him.

For his part, Robinson, in addition to getting plunked by Drysdale, doubled, hit two home runs, and drove in seven. You could knock him down, but you couldn't beat him.

Anyway, back to Drysdale's book for the thrilling conclusion of our story . . .

> So I owed the National League $100 and the next time we went into Cincinnati, I decided to pay my debt in person. I went to a bank and got $100 worth of pennies in those rolls, emptied them out, then put all the loose coins in a sack, and delivered them to Mr. Giles's office at the league headquarters in Carew Tower. I dumped the sack on his secretary's desk, she gave me this little smile, and I took off in a hurry. I was pretty proud of myself when I headed back to my hotel room, but I wasn't there too long before the phone rang. It was Mr. Giles's secretary.
>
> "Mr. Giles would like to see you," she said.
>
> I went back to the office and had a bit of a conversation with Mr. Giles. He told me to be careful about the way I was pitching, and I told him that I wasn't going to change my philosophy of keeping batters off the plate. It was all very amiable.
>
> "And by the way," Mr. Giles added, "I want you to take those pennies of yours and roll them back up for me."

According to Drysdale, it took him hours to put those "damn pennies" back in the containers.

This is probably as good as any time as any to mention something that does bear heavily on our tale: Drysdale had a reputation. Drysdale was the cover boy on the June 1960 issue of *Sport*. The article within, credited to Drysdale ("as told to Steve Gelman"), was titled "You've Got To Be Mean to Pitch". Drysdale learned from Sal Maglie, the master, in 1956, when Drysdale was nineteen and the Barber was thirty-nine. Drysdale insisted that he had never purposely tried to hit a batter with a pitch. But he wasn't shy about moving the hitters off the plate. "It is, I insist, strictly a matter of pitcher's rights."

When I read Boggess's account, I was *highly* skeptical. Could one lecture/fine/suspension really represent a turning point in a pitcher's career? There's no way to make an absolute determination, but thanks to Retrosheet it's not all that hard to find out if Drysdale's control did, indeed, improve after his suspension. Here are his 1961 control numbers, before and after:

Another story from Boggess's book, about his early days umpiring in the minors . . .

The one great lesson Dusty learned in that freshman year was to command the respect of players, managers, and owners. . . . One of his big tests came with a player who was to become a major league star in later years—Bob Dillinger. He was playing third base for Lincoln, Nebraska, at the time.

One night in Norfolk, Al Schacht, the Clown Prince of Baseball, had set the stage for fans and players alike to be in a joyful mood prior to the game. But, after an ump shouts "Play ball," everything becomes serious. Dillinger was at bat in the early innings.

"Strike one!" Dusty called as the first pitch hit the inside corner, knee high. Bob, who was ever the gentleman on or off the field, remarked, "Dusty, I thought that was inside." Only the catcher and the ump had heard his soft voice.

The next pitch was over the outside corner, a good curve ball which completely fooled Dillinger. "Strike two!" was Dusty's call again. Dillinger was silent, but he reached up and took off his big thick-rimmed glasses and handed them to the startled umpire. The crowd roared for their favorite player. Dusty was about to be "shown up" by a ball player; the cardinal sin for any umpire in any league. . . .

Dusty had to think fast, as this was his first real challenge. He took off his mask, put on Dillinger's

➨

glasses, returned the mask, stomped behind the catcher and shouted, "Play ball."

The young ump had made a good guess. Bob could not see a thing without those thick glasses but with the glasses on neither could Dusty see; but he waited until he heard the sound of the ball hitting the middle of the catcher's glove and shouted, without hesitation, "Strike three!"

Dillinger, real pro that he was, knew that he had become the straight man in this comedy act. He calmly accepted the decision, asked for his glasses back, bowed slightly, and returned to the dugout with a sheepish little grin on his face. The crowd went wild with glee.

Boggess did umpire in the Class D Western League in 1939, when Dillinger did play for the Lincoln Links. But "the crowd roared for their favorite player"? Why would Dillinger be a favorite in Norfolk? As for Dillinger being a "real pro," he was a first-year professional, just like Boggess, and wouldn't turn twenty-one until after the season. Which isn't to say these questionable details mean the story is not true.

Boggess and Dillinger were reunited two seasons later, when both toiled in the Texas League. The war interrupted Dillinger's career, but he reached the majors in 1946 with the St. Louis Browns, and in the early '50s he played for a spell with the Pirates and once again would have crossed paths with Dusty.

	IP	K	BB	HB	WP
Through July 9	126	103	54	15	5
After July 9	118	79	29	5	2

Obviously, after the suspension Drysdale's control improved *and* he didn't hit as many batters (his strikeouts went down some, too). Was this newfound control just temporary? Hardly. Here are career numbers, before and after:

	IP	BB/9	HB/9
Career through 7/9/1961	1197	2.88	0.50
Career after 7/9/1961	2235	1.90	0.35

Post-ejection, Drysdale's walk rate dropped by forty percent, his HBP rate by 30 percent. Maybe it was the admonitions from Boggess and Giles. Maybe it was the five-day suspension. Maybe it was the 10,000 pennies. In Drysdale's book, he doesn't even acknowledge that his control improved after the ejection, let alone admit a causal relationship. But it sure looks as if *something* happened that afternoon, because Don Drysdale really was, statistically speaking, a different sort of pitcher after July 9, 1961.

Postscript: Some of you, I suspect, are wondering about Dodger Stadium into which the Dodgers moved in 1962. It's certainly possible, isn't it, that Drysdale's post-suspension numbers in 1961 were something of a fluke, while his improved control afterward was mostly a product of pitcher-friendly Dodger Stadium?

Sure it's possible, and I do think that Dodger Stadium played a part. But Drysdale's walk rate in 1962 (1.9 per nine innings) was roughly the same as the second half of '61 (1.8). Johnny Podres's walk rate dropped, but not by a huge degree (17 percent, from 2.4 to 2.0 per nine innings). Sandy Koufax's walk rate fell similarly, by 19 percent (3.2 to 2.6). As a team, the Dodgers in 1962 actually walked slightly *more* hitters per nine innings than they had in '61.

Drysdale's post-suspension walk rate in 1961 was 42 percent better than his pre-suspension walk rate in 1961. His 1962 walk rate was 28 percent better than his career walk rate through July 9, 1961. I think those differences are real.

In terms of his *career* numbers, on the other hand, his walk rate—and everybody else's in that era—was greatly assisted not by his home ballpark, but by the expanded strike zone introduced in 1963. In 1962, Dodger pitchers walked 3.16 batters per nine innings. In 1963, Dodger pitchers walked 2.01 batters per nine innings. That wasn't Dodger Stadium; that was the big strike zone.

WILLIE MAYS & SAL MAGLIE

When Sal Maglie was pitching for Brooklyn he took a couple of shots at Willie Mays. I had the plate that day. Maglie's first pitch wasn't all that close, but it was a genuine brushback. Willie went down on the next pitch, a duster.

I went to the mound and told Maglie, "There'll be no more of that. The next one you throw, you're going to go with the ball."

Sal says, "Tom, it's a hot night, I'm sweating like hell. The ball just got away from me."

I said, "Bullshit," and started back to home plate.

Maglie says, "Hey, Tom?"

"Yeah, what do you want?"

"Tell Willie I'm sorry."

I get back to the plate. Willie is still brushing himself off. I said, "Willie, Maglie says he's sorry."

Willie had that high-pitched voice. He gave me sort of a quizzical look and said, "Is that right?"

This was in Brooklyn, at Ebbets Field, and Willie hit the next pitch out on Bedford Avenue, a four-hundred-foot home run.

And when Willie was rounding second he yelled, "Hey, Maglie, I'm sorry!"

—Tom Gorman as told to Jim Enright, *Three and Two!* (1979)

Umpire Tom Gorman worked in the National League for twenty-six seasons, 1951 through 1976. Umpires tend to have some of the best stories, because many of them spent their off-seasons on the rubber-chicken circuit, so they needed good stories to supplement their relatively meager baseball incomes.

And this is one hell of a story. You've got the Dodgers and the Giants. You've got Sal Maglie, the "Barber," famous for his enthusiastic knockdowns. And you've got Willie Mays, the greatest player since Babe Ruth.

For most of Maglie's career, he and Mays both were Giants. If this happened, it happened in 1956 or the first five months of the '57 season, which comprises Maglie's tenure with the Brooklyn Dodgers (Maglie did pitch in ten games with the Cardinals in '58, but none of those games were against Mays and the Giants).

I first began researching Gorman's story in the early 1990s, when I was working for Bill James. I'm not sure why I never finished, but I found my notes in a dusty file folder, and it reminded me of just how far we've come in fifteen years. At that time, I didn't have an easy way of finding out when the Dodgers and the Giants played each other, so I would look at the schedule published in the *Official Baseball Guide,* before the season, and just check the scheduled games in Brooklyn. Two Dodgers-Giants games in 1956 were rained out, though, and after going through reels of microfilm I'd found only one of the makeup games. I could have asked the Hall of Fame for a log of Dodgers games, but in those days I was oddly self-reliant when it came to these things. So I just gave up on this one.

Today, I don't have to touch a microfilm reader or call Cooperstown. Today I can simply ask a friend at Retrosheet to send me a list of the games in which Mays faced Maglie. And not only in Brooklyn's Ebbets Field— because even umpires' memories are not always perfect—but also in Harlem's Polo Grounds (home of the Giants) or Jersey City's Roosevelt Stadium (where the Dodgers played a few home games in both seasons).

Before we go any further, let's review exactly what we'll find *if* Gorman's story is precisely correct: 1) It's a hot night in Brooklyn, 2) Mays homers off Maglie, and 3) when it happens, umpire Tom Gorman is behind the plate.

In 1956, Maglie pitched in twenty-eight games for the Dodgers after being purchased from Cleveland. He pitched brilliantly, too: 13-5 with a 2.87 ERA. Oddly, though, he pitched against the Giants only twice all season: August 14 and September 1. The first game was in Flatbush, the second in Harlem.

Photo courtesy of Transcendental Graphics

Sal Maglie joins the Dodgers

In that game on the 14th of August, Mays did hit a home run. But not against Maglie. Against Maglie, Mays went hitless in his first three at-bats. Maglie was pulled for a pinch hitter in the seventh, with the score nothing–nothing, and in the eighth Mays homered off reliever Clem Labine. Aside from none of the details matching our story, there's one more problem: Tom Gorman wasn't anywhere close. He was in Philadelphia, working a Phillies-Pirates doubleheader.

On September 1 at the Polo Grounds, Maglie got Mays on a double-play grounder in the first inning and struck him out in the fourth. In the sixth, Maglie got ejected, after throwing his glove in disgust over an umpire's call, before Mays came up again.

And that's it for '56. Mays didn't get even a measly single off Maglie that year. Let alone a home run.

In 1957, Mays and Maglie had one notable meeting. On May 10, Mays was back in the lineup after spending sixty hours in the hospital with a "low-grade virus." As the *Times'* Joseph Sheehan wrote:

> Sal Maglie, the Giant hero of yore, started for the Dodgers. The crafty 40-year-old right-hander, previously unscored on by his old teammates in twelve and one-third innings, added two and one-third innings to that record of success.
>
> Then the roof fell in on the ancient Barber, whose razor curves have not been sharp since he was sidelined with a stiff neck three weeks ago.
>
> With one out in the fateful third, Whitey Lockman beat out a drag bunt. Mays followed with a 420-foot blast off the left-field wall that scored Whitey. After Maglie had issued a judicious walk to Gail Harris and Ray Katt had raised a fly ball too shallow for Willie to venture from third, Don Mueller plunked a single to center that delivered Mays.[1]

This *was* a night game, and it *was* a long, long drive hit by Mays. But it wasn't in Brooklyn, it wasn't a home run, and (most pointedly) Gorman was not within five hundred miles of the drama. Working the plate? Arbiter Bill Baker. Around the bases? Frank Dascoli, Frank Secory, and Stan Landes. And Gorman? He was in St. Louis that night, working third base in the Braves-Cardinals game.

That season, Maglie pitched twenty-four innings against the Giants. He didn't pitch particularly well, aside from a four-hit shutout on July 2. Gorman did work that game, but obviously Mays didn't homer; quite the opposite, as he was forced to retire in the fourth inning after fouling a ball off his foot.

In those twenty-four innings, Maglie gave up only one home run, and that was hit by third baseman Ray Jablonski on the last day of August in Brooklyn. Coincidentally or not, Tom Gorman *was* behind the plate for that game. It was Maglie's last appearance as a Dodger. Mays did hit a couple of singles, both of them off Maglie. And after the second of them, he scored on Jablonski's homer. It's certainly possible that Mays, as he trotted home from first, said something to Maglie. But we'll probably never know.

The next day, the Dodgers traded Maglie to the Yankees, and he never faced Mays again in a regular-season game. The final log included four hits—all of them in 1957—in thirteen at-bats, including the triple and three singles. Still, Gorman's story is a real good one. I'd love to know who told it to him.

WILLIE MCCOVEY & WILLIE MAYS

You know a great slugger who used to be a good bunter, Joe? Willie McCovey, one of your fellow Hall of Famers. You know, Willie McCovey one day at Candlestick Park when they had the artificial turf for a few years . . . Willie Mays was at first base, and they had the shift on for McCovey, and he bunted *hard* down the third-base side, and not only got a hit, it scored Willie Mays from first base on a *bunt*.

—Jon Miller on ESPN, August 20, 2006

McCovey and Mays were teammates for a long time, of course; from McCovey's debut on July 30, 1959, through Mays's return to New York on May 11, 1972. Nearly thirteen years. And for much of that time, Mays batted third and McCovey fourth, meaning ample opportunities for McCovey to bat with Mays on first base.

Fortunately, we've got one more detail here: the artificial turf. If Miller's right, and this happened at Candlestick Park, then we can narrow the time frame considerably. According to Philip J. Lowry's *Green Cathedrals* (2006 edition), Candlestick featured the carpet from 1970 through 1978, which leaves a small window: the Giants' 175 home games from Opening Day in '70 through May 3, 1972 (when Mays played his last game with the Giants).

And of course we can make the window even smaller by eliminating the games in which Mays and McCovey didn't both play (and in that order). Mays was still an everyday player, for the most part, but in a nod to his age—he turned forty early in the '71 season—he did get the day off every week or so.

And McCovey missed a bunch of games in both '71 and '72 with various injuries. In fact, McCovey didn't play any home games in '72 before Mays went to the Mets.

Anyway, I'll start in 1970 and look for box scores—again, courtesy of Retrosheet in which McCovey bats after Mays, and Mays scores at least one run, and McCovey drives in at least one run. When I find all those things in a box score, I'll move along to the play-by-play account and look for Mays scoring from first base on a McCovey single or double.

Surprisingly (at least to me), all those criteria were not met until the Giants' sixteenth home game of the season, on the 2nd of May. McCovey knocked in Mays from first base twice: in the fourth on a homer and in the sixth on a double. That double could have been a bunt, but according to the account, the double was to center field. So that's probably not it.

The next possibility was the very next evening, in the second game of a doubleheader against the

Phillies. And there it is, in the first inning. Bobby Bonds led off with a ground-out. Ron Hunt doubled. Mays singled to center, scoring Hunt. According to the *San Francisco Chronicle*, here's what happened next:

> The Giants introduced a new play in the scoring of their first-inning storm of runs. After Ron Hunt doubled and Willie Mays singled, Willie McCovey bunted down the third base line against a right side over-shift and by the time leftfielder Tony Taylor ran it down, Mays had scored from first base and McCovey strolled into second for a double.[1]

So Jon Miller's memory was dead-solid perfect. I'd have expected nothing less of him. But what about Larry Dierker's? In his blog last summer, he wrote this:

> Which brings me back to Mays. I probably saw him play 200 games. Who knows what his teammates saw him do? But, I saw him do two things that I'd never seen before and haven't seen since. Get this: Willie Mays bunted for a double in the Astrodome and scored from second on a bunt there too. Each time, the third baseman was facing the third base dugout, hoping the ball would go foul, and then panicked. Willie could run full speed, looking back to make sure nothing was gaining on him.

Dierker joined the Astros—actually, then they still were the Colt .45's—in 1964 when he was seventeen years old, and debuted on his eighteenth birthday. In '65 the team changed its name and moved into the Astrodome, and Dierker was still pitching for the Astros in 1973, Mays's last season. So that's nine seasons in which Mays played in the Astrodome: '65 through '73. First thing we'll do is check every double he hit in Houston in those seasons . . .

While Dierker undoubtedly saw Mays play a lot of games (if not 200), he didn't see him hit many doubles. Not in Houston, anyway. From 1964 through '73, Mays hit 190 doubles, but only 7 of those were hit in Houston (and none in '64, which means all seven were in the Astrodome). What's more, Dierker was never on the mound when it happened. Mays faced Dierker seventy-four times and never doubled off him, in Houston or anywhere else.

Anyway, back to those seven doubles in Houston. The Retrosheet accounts list outfield direction for five of them: three to left field, two to right. With the other two unidentified, I turned to the *San Francisco Chronicle* and checked all seven in the game stories published the next day. Sorry, Larry, no bunts among them. Which isn't to suggest that Dierker didn't see Mays do some amazing things over the years.

J. R. RICHARD & WILLIE MAYS

It was unbelievable the way J.R. handled those big bombers. He just blew them away with that overpowering fastball and one of the greatest hard sliders I've ever seen.

The first time Mays came to bat, J.R. just threw that fastball by him. I was coaching first base, and as Willie passed me on his way out to the outfield he said, in that high-pitched voice, "Man, where'd they get that big, black dude. He scared me half to death."

J.R. struck Mays out two more times, and Willie said to me, "Nobody ever struck Willie out four times in a game. I ain't playin' anymore," and he took himself out of the game.

—Giants coach Hub Kittle quoted in *Talkin' Baseball:*
An Oral History of Baseball in the 1970s (Phil Pepe, 1998)

Kittle is remembering Richard's major league debut, which came on September 5, 1971. And Richard was awfully impressive against the Giants that afternoon in San Francisco. He pitched a complete game to beat the Giants 5–3, and his fifteen strikeouts set a new major-league record for a pitcher in his first game. As Bob Stevens observed in the next day's *San Francisco Chronicle*, Richard was plenty intimidating.

> Richard, a towering 21-year-old righthander, put 222 pounds of power behind almost every one of his pitches and lived up to his reputation as a man who thrives on strikeouts. In one game in Oklahoma City this summer, he struck out 17, 16 of them in the first six innings.
>
> He comes down off the mound like a huge crane. There were very few Giants who dared dig in on him, and you certainly can't fault them for that.

So what did Mays do against the huge crane?

In the first inning, he struck out.

In the third inning, he struck out.

In the fifth inning, he struck out.

Mays was due to lead off the bottom of the eighth. This would be his fourth time up, and probably his last of the game. Did he, having struck out three times already, excuse himself from the proceedings?

He did not. Mays led off, walked, and eventually scored the Giants' third run.

In the bottom of the ninth, Dick Dietz led off and struck out. Steve Henderson struck out. And with Mays due next, Hal Lanier struck out.

I should say this: it's *possible* that Mays was *not* on deck when Lanier struck out, that he'd taken himself out of the game, just as Kittle remembered. But what's more likely, I think, is that Mays—still a real good hitter in 1971, even at forty—made a joke to Kittle. Because with the Giants in a pennant race

I was watching a game last summer, and a rookie starter was struggling in his first major-league start, when Rangers broadcaster Josh Lewin—one of my favorites, by the way—told this one . . .

I know in Jack Morris's big-league start, he walked the first four batters he faced, Tag. But Ralph Houk left him in, and he ended up throwing a complete game with twelve strikeouts.

Well, not exactly. Morris made his first start on July 31, 1977, in (coincidentally) Arlington, Texas. The first inning did not go walk-walk-walk-walk. Instead it went walk-walk-single, followed by an out on the bases, a stolen base, a run-scoring wild pitch, and—with the bases empty—two straight outs. So yeah, Morris got off to a rough beginning, but it wasn't THAT rough. He did pitch nine innings and struck out eleven Rangers (not twelve), but didn't throw a complete game. He exited with the score 2 to 2 (the Tigers hit a couple of solo homers off Bert Blyleven). The Rangers won in the bottom of the tenth on Mike Hargrove's run-scoring single. And who scored that run?

Tom Grieve. "Tag." Josh Lewin's broadcast partner . . . who didn't say a word about having been played a key role that night in Arlington. Ah, memory.

with the Dodgers—they eventually finished one game ahead—the notion that Mays would remove himself from a close game seems preposterous, at the very least.

Postcript: By the way, this sort of story has a long history. I don't have any idea about whom it was first told—Amos Rusie, maybe—but the earliest I've seen involves Ray Chapman and Walter Johnson. From Dan Okrent and Steve Wulf's *Baseball Anecdotes* (1989):

> Earlier in the same season in which he would be killed by a pitch thrown by Carl Mays, Cleveland's Ray Chapman was facing Walter Johnson. When the pitcher quickly brought the count to two strikes, Chapman left the batter's box for the dugout. Reminded by Umpire Billy Evans that he had one strike left, Chapman said, "You can have it. It wouldn't do me any good."

This one is probably as apocryphal as the rest of them . . . *but* . . . things were different in 1920. Players were competitive, certainly. But there was a certain amount of clowning around, and it's not unreasonable to guess that Chapman might really have given up a strike, particularly if the Senators were a few runs ahead and the Indians had a train to catch.

Post-Postscript: Oh, one more thing! If Mays had struck out four times against J. R. Richard, would that really have been the first time in his career?

No, it wouldn't have been.

On May 15, 1957, Mays struck out four times against four different St. Louis pitchers. But the last of his strikeouts came in the fourteenth inning, so maybe that game gets an asterisk.

No asterisk ten years later, though, as Mays struck out four times straight against Gary Nolan, Cincinnati's nineteen-year-old phenom, on the 7th of June in 1967.

When Mays was young, he didn't strike out a ton. In 1971, though, with his skills deteriorating—he turned forty that spring—Mays compensated by taking more pitches, and set career highs in both walks (112) and strike-outs (123) despite playing in only 136 games. Ten days after *not* striking out four times against Richard, Mays did strike out four times against Pittsburgh's Bob Johnson.

MAZEROSKI & CLEMENTE

One day soon after I joined the Pirates, Maz was playing second base, left-handed pull hitter up, while I was on the mound checking a runner on second base, the tying run. Winning run at bat, two outs, ninth inning, I check the runner on second, and see Maz playing up the middle. . . . I stepped off and said, "Hey, Mazzie!" I motioned for him to get over in the hole. Saw him take two or three steps over in the hole and that was fine. Took my stretch again, checked the runner, Maz is back up the middle! I stepped off, he trotted in and said, "Nellie, all I'm gonna tell ya is trust me." He went back to second base. Got my sign, checked the runner again, Maz was still up the middle! I fired a pitch and the left-handed pull hitter pulls the ball in the hole between first and second base. . . . Running in, backing up home plate, I'm swearing under my breath at Mazzie . . . and now I'm behind home plate, I see the throw coming in from Clemente. Perfect throw, the catcher tags the runner out, we win the ballgame. Everybody's happy.

I'm upset. Not that we won, but because Maz put 100 more gray hairs on my head. I go in the clubhouse, Maz is sitting by my locker and he says, "Sit down. You think that's luck, that Clemente saved you, don't you?"

I said, "I thought he'd saved you, not me."

Maz said, "Clemente and I have been working that play for a long time. If there's a base hit up the middle to center field, can Al Oliver throw somebody out at home? Or if there's a sharply hit ball to right field to Clemente, can he throw the runner out at home? With a left-handed pull hitter, I'll play up the middle, I'll take away the ground-ball base hit or a possible line drive, gambling that if the ball is hit sharply enough on the ground or lined near Clemente, one of two things can happen. They'll hold the runner at third, or they'll send him and Clemente has an excellent shot at throwing him out at home plate. How did we make out?" Now I understood. I was in the presence of two great players, Clemente and Mazeroski, who were thinking of ways to help win ballgames.

—Nellie Briles in *Twin Killing: The Bill Mazeroski Story* (John T. Bird, 1995)

Thanks to Retrosheet, of course, it's exceptionally easy to check the specific details of this story (if not the postgame conversation between Mazeroski and Briles).

Nelson Briles reached the majors in 1965 with St. Louis and spent six full seasons there. He joined the Pirates in 1971 and remained through 1973; by '73, though, Mazeroski had retired and Clemente was

New York Post columnist Milton Gross told this one about Lefty Gomez—for many years a reliable source of material for the scribes—in 1971 . . .

When the all-time All-Star team was picked a few years ago, Joe DiMaggio was named the all-time center fielder. I saw him the day after the announcement was made.

"I can't get over it," he said. "They picked me over Tris Speaker. Tris was my idol." Then he told this story:

"I was in my second year in the majors and my roommate was Lefty Gomez, the pitcher. Lefty did most of the talking for both of us. I rarely said much. In the cab on the way out to the park, Lefty said, 'You play too shallow. I'm pitching today. I'll tell you where to play.'

"I said, 'Tris Speaker played shallow. Someday I'm going to make the fans forget him and talk about me.'

"During the game Rudy York was at bat, and as usual I played fairly shallow. Lefty looked around and saw me. He waved me back. York had great power.

"I shook my head.

"He yelled, 'Get back.' Again, I refused.

"York hit the first pitch over my head, and I couldn't catch up with it. I managed to touch the ball with one finger. We lost by one run.

"On the way home from the park, I vowed to Lefty, 'I'm still going to make them forget Speaker.'

" 'Forget about that,' he said. 'You keep it up, and you'll make 'em forget about Gomez.' "

gone. So even if Briles didn't specify this incident as happening "soon after I joined the Pirates," we'd have only two seasons to check.

In 1971, Briles pitched mostly out of the bullpen, but did start fourteen games. He completed four of those fourteen starts and finished eight games as a reliever. So that gives us twelve games in 1971.

Of the eight he finished as a reliever, the Pirates lost six. The two victories were lopsided: 9–3 and 15–4. So that leaves only the four starts that Briles completed (at least in 1971).

Briles pitched his first complete game of the season on July 9, then finished in a rush, with complete games on September 6, September 12, and September 23; the latter two were shutouts.

On July 9 the Pirates beat the Braves 11–2.

On September 6 the Pirates beat the Cubs 4–1.

On September 12 the Pirates beat the Expos 4–0.

On September 23 the Pirates beat the Cardinals 5–0.

Clemente didn't play on September 23. In the other three games, he did play right field . . . but didn't get an assist in any of them.

Actually, there's a bigger problem than Briles's games finished not matching up with Clemente's assists, and it's this: Mazeroski wasn't playing much at all. Mazeroski's last full season as an everyday player was 1968, and in '71 he played second base in only forty-six games. It stands to reason, then, that there simply weren't many games in which Briles pitched, Mazeroski played second base, and Clemente played in right field. So let's ignore all the other details and focus only on these particular games: the games in which all three appeared at the same time. And we might as well forget about the ninth inning—that's the sort of detail that might easily be imagined—and look at *all* the innings in *all* the games.

In 1971, Briles pitched in thirty-seven games. In only eight of those thirty-seven games was Briles pitching, Mazeroski playing second base, and Clemente playing right field all at the same time. Eight games.

In none of those eight games did Clemente get an assist. None.

In fact, in Briles's thirty-seven games, Clemente was credited with just one assist. It happened on September 30 in Philadelphia, in the Pirates' last game of the regular season. This doesn't do us any good, though. Mazeroski didn't play, Briles was lifted for a pinch hitter in the fourth, and Clemente's assist came at the tail end of a fly double play in the fifth. Briles was never on the mound, in 1971, when Clemente nailed a runner.

In 1972, Mazeroski played so rarely that it's easier to look at his games than Briles's. Maz played second base in only fifteen games. Clemente played right field in eight of those games. Briles pitched in three of those games. And wouldn't you know it, Clemente did record an assist in one of *those* games: on August 27 against the Dodgers.

Again, though: problems. Briles started the game, and he was still on the mound in the top of the eighth when Clemente got his assist. But this was not a game-ending play at the plate. With two outs, runners on first and second, and the score tied at four runs apiece, Chris Cannizzaro rammed a pitch into right field. Cannizzaro was out trying for third base—Clemente to Mazeroski to Sanguillen to Hebner—but two runs scored and the Dodgers took a 6–4 lead. The Dodgers made it 7–4 in the ninth, and that's how it ended.

Summing up, then: according to Briles, he finished a game that ended with Clemente throwing out a runner at the plate, everything according to Mazeroski's plan. There is, however, nothing in the books that even remotely resembles this story. Clemente was credited with exactly one assist while playing behind Briles and Mazeroski, and it was neither game-ending, nor at the plate, nor in a Pittsburgh victory.

There are, however, two remaining possibilities: preseason and postseason. I'm not going to check spring-training games because 1) I don't find them particularly interesting, and 2) it's a real pain in the ass. But Briles did pitch once in the 1971 World Series and once in the 1972 National League Championship Series, and we really should check those games.

In the '71 World Series, Briles started Game 5 and tossed a two-hit shutout. Mazeroski did not play. Clemente did, but did not get an assist.

In the '72 NLCS, Briles started Game 3 and pitched six strong innings. Mazeroski did not play. Clemente did, but did not get an assist.

Maybe I'm missing something here. Maybe there's some combination of circumstances that would match, however slightly, Briles's memory. But this is one of those stories that just seems far too good to be true. And it almost certainly is.

DiMaggio's second year in the majors was 1937, which also was York's rookie season, in which he played in only 104 games but mashed thirty-five homers and slugged .651. Gomez started eight games against the Tigers in '37, and lost three close games to them, including two by just one run: 4–3 on June 7 and 5–4 on August 30.

In the June game, York didn't play, and the Tigers's only long hits were Pete Fox's triple and Hank Greenberg's home run. In the August game York did play, but his only hit was a first-inning homer that gave Detroit a three-nothing lead.

Gomez also lost a 5–3 game to the Tigers, on the 26th of June. Again, York's only hit was a home run, this one dropping into the left-field stands, presumably far from DiMaggio's outstretched finger. It's not hard to understand why the rookie York stuck in DiMaggio's mind, though. While he never doubled or tripled in four starts against Gomez that season, he did homer in three of them.

THE HIDDEN GENIUS OF LAWRENCE S. RITTER

The readers may wonder at the detail contained in these narrations, the near total recall of events that took place a half century or more ago. If so, he can join me in that wonderment. The memory of man is a remarkable storehouse indeed. Many of the people I talked to had to think longer to get the names of all their great-grandchildren straight than they did to run down the batting order of the 1906 Chicago Cubs. Psychologists assure me, however, that it is not at all unusual as one gets older for the more distant past to be remembered more clearly than what happened three weeks ago, especially if the distant past was particularly memorable.

Initially skeptical, I spent weeks checking a great deal of what was told me. I pored through record books and searched out old newspapers and other primary sources to verify a fact or an incident. But almost without exception I found that the event took place almost precisely as it had been described. And in those instances where something had been added, the embellishments invariably were those of the artist: they served to dramatize a point, to emphasize a contrast, or to reveal a truth.

This, then, is the way it was.

Listen!

—from the preface to Lawrence Ritter's *The Glory of Their Times* (1966)

On any short list of the greatest baseball books, you will find Larry Ritter's *The Glory of Their Times*, his collection of interviews with players from (mostly) the early part of the twentieth century. *Glory* certainly was not the first published collection of oral history; for example, nearly a decade earlier Studs Terkel put together thirteen interviews for his first book, *Giants of Jazz*. But *Glory* was the first collection of baseball oral history, and more than forty years later it remains the best.

Nevertheless, Ritter's probably never gotten the credit he deserves, because it's always been generally believed that he just turned his tape recorder on and got out of the way, a perception that Ritter only encouraged in his preface to the book. In addition to that passage above, there's also this:

> Of course, this book was really not "written" at all. It was spoken. And, as spoken literature, it is characterized by the simplicity and directness of the spoken word as contrasted

with the written word. My role was strictly that of catalyst, audience, and chronicler. I asked and listened, and the tape recorder did the rest.

In preparing these interviews for publication I have done very little editing of the tapes. I have eliminated my questions and comments and have selected and rearranged the material to make it more comprehensible than the verbatim transcript of a six-hour interview could possibly be. . . .

Snippets of Ritter's interviews had been heard over the years in various formats, but in 1998 the HighBridge Company released a set of four compact discs including five-plus hours of material from a dozen of the players in the book, which allows for extensive comparisons.

With all that in mind, let us examine two versions of a story told by Hall of Famer Sam Crawford. The first version, on the left, is the one that Ritter got on a Tandberg tape recorder and is entertaining in its own right. The second is what appears in *The Glory of Their Times* and is so vivid you're taken back more than a century to a hot, dusty field surrounded by men wearing white shirts and straw hats.

They used to tell a story about Tim Hurst, he was an old umpire. He was a tough character, Tim Hurst. He was wise to this deal, where they cut. Well, he was umpiring one time, and somebody, Jake Beckley, I think it was Jake Beckley, the old Cincinnati first baseman, Jake come in there, you know, made a big slide in, you know, and got up and Tim called him out, "Yer out." And a big argument started, you know, cussing and all.

"What do you mean I'm out, they didn't even make a play on me!"

He says, "You big S.B., you got here too quick!"

Did you ever hear of Tim Hurst? He was a very famous umpire back then. A real tough character. He was wise to this deal, of course, where the runner doesn't come anywhere close to touching third base. Well, Jake Beckley was playing first base for us—with the Cincinnati club in 1899 or 1900 or so—and he came sliding into home one day. A real big slide, plenty of dust and all, even though no one was trying to tag him out. Tim had been watching a play at second all the while.

"You're out!" yells Tim.

Jake screamed to high heaven. "What do you mean, I'm out?" he roared. "They didn't even make a play on me."

"You big S.O.B.," Tim said, "you got here too quick!"

Ritter's done a masterful job of editing this story, but one can hardly say that he has done "very little editing," or that he has merely "selected and re-arranged the material" here. For one thing, Ritter implicitly has Crawford actually witnessing the event, and he's sort of sneaky about it, throwing in the information that the incident occurred in "1899 or 1900 or so"; Beckley and Crawford were teammates with Cincinnati from 1899 through 1902 (what Ritter probably didn't know was that Hurst didn't work in the National League in 1899; 1900 was the only season in which Hurst, Crawford, and Beckley could have been involved in the same game).

So that—making the storyteller an actual witness rather than just a middleman—is Ritter's first move. And his second is to . . . well, it's to make a good storyteller a *better* storyteller. Compare this:

> *and he came sliding into home one day. A real big slide, plenty of dust and all, even though no one was trying to tag him out.*

to this:

> *Jake come in there, you know, made a big slide in, you know, and got up and Tim called him out, "Yer out."*

Obviously, Ritter was smart to remove the *you knows* from the narrative (and by the way, did you know that even the old-timers, raised in a story-telling tradition, so often resorted to that ubiquitous conversational place-holder? I sure didn't). But it's the details Ritter adds that really make the passage sing, the *real big slide, plenty of dust and all,* little of which Crawford actually described with his own words.

Of course, that is just one example. There are many, many others. Some of the stories in *Glory* are so well told that they'll stick with you for many years. Davy Jones tells this wonderful story about the day his teammate Germany Schaefer, one of the game's more colorful personalities, was called upon to pinch-hit for pitcher Red Donahue in the ninth inning. Here's what happened next, as presented in the book.

> "Hey, Red," yells Schaefer, "the manager wants me to hit for you."
>
> "What?" Red roars. "Who the hell are you to hit for me?" And he slams his bat down and comes back and sits way down at the end of the bench, with his arms folded across his chest. Madder than a wet hen.
>
> Well, Schaefer walked out there and just as he about to step into the batter's box he stopped, took off his cap, and faced the grandstand.
>
> "Ladies and gentlemen," he announced, "you are now looking at Herman Schaefer, better known as Herman the Great, acknowledged

by one and all to be the greatest pinch hitter in the world, I am now going to hit the ball into the left field bleachers. Thank you."

A moment later, Schaefer hit a home run into the left-field bleachers. He then sprinted to each base, into which he slid, then yelled an announcement to the crowd, and finally finished with a proclamation to the grandstand: "Ladies and gentlemen, I thank you for your kind attention."

At least according to Davy Jones. We do know that Schaefer, on the 24th of June in 1906, did hit a pinch-hit homer in the ninth off Doc White, in Chicago. But again, it's not the facts of the incident that interest us here, it's how they're described. And here's what Jones actually told Ritter and his tape recorder.

> Schaefer says to Red, "Manager wants me to hit for you."
> Red looked at him, says, "Who in the hell are you, to go to hit for me?"
> He folded his arms, and he sat there, you know, madder than a wet hen, you know, because they took him out, and put in a pinch hitter for him.
> So Schaefer walks over in front of the grandstand, took off his cap, and he says, "Ladies and gentlemen, you are now looking at Herman Schaefer, better known as Herman the Great, and the greatest pinch hitter in the world." He says, "I'm going up there and I'm going to hit the ball in that left-field bleachers and win this ball game." Finally, he turned around and he says, "Thank you."

Ritter's changes here are more subtle, but no less effective. How mad was Donahue? So mad that he "slams his bat down" . . . even though Jones says no such thing. And Ritter makes Schaefer's speech funnier than it was; instead of Schaefer claiming to be "the greatest pinch hitter in the world," Ritter adds that Schaefer boasts of being *acknowledged by one and all* to be the greatest.

Nearly forty years after *Glory* was published, Ritter did admit—for the first time, near as I can tell—that he'd been less than forthright about his role in the shaping of the source material:

> The weaving process? Well, you know that quote in the preface, where I say, "I asked, I listened, and the tape recorder did the rest?" That's a misstatement. Of course there was a lot of work that went into arranging the various elements. I had a typed manuscript of the conversations, and I would listen to the tapes I made—there are over a hundred hours of them—and after hearing them a few times, I would begin to hear the voice, its cadence, its peculiarities, so that I could recall its

The most affecting character in *The Glory of Their Times* is Rube Marquard. As Larry Mansch wrote in *The National Pastime* in 1996, "Marquard's is the most classically American. It is the story of a boy who pursued his dream and rose, against all odds, from the bottom to the very top of the baseball world."

But as Mansch discovered, most of Marquard's story—outside of the facts of his major-league career—turns out to be largely a figment of Marquard's apparently active imagination.

Perhaps the most dramatic example is Marquard's story about the rift between him and his father when he chose baseball as a profession . . .

"Now listen, I've told you time and again that I don't want you to be a professional ballplayer. But you've got your mind made up. Now I'm going to tell you something: when you cross that threshold, don't come back. I don't ever want to see you again."

"You don't mean that, Dad," I said.

"Yes I do."

"Well, I'm going, and some day you'll be proud of me."

"Proud! You're breaking my heart, and I don't ever want to see you again."

That's Ritter's version in the book, and it essentially matches the actual recording. The rest of the story we'll take from the recording, which is actually a bit better than what's in the book.

"So, I never saw my dad until, oh, about fifteen years—"

sound and character just by reading the transcript. Then I'd begin weaving the material into a narrative.[1]

An intimate familiarity with a voice's cadence and peculiarities would be helpful when "weaving material into a narrative," but it would be *particularly* helpful if one wanted to *add* material to a narrative. And that's exactly what Ritter does, again and again. Consider the following section from Ritter's interview with Rube Bressler, who was playing for the Dodgers when Babe Herman famously "tripled into a triple play," though he actually doubled into a double play (again, the first version is the recorded version, the second Ritter's). When the play begins, Dodgers pitcher Dazzy Vance is the runner at second base, Chick Fewster is at first base, and Babe Herman has just lashed a line drive. It ends with all three Dodgers laying claim to third base.

In the audio introduction to the Bressler interview on the CD collection, Ritter says of Bressler, "He was very articulate. . . . So words, he was used to

Photo courtesy of Transcendental Graphics

Rube Bressler

And the umpire hesitated, you know what I mean? What the hell, it was an odd situation for him, to figure out *which* man is out. And during the interval, Daz is laying down the ground like this, you know, the most impromptu speech ever made, he said, "Mr. Umpire, members of the opposition, fellow teammates . . . if you'll carefully scan the rules of our National Pastime, you'll find that the only gentleman safe on this hassock is Arthur C. Vance."

And the umpire hesitated, trying to decide which two of these guys are out and which one is safe. Rather an unusual situation, doesn't exactly come up every day, and they started arguing about who's what.

Well, while all this discussion is going on, Daz is still lying there flat on his back, feet on third and head toward home. Then he lifts up his head.

"Mr. Umpire, Fellow Teammates, and Members of the Opposition," he intones, "if you carefully peruse the rules of our National Pastime you will find that there is one and only one protagonist in rightful occupancy of this hassock—namely yours truly, Arthur C. Vance."

"Didn't your father try to get in touch with you, all this time?"

"No, no. He was stubborn, so was I. So one day the batboy came in and said, 'Rube, there's an elderly man outside, and he wants to see you. He says he's your father from Cleveland.'

"I said, 'My father wouldn't go across the street to see me. But you go out and get his autograph book and bring it in and I'll autograph it for him.'

"So instead of bringing the book he brought in my dad, and we were both glad to see one another."

According to Mansch, "there is probably little truth" to this tale of paternal estrangement and reconciliation. "Rube's family was featured prominently in many newspaper articles and features over the years covering his big league career, particularly during the winning streak of 1912, and always the family (including the elder Marquard) is portrayed as proud, supportive, and among Rube's biggest fans."

This is far from Marquard's only foray into fictional autobiography. He told Ritter that he was born in 1889 and thus was only sixteen when he left home to play baseball, and only eighteen when he debuted in the majors. Until well after Marquard's death in 1980, his 1889 birthday was accepted. But researcher Fred Schuld discovered that Marquard actually was born in 1886. Which means, as Mansch wrote, that Marquard "was 19, and not 16, when he left home— shattering the image of an innocent boy riding freight trains

words, he liked words, and you could tell when you talked to him because he was very expressive. So he was a pleasure to interview, because he played with thoughts and made them even more interesting than they were by the way he expressed himself."

Look at those two versions. When recalling Vance's little speech at third base, Bressler did not use the word *intone* (at least not here), nor did he use the words *peruse, protagonist,* or *occupancy* in his story. But Ritter did, presumably because he considered Bressler a particularly articulate fellow, and those were the sort of words that a particularly articulate fellow might use.

Of course, what we end up with is a baseball version of the telephone game; who *knows* what Vance actually said, but we can guess it bears little relation to Ritter's ultimate version. And it's Ritter's version that will forever remain the popular account.

And I'm okay with that. Ritter's not done anything different from a thousand biographical collaborators before and after him. The only real difference is that Ritter went to such great lengths to deny that he'd done any writing of consequence, when he knew the truth was something quite different. Why the denials? Well, one might argue that he did it out of self-

across the country in search of adventure. And if Rube entered the big leagues not at age 18, but at 21, he was no 'teenage phenom,' but a young adult."

Marquard suggested to Ritter that he'd been a teetotaler during his career, not one to hit the town for a late night of booze and broads. "I always said you can't burn a candle at both ends," he said, and "I never drank a drop." In fact, Marquard married famous vaudeville and burlesque performer Blossom Seeley and was far from a stranger to spirits and the nightlife.

These are just the highlights. In essence, Marquard's chapter in *The Glory of Their Times* is a fanciful work of fiction.

interest, that he believed his book would be better received if there didn't seem to be some all-powerful Oz behind the curtain. If that was his aim, he was brilliant, as he wound up with a huge commercial success.

I don't think that's it, though. According to Ritter, he received a small advance from his publisher, which suggests nobody had high hopes, financially. Rather, I believe he simply held a deep affection for the players he interviewed, and more than anything else, he wanted them to come across well in the book. I believe he felt indebted to these one time greats for their time and their wonderful stories, and he repaid them many times over. For as long as they were alive, Ritter gave them a cut of his royalty payments from book sales (even though he was under no legal or ethical obligation to do so). Quite possibly due to the book's success, within a few years after its publication subjects Rube Marquard, Goose Goslin, Stan Coveleski, and Harry Hooper were elected to the Hall of Fame. Chief Meyers became something of a celebrity, reciting "Casey at the Bat" on national television. And Ritter, in addition to giving all of us a great gift, gave his collaborators perhaps the greatest gift of all: he made them even more interesting than they really were.

HONUS WAGNER & THE YOUNGSTER

I made a hit once that I always will remember, though it wasn't a freak.

The St. Louis club was playing the Pirates at Pittsburgh. Miller Huggins was the St. Louis manager. A fresh young pitcher had joined them and was rarin' to go. He was quite a wise boy, according to his own way of thinking—full of ideas and conversation. For several days he had been telling the other St. Louis players how he could make the so-called good hitters sidestep. He was eager for a chance to show us all up.

"How'll you pitch against Wagner?" Huggins asked him.

"There's only one way to do it," he said. "I don't see why others haven't thought of it. Why, I'll pitch three fast balls right at his head and drive that Dutchman from the plate. If he doesn't get away he'll get his head knocked off. Then I'll curve the next three and strike him out."

Now, that sounded simple enough, didn't it?

While he was doing this talking on the bench two of the St. Louis pitchers were being hammered out of the box.

"All right, here's your chance," Huggins told the fresh youngster. "Get in there and show us some of that pitching. Make sauerkraut out of that big Dutchman."

Several of the St. Louis players waved to me in mock fear, but I didn't know the joke.

We had the bases full when the youngster started and I was up. He really did pitch at my head, but I backed off a little as I swung and happened to hit the ball squarely on the nose, knocking it over the wall for a home run.

"That'll be all," Huggins yelled at him. "The scheme doesn't work."

In a few days Huggins released him. That boy, who was going to knock our heads off, had the unique record of having stayed in the big league just long enough to pitch one ball. And he never came back.

I've often wanted to know how his work appeared in the official records. The papers didn't print it. To tell the truth, though, I felt sorry for that kid. I like to see them come in fresh and full of pep and vinegar.

—Honus Wagner in *Honus Wagner: On His Life and Baseball*
(ed. William R. Cobb, 2006)

This story certainly doesn't lack in details, notwithstanding the anonymity of the fresh pitcher. But of course, details—invented or otherwise—are the hallmark of a good story. This one first appeared in a series of articles that were published in at least two newspapers—the *Los Angeles*

Of course there's a whole genre of stories about young players who didn't know shit from shinola, this being just one more example . . .

When Billy Murray was managing the Phillies in the 1900s, an earnest young bush leaguer joined the club, determined to make good.

In his first game, he played acceptable ball for eight innings. In the ninth it came his time to bat. Philadelphia was trailing by a run, two men were out, and there was a runner on third. The rookie got his bat and then stepped over the Manager Murray.

"What do you want me to do?" he asked.

Murray stared at him for a moment, then snorted sarcastically, "Strike out."

The rookie walked to the plate, swung listlessly at the first three pitches, and struck out.

By suppertime he was on his way back to the minors.

—Ira L. Smith and H. Allen Smith, Low and Inside (Doubleday, 1949)

Billy Murray managed the Phillies for three seasons, 1907 through 1909.

In 1907 no Phillie played in just one game. The closest was Paul Sentell, who played in three games and batted only four times. But Sentell had played in sixty-three games the season before.

In 1908 someone named Pep Deininger played in only one game, but he didn't bat and, at thirty years old, was no young busher.

In 1909, young bushers—and catchers—Ben Froelich and Ed

Times and the *Pittsburgh Gazette Times*—in late 1923 and early 1924. The pieces were recently compiled and published as a book, edited by William R. Cobb. In the book's foreword, Cobb writes of Wagner:

> By 1924 he was comfortable in the spotlight as a public speaker, and had grown to thoroughly enjoy the reaction of his audience to his anecdotes and his sometimes embellished tales of the diamond. In the later years of his life, Wagner developed a reputation for making up outlandish and even unbelievable stories to capture the attention of his audience. The stories in this autobiographical work seem not to fall into that category, however, the timing being a decade or so before Wagner's wild creativity in storytelling reached full bloom.

Further, Cobb says, "The editor feels that Wagner most likely penned this work on his own. Certainly not without editorial assistance that would accompany any widely printed article, but quite possibly without a major influence by what would now be considered a ghostwriter."

Okay, enough introducing. Do you remember the details? Our brash-but-unfortunate youngster pitches for the Miller Huggins–managed Cardinals, and in his first game he throws a single pitch, which Honus Wagner turns into a grand slam. Poor kid is never allowed to show his face again on the mound.

Huggins managed the Cardinals from 1913 through 1917. He didn't manage somewhere else before 1913, and 1917 was Wagner's last season. So if Huggins really was on the bench when Wagner hit this home run, it would have happened in that five-season span.

If I were checking this story five years ago, I would look for Cardinal pitchers who a) appeared in just one game, and b) gave up a homer in that game.

But that presupposes a lot of details that might not exist in real life. Today it's easy to check every home run Wagner hit during those five seasons. SABR's Home Run Log—unfortunately, available to SABR members only—will tell me whom he hit them against, and how many runners were on base. If Wagner hit a grand slam against the Cardinals, that'll show up real quick.

Especially considering how few homers Wagner hit. It's not that he wasn't a power hitter. It's that he was getting old, and anyway, hardly anybody hit home runs. It was the Dead Ball Era. In fact, Wagner didn't hit any homers at all in 1917, which narrows our search to four seasons, and in those four seasons he hit only eleven homers. Without checking, I will guess that none of them were grand slams. But of course that's why we check. . . .

Art courtesy of Transcendental Graphics

The Great Wagner

In 1913 he hit three home runs. None were grand slams, and none came against the Cardinals.

In 1914 he hit one home run. It wasn't a grand slam. It wasn't against the Cardinals.*

In 1915 he hit six home runs. One of them was a grand slam (I guessed wrong), but it didn't clear the fence and it came against Brooklyn's Jeff Pfeffer, who would win 158 National League games. Four of the homers came against the Phillies—including one apiece off future Hall of Famers Eppa Rixey and Pete Alexander—and the other against Chicago's Karl Adams. Adams easily ranks as the least distinguished of Wagner's 1915 homerees, but he did throw 107 innings that season.

In 1916, Wagner hit one home run. It was against Cincinnati's Elmer Knetzer with the bases empty; Knetzer was no star, but he was no youngster, either. He was thirty years old, and his career record included thirty-one wins in the majors (and another thirty-eight in the Federal League). After allowing the homer to Wagner, Knetzer pitched 128 more innings that season.

So that's four seasons, with nothing close to a match. Just for fun,

---

* Wagner's only homer in 1914 was one of sixteen given up by Christy Mathewson that season; he never allowed more than nine in any other season.

One thing I wish I'd done for this book but didn't: compile a comprehensive list of stories that are almost exactly the same, except the characters are different. Anyway, here's one excellent example . . .

Crazy Schmidt was a pitcher with a poor memory. Whenever he was at work on the mound he always had a little notebook in his hip pocket. As each batter came to the plate, Schmidt got out the book, riffled through it, and checked his private record of the man's potential weakness. One day in 1894 Cap Anson, four times batting champion of the National League, stepped to the plate and faced Crazy Schmidt. The pitcher got out his notebook and studied it a few moments. Then in a loud voice he read from it: "Base on balls." Anson walked.

—Ira L. Smith and H. Allen Smith, Low and Inside (Doubleday, 1949)

Years back, Crazy Schmidt of the Cincinnati Reds was troubled by a sievelike memory and actually kept his book on his person—in a loose-leaf notebook which he tugged from his hip pocket for reference as each batter approached the plate. "Base on balls" he is supposed to have written opposite the name of Honus Wagner . . .

—George Plimpton, Out of My League (Harper & Row, 1961)

The only Schmidt who's ever pitched for Cincinnati was Willard Schmidt, and that was in the late 1950s, roughly half a century after

though, let's check the rest of Wagner's long career—he began with Louisville, then a National League club, in 1897—for grand slams, and homers against the Cardinals, and homers against young pitchers who spent little time in the majors. This time, though, I'll spare you most of the details. Except these . . .

Wagner hit 101 homers during his career. Five of them were grand slams. Oddly, only 7 of the 101 came against the Cardinals. A number of the 101 were surrendered by young pitchers who were either just beginning obscure careers or who didn't really have major-league careers at all.

Here's one intriguing possibility: Howard McGraner. He pitched for the Reds in 1912, just briefly. He debuted on September 12 and pitched his last game on October 6. His entire career consisted of four games and nineteen innings. That October 6 game was the last game of the season for both the Reds and the Pirates. McGraner entered in the sixth, and with two outs and nobody aboard in the seventh, Wagner hit the home run. According to the box score, McGraner did finish the inning—so he must have pitched to at least one more batter—but was replaced in the eighth and never threw another pitch in the majors. He had turned twenty-three just a few weeks earlier.

So a lot of things match up. But it wasn't a grand slam, that wasn't his only pitch in the majors, and he wasn't a Cardinal (let alone managed by Miller Huggins).

Plus, I found a more intriguing possibility.

When going through all of Wagner's homers, I used a "pen" and some "paper" and designated one row for each year and drew three columns: one for Wagner's grand slams, one for home runs hit against St. Louis, and one for young pitchers with short careers. Only one name showed up in all three columns: Bunny Hearn.

On May 4, 1911, Honus Wagner hit a bases-loaded homer off St. Louis left-hander Charles Bunn Hearn.

As you might recall, Miller Huggins didn't manage the Cardinals until 1913. In 1911, Roger Bresnahan was the manager. Bresnahan also was one of the Cardinals' two semi-regular catchers. Huggins was the Cardinals' regular second baseman. On the day in question, both were in the starting lineup. Retrosheet actually has the play-by-play account for this game, so we know that when Hearn entered the game with one out in the bottom of the seventh, Bresnahan had already removed himself from the proceedings, and Huggins was still at second base. We also know that Wagner was the first batter that Hearn faced. And of course we know that Wagner homered.

The pitch that Wagner hit was not Hearn's last of the game. He retired the next two batters and pitched the bottom of the eighth, too. The game wasn't his last of the season; he pitched one inning on May 30. The season wasn't the last of his career. After spending 1912 in the minors, Hearn returned to the majors in 1913 and started two games for the Giants, but neither of them were against the Pirates. And even if Wagner were a religious reader of box scores, he might not have recognized *Hearn* if he saw it.

Hearn apparently returned to the minors in 1914, then pitched for Pittsburgh's Federal League team in 1915. Next, a couple more seasons in the minors. Hearn was back in the National League in 1918, with the Boston Braves, but by then Wagner was retired. So it's quite possible that, though Hearn did kick around for years after Wagner hit that home run, Wagner never actually saw him pitch again.

And even if he did know that Hearn pitched in the majors again, he might still have happily told his story. Remember what Wagner wrote: "I've often wanted to know how his work appeared in the official records. The papers didn't print it."

Maybe he believed that. Or maybe he was just covering his tracks. Saying that something wasn't printed in the papers might discourage some humbug skeptic with too much time on his hands from actually, you know, checking.

Honus Wagner's heyday. In fact, there has been no pitching Schmidt, Crazy or otherwise, who could have faced Wagner or Cap Anson.

The pitcher in question is actually Frederick M. Schmit (no d). He couldn't have pitched against Cap Anson in 1894, because Schmit was missing from the majors from 1894 through 1898 (though he presumably was pitching somewhere, and could have faced Anson in a nonleague game). He did pitch in the National League in 1890, 1892, and 1893, and probably faced Anson a few times (Schmit didn't actually pitch much, because he wasn't much good). Schmit also pitched in the majors in 1899 and 1901, but he was an American Leaguer in the latter season and probably would not have faced Honus Wagner. In 1899, though, Schmit certainly would have pitched to Wagner, who played in almost every game the Louisville Colonels played.

Almost as certainly, Schmit's little notebook didn't do him much good. Pitching for the infamous Cleveland Spiders—who went 20-134 and were disbanded after the season—Schmit went 2-17 with a 5.86 ERA (which was, believe it or not, better than those of most of his colleagues).

CY RIGLER & JOHN MCGRAW

Those old umpires were colorful characters. Charlie Rigler, for instance. He was six feet four and he weighed about 260 pounds. When John Tener was president of the National League he told Rigler, "Any time you're in town, I want you to come up to my office and see me." Rigler was a great storyteller, and Tener wanted him to come in just so he could sit there and listen to him. He'd listen to Rigler tell stories, and he'd laugh all morning long.

Rigler had a big argument one day with a New York Giant player and he ended up by punching him. John McGraw wanted Rigler fired; he wanted him thrown right out of baseball. Tener called Rigler in and he said, "Charlie, how could you do such a thing? Hit a ballplayer, oh dear. Charlie, I'm going to have to let you out. Why did you do it, Charlie?"

"Well, I'll tell you, Governor," Rigler said. "I want you to know that I kept my temper when he called me an ugly, stupid this-and-that, and I controlled myself when he said I was a blind, no-good so-and-so and every other name you could think of. That was all right. I'm an umpire. I can take that. But when he said, 'You're just as bad as that blankety-blank Tener that you work for,' I couldn't hold back any longer, Governor. I let him have it."

Tener jumped up and yelled, "You should have *killed* him!" And he wasn't fired. He was suspended for a while, though.

—Jocko Conlan in *Jocko* (Conlan and Robert Creamer, 1967)

Rigler umpired his last game in 1935 and died shortly after that season. Jocko Conlan played in the American League in 1934 and '35 and became a National League umpire in 1941. McGraw managed his last game in 1933, and of course the majority of his managing was done before Conlan was involved at all with professional baseball.

Point being, Conlan almost certainly didn't come by this story firsthand. I should mention, too, that according to Retrosheet, Rigler was not 6'4" and (about) 260 pounds, but 6'1" and 270, which still was plenty big, especially in that era. And Rigler, like a lot of the other umpires who came in before World War I, wasn't shy about using his fists to enforce discipline.

Looking for a fight involving Rigler, I found a game in 1912 between the Giants and the Dodgers, on the 21st of April. Early in the game, Giants shortstop Art Fletcher was "banished to the clubhouse" for his complaints from the dugout, and in the ninth Rigler ejected Giants catcher Chief Meyers. And then things got rowdy . . .

A fist fight between Manager Bill Dahlen of the Brooklyn Club and Umpire Charles Rigler marked the close of the baseball game between the Giants and Brooklyn at the Polo Grounds yesterday afternoon. As Dahlen and Rigler stood at the plate punching each other the crowd immediately became inflamed with excitement and swarmed on to the diamond until the fighters were surrounded by a riotous mob. The scene which followed the Giants' sudden victory was one of the most pronounced outbursts of rowdyism witnessed at a National League ball park in many years.

The trouble was caused by Arthur Wilson's terrific home run smash into the right field grand stand with one batsman out in the ninth inning. The hit sent Groh home ahead of Wilson and won the game for the Giants. As soon as the ball fell in safe territory in the upper tier of the grand stand, Dahlen rushed in from the Brooklyn bench yelling that the ball was a foul. Catcher Erwin of the Brooklyn team also protested. Rigler had watched the ball closely and called it fair.

Defiantly, Dahlen rushed at Rigler, shaking his fist in the umpire's face. The crowd of more than 20,000 people were in a deafening uproar and it was impossible to tell what the manager and umpire were yelling at each other. As Dahlen stood in front of Rigler waiving his arms in a wild rage, the umpire struck him full in the face. Then Dahlen punched Rigler and the umpire delivered another crack on the infuriated manager.[1]

Dahlen wasn't a "New York Giant player" (as Conlan describes Rigler's partner in pugilism); he was a Brooklyn Dodger manager. But Dahlen had *been* a New York Giant; he'd been McGraw's everyday shortstop with the Giants from 1904 through 1907, and he'd learned the dark arts from the master himself. According to the same *Times* story, "Dahlen is known as one of the worst umpire baiters in the league. Only yesterday he was released from a three days' suspension inflicted by President Lynch for making trouble for the umpires in Brooklyn. This mild form of punishment did no good for his outburst yesterday was of the rabid sort."

Which brings up another contradiction: in 1912, John K. Tener wasn't yet serving as National League president; that position was then held by Thomas J. Lynch. Tener, who'd played in the National League in the 1880s, was in 1912 the governor of Pennsylvania. His tenure as NL prexy ran from 1914 to 1918 (and he did hold both jobs for a while).

A few days later, Lynch announced punishments: Dahlen and Rigler both were fined $100—a substantial sum, in those days—and Dahlen also drew a ten-day suspension. Lynch "did not state in his decision who struck the first blow," and there's no mention of a suspension for Rigler.[2]

Bobby Bragan told this one about Hall of Fame umpire Bill Klem . . .

Klem's method of handling complaints was simple. When he'd heard enough he'd draw a line in the dirt with his baseball shoe and tell whoever was disputing with him, "If you cross that line, you're gone."

In a game at Philadelphia in 1940, the Pirates had us beaten 6–2 in the bottom of the ninth with two out. I came to bat for the Phillies. Danny MacFayden, a sidearming right-hander, was on the mound. With a count of one ball and two strikes, MacFayden threw me a superb sidearm curve that started at my belt and broke right over the heart of the plate. It was one of the plainest strikes in history, but Klem called it a ball. Al Lopez, who was catching for Pittsburgh, immediately started yelling. Klem drew his famous line. Lopez jumped across it and Klem threw him out of the game. MacFayden came running in, crossed the line, and was ejected. Frankie Frisch, the Pirate manager, came racing toward Klem, crossed the line, and found himself tossed, too. Well, when things calmed down Bill Baker came in to replace Lopez behind the plate, and Pirate reliever Bob Klinger was taking his warmup tosses when Bill Klem sidled up to me and whispered very softly, so nobody else could hear him, "How in the hell could you take such a beautiful pitch?"

—Bobby Bragan with Jeff Guinn, You Can't Hit the Ball

With the Bat on Your Shoulder:
The Baseball Life and Times of
Bobby Bragan *(Summit Group,
1992)*

*✎ When's the last time you saw a
rule book on the field?*

Scrappy infielder Ivy Olson loved
nothing better than a good
argument with an umpire—and
to prove his point in disputes, he
always lugged a rule book in his
back pocket.

Ivy made umpires break out in
a rash. At the screaming height of
a squabble, he'd yank out his book
and start flipping through the
pages with an exaggerated
flourish. But Ivy rarely had time to
find the appropriate rule before the
apoplectic ump thumbed him out of
the game.

Ivy, whom arbiters nicknamed
"Ivan the Terrible," carried his
trusty rule book in every game for
fourteen years.
—Bruce Nash and Allan Zullo,
The Baseball Hall of Shame's
Warped Record Book *(Pocket
Books, 1991)*

Things were different in those days, and physical confrontations between uniformed personnel and umpires were not particularly uncommon. In 1915, Tener suspended Reds manager Buck Herzog for five days as a result of Herzog's "fisticuffs" with Rigler.[3]

It wasn't the last time Rigler would be fined. In a 1934 game, Cardinals manager Frankie Frisch, upset when Rigler called Joe Medwick out at the plate in the twelfth inning, grabbed Rigler's arm. Rigler responded by swatting Frisch with his mask. Both men were fined $100 (which, this being in the middle of the Depression, still was a considerable sum). Looking at Rigler's career record, though, it's clear that he was never suspended for a considerable number of games

Shortly after Rigler died of a brain tumor, *The Sporting News* editorialized, "He was an easy man to love and he loved everyone else. Buff, hearty and even tempered, he bubbled with good nature and good stories. . . . Like the proverbial Santa Claus of this Yuletide season, his belly shook with mirth as he related his yarns and anecdotes, stories on himself, fellow members of his craft and ball players with whom he came into contact."[4]

HAL CHASE TRIES TO THROW ONE . . .

Clark Griffith recently recalled to Shirley Povich a vivid incident in the Chase career. Said the Old Fox: "Chase and a couple of other players were betting against their own team, the Reds, and were all ready to collect in the ninth inning, with the Braves having a 2–0 lead. Chase was first up for Cincinnati in the ninth and struck out. The next batter, who was in the fix, laid down a bunt, expecting to be thrown out, but was safe when the pitcher threw wild to first. They had three hitters in a row trying to throw the game and the third of these hit a grounder to the Boston shortstop, who also made a wild peg, and the Reds had two on.

"A bit later a Cincinnati batter, who wasn't betting on the game, knocked a three-run homer and won it for the Reds. There's no sure way to fix a ball game."

—Arthur Daley in *The New York Times* (May 29, 1947)

Hal Chase, baseball's top non–Black Sox crook, played for the Reds from 1916 through 1918. Some of the details here are fairly easy to check: Reds beat the Braves 3–2 on a three-run homer in the ninth. We can find the scores in Retrosheet, and the Reds didn't hit many homers in those seasons: only fourteen in 1916, twenty-six in 1917, and fifteen in 1918. And of those fifty-five home runs, Chase himself hit ten. Which leaves only forty-five homers among his teammates. If we find that one of those home runs was a game-winner against the Braves, we've got our story. Of course, usually it's not nearly so easy.

We'll start with 1916. Chase hit four of the Reds' fourteen homers that season, which leaves only ten to check. Of those ten—and my source here is SABR's Home Run Log, available only to members—only two came against the Braves, and one of *those* was hit by Chase (on September 20). Which leaves only one home run, hit by outfielder Red Killefer. It was just the third homer—and the last—of Killefer's career. It came on May 18 in Cincinnati, in a game the Reds won. The score? 3–2.

So every detail checks out, so far. This is the game, right?

Not so fast there, pardner. Here's the short summary in the *Times* the next day:

> CINCINNATI, Ohio. May 18.—Cincinnati broke its long losing streak here today by defeating Boston, 3 to 2. The visitors took the lead in the first inning, when Evers was passed and scored on singles by Collins and Konetchy. In the fourth inning Herzog was given a base on balls and Killifer sent the ball into the right field fence for a home run. Boston tied it up in the fifth, then Cincinnati put the winning tally over the plate in the seventh.

So now every detail doesn't check out. Or rather, *each* detail doesn't check out. Killefer's home run comes in the fourth inning and (according to the line score accompanying the recap) gives the Reds a 2–1 lead. The Bostons pick up the equalizer in the fifth, but the Cincinnatis go ahead for good in the seventh. Also, the only error in the game was made by Boston first baseman Ed Konetchy; no pitcher from either side erred in the contest.

All of which leaves us where? Right: off to check 1917, and then perhaps 1918.

Unfortunately, the Reds and Braves didn't play a single 3–2 game in either season. Where does that leave us? Well, we could check every game in which the Reds beat the Braves, looking for late home runs. Or we could check every 3–2 game the Reds played in those three seasons.

Those are half-measures, though. Seems to me there's only one way to proceed: make a list of all forty-five non-Chase homers in those three seasons, then see if any of them reasonably match the circumstances described in the story.

Well, we—Jason Brannon and I—checked all forty-five home runs, and we found only five candidates. The No. 1 candidate? It came in the first game of a doubleheader in Boston on July 25, 1918. Given the date, I found a great deal of information about this game in Martin Donell Kohout's biography of Chase. As it turns out, the obvious villain in this *particular* game is not Chase, but *another* crooked Red, second baseman Lee Magee. In the bottom of the ninth, with the Reds leading the Braves 2 to 1, Magee had a chance to end the game with a routine play. Instead he threw toward the wrong base, and wildly, which allowed the tying run to score.

The game was still tied after twelve innings. In the top of the thirteenth, Magee hit an easy grounder to shortstop Johnny Rawlings, but the ball took a bad hop and broke Rawlings's nose, with Magee safe at first. Boston's center fielder came in to play shortstop, and a Boston pitcher took over in center; left field already was manned by a pitcher (the rosters weren't nearly as large then as they would become in later years).

Next up was Edd Roush, and he shot a long drive into left-center field, sending the two pitcher-outfielders in desperate chase. According to Kohout, "Magee circled the bases so slowly that Roush, hard on his heels, reportedly shouted, 'Run, you son of a bitch!' and barely beat the throw home for a two-run, inside-the-park home run. The Reds now led 4–2."[1]

That was the final score. You'll notice that a great number of details don't match the story in Daley's column—for one thing, the many accounts of this incident name only two conspirators, Chase and Magee—but this almost certainly is the game in question. Especially considering what happened next. Over the next few games, Magee flubbed a few more plays in the field. And things came to a head on the 5th of August in Brooklyn. When Magee threw the ball over outfielder Greasy Neale's head in pre-game practice, Neale went after Magee. Under the headline "Magee and Neale Put on Fist Fight," the following item appeared in the *Times*:

> The fans who daily straggle into Ebbets Field for batting practice had their patience rewarded yesterday by Lee Magee and Earl Neale. Lee and Earl engaged in a hurricane bout shortly before game time in front of the Cincinnati dugout. Though there was a question as to the methods he employed, the popular verdict went to Neale.
>
> The Neale-Magee added attraction, while it did not last long, produced more action than was seen in a number of ten-round bouts at local clubs during the Frawley law regime. The reason for the combat went unexplained. The players were practically all out on the diamond throwing the ball around when Neale and Magee lit into each other. For a space there was a lively scrimmage, and the combatants separated and charged at each other again.
>
> Magee was met with a left uppercut as he neared Neale and the Redleg second baseman went down, slightly stunned. He arose and then players separated the fighters. The intermission was short-lived, however, for suddenly Neale started thumping the second baseman again. Once again Magee hit the ground and Neale piled on top of him, pummeling the former until a cordon of players pried him away, and then the battle was over.
>
> Magee's face as he arose was smeared with blood and his left eye was said to be swollen. Neale didn't have a scratch, but only played three innings.[2]

Two days later, Reds manager Christy Mathewson suspended Chase. Meanwhile, Magee spent a few days on the bench, but finished out the season with the club. The following spring, the Reds sold him to the Dodgers. With Magee and Chase gone, the Reds would win the National League pennant, then beat the Black Sox in the crooked World Series that fall. Prior to the 1920 season, Magee—then property of the Cubs—admitted to the National League president John Heydler and Cubs owner William Veeck that he'd tried to throw that game against the Braves in 1918. Magee apparently thought his admission would result in a clean slate, but instead it got him released. Chase had already unofficially been blacklisted from Organized Baseball, and neither of them played again.

JOHN MCGRAW & "BUCK LAI"

Clark Griffith needn't think he's pulling something new when he introduces a Chinese into the American League this year. Twenty years ago, John McGraw unveiled a Chinese utility infielder named Buck Lai, who broke into a few games for the Giants.

—Eddie Brietz in *The New York World-Telegram* (reprinted in *Baseball Digest*, March 1945)

There's an awful lot about baseball I don't know. I don't know one percent of one percent of what there is to know about baseball. Actually, I don't know one percent of one percent of one percent. Nevertheless, I've read a lot of books and a lot of well-researched articles over the years, and when I came across this item, my reaction was "Really? There was a Chinese ballplayer? That would have been a big story, right? Wouldn't I have read about that? Wouldn't somebody have mentioned Buck Lai at a SABR convention, at some point?"

Anyway, after that reaction I did the obvious thing: I looked up *Buck Lai*—or rather, just *Lai*—on baseball-reference.com.

Nothing.

Next, I looked up the list of countries in which major leaguers have been born, to see if there's ever been a Chinese-born major leaguer.

Nothing again.

I almost gave up then. But instead I looked up *Lai*

in the Professional Baseball Player Database (PBPD), a CD-ROM that lists every player in Organized Baseball—majors and minors—since 1922 (there might actually be a more recent version that goes back farther, but that's the one I've got).

Bingo.

Somebody named Bill Lai played for Jersey City in 1928 and batted .188. The PBPD lists batting average, home runs, and runs batted in for each player in each season, but Lai didn't show up with any homers or RBI. Just that batting average. What this means, usually, is that he didn't play enough that season to get a full statistical line in the baseball guides; that instead he garnered just a short summary in a section of little-used players.

Which in this case was the International League.

When I think of Jersey City, I think of the Jersey City Giants, a New York Giants farm club, which immediately suggests that Lai was indeed property of the Giants. However, a quick check of the book

Professional Baseball Franchises: From the Abbeville Indians to the Zanesville Indians reveals that in 1928 they were the Jersey City Skeeters and had been the Skeeters since 1918. The franchise disbanded in 1933. Jersey City was without a team for four years, and then the Jersey City Giants were born in 1937. Further, according to *The Encyclopedia of Minor League Baseball*, the Skeeters weren't officially tied to any major-league team until 1932, when they began a one-year relationship with not the Giants, but the hated Dodgers.

Okay. I'm sure that's more than you really wanted to know about the history of Jersey City baseball. But I needed to know it. And now, back to the International League. I expected to find Bill Lai batting .188 in my 1929 *Reach Official Base Ball Guide*. I didn't find Bill Lai at all. Not batting .188 or doing anything else. The guide lists only players with at least ten games. And I'm guessing that Lai, if he did play for the Skeeters, went 1 for 8 or 2 for 16 in fewer than ten games.

Next stop: *The New York Times*. The archives are searchable.

Bingo.

In the March 14, 1928, edition, a report from spring training by Richards Vidmer noted that the Giants had just spent a weekend away from camp, playing minor-league clubs. When they returned to Augusta, Georgia, their spring home, McGraw seemingly knew everything his players had done, even though he'd not accompanied them to St. Augustine and Jacksonville. Meanwhile, in the Giants' absence some things had happened in Augusta: "Clarke Barnes had been operated on for appendicitis, Edd Roush had reported and Buck Lai, the Chinaman who never had a Chinaman's chance, had been sent to Little Rock."

I'd searched for *Bill* Lai, but apparently he really was *Buck*, at least in the *Times*. So I searched again, this time for *Lai + Giants*. I checked four years: January 1, 1926, through December 31, 1929. I got eight hits, all from the spring of 1928: the note above, and seven others . . .

Lai's story with the Giants apparently began in 1928, on the 9th of January:

> The Giants, having exhausted all the resources of these United States, went out yesterday and signed a Chinese infielder, William T. Lai by name, who will report for examination at the Southern training camp in Augusta, Ga., in the Spring. Lai has had quite a number of years of experience as a professional ball player. For four years he was with the Bridgeport Club of the Eastern League. Later he drifted to Brooklyn and became a member of the semi-pro Bushwicks, where he made such a reputation that John J. McGraw signed him. Lai can play all the in-

field positions and may prove to be a useful utility infielder for the Giants.[1]

March 1: Lai among a list of players present in the Giants' spring camp.

March 4: "Buck Lai, the Chinaman, showed that he can field with the best of them, but his only claim to hitting prowess is his own assertion that he was the second-best batter on the Bushwicks."

March 14: Lai sold to Little Rock, as mentioned above.

March 15: "Buck Lai, the Chinaman, hasn't been sold to Little Rock at all. McGraw only thought he had sent him to that club. 'I'll go in the laundry business instead,' Buck declared, refusing to leave the Giants." (We can guess that this quote might have been the invention of a typically insensitive sportswriter.)

April 13: "Secretary Frank Donnelly of the Jersey City International League Club announced last night through The Associated Press that Buck Lai, Chinese infielder, had been obtained from the New York Giants on option.

"Lai joined Bridgeport in 1918 after coming to this country with a touring team of Chinese ball players from Hawaii. He remained in the Eastern League until 1921. Since then he has played with various independent teams before signing with the Giants this Spring. Jersey City plans to carry Lai as an extra infielder."

April 15: In a Sunday Special Feature about ex-collegians in the majors, Lai was listed in passing as a product of the University of Hawaii.

April 16: "Buck Lai, the Chinese player recently turned over to the Skeeters by the Giants, broke into the game for Jersey City in a most auspicious manner. He filled in cleverly at short, but it was at bat where he impressed most favorably, and he was responsible for three of the Jersey City tallies."

According to the record books, he played in only four games with Jersey City, after which we lose track of him. Or rather, the *Times* lost track of him, which for the moment is the same thing, and we don't find him again until 1944. Reporting from a Giants-Phillies doubleheader in Philadelphia, James

P. Dawson mentioned this: "Buck Lai, only Chinese member of the club in Giant history, was a visitor. Lai played third under the late John J. McGraw."

Frankly, I don't have any idea what came next, except that William "Buck" Lai's son—William "Buck" Lai Jr.—became a legend at Long Island University, as basketball coach, baseball coach, and athletics director for many years. He also worked as a scout for the Dodgers and authored a book, *Championship Baseball: From Little League to Big League*. The book, published in 1954, includes Lai Jr.'s line drawings, and the dust jacket includes this author bio:

> "Buck" Lai received his own early sports education from his father, a former New York Giant third baseman, and then went on to become an outstanding athlete at L. I. U., where he paced the Blackbirds to the Metropolitan baseball championship in 1940
>
> In 1950 he was named faculty manager of athletics, serving as assistant varsity basketball coach, instructor of physical education, and varsity baseball coach. He was appointed to his present post as Director of Athletics in February 1952, succeeding Clair Bee.[2]

Still so little about Jr.'s dad, though. Now, some of you are probably wondering why I didn't just Google the elder Buck. I did. But most of the results for *Buck Lai* and *William Lai* were about the younger Buck. One of those identified Jr. as "the son of . . . the first Chinese major league baseball player." Which wasn't exactly helpful.

I also ran across a note from a woman identifying herself as Sr.'s greatniece. But she seemed to be looking for nearly as many solid facts as I was. Fortunately, I found one more note, this one by someone named Bob Timmermann. According to Timmermann, in 1928 Lai was described as "Chinese-Hawaiian" and "had been signed by the Pirates in 1918 but never appeared in a game."

Well, that's interesting. But I'm doing my best to track down sources. Fortunately, Bob Timmermann is a friend, a fellow SABR member. And Bob pointed me to a 2001 article in the San Francisco newspaper, *AsianWeek*, written by Keoni Everington.

Therein, we learn that William Tin "Buck" Lai was born in 1895 in Honolulu, the son of Chinese immigrants. Buck learned to play baseball on the Honolulu sandlots, and set a long-lasting high school record in the long jump. When Buck was seventeen, he earned a spot on the Hawaiian Chinese University Nine, a local baseball team that spent much of each year traveling around the United States. While playing in New York, Buck met a Brooklyn girl named Isabel Reynolds; they later married and had two chil-

🦅 *Speaking of major leaguers who weren't (or if you prefer, non-major leaguers who were), consider this from Bill Sharman's Wikipedia entry:*

From 1950 to 1955, Sharman played professional baseball in the Brooklyn Dodgers' minor league system. He was called up to the Dodgers late in the 1951 season but did not appear in a game; as a result of a September 27 game in which the entire Brooklyn bench was ejected from the game for arguing with the umpire, Sharman holds the distinction of being the only player to have ever been ejected from a major league game without ever appearing in one.

I read about this somewhere many years ago, but the story does not appear in any of the many, many books about the Dodgers I've checked. There was an incident on the 27th of September. In the eighth inning of a big game against the Braves, with the score 3 to 3, a Boston runner was called safe at the plate by umpire Frank Dascoli. Catcher Roy Campanella, who apparently threw his mask or glove (reports differ) in the air, was immediately ejected. Dodgers coach Cookie Lavagetto got the heave-ho, too; some sources say it was the first of his career (he'd reached the majors as a player in 1934). Two outs later, having heard a great deal of abuse from the Dodger dugout, Dascoli, according to the Times, *"suddenly wheeled and ordered the Brooklyn bench cleared. Jocko Conlan, second-base arbiter, went to the bench and*

dren (including young William). Buck settled in Audubon, New Jersey, worked for the Pennsylvania Railroad, and played semi-pro ball in his spare time.

According to Everington,

> In 1918, Buck was signed on to participate in spring training with the Philadelphia Phillies under manager Jack Coombs, who was quoted as telling him: "I am doing a lot of experimenting and your chances are as good as anyone else's." However, it was decided that he needed more experience and was sent to a farm team in Bridgeport, Conn.*
>
> He was a sensation in what was known as the Eastern League until he developed a chronic hand injury. After a brief retirement, he returned to spend the next several years playing for one of the best and highest paying semi-pro, white teams in the United States, the New York Bushwicks. The team had the distinction of being one of first teams to own their own portable lights to enable them to play night baseball games at any venue, which were played four times a week.
>
> Late in the season, after the major league World Series, they would play teams consisting of major league players that would barnstorm around the country such as Babe Ruth's Bustin' Babes and Lou Gehrig's Larrupin Lous. It was at this time that he posed for photographs with Babe Ruth and Lou Gehrig. The picture with the Babe is personally autographed by the Sultan of Swat himself.[3]

In 1935, Lai returned to Hawaii and created his own traveling team. He continued to play for a few years, then "retired" in 1939 or '40; "he had played in forty-four states, Cuba, Mexico and Canada." Everington doesn't have much to say about the rest of Lai's life, except that he "took great pride in his health and maintained a strict exercise regimen well into his 80s. He continued to strive to spread the sport of baseball in the community until he passed away in 1978, at the age of 83."

Let us return to our original question. Was Buck Lai a Giant? Well, no. Not as we typically answer that question. But then, there's more to being a Giant—or a Yankee, or a Marlin, or anything else—than playing in an official game, right? In those days, there wasn't the distinction between "regular season" and everything else, as there is now. In those days, teams barnstormed, in late March and early April, from their training site to wherever they were playing on Opening Day. There were exhibition games, too, on

---

* **Late note**: Among Lai's Bridgeport teammates in 1918 was one "Andy Yim," a Japanese-American whose actual surname was Yamashiro. I only wish I'd come across this information early enough to get a photo of them together.

off-days during the regular season. A lot of people saw these games, and a lot of them never got another chance to see the big leaguers. So those games were, to a lot of people, important. In those days, it was not uncommon for a player to be considered a Giant—or a Yankee, or an Indian, or whatever—if he'd worn the uniform, regardless of when and where he'd worn it. Too, in those days teams could carry as many players as they liked on the active roster until the middle of May. Lai wasn't acquired by Jersey City until April 13; perhaps the evening of the 13th. The Giants had played a game on the 11th, and another on the afternoon of the 13th. I can't prove this, but it's quite possible that Lai was in uniform for one or both of those games, and available to McGraw.

If so, then wasn't he a Giant in most of the ways that matter? For those three days, he was just as much as Giant as anybody else on the roster.

Postcript: Here—for the first time, as far as I know—is Buck Lai's career in Organized Baseball (his statistics with the Bushwicks merely await a few hundred hours of work with microfilm of the Brooklyn newspapers):

	League	Team	Pos.	Games	At-Bats	Hits	Avg
1918	Eastern	Bridgeport	?	55	188	55	.293
1919	Eastern	Bridgeport	3B	107	407	106	.260
1920	Eastern	Bridgeport	?	118	441	117	.265
1921	Eastern	Bridgeport	OF/3B	73	275	63	.229
1928	National	New York	–	0	0	0	–
1928	I'national	Jersey City	?	4	?	?	.188

herded the players out. The boys took their time, many of them pausing en route to pay their compliments to Dascoli."

However, according to Lee Heiman and Bill Gutman in their book about the 1951 pennant race, "The players weren't banished, just removed from the dugout so some semblance of order could be restored." Which sounds strange but must be true, because in the ninth inning Brooklyn's Wayne Terwilliger—presumably among those removed from the dugout—entered the game as a pinch hitter.

So it seems the story is not true. Sharman was removed, not ejected. Though we might assume he's still got that particular distinction to himself.

JIMMIE REESE & JEWISH YANKEES

Until I made my major league debut in 1969, the only Jewish player to ever don the pinstripes was Jimmie Reese, a utility infielder who once roomed with Ruth. Reese had hidden his Jewish identity by changing his name, which was really James Herman Solomon.

Reese was not above sharing his true religious background on one occasion, however. He had such great success against a pitcher that the catcher that day asked him point blank if he knew what pitches were coming. The pitcher and catcher, both also Jewish, had been communicating their signals verbally in Yiddish. Jimmie looked down at the catcher and said, "I'll tell you a secret. My real name is Hymie Solomon."

—Ron Blomberg in *Designated Hebrew: The Ron Blomberg Story*
(as told to Dan Schlossberg, 2006)

This one doesn't seem even remotely likely, does it? I think we might dispense of it quickly. Reese played in the majors during three seasons: 1930 and '31 with the Yankees, 1932 with the Cardinals. I piled every pre-1970 Jewish major leaguer into an Excel file, and would you like to guess how many Jewish catchers were active during Reese's brief career?

One: Moe Berg, whose career began in 1923 and ended in 1939.

Would you like to guess how many Jewish pitchers were active during Reese's brief career?

One: Izzy Goldstein, whose career consisted of sixteen games in 1932.

Both Berg and Goldstein were in the American League at the same time, but they were not teammates, and anyway, by then Reese was a National Leaguer. So on the off-chance this did happen, it happened in the minor leagues, or perhaps in an exhibition game. Sure enough, in the middle of my re-

search I happened to pick up *The Big Book of Jewish Baseball* and found the following passage:

One of the greatest baseball enthusiasts of all time was Jewish songwriter Harry Ruby, whose songs include "Babyface" and "Who's Sorry Now?" Ruby had grown up in the same neighborhood as Al Schacht and the two men were friends from childhood. They often played ball together, and Ruby continued to fancy himself as a pitcher well into his later years. Red Smith called Ruby the "world's greatest baseball fan." Sometime during the mid-1920s, Ruby was pitching in an exhibition game with a mixed team of celebrities and players of the Pacific Coast League. Ruby's catcher was Ike Danning, and the two men decided, instead of using signals, because no one else on the field appeared to be Jewish, to simply indicate their choice of pitches in Yiddish. Jimmie Reese got 4 hits for 4 at-bats. After the game, Ruby, who followed the doings of the Pacific Coast League very closely, complimented Jimmie, but told him he was surprised—as he wasn't aware that Jimmie was such a good hitter. "I guess you also don't know," replied Jimmie, "that my name used to be Hymie Solomon."[1]

This makes more sense, doesn't it? Instead of giving up his edge during the game, Reese waits until afterward. And of course the entire scenario seems more likely in a loosely played exhibition. Aside from his three years in the majors, Reese played in the Coast League from 1925 through 1938. Danning spent a bit of time in that league and also was a California native and presumably wintered there and would have been a likely suspect if somebody was recruiting players for an exhibition game.

I think there's something else in Blomberg's story of greater interest. Jimmie Reese really was born James Herman Solomon (or perhaps Soloman), and he really was Jewish. But was he really the first Jewish Yankee? And was Blomberg really the second?

Reese reached the majors in 1930, as a Yankee. According to *The Big Book of Jewish Baseball*, thirty-one Jews debuted in the major leagues before Reese. Granted, five of them played in the nineteenth century, before the American League and the Yankees even existed . . . but at least one of the other twenty-six must have played for the Yanks, right?

Right. In 1905, Phil Cooney—born Philip Clarence Cohen—got into one game with the New York club, then popularly known as the Highlanders (because they played in upper Manhattan's Hilltop Park). Considering Cooney's name change, it's quite possible that Reese never knew about him. Plus, it was just one game and the Highlanders weren't wearing pinstripes in those days.

But what about Guy Zinn? The Jewish outfielder debuted with the Yankees on September 11, 1911, and batted .148 in nine games that fall. And in 1912 the Yanks sported new uniforms. As *The New York Times* observed upon Opening Day, "The Yankees presented a natty appearance in their new uniforms of white with black pin stripes."* Zinn played 106 games with the Yanks that season.

So Jimmie Reese was the third Jewish player with the franchise, and the second "Yankee" to wear pinstripes.† Whether he knew it or not.

---

* For many years, it's been said the Yankees adopted pinstripes to make Babe Ruth look thin; or rather, less fat. But of course he didn't join the club until 1921. After adopting the pinstripes in 1912, the Yanks junked them for a couple of years, but they brought them back in 1915 and they've been a part of the home livery ever since.

† In addition to being the first Jew in pinstripes, Zinn later was the only known Jew to play in the Federal League.

🐟 *Tigers pitcher Harry Eisenstat told this one . . .*

Only once in my major league career did I ever intentionally try to hit a batter, and I was under orders to do so.

It was in 1938, right after Hitler had come to power in Germany. I was pitching against Chicago and heard a bench jockey yelling from the White Sox dugout, "Hey, Eisentat. Hitler is looking for you and Greenberg." At that time there were not many Jewish players in the major leagues.

Cochrane also heard what the guy was yelling and came out to the mound. He told me, "When that sonofabitch comes to the plate, if you don't hit him right between the eyes with your first pitch, you'll be on a bus to Toledo tomorrow. And if he starts to come out after you, I'll toss you the ball, and you hit him with it again."

So I did. I threw at him and he ducked, but the ball hit the peak of his cap. When he got to first base I saw Greenberg talking to the guy and pounding his finger on his chest. The minute the game ended Greenberg ran into the White Sox clubhouse, chasing the guy who'd been yelling at me, and had to be restrained by Jimmy Dykes, otherwise he'd have killed him.

—*Russell Schneider*, Tales from the Tribe Dugout *(Sports Publishing, 2002)*

Actually, Hitler was sworn in as Germany's Chancellor in 1933, and assumed the powers of head of state—Führer—in 1934. Which ☞

isn't to say that 1938 was not momentous for the Third Reich, which added Austria and the Sudetenland districts to its territory that year.

It was also a momentous year for Hank Greenberg, who entered the final week of the season with a real shot at breaking Babe Ruth's record of sixty home runs in one season. It didn't happen, in part because Greenberg was walked a number of times, and it's been suggested that the pitchers didn't want a Jewish player breaking the record. Eisenstat, though, would later say, "Frankly, I think the pitchers were just trying to get him out and they were trying to be too fine . . . I don't think they were deliberately walking him."

In Greenberg's autobiography he doesn't mention the incident involving Eisenstat and the White Sox. He does write this: "Sure, there was added pressure being Jewish. How the hell could you get up to home plate every day and have some son of a bitch call you a Jew bastard and a kike and a sheenie and get on your ass without feeling the pressure."

And after Reese? He last played for the Yankees in 1931. Blomberg debuted with the Yanks on September 10, 1969. Were the Yankees really 100 percent Jew-free for thirty-eight years? Over that span, sixty-seven Jews (not including converts) debuted in the majors. At least one of them must have played for the Yanks, right?

Right. But only one. Only one, and for only a moment. Two moments, really.

Herb "Lefty" Karpel, who grew up in Brooklyn with Phil Rizzuto, made his major-league debut in the Yankees' 1946 home opener, having spent the previous three seasons in the U.S. Army, with whom he saw combat in Europe.

Karpel's first professional outing since 1942 was a good one, as he stopped a Washington rally in the eighth inning (in the ninth the Yankees scored twice to win). Karpel pitched again the next day, in front of another big crowd, but this time didn't fare so well, giving up a single, a double, and two triples while recording only four outs. He would never pitch another inning for the Yankees, or any other team in the majors. Karpel spent the rest of that season with Newark and went 14-8 with a 2.41 ERA, and he would later finish his professional career with four seasons in the Pacific Coast League.

It's not clear that the writers of the time knew that Karpel was Jewish. The Giants employed a fair number of Jewish players in the 1930s and '40s, and they got plenty of attention in the newspapers. But the *Times* didn't mention Karpel's religious background, nor did any of the other papers I checked. It was not uncommon then for Jews to keep quiet about their religion, but there certainly was not the same stigma in 1946 that there might have been twenty years earlier, as Hank Greenberg had long established himself as a superstar. And it's not as if the Yankees played in St. Louis or Chicago. When John McGraw managed the Giants, he'd searched far and wide for a Jewish star, in hopes of boosting attendance at the Polo Grounds. The closest he came was second baseman Andy Cohen, who lasted just a couple of seasons. But later on, catcher Harry Danning starred for the Giants in the late '30s, and in '41 Danning was joined on the roster by outfielder Morrie Arnovich.

Then again, the Yankees were not exactly the most liberal franchise in the sport, and they never had to worry much about attendance. So it's possible that Karpel just didn't talk about being Jewish (though according to my Jewish friends, with a name like Herbert Karpel, he wouldn't have needed to say anything at all).

DON DRYSDALE & WALT ALSTON

. . . But over the final days of the season one big caution flag had been raised. The series was scheduled to begin on October 6, the Jewish holiday of Yom Kippur. Koufax didn't wear his religion on his sleeve, but he wouldn't pitch on Yom Kippur. The decision made him a hero to many Jews, but scared other Dodger fans to death.

At first it didn't seem like a big deal. Drysdale had been untouchable down the stretch, and he would open the Series. What was more important was that the decision seemed to preclude Koufax pitching three times in the Series. . . .

After the pressure cooker of the pennant race, the Dodgers came out flat. Drysdale was routed in the second inning of game one when Zoilo Versalles, the AL MVP, cracked a three-run home run. Minnesota won going away, 8–2, leading Drysdale to quip to Alston, "I bet you wish I was Jewish too."

—*The Dodgers: 120 Years of Dodgers Baseball* (Glenn Stout and Richard A. Johnson, 2004)

It's a great line, and one that's been reprinted many times over the years, including in Jane Leavy's lauded 2002 biography of Koufax: "The score was 7–1 when Alston came to the mound to relieve him. 'Hey, skip, bet you wish I was Jewish today, too.'"[1]

Funny thing, though . . . We can identify three men who would have been on the mound to hear Drysdale say those words: Drysdale, manager Walter Alston, and catcher John Roseboro. All three of those men later composed their memoirs (Alston twice), and yet none of them happened to mentioned this seemingly memorable joke that Drysdale made.*

In Drysdale's autobiography, he devotes exactly one paragraph to the '65 World Series and doesn't mention this funny thing he supposedly said after getting knocked out of the biggest game (until then) of the year.[2]

Walter Alston's first autobiography was published in 1966, when the events of the previous October would have been quite fresh in his mind. Here's what he said about Game 1:

> When the Series opened on the following Wednesday, a well-rested Drysdale faced the Twins' Mudcat Grant, but it was the Mudcat's day all the way. I may have made a mistake by not letting Don work a few innings on the last Sunday of the year, when we'd already sewed up the pennant. With five days of idleness behind him, the big right-hander was anything but sharp and apparently was suffering from, of all things, too much rest. We lost, 8–2, in a game that, save for his Holy Day, Koufax would have started. In the press room that night, Lefty Gomez, the baseball

---

* I've found another variation, with the famously stoic Alston saying, "Why couldn't you be Jewish, too?"

comic, drew a hearty laugh with this quip: "I'll bet Alston was wishing today that Drysdale was Jewish."[3]

In Alston's later autobiography, published in 1976, he repeated his self-doubts about giving Drysdale five days off, but didn't mention Gomez's joke at all.[4]

In Roseboro's 1978 memoir—unfairly ignored, by the way, as it's more thoughtful and revealing than most such books—he devotes one short paragraph to Games 1 *and* 2 (the latter was started and lost by Koufax), and again there's nothing about Drysdale making a cute remark when yanked by Alston.[5]

Drysdale was forced to quit in 1969 because of arm problems, and he would later make a solid living as a broadcaster and ex-Dodger superstar. If you keep your nose clean and tell the right stories, both can be lucrative work, and Drysdale seems to have eventually adopted the story about Game 1 as one of his favorites. But a check of various newspaper archives doesn't find it attributed to Drysdale until the 1980s, usually in reference to Sandy Koufax and the status of the Jewish ballplayer.

After Drysdale died a surprisingly early death in 1993, Ira Berkow wrote in the *Times*:

> A few years ago he told me this story: Drysdale started Game 1 for the Dodgers in the 1965 World Series against Minnesota. Koufax had originally been scheduled to pitch but the game fell on Yom Kippur, the Jewish high holiday, and Koufax sat out the game in deference to his religion. The Twins scored one run off Drysdale in the second inning and six runs off him in the third and there were still only two outs when Walter Alston came out of the dugout to remove Drysdale. As the manager approached the mound, Drysdale said: "I know, Skip. You're wishing I was a Jew."[6]

Jim Murray, writing in the *Los Angeles Times* a day later, also referenced the line, in slightly different form: "I bet you wish I was the one who was Jewish."[7]

Either way it's a wonderful line, and one can hardly blame Drysdale for taking it for himself. After a while, he might even have believed it.

JOE TAYLOR & CHARLIE METRO

Joe Taylor was a great Triple-A ballplayer. He could do it all. He had a cup of coffee in the big leagues, but he really should have had a career in the majors.

Anyway, one day in 1959 when Joe and I were on the Vancouver club in the PCL, Joe came to the ballpark drunk. We tried to sober him up by getting him to drink a lot of coffee and juice, but that didn't help a whole lot, so when the game started Joe was not in the lineup.

When the ninth inning rolled around, we were trailing 2 to 1, but we had the tying and winning runs on base with two outs. Joe was feeling better at that point, and he started pestering our manager, Charlie Metro, to let him pinch hit. "Come on, Charlie. Put me in, and I'll break this thing wide open."

Metro pinch hit him, and Joe struck out on three pitches. Three fastballs right down the middle, and Joe didn't even take the bat off his shoulder.

Of course, Metro was pissed. And as he started walking down the concrete corridor to our locker room, Joe came up behind him and said, "Charlie, you dumb ass . . . You knew I was drunk. Why'd you put me in?"

—Dick Fitzgerald in *Tales from the Ballpark: More of the Greatest True Baseball Stories Ever Told* (Mike Shannon, 1999)

Taylor and Fitzgerald played together with Vancouver in 1959. Taylor certainly was a good Triple-A ballplayer, but "great" probably is a stretch. In 110 games that season, he batted .292 with twenty-four homers, which would have been more impressive if he hadn't been thirty-three. Taylor did enjoy other fine AAA seasons. In 1954, Taylor batted .323 with twenty-three homers in the International League. But looking at his playing record—in SABR's *Minor League Baseball Stars Volume III*—what's most striking is that Taylor didn't play his first game in Organized Baseball until 1951, when he was twenty-five.

That got me to wondering. So I did what I could probably have done in the first place: look for references to Taylor in Charlie Metro's autobiography. The first thing I found was this: "Vancouver was the first club on which I had black ballplayers. I eventually had Joe Taylor, Joe Durham, Charlie White, Charlie Beamon, Lenny Green, and Connie Johnson. They stayed in our hotel. Wherever we went—Sacramento, San Diego, Phoenix—they stayed right with us."[1]

So that's a clue. My next stop: Jim Riley's *Biographical Encyclopedia of the Negro Baseball Leagues*, where I discovered that Taylor really got his professional start as a catcher with the Chicago American Giants in 1949. According to Riley, "At that time the Negro American League was struggling to survive the loss of players to organized baseball, and during the

Bill Giles, who worked for the Houston club in the early '60s, tells this one about Colt .45's pitcher Turk Farrell.

Turk Farrell—our resident snake-shooter—was one of my favorties. He drank about as much as Jim Owens but didn't throw as many punches. He was a big, fun-loving guy with a huge heart, but he did like his booze, women, and staying up late—often at the same time. One Saturday night in Philadelphia, I returned to the Warwick Hotel around 2:00 AM to find Farrell coming out of the elevator all dressed up and heading out.

"Turk, don't you have to pitch tomorrow afternoon at 1:00 PM?" I asked.

"Yes."

"Shouldn't you be in bed?"

He shook his head. "Come with me, and I will show you the after-hours spots of Philadelphia."

He took me to Sinatrarama, where they played Sinatra records all night, and then to the CR Club, which was rumored to be Mafia connected. We got back to the hotel at 6:00 AM, got up at 9:00 AM, and Turk pitched a four-hitter, winning 4–1.

—Bill Giles and Doug Myers, Pouring Six Beers at a Time: And Other Stories from a Lifetime in Baseball (2007)

Farrell was an original Houston Colt .45 and won more games (52) than anybody else on the team during the franchise's first five seasons, mostly as a starter. In 1967, he pitched out of the bullpen for the season's first few weeks, then

1950 season he became one of the defectors, playing with Winnipeg in the Mandak League and batting .237 in 34 games."[2]

But I still don't know why Taylor got such a late start. In 1949, he'd have been twenty-three, which obviously is an advanced age for a professional debut. Next stop: Larry Moffi and Jonathan Kronstadt's *Crossing the Line: Black Major Leaguers, 1947–1959*, which includes an entry for every black player in those years. Those guys—Moffi and Kronstadt, I mean—don't really solve this little mystery, but they do offer this nugget by way of introduction: "Joe Taylor's baseball career was launched by a sportswriter. Writing for the Pittsburgh *Courier*, Earl Johnson covered Taylor's exploits as a sandlot catcher in the Pittsburgh area. Johnson's articles and personal encouragement helped Taylor gain the confidence to pursue a career in baseball."[3]

Getting back to our story, here's the second (and last) reference to Taylor in Charlie Metro's book:

> Speaking of players performing under the influence of too many spirits, I recall another episode at Vancouver. Joe Taylor showed up one game having had a bit too much. Late in the game, a close one, I needed a pinch hitter. Joe volunteered. I had my doubts, but he kept at me until I let him go up to the plate. "I can do it, Charlie. I can do it," he kept saying. Well, he went up to the plate and took three quick strikes. Never even lifted his bat off his shoulder. After the game, he came up to me and chewed me out. "Charlie, you shouldn't have sent me out there. You know how drunk I was," he said.

Metro's recollection so closely mirrors Fitzgerald's that one can't help but wonder if one is somehow a source for the other. Hard to figure how, though. Especially considering this: according to the box scores, Joe Taylor did not enter a game as a pinch hitter in 1959. Not while he was with Vancouver.

According to *The Official Baseball Guide*—and the final standings published in the newspapers—the Vancouver Mounties played 151 games that season. According to the same source, Joe Taylor played in 110 games; he didn't play from June 16 through July 26 because he was in the majors with the Orioles.

Well, we (me, with a lot of help from Calvin Bohn) started on Opening Day and, going through the microfilm, found box scores for all 151 games the Mounties played, and we found Taylor in 110 of those box scores. According to those 110 box scores, Taylor started every game that he played. He did not, according to the box scores, pinch-hit in one Pacific Coast League game in 1959.

In 1957, Taylor played for the Seattle Rainiers. According to Moffi and Kronstadt, Taylor hit three homers in the Rainiers' home opener, and afterward manager Lefty O'Doul said, "When Taylor is right, he is definitely a major league hitter."

Taylor did play for four major-league teams, hitting nine homers in 297 at-bats. He could hit. But it seems he wasn't often enough right, and Fitzgerald's/Metro's anecdote would seem to be one piece of evidence for that. But like so many stories in this book that are supposed to help explain something, we wind up with more questions than when we started.

was sold to the Phillies. So we've got five years to check, 1962 through '66.

In those five years, Farrell started ten games in Philadelphia. But only two of those starts were afternoon games, and Farrell lost one of those games in the bottom of the ninth. Which leaves only one possibility, and it's a reasonable match: On the afternoon of May 5, 1963, Farrell beat the Phillies 6–2 with a complete-game seven-hitter. It wasn't a four-hitter and he didn't win 4–1.

But Farrell did pitch a four-hitter in Philadelphia. It was a night game, not a day game, and the score was 4–2, which isn't 4–1 but you can't get much closer. And that game was also in 1963, on September 11. It seems highly likely that Giles has simply combined—unwittingly or otherwise—these two 1963 games in his mind, which does make for a slightly better story.

JOE FOY & GIL HODGES

Joe Foy was from the Bronx, so now he was back in town with his old cronies, and pretty soon he started walking down the wrong sidewalk again.

We saw it gradually coming on. I remember a doubleheader in New York. The first game Hodges didn't play Foy, and you could tell in the dugout he was high on something. One thing you didn't do was walk in front of Gil Hodges during a pitch. Foy not only walked in front of him, he stood in front of him, cheering. We could see right away this was a no-no. Here was a disaster about to happen. We could see he really wasn't in his right mind.

Well, Gil put him in to play third base for the second game. And we knew he wasn't capable of playing that day. I remember the first batter hit a hard ground ball by Foy, and after the ball went by him, he was still patting his glove and saying, "Hit it to me. Hit it to me." He never even saw it.

We were looking at each other and saying, "Oh, my God, you gotta get him out of there." But Gil left him in a little longer just to let everyone see that he didn't fit on that ball club.

And it was not long after that that Joe was gone.

—Jerry Koosman in *Amazin': The Miraculous Story of New York's Most Beloved Baseball Team* (Peter Golenbock, 2002)

This story supposedly goes some way toward explaining why third baseman Joe Foy—traded to the Mets for Amos Otis, by the Royals—failed so miserably in New York after coming over prior to the 1970 season. And this one's easy to check, because Foy lasted for just one season with the Mets, after which he was left unprotected and claimed by the Washington Senators (who also quickly tired of Foy).

I certainly *hope* this story is true . . . because in my last book I reprinted it without even a cursory check to see if it actually happened. But thanks to the urging of a skeptical (though forgiving) reader, I will do that now.

As we've seen, Koosman remembered a double-header in which Foy didn't play the opener but did play the nightcap. But that's about all we "know," right? When Koosman says the hard ground ball "went by" Foy, we don't know if an error was charged, or if he simply didn't make a move to field the ball (in which case an error would probably not have been levied). Similarly, when Koosman says Hodges left Foy "in a little longer," we don't know if he means Hodges left Foy in that game a little longer, or in the lineup a little longer. And when Koosman says, "It was not long after that that Joe was gone," it's not readily apparent what that first *that* refers to.

Let's start with the doubleheader, though.

In 1970 the Mets played eight doubleheaders at home (and five away). In two of those eight home doubleheaders, Foy did sit during the first game and play third base in the second game. Both twin bills were in September: the 7th against the Expos, the 9th against the Phillies. And that game on the 7th might just be the one we're looking for. Foy did not get charged with an error, but he didn't field any ground balls, either (so he might have waved at one). At the plate, he went 0 for 3 with a strikeout. And after the seventh inning, with the Mets leading 5–1 and Foy due to lead off the bottom of the eighth, Hodges lifted Foy in favor of Ken Boswell (who went to second base, with Wayne Garrett shifting from second to third).

Two nights later, Foy again started in the second game of the twin bill, and this time he did make a couple of plays on ground balls (and also walked twice before being lifted for a pinch hitter in the eighth). But that was just about it. Foy, who'd more or less been the regular third baseman throughout the season, started only three of the Mets' last twenty games. And those twenty games seemed, at that time, mighty important. The Mets won that second game on the 9th, thus pulling into a first-place tie in the National League East with the Pirates (and the Cubs were just one game behind). So when Hodges essentially yanked Foy from the lineup, he presumably was doing it because he thought that gave his club the best chance to win the division title.

The Mets didn't win. They lost twelve of their last twenty games and finished six games behind the division-winning Pirates. After the season, Jack Lang, writing in *The Sporting News*, summed up Foy's season with the Mets:

> To say that Joe was a major disappointment would be putting it mildly. He was much more than that. He was a complete puzzle to all who came in contact with him. A happy-go-lucky fellow, his exuberance at times raised eyebrows and brought whispers from teammates as well as rival players.
>
> Ugly rumors began to circulate. When Manager Gil Hodges was questioned about them, he issued a quick denial. Still the rumors persisted and the more they did, the less Foy played.
>
> In fact, once when he was scheduled to play—on September 12—Foy's name was a late scratch from the starting lineup. The official announcement was that Foy had a "pulled muscle." It's possible he pulled it rushing to get into uniform after arriving at the park long after his mates were out on the field.[1]

Nearly forty years later, we perhaps cannot know the exact nature of the "ugly rumors," but later there was talk of heavy marijuana use. At the time,

One could do a book just about Casey Stengel's Mets . . . What's that? Somebody's already done it? Oh, well, here's a Tracy Stallard story to whet the appetite . . .

In a game the following year, again at the Polo Grounds, I was pitching against the Phillies. This was the year before they were going to raze the Polo Grounds because Shea Stadium would be ready for the 1965 season. The first two times Johnny Callison came up, he hit two rifles into the upper deck down the right-field line. They were both smoked, and you could hear the balls rattling and bouncing around in the seats. After the second one, Casey came out to the mound and said, "Hey, young fella, how you doin'?"

"Okay, I guess," I said.

"Well, just keep on doin' that, and there'll be one section up there they won't have to tear down next year."

—*Tracy Stallard in* Tales from the Ballpark: More of the Greatest True Baseball Stories Ever Told *(Mike Shannon, 1999)*

Stallard is famous for giving up Roger Maris's sixty-first homer in 1961. He did not, however, give up two homers to Johnny Callison in 1964. Stallard pitched against Callison's Phillies six times that season, and in each game he allowed one home run. One of those was hit by Callison, at the Polo Grounds on June 21.

He just got the year wrong. On September 17, 1963, Callison took Stallard deep in the first inning, and then again in the third. Stengel did not yank Stallard immediately after the second home run, but two batters later he was gone.

there was talk that Foy, a native New Yorker, needed to get away from his hometown and his old friends. He did get away in '71, but got into only forty-one games with the Ted Williams–managed Washington Senators before being sent to their farm club in Denver. After just a few weeks there he drew his release and never played professionally again. When he was forty-six, he died of a heart attack.

REX BARNEY & BURT SHOTTON

Then another time, we're playing the Giants in the Polo Grounds. This is in 1947, when Burt Shotton was managing. Barney is pitching for us, and the score is either tied or we're a run ahead. There's a runner at second and Sid Gordon is the hitter. Shotton sends Clyde Sukeforth, one of our coaches, out to the mound with a message: "Throw the fastball. Stay with the fastball." Sukeforth does that and then comes back and sits down next to Shotton. The next pitch Barney throws is a curve that bounces on home plate and goes over the catcher's head, and the guy scores from second.

After the game, when we got in the clubhouse, Shotton called Barney over and said, "What did Sukeforth tell you when he came to the mound?" Barney looked at him and said, "Sukey? He didn't come to the mound." He hadn't even been aware that Sukeforth had been out there to talk to him. That's hard to believe, isn't it?

—Bobby Bragan in *The Man in the Dugout* (Donald Honig, 1977)

Yeah, it is sort of hard to believe. Bragan continues, "But that's probably one of the things that kept him from being a great pitcher—his mind wandered while he was working, and the ball wandered with it. It was heartbreaking because he probably threw as hard as any man who ever lived. And a nice fellow, too. Very likable."

Bragan's opinion about Rex Barney's fastball is not uncommon. Nevertheless, in Barney's best season—his only good season, actually—he struck out only 138 batters in 247 innings and walked 122. Granted, that was a low-strikeout era and Barney actually finished second in the National League in strikeouts. But 138 doesn't seem like a lot for the guy with the fastest fastball in the league.

Barney's control problems would get much worse, and by 1950, when he was still only twenty-five, Barney was back in the minors for good.

Barney's exact statistics from his 1951 stint in the Texas League are not readily available, but according to his autobiography he walked thirty-eight batters in roughly thirteen innings before the Dodgers shut him down for the season. The Dodgers sent Barney to St. Paul in '52. In two innings he issued fourteen walks, and that was it.

"I was twenty-seven," Barney later wrote. "I was finished. I get weepy thinking about it now. It's a part of my life I cannot forget, ever. When you have to face yourself with that memory every day of your life, it's not very pleasant." [1]

Here is Barney's version of Bragan's story:

> When we walked into the clubhouse on opening day, we had no manager. Clyde Sukeforth ran the team for the first two games, which we won. We did not know

who Burt Shotton was until Sukey told us about him: an outfielder with the St. Louis Browns when Mr. Rickey managed that team, later a coach at Cleveland, then a scout. As our manager, Shotton, like Connie Mack and a few others, did not wear a uniform.

Some of us really missed Leo. We felt sorry for Sukeforth having to do all the dirty work for Shotton. As far as I was concerned, there was a sort of vacuum. I never cottoned to kindly old Burt. We just never got along. I didn't like him and he didn't like me. I needed the Durocher type of fire-eating manager. That's no excuse for how things turned out. It's just the way things were.

One day I was pitching and Johnny Mize was the batter and Sukeforth came out to the mound.

"Shotton says to pitch him high and outside."

"Last time up I struck him out pitching him low."

"Well, *he* says to pitch him high."

I threw a low fastball and Mize popped it up.

After the game Shotton called me into his office. "What did Sukeforth say to you when he went out to the mound with Mize at bat?"

I said something flip like, "Oh, was Sukeforth out there?"

Of course I knew he'd been out there, and I would never have spoken to Leo Durocher that way. That's what I mean about something missing between us.

You'll notice that Barney recalls the hitter as Johnny Mize. And more to the point, Barney recalls a vastly different outcome: an easy out, instead of the run-scoring wild pitch (and by the way, how often does a runner score from second on a wild pitch?).

So what really happened?

Shotton managed the Dodgers in 1947—after the first two games—and then again in the second half of 1948. Barney and Bragan both spent all of both seasons with the Dodgers. Barney was charged with five wild pitches in '47, and three in '48 after Shotton took over again.

So that's eight wild pitches. None of them came against the Giants.

In '47—the year in which Bragan places this story—Barney pitched against the Giants only twice: on the 4th of July and the 24th of September. On the 4th, with Gil Hodges behind the plate, Barney did not throw a wild pitch but did get knocked out in the second inning (the Dodgers came back and won, 16 to 7; and, yes, Gil Hodges began his career with the Dodgers as a catcher). On the 24th (again Hodges was catching), Barney pitched the ninth inning of a 6–5 loss. He didn't throw a wild pitch or allow a hit, but he did strike out two Giants. Was one of them Mize?

No. In that game, he didn't face Mize. In the earlier game, Barney faced

Photo courtesy of Transcendental Graphics

Rex Barney after his no-hitter

Mize just once before getting knocked out and got Mize on a fly ball to right field. So while Bragan says the incident happened in 1947 against the Giants, it almost certainly didn't.

Barney doesn't specify the year, but if Bragan and Shotton really were around, the only other possibility is '48. Barney pitched against the Giants in six games that season. We've already seen that he didn't throw a wild pitch in any of those games. But what about the Mize connection?

Barney faced Mize nineteen times in 1948. Mize walked twice, singled once, tripled once, and made outs the other fifteen times. But Mize did *not* strike out against Barney even once. Even on September 9, when Barney threw a no-hitter, he didn't strike out Mize, who walked, lined out to Furillo in center, and popped out to Pee Wee Reese.

One more question . . . Was Bragan behind the plate for any of Barney's outings against the Giants? No, he wasn't. Hodges caught four of them, Roy Campanella and Bruce Edwards two apiece.

Speaking of Bragan—and I didn't realize this until I checked his autobiography for references to Barney (I didn't find any)—he didn't really catch much at all. He was behind the plate only twenty-one times in 1947, and only five times in '48. In fact, he didn't last the whole '48 season. With Roy Campanella in the minors and the Dodgers needing a manager for their farm club in Fort Worth, on the 29th of June Bragan was released by the Dodgers and sent to manage the Cats.

Four of Barney's six outings against the Giants in '48 came *after* Bragan left for Texas. Which only throws another doubt on his version of events. If something like this *did* happen, he might have heard about it from somebody who actually was there. Which doesn't mean it's not true. But remember, both Bragan and Barney say Shotton was managing the Dodgers, and both Bragan and Barney say the Dodgers were playing the Giants. Whether Bragan was there or not, aren't we limited to those eight games?

And as we've already seen, Barney did not throw a wild pitch in one of those games, nor did he strike out Mize. I do believe that Barney did claim to Shotton that he'd forgotten about Sukeforth's mound visit, and I believe it happened in a Giants game. As for the other details, who knows?

But I just don't trust Bragan's account. Rex Barney was one of the great mysteries of post–World War II baseball. If Steve Dalkowski was the original Nuke LaLoosh, Barney was the original Steve Blass, except with a better arm. I suspect that Barney suffered from some sort of arm problem. But in the absence of magnetic resonance imaging and arthroscopic surgical techniques, those trying to understand what happened to Barney were reduced to X-rays and armchair psychology, neither of which are particularly effective when it comes to diagnosing a pitcher's control problems. Bragan's story about Barney is simply an attempt to explain Barney's vanishing promise, but the story is not true and thus does not explain much at all.

LEO DUROCHER & RED EVANS

Red Evans was a hard-luck guy. He pitched our opening game of the season that year against the Giants, and Zeke Bonura beat him with a homer with a couple of men on.

One day soon after that he was pitching a whale of a game against the Cardinals, and the score was 0–0 in the ninth, with Pepper Martin on third.

Red took a lot of time with his delivery, and Pepper made a trial run toward the plate, skipping back to third at the last second.

"Time!" I hollered. "Evans, Martin will steal home on you if you don't watch him."

Red shook his head, sagely.

But, just as I had warned, Martin stole home on the next pitch, and we lost, 1–0!

Red lost another game in which he led the Phils, 1–0, in the ninth. He balked the tying run over.

He had enough stuff to win, but we could never get him to go to bed, and finally we had to send him to the Southern League. About a month later I got a letter from him saying that things were tough. He was broke—and could he please have back that C-note I had fined him?

I sent Evans the money.

—Leo Durocher, *The Dodgers and Me: The Inside Story* (1948)

Evans pitched for Durocher's Dodgers in just one season: 1939. And he didn't pitch much: twenty-four games, only six of them starts, and sixty-four innings. Durocher's vignette—and frankly, it's surprising that Durocher found room for such an unexceptional player in his book—is wonderfully drawn, and considering the level of detail and the recentness of the recollection, it's easy to check one's skepticism at the door. Still, I'm here and you're here, so . . .

1. "He pitched our opening game of the season that year against the Giants, and Zeke Bonura beat him with a homer with a couple of men on."

Well, yes. Sort of. Evans did start the Giants' first game of the season, and it was against the Giants. But this passage suggests, if not explicitly, that Evans was cruising along in good order until late in the game, when Bonura went deep. Which wasn't the case. Before we get to that, though, a question: Why was Evans, with little experience in the majors—he'd pitched in seventeen games with the White Sox in 1936, but strictly as a reliever—starting on Opening Day? According to the *Times*:

> In a surprise move, Manager Durocher started Russell (Red) Evans, purportedly a "steal" from the Giants' Jersey City farm. A Southern Association pitcher last year, the right-hander had conquered the famed Yankees in Spring exhibition play. He was the one pitcher on the Flatbush roster who had gone nine innings this year.
>
> Evans had belonged to the Giants, but was obtained by the Dodgers from New Orleans in the draft, and the Giants were irked. Evans might by his very presence on the hill in the murky air of the soggy day wield a strange influence to upset the Terrymen completely, thought Durocher.
>
> But all this astute strategy worked in reverse. What the Giants did to Evans was a shame.[1]

Bonura did hit a three-run homer, but it came in the third inning. And Evans got lifted after five innings, having surrendered eight hits and seven runs. Considering how poorly Evans pitched that afternoon, he would probably have lost even if Bonura had never been born.

2. "One day soon after that he was pitching a whale of a game against the Cardinals, and the score was 0–0 in the ninth, with Pepper Martin on third. . . . But, just as I had warned, Martin stole home on the next pitch, and we lost, 1–0!"

Evans pitched against the Cardinals six times. On the 8th of May, in his first start since Opening Day, Evans did fall asleep with Martin on third base, and Martin did steal home to score the game's only run. It wasn't the ninth inning, though; it was the sixth, and Evans was lifted for a pinch hitter in the bottom of the seventh. The Dodgers did lose, one to nothing.

3. "Red lost another game in which he led the Phils, 1–0, in the ninth. He balked the tying run over."

Evans committed one balk in 1939. It did come against the Phillies, on April 22nd, which was the only game in which he appeared between the 18th and the aforementioned 8th of May. But again, the devil's in the details. We're again led to believe that Evans was pitching a gem, only to be undone at the last moment by a mental lapse. But he wasn't pitching any sort of gem. Durocher summoned Evans from the bullpen in the bottom of the ninth, with two runners on base and nobody out, the Dodgers leading 4–2.

He walked the first man he faced (on four pitches!) to load the bases. He got the next man on a pop fly. But the next man doubled, scoring two runs and tying the game. After a pinch hitter was intentionally walked, Evans struck out Del Young. Which brought up Hershel Martin. Again the *Times*:

> Then, for some reason that probably not even Evans could explain, he tried to stop the next pitch, and finally let it go with a stiff-arm sweeping motion. Martin fouled it off, but Moran already had called the balk. Because he was having difficulty with his mask, Moran couldn't wave May home. So Magerkurth took care of that, and two seconds later was surrounded by wildly protesting Dodgers, led by Lippy Leo Durocher, the manager.[2]

The details Durocher invents do make this a more dramatic story . . . but he leaves out a fact that would have been just as dramatic: Evans's three most memorable miscues happened in his first three games. After those three games, it would have been really tough for Evans to redeem himself, even if he were a good major-league pitcher. Which he was not. Which isn't to say he wasn't talented. Durocher was a pretty shrewd judge of talent, and in 1938 Evans had been one of the best pitchers in the Southern Association, going 21–14 with a 2.83 ERA. Then again, Evans was thirty-one that season; he should have been one of the best pitchers in the Southern Association, which was a full rung beneath the best minor leagues of the day.

Evans lost eight games with the Dodgers. His only win came on July 16, when he beat the Cubs with six and one-third shutout innings in a relief outing, his first appearance in a month (I've not been able to find evidence that Evans was injured, he apparently was just benched for cause). One week later he drew a starting assignment and got hammered by the Cardinals. Evans last pitched for the Dodgers on August 27, tossing a couple of scoreless innings in a 9–5 loss. On the 2nd of September, the following note appeared in the *Times*: "Yesterday saw the departure of Pitcher Red (Donald Duck) Evans from Brooklyn. He was sold to the Louisville Colonels, and

According to this story, the Phillies once discovered an unusual way of busting a long losing streak . . .

Picture this: The Phillies are playing in Ebbets Field against the Brooklyn Dodgers. It's the early 1920s, and naturally, the Phillies are just a step in front of a condition called disaster. And they're wearing Dodgers uniforms.

"We'd lost 11 games in a row," explained Huck Betts, a Phillies pitcher at the time. "We stopped in Brooklyn, but all our trunks had gotten lost. We had no uniforms, no nothing. So we took the field in Brooklyn's away uniforms with the Dodgers' shoes and gloves. And we beat them. Then darned if we didn't get home and lose 12 straight."

Maybe the Phillies, as they say, should have stayed in Brooklyn.

—*Rich Westcott*, Tales from the Phillies Dugout (*Sports Publishing, 2006*)

Huck Betts pitched for the Phillies from 1920 through 1925. In those six seasons, the Phillies did suffer through one eleven-game losing streak and one twelve-game losing streak . . . but those came in different seasons. What Betts might be remembering is a stretch in 1922 when the Phils lost twelve straight, beat the Dodgers, lost to the Giants, won three of their next four games, then lost seven straight, with the first of those seven losses coming against the Dodgers.

But the game that busted their

twelve-game losing streak? It was in Philadelphia, not Brooklyn. I suspect the Phillies did, at some point, wear Dodger uniforms in a game. But the details here just don't check out.

goes there probably as part payment for the shortstop sensation, Pee Wee Reese."[3]

So let that be Red Evans's epitaph. Not that he wouldn't stop drinking and benefited from Leo Duorcher's charity. Let us instead remember him as perhaps providing an assist (albeit unwillingly and unwittingly) in the Dodgers' acquisition of their Hall of Fame shortstop.

LEO DUROCHER & ED BARROW (& BABE RUTH'S WATCH?)

Once, a young tough Yankee infielder came roaring into Ed Barrow's office demanding more pay for his baseball services. Ed Barrow patiently listened to the angry player, and when the tirade ended, he quickly put that tough player in his proper place by saying:

"Close the door quietly on your way out."

The next day, that Yankee ballplayer was fired from the team. The name of that player was Leo Durocher.

—Bill Stern, *Bill Stern's Favorite Baseball Stories* (1949)

This little vignette concludes a two-page of summary of Ed Barrow's accomplishments, of which there were many; he is one of the few men elected to the Hall of Fame purely because of his work as an executive.

Barrow published his memoirs in 1951. Here's everything he has to say about Durocher, by then one of the game's more famous figures:

At one time we had Leo Durocher, now the manager of the Giants.

Krichell watched him play at Hartford, then owned by Jim Clarkin.

"I saw the best fielding shortstop I've ever looked at," Krichell told me. "If only he could hit."

"Get him," I said. "We'll teach him to hit." We paid $6,000 for him.

We never did teach Leo to hit, though he tried hard to learn, batting left-handed for a while, and then right-handed.

One day he said to Miller Huggins,

"Well, I've tried hard and I've made it. I'm a .400 hitter now—.200 left-handed and .200 right-handed."

Because of his batting weakness I sold Leo to Cincinnati a couple of years later for $10,000. When he was passing through New York on his way to Cincinnati he stopped into my office on 42 Street. He had on a derby hat, spats, and a velvet-collared overcoat.

"Good-by, Mr. Barrow," he said. "I'm on my way to Cincinnati."

"What time does your train go?" I asked.

He led me over to the window, and there in the street outside was a crimson convertible with a blonde sitting in it.[1]

Durocher would later tell the story quite a bit differently . . .

In a roundabout way, it could be said that I was sold because of all those debts I kept running up. . . . After two seasons with the

Yankees, I still owed money all around town. Instead of using my World Series check to pay off the old debts the previous year, I had blown it on a new Packard. What the hell, I deserved it. In particular, I owed the Picadilly Hotel around $800. My plan, therefore, was to ask for $7,000, a thousand-dollar raise, with the thousand being paid to me in advance so that I could get myself out of hock at the hotel.

In those days the Yankee offices were on 42nd street, overlooking Bryant Park and the old Sixth Avenue El. When we got together to sign the contract, Mr. Barrow informed me I wasn't going to get either the raise or an advance. I was going to sign for $6,000 again, he said. Take it or leave it.

"Don't hold your breath," I snapped. "Because that's never going to happen."

Mr. Barrow just turned around in his swivel chair and stared out the window, his back firmly to me, as much as if to dismiss me. As if, you know, I wasn't worth his time. Boy, that burned me. I turned away and went stalking off, and if it had been an ordinary-sized office I might have got out of there without any more trouble. It was a huge office, though, and by the time I reached the door I felt the urge to make it clear to him that I meant what I had said. That I was never going to sign for any lousy $6,000.

When I still found myself talking to his back I said, "Ahhh, go and fuck yourself," taking care to make it just loud enough so that he could hear me but still soft enough so that he could pretend he hadn't.

Unfortunately, Mr. Barrow wasn't playing by my rules. He came spinning around in his chair—now I had his attention all right—and he yelled, "What did you say?"

"Didn't you hear me?" I yelled back.

"Yes, I did hear you."

And so I looked him right in the eye and I said, "It still goes."

Mr. Barrow raised up out of that chair, leveled his finger at me and said, "And so do you!"

The next morning I picked up the paper and learned I had become the property of the Cincinnati Reds. He had sent me out of New York, out of the league and onto a last-place club.[2]

After reading those accounts, you might be wondering how they might possibly be reconciled, as so many of the particulars just don't match up.

Read them again, though, and you might be surprised.

Notice, for instance, that both men recall a face-to-face meeting in Barrow's office on 42nd Street. Notice, too, that both men mention a fancy car: Barrow, a "crimson convertible"; Durocher, a "new Packard."

Yes, Durocher says he visited Barrow to discuss his next contract, while Barrow says Durocher stopped in New York on his way to Cincinnati. But are those things mutually exclusive? In a way, the moment Durocher stepped into Barrow's office, he already *was* on his way to Cincinnati, whether he knew it or not. And finally, the root cause of Durocher's departure. Durocher suggests that he was sold because he wanted more money; Barrow says it's because Durocher couldn't hit. Again, though, is there a real difference here? Barrow would probably have been willing to give Durocher more money if he were a better hitter . . . so in a sense, he got dumped because he didn't hit enough to justify the contract he wanted.

Read separately, the accounts of that meeting on 42nd Street don't explain what happened. Read together, though, they might tell us almost everything.

Or not.

Another story about Durocher's departure has been told many times over the years, perhaps most recently by 1930s pitcher Elden Auker, who published an autobiography a few years ago (he died in 2006, just a few weeks shy of his ninety-sixth birthday). Chapter 3 of Auker's book is "Stealing from the Babe and Other Baseball Black Eyes," and it begins with a lovely piece of information about Ruth.

Photo courtesy of Sporting News/ZUMA Press/Icon SMI

Leo Durocher, Yankee

In '29, the Yankees couldn't pay someone to be the Babe's roommate. Not that he wasn't a nice guy. He was a very nice guy and treated everybody well. It's just that he wasn't an easy man to share a room with, not when you had to play a game the next day and needed your rest.

Babe was always carousing at night. He'd burst into the room in the middle of the night and start eating loudly, or worse. He was famous for drinking beer in his room, or worse. OK, no point in sugar-coating it, I guess: a big reason the Yankees had so much trouble finding a roommate for Ruth was his penchant for burping and passing gas. Some things a man just can't sleep through, and by all accounts, Ruth's gas was definitely one of those things.[3]

As Auker tells the story, the Yankees finally found a roommate for Ruth when they brought up a brash rookie shortstop who didn't seem to mind the Babe's many eccentricities. This went well for a while, but somewhere along the Yankees' third road trip, "the Babe noticed that he had been spending his money even more rapidly than usual. At the same time, some of the guys in the clubhouse noticed that they were missing some valuables, including money, watches, and rings."

The Babe becomes suspicious, particularly after a gold pocket watch disappears, and sets a trap with five marked $100 bills. That night, Ruth comes back to his room at two in the morning, checks an "out-of-the-way compartment" in his roommate's bag, and discovers the marked bills *and* the gold watch. Ruth kicks the hell out of his thieving teammate. By the time somebody was finally able to break into the room, "the big man had beaten the little man seemingly to within inches of his life." Within a few days, the little man was released by the Yankees.

The little man in the story is, of course, Leo Durocher.

I've presented Auker's version—there are many versions of this story—because it's the most recent I've found, and because, quite frankly, it might be the most ridiculous of them all.

Auker places Durocher's release during his rookie season, which was 1928. But he didn't leave the Yankees during that season, or the next one. He was a Yankee for all of both seasons. More troublingly, Auker didn't even join the Tigers until late in the '33 season, nearly four years after Durocher played his last game as a Yankee.

So what of this story? Robert W. Creamer, Ruth's first serious biographer, wrote this:

And there is a legend, seldom printed but often talked about in baseball circles, that says Leo Durocher stole Babe Ruth's watch, which is not true. What is true is that Ruth did not like Durocher. . . . He resented Leo's cockiness, and the two never got along, although Leo tried to—at first.

Durocher was in a hotel elevator late one night with a couple of other players when Ruth got on. "Oh, am I drunk," said the Babe. "Somebody's got to undress me and put me to bed. You guys have to help me."

The other players backed away rapidly, but Leo said, "I'll help you, pal."

"Thank you, pal," Ruth said. Leo helped him get off the elevator and down the hall to Babe's room. The next morning Ruth decided that he was missing something—money in one version of the story, his watch in another. Although he was drunk on the town the night before and had been in the Lord knows what places, he blamed Durocher. As Leo said, in a half-angry, half-mocking tone, "Jesus Christ, if I was going to steal anything from him I'd steal his god damned Packard.[4]

One might reasonably wonder who Creamer's source was for this passage. It wasn't Ruth, who'd been dead for a long time when Creamer set to his task. Which basically leaves Durocher, who wrote the following in *his* book about the Babe, the Babe's money, and (again) that shiny Packard.

A great big boy was what he was, alternately generous and mean. And, unlike me, born under a lucky star. A Saturday afternoon exhibition game in New Orleans was rained out and so Babe went to the racetrack and won about $9,000. The players didn't get paid until the season started in those days, and so naturally everybody was broke. Babe walked into the clubhouse on Sunday, threw the whole wad of money on top of the equipment trunk and said, "Well, boys—come and get it."

Boy, it was like feeding time at the zoo.

After everybody had taken what they wanted, Babe just picked up what was left, put it in his pouch and dropped the pouch into the money trunk. The Babe would give you anything, but he was funny about one thing. If you took the money you had better be there when you got your next paycheck. Because if you weren't, he'd come around with a bat in his hand and tell you to get it up. . . .

In certain ways, though, I was as good a friend as he had on the team. The Babe had a big brown Packard roadster, and we used to ride to the Stadium together almost every day. And there was many a time I put him to bed on the road after he had been out on the town.

Frankly, none of this is conclusive. It's clear that Auker didn't have the straight story, but it's nearly as clear that Creamer didn't have an authoritative source for dismissing out of hand the allegation against Durocher. I do not think Durocher was waived to the National League because he stole from Ruth. But if you've read much about Durocher, you know that he was well stocked in some qualities that we would find less than admirable in a prospective son-in-law. We also know because Durocher habitually spent more money than he was making. Is it really far-fetched to think that, at some point, he said to himself at two o'clock in the morning, "Damn it, here I am again, dragging this fat asshole off to bed. He's making one hundred thousand dollars a year and I'm making six grand, and will he really miss this hundred bucks in the morning?"

Of course we'll never know. But Durocher was a brilliant narcissist and would probably have had little trouble justifying to himself all manner of ill behavior. Is it really so far-fetched to imagine Durocher, saddled with debts and sick of carrying this drunken-but-wealthy lout to bed one more time, figuring it wouldn't hurt if he just helped himself to a few of the lout's greenbacks? After all, who would ever know?

But I don't believe Ruth beat up Durocher, and I don't believe Durocher was waived to the National League because he was an ingrate. He was waived to the other league because he was a pain in the ass who couldn't hit water if he fell out of a fucking submarine.

PETE ALEXANDER & JOE MCCARTHY

Here's Grover Cleveland Alexander's own version of why the Chicago Cubs suddenly decided to send him away. It was one day in 1926 against the Giants—but let Alex tell it:

"Joe McCarthy was our new manager. I've got the bases full with Long George Kelly up. McCarthy comes out and says, 'Pitch high to him.' I say, 'He's a high-ball hitter.' McCarthy says never mind. I pitch high, and a man in the left field bleachers has a souvenir.

"I walk to the dugout, hand McCarthy my glove, and tell him, 'Here, you know how to pitch to them.' He tells me, 'I just want you to know who's the manager.' Next morning I read in the paper where I belong to St. Louis."

—Pat Conger in the Los Angeles *Mirror* (reprinted in *Baseball Digest*, July 1950)

Why does this story matter? Because the St. Louis Cardinals won the World Series in 1926—more about that in a moment—and they almost certainly wouldn't have won without Pete Alexander. And by extension, the Cardinals wouldn't have won without Joe McCarthy's pig-headedness. Which is, when you get down to it, really the point of this story.

We'll never know what McCarthy said to Alexander, but we can check the facts cited here.

On June 22nd, the Cardinals plucked Alexander off waivers.

While with the Cubs, Alexander pitched in only seven games, all starts. Thus, we can easily check the dates of those starts:

Alexander's last appearance as a Cub was on May 22, a full month before he joined the Cardinals. And he didn't give up a homer to George Kelly on May 22, because on May 22 the Cubs played the Boston Braves, not George Kelly's Giants.

Did Alexander perhaps give up a home run to Kelly earlier in the season? Actually, Alexander didn't give up a home run to anybody earlier in the season; in his seven starts as a Cub, he pitched fifty-two innings and didn't give up a single homer (he would allow eight as a Cardinal). So we don't have to check Alexander's home-run log, because there weren't any home runs to log. What we can check is Alexander's one start against the Giants, on May 8.

On the 8th he pitched a complete game, beating the Giants 6–4. Here's a colorful passage from the game story in the *Times*:

> The shadow of Alexander hovered over the Giants like Banquo's ghost. His easy swinging motion sent the ball soaring over the corners of the plate, and when the ancient arm began to weaken in the sixth his stout heart carried him through. An inspiring figure was Alex the Great as he stood unmoved in the face of New York's vicious blows.[1]

George Kelly did play and went 0 for 3 with a walk. That was Alexander's last win as a Cub.

No doubt about it, Alexander was a workhorse. He pitched in more than 300 innings in nine different seasons, including all seven years with the Phillies. On occasion, he exceeded the call of duty.

Such was the case in 1916 at a doubleheader on a getaway day in Philadelphia. Alexander had already won the first game against the Cincinnati Reds when Phils manager Pat Moran came to him with a special request.

"I have to ask you to pitch the second game, too," Moran said. "We only have a little more than an hour to catch the train. Get it over fast."

Ever the dutiful player, the likeable Alex complied. He pitched a shutout. The game was played in fifty-eight minutes.

—*Rich Westcott*, Tales from the Phillies Dugout *(2006)*

Alexander did beat the Reds in both games of a 1916 doubleheader; on the 23rd of September, he beat them 7–3 and 4–0. However, according to The New York Times— *and it should be mentioned that game times were not then officially kept—the second game was played in one hour and seven minutes.*

From the schedule, it doesn't look like a "getaway day"; the doubleheader was played in Philadelphia on Saturday, and after an off day the Phillies and Reds resumed their series on Monday. But baseball was different then.

So nobody homered, and Kelly didn't even get a hit against Alexander. Not in 1926 while Alexander was pitching for the Cubs. But what about later, when Alexander was pitching for the Cardinals?

Bingo. On August 1 in New York, Alexander gave up two home runs. In the fourth, Giants shortstop Travis Jackson hit one. In the eighth, with two runners aboard, so did Kelly. Alexander pitched a complete game, but the 7–2 loss was one of his worst outings of the season. Somehow Alexander apparently conflated Kelly's home run with McCarthy's feelings, which certainly were not positive toward him.

So why *did* Alexander go for a month without pitching for the Cubs, and why *was* he placed on the waiver wire? According to teammate Jim Cooney, Alexander "kept a bottle of booze in the locker room. He knew McCarthy was on to him, so he would hide it in the locker of one of the rookie pitchers. He'd slip down there during the game and take a few slugs. Things got pretty bad after awhile and it was no surprise when the Cubs cut him loose."[2] According to Alexander biographer Jack Kavanaugh:

> On May 16, Alex was knocked out of the box in the first inning by the Phillies and on May 22 took a 7–1 beating from the Braves as the Cubs ended a long homestand. Before the game Grover Cleveland Alexander was given the keys to a car he should not have been permitted to drive. The fans bestowed what proved to be a going away present, a $5,500 Lincoln sedan, on their favorite.
>
> Alex remained behind when the Cubs, slipping down in the standings after a quick start, made an eastern trip. He joined the team in Philadelphia, in no condition to pitch and seemed in no mood to get back in shape.

On June 15, McCarthy suspended Alexander, saying the pitcher had arrived at the ballpark "out of condition," which in those days meant drunk or hungover.

"This isn't the first time by any means," McCarthy told the press. "This is the sixth time it has happened in the last nine or ten days. He can't hope to get his arm cured by such things as he is doing, and those things don't fit in with my plans to build up a team. I absolutely refused to allow him to disrupt our ball club and will not have him around in that condition. Any player may drink and get away with it if he is winning . . . but no player can get away with it if he isn't winning. I refused to stand for it any longer."[3]

Alexander requested a meeting with Cubs president Bill Veeck Sr. (father of you know who), but Veeck backed up McCarthy, both privately and publicly. Faced with this public and professional embarrassment, Alexander promised to mend his ways, but it was too late. The Cubs placed him on waivers, the Cardinals claimed him, and the two clubs wound up working out a deal: the Cubs got $4,000 and the Cards got a future Hall of Famer with (as events would make clear) plenty left in the tank.

Many years later, McCarthy told interviewer Donald Honig:

> Grover Cleveland Alexander was with the Cubs when I took over in 1926. He was getting along in years then but still quite a good pitcher. I had to get rid of him though. He didn't obey orders. Wouldn't get along with me. A fellow asked me one time if Alex followed the rules. "Sure he did," I said, "but they were always Alex's rules." So I had to let him go. St. Louis took him and he helped them win the pennant. That didn't bother me; he'd been with the Cubs the year before, and they had still finished last. If they finished last again, I'd rather it was without him. That's how I figured it. But he was a nice fellow. Alex was all right. Just couldn't keep to the rules, that's all.[4]

A couple of postscripts . . .

Alexander pitched quite well for the Cardinals, going 9-7 with 2.91 ERA in twenty-three games. His wife would say, in 1951, that he'd pitched so well because the Cardinals brought her on all the road trips. "I didn't shut him off from liquor completely, but I tried my best to keep him under control and he seldom gave me any trouble."

It's long been rumored that Alexander was drunk when he struck out Tony Lazzeri in Game 7 of the World Series that fall. That he'd actually visited a saloon during the game. That's almost certainly not true, but Alexander had pitched nine innings to win Game 6, twenty-four hours earlier. And it's not hard to imagine him celebrating afterward with a drink or six. So he might have been hungover when he struck out Lazzeri in the seventh and finished off the Yankees in the eighth and ninth. But he wasn't drunk.

Joe McCarthy managed the Cubs to a pennant in 1929, was fired in 1930, almost immediately signed with the Yankees, and led them to eight pennants and seven World Championships. He left the Yankees in 1946 and took up with the Red Sox in 1948. When he quit in 1950, he had a reputation among his players and everybody else close to the team as a serious alcoholic. He had his own rules, too.*

---

* When McCarthy quit, his wife said, "He's just physically exhausted. It's later than you think." Randy Gumpert, who pitched for McCarthy in 1946, would later say, "McCarthy had a drinking problem. It was uncontrollable. It got so bad they would have to take his wife on road trips to keep him sober."

Sunday baseball was illegal in Philadelphia, and the Phillies might well have jumped on a train that evening to play a non-league game on Sunday in another state.

Regardless, it was an impressive achievement, especially considering that the Phillies were still in the pennant race. And here's something else worth mentioning: just three days earlier, Alexander's teammate Al Demaree had pulled off the same feat, beating the Pirates 7–0 and 3–2.

GERRY PRIDDY & THE YANKEES

The thing that Gerry Priddy, the old second baseman who has just turned golf pro, likes to remember most about his baseball career is the way he hit against the Yankees after they'd traded him away following the 1942 season. For ten years thereafter with the Senators, Browns and finally the Tigers, he was a murderous hitter against his old mates, especially with men on bases.

"It wasn't just pride or revenge or anything like that," Gerry explained the other day. "Actually, I had a secret. I never told anybody till now. You know when I was a rookie breaking in, Joe McCarthy always had me sit on the bench next to him. And I can still hear him yelling to our pitchers whenever they were in a tough spot. 'Make him hit the hook. Give him the curve ball.'

"I always remembered that and whenever I came up against them with men on bases, I was always looking for the curve. I usually got it, too, even after McCarthy had gone. One year I hit .500 against them and the other years I was much better against them than any other club in the league."

—Arch Ward in the *New York Post* (reprinted in *Baseball Digest,* March 1960)

Unfortunately, there's only so much here that we can check, because we don't yet have comprehensive play-by-play accounts for games in the 1940s. When Priddy says he "hit .500 against them," does he mean he hit .500 overall against the Yankees, or does he mean he hit .500 against them with runners on base? We can check the former—using Priddy's daily sheets—but not the latter.

Priddy never hit .500 against the Yankees over any particular season. He did fare *quite* well against the Yankees in four different seasons, though: from 1948 through '51 he batted .329, .284, .329, and .305 against them. In each of those seasons, the Yankees ranked either second or third in the league in team ERA. Overall, Priddy batted .311 against the

Yankees from '48 through '51, and .275 against the rest of the American League.

Did it really have anything to do with McCarthy, though?

Sure doesn't seem like it.

In 1943, his first season after the Yankees traded him to Washington, Priddy batted .266 against McCarthy and his old mates. Priddy spent the next two seasons in the service, then returned as the Senators' everyday second baseman in 1946. That season, a) McCarthy managed the Yankees for only thirty-nine games—six of them against Priddy's Senators—before resigning, and b) Priddy hit just .228 against the Yankees. He did do particularly well *before* McCarthy resigned, going 8 for 22 (.364) in those six games. So in twenty-eight games against the Yankees when McCarthy was managing, Priddy batted .287. With McCarthy gone in '46 and '47, Priddy batted .228 in thirty-eight games. Not until '48, with McCarthy—and presumably his influences—long gone, did Priddy *really* start hitting the Yankees; from '48 through '51, he batted .311 over 336 at-bats, which is particularly impressive considering the Yankees were obviously the best team in the league, winning three World Series in those years.

It just doesn't seem likely that it had anything to do with McCarthy.

JOE McCARTHY & ROOKIES

That rookie year of 1941 I learned firsthand the McCarthy system with rookies. He would put a player in for a month and a half, then he would bench him and sit him next to the manager for a few weeks. That is what happened to me. I opened the season at shortstop, played for about six weeks, then was benched for Frank Crosetti. Each day I sat on that bench next to McCarthy and he would explain everything that was going on. It all looked so easy listening to him. And you had to listen. Often he would try to catch you daydreaming. All of a sudden, he'd bark, "Don't look at the scoreboard; what's the count?" You had better know what the count was. His magic worked with me all right. I got back into the lineup, fielded pretty well and hit .307. One of my big thrills came against Philadelphia the day our infield participated in seven double plays, which is still a record. I was in five of them myself.

—Phil Rizzuto in *The "Miracle" New York Yankees* (Rizzuto and Al Silverman, 1962)

This one has it all, don't you think? A Hall of Fame shortstop and the (supposed) regular strategy of a Hall of Fame manager?

Questions to answer:

- Did this happen, at all?
- If so, when was Rizzuto yanked from the lineup, and what were his stats at that time?
- When was he put back in the lineup, and what were his stats afterward?
- What did McCarthy say to the press about Rizzuto at the time?
- Did McCarthy really do this with other players? Or was it just the Scooter?

I sent away to the Hall of Fame for Rizzuto's day-by-days, and the answer to the first question is, yes, this did really happen.

Rizzuto was in the lineup on Opening Day and remained in the lineup for every single game for a month (McCarthy liked to play the same guys every day, especially in the infield). On May 15, Rizzuto doubled and scored a run, which made his batting average .248.

And then he sat. Rizzuto did occasionally get into a game as a pinch hitter or defensive replacement, but from May 16 through June 15 he didn't start a single game. On the 17th, though, Rizzuto got back into the lineup and, playing just about every day, batted .332 the rest of the way (and finished at .307, exactly as he or his ghostwriter said in the book).

So this is basically right, with the caveat that he was benched after the first four weeks of the season (which started for the Yankees on April 14) rather than the first six (as Rizzuto remembered).

Did McCarthy really do this with other players? With apologies to Billy Johnson and Jerry Priddy, these are the seven best players (not including pitchers or Rizzuto) who joined the Yankees while McCarthy was managing the club (1931–1946):

In 1932, Frankie Crosetti joined the Yankees and played 116 games.
  In 1933, Dixie Walker joined the Yankees and played 98 games.
  In 1934, George Selkirk joined the Yankees, but he didn't play his first game until August 12 (and he played most of the games down the stretch). Though Selkirk batted .312 in those first 46 games, he played in only 128 games in 1935, his first full season.
  In 1936, Joe DiMaggio joined the Yankees and played 138 games.
  In 1937, Tommy Henrich joined the Yankees and played only 67 games.
  In 1938, Joe Gordon joined the Yankees and played 127 games.
  In 1939, Charlie Keller joined the Yankees and played only 111 games.

Taking those guys one by one . . .

In '32, Crosetti played third base on Opening Day and remained in the lineup virtually every day through June 11. By that point he'd been moved to shortstop and was batting .262 with nine doubles, two triples, and zero homers in 145 at-bats. Not great, but certainly nothing that would embarrass a shortstop. Nevertheless, he got benched and apparently didn't start a game for almost exactly one month. But on July 11 he got back in the lineup and started almost every game the rest of the way.

In '33, Dixie Walker started the season on the bench, moved into the starting lineup for five games in late April and early May, then was relegated to pinch-hitting duties for six weeks. In the middle of June, Walker got back into the lineup and stayed there until late July. He finally got in there for good on August 15 and spent the rest of the season as the Yankees' regular center fielder.

In '35, Selkirk never sat for more than a few games in a row.

In '36, DiMaggio didn't debut until May 3, but he was in the lineup almost every day the rest of the season.

In '37, Henrich debuted on May 11 and played regularly until the middle of June, after he which he was in and out of the lineup for varying stretches.

In '38, Joe Gordon was the Yankees' Opening Day second baseman, but was yanked from the lineup at the end of April; at the time, he had just seven hits in forty-five at-bats. Roughly five weeks later he got back into the lineup, and it took a war to get him out.

Speaking of learnin' a rookie all your experience . . .

In 1960, the Chicago White Sox brought up a bonus baby from the Deep South for some big-league exposure. Sox manager Al Lopez had the kid sit beside him on the bench in order to absorb a few of the subtleties of the game.

One afternoon, Nellie Fox opened the second inning by drawing a walk. When the next batter lined a hit down the right-field line, Nellie rounded second and raced for third, but a perfect throw by outfielder Roger Maris cut him down.

"He was right to try for third," Lopez told the kid. "You won't see another throw like that in a hundred years."

In the seventh inning, with Fox again on first, the same batter lined a hit to the same spot, and the same Roger Maris cut down Fox at third.

"Mister Lopez," the Southern rookie dryly drawled, "time sure does fly by here in the North."

—*John Thorn*, A Century of Baseball Lore *(1974)*

🖎 Norman Macht, as Dick
Bartell's co-author of *Rowdy
Richard*, tells this story about Joe
McCarthy's patience . . .

He had a way with young players.
He was managing Louisville when
Earle Combs, a Kentucky
schoolteacher, broke in.

Playing center field for the first
time, Combs was so nervous he
dropped a fly ball hit right to him.

McCarthy said nothing.

A couple innings later, Combs
booted a single into a triple.

McCarthy never said a word.

In the eighth inning, score tied,
two men on base, the batter
singled to center. Determined,
Combs said to himself, "I'll stop
this ball if it kills me."

It rolled through his legs to the
fence. Chasing it down, he decided
he was through. He'd quit if he
wasn't fired. After the game,
McCarthy said to him, "Forget it. I
told you today you're my center
fielder. You still are." He laughed,
then added, "Listen. If I can stand
it, I guess you can."

*I have not checked the Louisville
newspapers, but this story reeks of
apocryphalness.*

*When Combs joined the
McCarthy-managed Louisville club
in 1922, he was almost twenty-
three but had never played an
inning in Organized Baseball. That
season he batted .344, and in '23
he batted .380 with 145 RBIs. The
Yankees paid Louisville $50,000 for
Combs, then a huge sum for a
minor leaguer. Combs's first season
with the Yankees, 1924, was ended*

In '39, Keller didn't start his first game until April 29, but actually led
Yankee outfielders with 462 at-bats, as DiMaggio missed a good chunk of
the season with an injury, and McCarthy worked Selkirk and Henrich into
the lineup, too.

So "the McCarthy system," if it really existed, was rarely employed.
Crosetti sat for a month, Walker for six weeks, and Gordon for five weeks.
Toss in Rizzuto, and we're talking about four rookies in the span of roughly
a dozen seasons. It does suggest a pattern, though, doesn't it? And of the
four players, three were middle infielders. Just like McCarthy, who'd been a
second baseman for nine years in the minors.

Then again, the vague appearance of a pattern does not prove design.
When Rizzuto was benched in 1941, fellow rookie Jerry Priddy was
benched right along with him, and there wasn't any talk of Crosetti in '32 or
Gordon in '38.

After winning four straight pennants from 1936 through '39, the Yankees
had finished third in 1940. So when they got off to a slow start in '41, something had to be done. When Rizzuto and Priddy got benched on May 16,
the Yankees had lost eight of ten, and they were in fourth place with a
14–15 record. Those two had been double-play partners the year before in
the minors, and although Joe Gordon had already established himself as
one of the game's best second basemen, when the '41 season opened, Gordon shifted to first base to make room for Priddy.

But with Priddy not hitting and the Yankees not winning, both
Priddy and Rizzuto got benched, which the *Daily News* described as a
"shakeup." At the end of the month, the *Times* published this letter to the
editor:

> In my opinion Joe McCarthy has been altogether too hasty in giving
> up on his rookie second-base combination of Jerry Priddy and Phil
> Rizzuto.
>
> I think the only hope the Yankees have of getting back on top in
> the American League is to rebuild from the bottom. Naturally, this re-
> quires some patience, but in the long run such a policy will pay divi-
> dends.
>
> Possibly, Priddy and Rizzuto will prove not of major league caliber.
> Nevertheless, it seems to me that it would be a more constructive move
> to give them a thorough trial than to go along with the aging Frank
> Crosetti at short and Johnny Sturm, who definitely is no major leaguer,
> at first.
>
> N. Glickman. New York, May 27, 1941

An editor responded, "I low about being 'constructive' to the extent of giving Johnny Sturm a 'thorough trial'? He has been doing good work for the Yankees at first base."[1]

Mr. Glickman was right. The aging Crosetti was an awful player by then, and Sturm, who spent the rest of the season getting his thorough trial, was easily the worst player in the lineup. Priddy never did get back into the lineup, regularly. As we've seen, Rizzuto did . . . but only after Crosetti was spiked by Hal Trosky in a game against Cleveland on the 16th of June.[2] It's highly likely that Rizzuto, one way or the other, would have been back in the lineup eventually. He was too good to sit and Crosetti was too old to play. But from this distance, McCarthy's intent in the spring of '41 is far from obvious.

early by a broken ankle. And in 1934 in St. Louis, he crashed into a concrete wall while chasing a fly ball, fractured his skull, and spent seven weeks in the hospital. He came back in '35 but wasn't the same player and retired after the season.

JOHNNY BABICH & THE YANKEES

Al Lyons, who moved to the Pirates this year from the Yankees, tells an anecdote about Johnny Babich, the pitcher, who had a brief trial with the Yankees.

Babich didn't do very well and, after the tryout, the Yankees let him go. He wound up with the Athletics.

One day when the Athletics played the Yankees, Connie Mack named Babich the pitcher. Inning after inning Babich set the Yankee sluggers down with an ease that had Manager Joe McCarthy tearing his thinning hair.

After Joe Gordon fanned, slammed his bat down disgustedly and returned to the bench, McCarthy asked:

"What has that guy got, anyway?"

"I dunno," retorted Gordon, "but whatever it is, it's something our scouts missed."

—Vince Johnson in the Pittsburgh *Post-Gazette*,
reprinted in *Baseball Digest*, November 1949

Babich first pitched in the majors in 1934, when he was only twenty-one. He went 7-11 with the Dodgers that season, and 7-14 the next. Early in 1936, the Dodgers traded Babich to the Boston Bees (as the Braves were then officially known). He pitched only six innings for Boston, giving up eight runs, and spent most of that season and the next three in the minors. In 1938 with Hollywood, Babich went 19-17 with a 3.27 ERA against top competition in the Pacific Coast League. Afterward, the Bees sent him to the Yankees to complete an August trade for shortstop Eddie Miller. So if Babich had a trial with the Yankees, it would have been in 1939.

He did *not* pitch for the Yankees in the regular season. He apparently spent the entire season with the Yankees' farm team in Kansas City, for whom he went 17-6 with a 2.55 ERA, good for third in the American Association.

Now, before you assume that a (still) young pitcher with the third-lowest ERA in the league certainly deserved a shot with the big club, know this: Babich's K.C. teammates held the first, second, and fifth spots on the ERA list. The Blues were a legitimately great team, going 107-47 and taking the Association pennant by eight games. And those three teammates who also ranked among the top five in the league? You've never heard of any of them.[*]

Anyway, in early October of 1939, the Athletics grabbed Babich from the Yankees in the Rule 5 draft. If the Rule 5 draft operated then as it does now—and frankly, I don't have any idea who would know if it did—this means the Yankees didn't place Babich on their forty-man roster, and the A's drafted him with the stipulation that if they didn't keep him

---

[*] On the other hand, the Blues' fifth-best starter, forkballer Tiny Bonham, became something of a star for the Yankees in the early '40s.

on their active roster all season, they'd have to offer him back to the Yankees for a small sum of money.

The A's kept Babich, and he performed magnificently, just as his stats in Kansas City would have suggested. Pitching for a lousy team—the A's lost 100 games and finished last for the fourth time in six seasons—Babich went 14-13 with a 3.73 ERA that was easily the best on the staff. The Yankees, meanwhile, struggled (for them) in 1940, going 88-66 and finishing two games out of first place, their first non-pennant season since 1935. The Yanks weren't used to losing to the Athletics, but one might argue that their inability to beat the A's in 1940 is what cost them the pennant, as they won only thirteen of the twenty-two games the teams played (they did worse against only the pennant-winning Tigers).

Did Babich pitch against the Yankees that season? Actually, he pitched against the Yankees a *lot*; of his thirty starts, six came against the Bombers. Here's how he fared against them:

	IP	Hits	K	ER	W/L
June 30	10	5	5	2	W
July 5	9	7	5	3	W
Aug. 9	6	7	1	2	L
Aug. 18	9	7	2	3	W
Sept. 2	9	5	3	0	W
Sept. 27	9	5	2	2	W 5-1, 2.08 ERA

Johnny Babich

Photo courtesy of National Baseball Hall of Fame, Cooperstown, New York

Babich pitched six times; he pitched five complete games and won all of those.

It was a rough season for the Yankees, generally. As late as August 20, they were nearly ten games out of first place and everybody was writing "What's wrong with the Yankees?" stories. But when Babich faced them on September 2, they were back in contention, having won fourteen of fifteen and eight in a row.

He busted that streak with a shutout, his only shutout of the season. The next time he faced them, the Yanks had almost been eliminated, but they still had a shot and were riding another eight-game winning streak.

He busted that streak, too, along with the Yankees' pennant hopes. As the *Times* noted:

> PHILADELPHIA, Sept. 27—Finis was written on the 1940 championship aspirations of the Yankees at Shibe Park today when Johnny Babich, their worst tormentor through the campaign, draped them over the ropes and counted the New Yorkers out of the race with a five-hit rout. The Athletics won by 6–2.
>
> However, the Yankees still have a chance for second place.
>
> It was ironic that Babich should be the one to kill McCarthy's last hope for a fifth straight pennant, a feat never accomplished in major league baseball. The 31-year-old right-hander was Yankee property at Kansas City last season until drafted by Connie Mack for service with the Athletics. Today Babich notched his fifth victory over the McCarthymen. It was his fourteen triumph of the season and snapped an eight-game winning streak of the New Yorkers.
>
> Handcuffed all the way by Babich's "slider," the Yankees offered little opposition.*

A variation of the Babich-McCarthy story popped up again some years later, in Al Silverman's book about Joe DiMaggio in 1941. With DiMaggio's '41 hitting streak at thirty-nine games, Babich started against the Yankees on June 28, and Silverman sets up that game like this:

> . . . Johnny Babich was the Philadelphia pitcher and that meant trouble.
>
> Babich had a reputation as a Yankee killer. Originally a Yankee farmhand, he had had a fine minor-league year in 1939, but the Yankees did not buy him. In 1940 he was so angry at the Yankees that he beat them five times. His fifth victory knocked the Yankees out of the American League pennant. After that game Joe McCarthy came into the clubhouse growling, Babich . . . Babich . . . BABICH! Who in the hell ever heard of Babich?
>
> Joe Gordon looked up calmly and said, "Well, apparently our scouts didn't." [1]

If McCarthy said that—"Who in the hell ever heard of Babich?"—he was engaging in a bit of locker-room irony, because McCarthy certainly had heard of Johnny Babich. Between spring training in 1939, Babich's season

---

* By the way, Babich was only twenty-seven in the summer of 1940, and it's odd that the *Times* would have him as thirty-one. Many, many of the listed ages in that era were off by a few years, but nearly always in the other direction.

Photo courtesy of the author

Gordon and McCarthy in '43 when the Yankees did win the pennant

with Kansas City, and—not least—Babich's four previous wins over the Yankees in 1940, McCarthy, famous for his memory, must have known Babich about as well as any manager could have.*

It's not hard to understand McCarthy's frustration, though. Letting Babich get away cost the Yankees both ways. He didn't win *for* them in 1940 *and* he beat them five times. The Yankees had all kinds of pitching problems that season, and it's not at all far-fetched to suggest that if they'd kept him, they would have won their fifth straight pennant. It was a weird year. Johnny Babich was right in the middle of it.

I know this one's appeared in many books over the years, but it's one of my favorites and I wanted it in my book, too.

This is Joe McCarthy's favorite story. Maybe it's the favorite of every man who ever managed a ball club. As McCarthy tells it, he had a dream that he'd died, gone to Heaven and promptly been ordered to assemble and manage a ball club. McCarthy's eyes glistened as he surveyed the talent around him—Christy Mathewson, Walter Johnson, Cy Young, Babe Ruth, Lou Gehrig, Tris Speaker, Honus Wagner, and all the other superstars.

"This will be the greatest team of all time," gloated the happy Marse Joe. "No one will ever beat us."

Just then the phone rang. It was Satan calling from downstairs and challenging the heavenly hosts to a ball game.

"But you haven't a chance of winning," protested McCarthy to the Devil. "I've got all the ballplayers."

"I know that," said Satan. "But I've got all the umpires."

—*Arthur Daley in* Sport
(February 1961)

---

* In the June 28 game, Babich retired DiMaggio on a grounder in the first inning. In the third, Babich threw three straight balls, far out of the strike zone. The fourth pitch was outside, but DiMaggio reached out and slapped a liner right through Babich's legs for a hit. Years later he said, "It was my most satisfying hit of the entire streak."

VIC RASCHI & JIM TURNER

Turner was a marvelous teacher, Raschi thought. He knew when to teach and when not to. . . .

Raschi had come to him desperate to learn—he was proud of his skills, and deeply wounded by the failure of Yankee management in the spring of 1947 to see his career as he did. Turner immediately saw Raschi's talent. But there were too many lapses—moments when he was pitching but not thinking. In an early Portland game, Raschi had a lead in the third inning. With two outs, two men on base, and the pitcher up, Raschi had allowed the pitcher to get a hit, and that had cost him the game. Turner waited a day and then took Raschi aside. "When you have a situation like a weak hitter up, you *crucify* him. You never let a pitcher beat you, Vic. Never!" Raschi's ability to concentrate improved immediately.

Turner taught him not just to study the hitters but also to prevail over them. "Vic—those hitters are your enemy. If they get their way, you're out of baseball," he would say. "I've seen pitchers with talent who might have made the major leagues, but they didn't hate hitters enough." Raschi proceeded to do that well with Portland, winning 9 and losing 2, and in mid-season the Yankees brought him back to New York. He won two games during their extraordinary 19-game winning streak.

—David Halberstam, *Summer of '49* (1989)

Two key and verifiable assertions here. One, giving up that hit to the opposing pitcher cost Raschi a game. And two, he lost only two games while pitching for Portland.

The second of those is true. He did not win nine games, as Halberstam says. According to the 1948 *Baseball Guide*, Raschi pitched in twelve games and went 8 and 2 with a 2.75 ERA. So all we have to do is check those two losses for an enemy pitcher getting a game-changing hit, right?

That does require a visit to the microfilm room in the Portland library. We do know, thanks to *The New York Times*, that Raschi opened the '49 season with the Yankees, but was sent to the minors in early May. As James P. Dawson reported from chilly Cleveland, "Vic Raschi, rookie right-hander, will leave the team here for Portland, Ore. He is being sent out on option to gain experience under the tutelage of Jim Turner, former Yankee relief hurler who is managing the Pacific Coast League club."[1]

On the 11th of July, Dawson reported, "The Yankees today recalled Pitcher Vic Raschi, a right-hander, from Portland in the Pacific Coast League, where he has won seven games and lost two. He will report in Chicago Sunday, ready to pitch."[2]

So Dawson got the wins wrong, too. But Raschi did start against the White Sox on Sunday, and he pitched into the seventh to earn his first major-league win. It was the Yankees' fourteenth straight win, and four days later Raschi won again for the Yankee's nineteenth straight. He was a regular starter for the rest of the season, but the Yankees had a lot of good starters and Raschi appeared just briefly in the World Series.

Anyway, back to Portland and Raschi's two months in the Pacific Coast League. Upon his arrival, *Oregonian* sports editor L. H. Gregory wrote of the new Beaver, "He's sizable and lives up to the reputation all Yankee farmhands have of being able to throw hard."[3]

I found all twelve games in which Raschi pitched, with box scores and game accounts (and I can confirm the eight wins and two losses). I also logged the at-bats and hits for all opposing pitchers in Raschi's games. Without benefit of play-by-play accounts we can't necessarily discover which pitchers' hits actually came when Raschi was pitching . . . except as it turns out, there are only two of them. In Raschi's twelve games, opposing pitchers totaled two hits in twenty-eight at-bats.

The first of those hits came in Raschi's second start, a rough one. He'd pitched exceptionally well in his first outing. But in his second, on May 22 in Hollywood, he was driven from the mound in the fifth, having given up nine hits and five runs. The box scores in the Portland newspapers somehow omitted Hollywood starter Pinky Woods, but *The Sporting News* shows him going 1 for 3. I do not know if that hit came against Raschi, but it seems somewhat likely, considering that Woods did drive in one run, and Hollywood scored only two runs after Raschi's exit.

So that's one possibility. The other shows up in Raschi's next start, on the 28th against the Seattle Rainiers. The Beavers finished with a convincing 11 to 4 victory, but our hero got knocked out in the fourth, when the Suds racked up five hits and four runs. The last of the five hits was made by pitcher Rex Cecil, and that was enough for Jim Turner, who yanked Raschi from the game.

So this seems like the origin of Halberstam's story, doesn't it? Sure, it was the fourth inning rather than the third. But that's nothing. And Cecil's hit didn't "cost him the game," as the Bevos won going away. But there *were* two outs in the fourth inning, and Cecil's hit did cost Raschi, personally, what should have been an easy victory. And however coincidental it might be, in Raschi's last nine appearances as a Beaver, he did not allow a single hit to a pitcher.

When it comes to baseball careers, I don't generally put much stock in

One can only wonder about the tales they'll someday tell about Joe Torre and Cap'n Jetes . . .

Joe Torre always tells the story, in '96 when Jeter was the rookie shortstop for the Yankees, he was on second base with nobody out, and tried to steal third and got thrown out for the first out. You don't make the first or third out at third. Rather than avoiding Torre, he went back to the bench and sat right next to him. And Joe said, "Get outta here." Because he knew he knew he had made a mistake, but he wanted to go next to Joe Torre to take his punishment.

—Yankees broadcaster
Michael Kay during game,
June 13, 2007

Well, not exactly. Jeter was caught stealing seven times in his rookie year. Once was at third base: August 12 against the White Sox. However, it was the third out of the inning—not the first—so Jeter couldn't have sat down next to Torre (at least not right away) because he had to immediately grab his glove and play shortstop. It was a dumb play, though, as it occurred in the eighth with the score tied. The Yanks lost in the tenth.

Eureka! moments, and I suspect that Vic Raschi would have become a fine major leaguer if he'd retired Rex Cecil, or if he hadn't but Turner hadn't turned that into a teaching moment. But unlike a lot of the stories that Halberstam casually passes off as factual in his book, this one seems to be essentially true.

CASEY STENGEL & VIRGIL TRUCKS

I remember one day I was clinging to a one-run lead with one out and first and third in the ninth. Casey came out and said that he wanted Johnny Kucks, because Johnny was a sinkerball pitcher, and he thought Johnny might get the double play. He had already called down to the bullpen and said that he wanted "Kucks," but Darrell Johnson, the bullpen catcher, thought Casey said "Trucks." Casey almost died when Virgil Trucks hopped over the fence. Well, Trucks came in and threw one pitch, a ground-ball double play, and the game was over. But Casey never let the press know the wrong man came in. The Old Man had style.

—Whitey Ford in *Sweet Seasons: Recollections of the 1955–64 New York Yankees* (Dom Forker, 1990)

This one should be exceptionally easy to track down, because Virgil Trucks spent just a few months of his seventeen-year career with the Yankees. On June 15, 1958—his last season in the majors—the Kansas City Athletics traded Trucks and Duke Maas to the Yankees for Bob Grim and Suitcase Simpson. Trucks was forty-one, but he could still pitch some; in '57 with the A's, he'd gone 9-7 with a 3.03 ERA, and in '58 before the trade he'd posted a 2.05 ERA in twenty-two innings and saved a few games. The Yankees in the 1950s loved to trade for old stars who seemed to have a bit left in the tank, and Trucks filled the bill (as did Sal Maglie and Murry Dickson, two other geezers who pitched for the Yanks that summer).

So he came over on June 15.* Whitey Ford started for the Yankees on the 17th, and would start eighteen games from then through the end of the season (including only three starts in September, due to an elbow injury).

Remember the basics of Ford's story: he's on the mound in the ninth inning of a close game and is replaced by Trucks, who escapes a big jam to seal a victory.

Of course, Ford is more specific than that: he says it's a one-run lead, runners are on first and third, and Trucks throws one pitch to get the game-ending double play. But let's cast our net a bit wider, because I've got a sneaking suspicion—based on my experience with Dom Forker's two books of Yankee recollections—that the specifics won't quite check out.†

Of those eighteen games Ford started after Trucks joined the Yankees, the Yanks won only eight. Of those eight wins, four were blowouts, the

---

* That same day, the A's traded Roger Maris to Cleveland.

† Forker's other book is *Men of Autumn*, featuring members of the Yankees' previous dynasty.

The Old Man used to play hunches once in a while. For example, we went into Detroit and one day we were tied 4–4 with two outs in the ninth. He brought me in to face a left-handed hitter, and I struck him out. I came up in the tenth with a run in, two on, and two out. They brought a left-hander in. It was a pinch-hit situation for Casey. I started to take one foot out of the box, but he let me hit. I hit the first pitch off the facing in right, and we won, 10–6. The pitcher threw me a fastball that sank. When I rounded the bases, the right fielder threw the ball in. I got the ball.

—*Dom Forker,* The Men of Autumn *(1989)*

It was the 16th of July in 1957. Byrne did enter with two outs in the bottom of the ninth and struck out lefty-hitting Charlie Maxwell to send the game into extra innings. And in the tenth, with lefty Al Aber on the mound, Byrne did hit a three-run homer off the facing of the upper deck beyond right field. Only three quibbles: (1) Byrne was actually the third hitter Aber faced, (2) when Byrne batted, the score was already 7–4, and (3) the final score was 10–4. So Byrne's home run, as memorable as it was, also was meaningless.

Two months later against Kansas City, though, Byrne, pinch-hitting for Bob Turley, hit a three-run homer in the seventh inning that was the difference in a 5–3 win. It was Byrne's penultimate game in the majors, as he quit

Yanks winning by at least six runs. That leaves only four games in which Ford started and the Yankees won by five or fewer runs:

June 17	Yankees 4	Indians 0
July 14	Yankees 5	White Sox 0
Aug. 8	Yankees 2	Red Sox 0
Sept. 14	Yankees 12	Athletics 7

The first thing you notice is that this story did not happen as Ford told it; the Yankees didn't win any of these games by just one run, and only the August 8 game seems like it might have been even close to what Ford remembered. So we'll start there.

In that game, Ford gave up only three hits and tossed his seventh shutout of the season (just one shy of Russ Ford's franchise record). So we have to check the other three games.

- On June 17, Ford pitched a complete game, shutting out Cleveland on three hits.
- On July 14, Ford pitched a complete game, shutting out Chicago on three hits.
- On September 14, Trucks enjoyed his greatest day as a Yankee . . . but it didn't have anything to do with relieving Ford.

Pitching for the first time since late August, Whitey held the A's to one run through five innings, but left then to rest his sore elbow.* The bullpen didn't fare well, but the Yankees scored a run in the ninth to force extra innings. And after they scored five runs in the top of the fourteenth, Trucks, who'd entered the game in the ninth, finished off Kansas City with his sixth shutout inning.†

By the time Trucks sealed the deal, Ford was probably showered, shaved, and enjoying a double martini with Toots Shor. So while I didn't want to do it, I'm going to have to check every game in which both Ford and Trucks pitched, and see if there's *anything* here.

Trucks pitched in twenty-five games for the Yankees. In only four of those twenty-five games did Ford also pitch. We already know about September 14. The other three:

---

* The game was meaningless, as the Yankees had clinched the pennant earlier in the afternoon by winning the first game of the doubleheader.

† Aside from this game, Trucks's tenure with the Yankees included 33⅔ innings and a 5.35 ERA.

- On July 9, Ford got knocked out in the eighth and was replaced by Trucks, who added more fuel to the fire as the Indians finished with a 12–2 laugher.
- On August 3, with the Yankees down a run in the eighth, Ford was lifted for a pinch hitter, and Trucks later took Ford's place on the mound. But Trucks was charged with a run, and Ford was hung with the 3–1 loss.
- On September 26 in a meaningless game—the Yankees had already clinched the pennant—Ford started and pitched six strong innings. Following two relievers, Trucks entered in the eleventh inning and took the loss after giving up two runs in the twelfth.

And that's it. Trucks did save two games, on August 12 and August 22. But in neither of those games did he enter in the middle of an inning with the bases loaded (and Johnny Kucks actually started the game on the 22nd).

So what do you think? Ready to give up on this one? Me, too. Almost. Let's check one more thing. Let's check every game in 1957 and '58 that Whitey Ford won and somebody else saved. There aren't many to check: four in '57 and just one in '58.

The one in '58 came on May 10, and by the rules of today there wouldn't have been a save at all. Ford pitched seven innings and left with an 8–0 lead. Ryne Duren finished up with two scoreless innings, and when saves were first credited, retroactively in 1970, they were essentially credited to any pitcher who finished a victory. A few years later the rule was changed—but not retroactively—and of course today Duren wouldn't get a save for protecting an eight-run lead unless he pitched three innings.

Anyway, that leaves four games in 1957. And only two of those four are remotely interesting.

On July 1, Ford, making his first appearance since May, relieved Johnny Kucks (yes, Kucks) in the eighth inning and snuffed out a rally to preserve the Yankees' 2–1 lead. He did blow the save in the ninth, though, and the game moved to extra frames. Mickey Mantle put the Yanks back ahead with a solo homer in the tenth. In the bottom of the inning, with a man on first and one out, right-handed-hitting Jim Brideweser was due next. Stengel summoned Brooklyn Bob Grim from the bullpen, who retired pinch hitter Tito Francona on a grounder to first base, then struck out Jim Busby to seal the victory.

On September 20, Ford started against the Red Sox and carried a 7–0 shutout into the ninth. But Ted Williams led off with a homer, and a few moments later Jackie Jensen homered to make the score 7–4. There were

the next spring to pursue his business interests, though he would later say, "If the opportunity to start games had been there, I never would have quit."

Stories buzzed. When Casey went to the mound to take a pitcher out, the pitcher said, "I'm not tired," and Stengel replied, "Well, I'm tired of you." Bob Cerv, the big outfielder, was sitting at one end of the empty dugout before a game when Stengel came down the runway from the clubhouse and sat down near him. He looked over at Cerv and said, "Nobody knows this, but one of us has just been traded to Kansas City."
　　—*Robert W. Creamer*, Stengel: His Life and Times *(1984)*

As my friend Mike Kopf observes, "Here's a tracer so easy a caveman could do it" . . .

Bob Cerv began his career with the Yankees, who did trade him—actually, they sold him—to the Kansas City Athletics in 1956. But the transaction was on October 15, five days after the World Series had ended. Case closed? Probably . . . but maybe not. According to the Times, *"This sale was believed to be the final move in a trade that started when the Yankees purchased Enos Slaughter from the Athletics late last season." Slaughter had come to the Yankees on August 25 in a waiver deal. So it's possible that the Yankees agreed to send Cerv to the A's then, and it's possible that Stengel told Cerv. But why he would do that, we don't have the slightest idea.*

two outs, but Stengel had seen enough. Again he summoned Grim, who quickly retired Ken Aspromonte on a grounder to third base.

Was one or both of these games floating around in Ford's brain when he told his tale? Kucks makes an appearance in the first, and in the second a reliever comes in and ends things with a ground ball (though not a double play). But if that's as close as we can get, we might as well not bother at all. It's of course a wonderful story, but it seems like a story that might been invented for the amusement of Whitey Ford's many audiences over the years.

WHITEY HERZOG & ROGER CRAIG

One game in 1987 really put that strategy to the test. We were at Busch Stadium playing Roger Craig's Giants, the team we ended up facing in the NLCS that year, and we had a good rivalry. Roger had a hell of a club, one with home-run power and good starting pitching. But we piled it on early. We were ahead 10–3 in the fifth, and Vince, who'd already stolen a base, took a purpose pitch on the arm and got a free pass. He decided to keep doing his thing. He swiped second. Then, on the next pitch, he swiped third. All hell broke loose. Roger stormed out of the dugout after me, both benches cleared, and we had a hell of a rhubarb, with players and coaches rolling all over the field, hollering and kicking and gouging. Roger was charged up, boy. "You're going to *run on me*, you SOB, when you're up by seven? You'd better tell them guys not to run!" he shouted. There's an unwritten rule in baseball that you don't run when you're far ahead; that's seen as showing the other team up.

Unwritten rule, my ass. People talk about the "book" in baseball. There ain't no damn book, and if there was, you'd rewrite it whenever you needed to. But Roger wasn't buying that. He didn't accept that the Cardinals had to steal their way onto the scoreboard. I said, "Roger, if that's the case, why don't we just give you fifteen outs, and you go ahead and hit, because we *don't* run, we ain't gonna score!" If he'd promise me Jeffrey Leonard and Will Clark wouldn't hit any more homers, I'd be happy to call off the hounds.

He didn't take me up on it. And the game proved my point: At the end, Chris Brown, their power-hitting third baseman, came to bat with two runners on base. The score ended up 10–8 for us. They could have won with one swing! Roger never argued the point after that.

—Whitey Herzog in *You're Missin' a Great Game* (Herzog and Jonathan Pitts, 1999)

Plenty of details here, obviously, and Herzog was writing (or dictating, probably) just a bit more than a decade after the events in question. Was his memory really that good?

The easiest to check is the score: did the Cardinals, in 1987, beat the Giants, 10–8?

They did not. According to Retrosheet, the Cardinals and Giants played a dozen games that season. The Cardinals won only five of those games, and by the following scores: 6–5, 7–6, 7–6, 7–5, and 3–2. The first two of those wins were in San Francisco, which leaves only the other three as candi-

You might say that Whitey Herzog wasn't exactly objective when it came to Tommy Herr, his second baseman for years in St. Louis . . .

The most amazing hitter I had those years might have been Tommy Herr. I can't think of a better example of how having a plan, a sense of the situations you're in, can help you succeed. If there was one guy I managed that I would want hitting for me in the stretch drive, in August and September, it'd be hard to pick between George Brett and Tommy. He didn't have much power, but he'd rope it to all fields, torch the lines, bleed it up the middle, even hit one out of the ballpark when you needed it. I don't know how he did that, but if he'd hit you ten homers a year, eight counted for something.

—Whitey Herzog and Jonathan Pitts, You're Missin' a Great Game (1999)

Let's start with that last contention: "if he'd hit you ten homers a year, eight counted for something."

There's one obvious problem here, which is that Herr didn't hit ten homers a year. Herr never hit ten homers in one year. Herr was the Cardinals' everyday second baseman, more or less, from 1981 through 1987. His home runs in those seasons: 0, 0, 2, 4, 8, 2, 2.

Perhaps Herzog was recalling Herr's eight homers in 1985. After all, that's the season everybody remembers, and it's also the season in which Herr became the

dates (assuming that Herzog was wrong about the score and right about everything else). Taking those games in order:

- ◆ On July 9, the Cardinals trailed 3–1 before scoring twice in the bottom of the seventh. The Giants scored three in the top of the tenth, only to see the Cardinals win with four in the bottom of the tenth.
- ◆ On July 10, the Cardinals led 4–2 after six innings, the Giants tied the game in the seventh, both teams scored single runs in the twelfth, and Jack Clark hit a walk-off homer in the thirteenth. Coleman didn't play, and the Cardinals didn't steal any bases.
- ◆ On July 12, the Cardinals won a close one, 3–2. Again Coleman didn't play, and again the Cards didn't steal a base.

For the moment, then, let's assume Herzog's tale is true, but didn't happen in 1987. Craig took over as Giants manager late in the '85 season; the club had already played their requisite games against St. Louis. Herzog managed the Cardinals from 1980 through the middle of the 1990 season. So that's four and a half seasons, 1986 through mid-'90, where they overlapped, and we already checked one of those seasons. We'll start with 1986, for an obvious reason (it's first). And wouldn't you know it? Check out the fifth inning of the game in St. Louis on July 22. Just the facts, ma'am, courtesy of Retrosheet:

> CARDINALS 5th: LaValliere made an out to third; Tudor singled to left; Coleman forced Tudor (second to shortstop) [Coleman to first]; Coleman stole second; Coleman stole third; Smith walked; Coleman was caught stealing home (catcher to pitcher); 0 R, 1 H, 0 E, 1 LOB. Giants 2, Cardinals 10.

Herzog, in his story, didn't mention Coleman trying to steal home, which is something you'd think he would remember. The other thing that gives one pause: Retrosheet accounts usually include a note about interruptions. No mention here, but that doesn't necessarily mean there wasn't a dugout-emptying situation that delayed the game for a while. First I checked *The New York Times* archives on the Web and discovered that, yes, there was a brawl in this game. Then I went to Missouri to look at microfilm, and here's how the *St. Louis Post-Dispatch*'s Rick Hummel described the action:

> There were 26 hits in the Cardinals' 10–7 victory over the San Francisco Giants on Tuesday night, but there were many more in a seventh-inning brawl that involved players, managers and coaches from both teams.

The flame for the fight was the Giants' indignation with Vince Coleman, who stole second and third with the Cardinals leading by eight runs in the fifth. Coleman was out at home trying to score on a wild pitch by Juan Berenguer, and when Berenguer made the tag, he spiked the ball. Both benches emptied after Berenguer yelled at Coleman and Coleman tipped his helmet, but there was not fighting—yet.

When Coleman came to bat in the seventh, Frank Williams threw one close to Coleman, and Bob Davidson issued a warning to both benches. The next pitch hit Coleman, prompting the automatic ejection of Williams and San Francisco manager Roger Craig.

When those ejections were made, San Francisco third baseman Chris Brown became upset and had to be restrained. Both benches emptied, and the melee was on. San Francisco pitcher Mike Krukow took a bull rush at Coleman, and Coleman tackled him.

Players were still milling around when Cardinals manager Whitey Herzog and Craig began arguing. Craig and Herzog shoved each other as umpire John McSherry tried to restrain them. The momentum of all the players carried them into a large pileup near the screen.

Herzog and Cardinals pitcher Rick Horton were involved in a double-team with Joel Youngblood of the Giants after Cardinals pitching coach Mike Roarke had been body-slammed by the Giants' Jeff Leonard.

Herzog then went for a clothesline on San Francisco's Randy Kutcher, and Kutcher threw him off.

Cardinals catcher Mike Heath wrapped up Coleman and kept him from more harm by carrying him off the field. Cardinals second baseman Tom Herr had to be removed from the game with a cut on his face.[1]

Clearly, this is what Herzog remembered. But how poorly he remembered it! He got the year wrong. He got the score wrong. The Giants did *not* have much "home-run power" that season; they finished ninth in the National League with 114 homers (of course, the Cardinals had no power at all, hitting only fifty-eight all season).

Herzog forgot when the festivities broke out; he remembered the fracas happening immediately after Coleman stole third, rather than two innings later. He forgot—or simply didn't bother to mention—that his second baseman wound up with eight stitches because of a spike wound, on his *face* (though in fairness to Herzog, Herr missed just one game). He remembered Chris Brown coming up in the ninth with a chance to tie the game. But that couldn't have happened, because Brown got kicked out of the game in the seventh after tackling Coleman.

first player since George Kell to top 100 RBIs while hitting fewer than ten homers, and only the eighth second baseman in National League history with 100 RBIs . . . and Herr drove in 110. Which is to say, he made a real impression.

So what about those eight homers?

The first, on May 29, was a solo shot in a 5–3 loss.

The second, on June 8, was a big one. Top of the ninth against the Mets—the Cardinals' top competition for the division title— and the game was scoreless. With two outs and nobody on base, Herr put the Cards ahead with a homer off Tom Gorman. And the game ended 1–0.

The third, on June 28, was a solo shot in the third inning and gave the Cardinals a 3–0 lead in a game they'd eventually win, 3–2.

The fourth, on August 18, was yet another solo shot. It must have seemed important at the time, though, coming in the eighth inning to tie the score at four against the Expos (the Cardinals did wind up losing in the tenth, 6–5).

So that's three "big ones" out of four, all of them before September 10. Which is when Herr really started doing his damage. That morning, the Cardinals and Mets were tied for first place in the National League East. Remember, there was no Wild Card in those days; this was a fight to the death. And beginning on September 10, Herr hit four home runs in three weeks.

Otherwise, though, Herzog wasn't far off about the game's conclusion. Moments after all those ejections, the Giants scored three runs in the top of the eighth. And in the top of the ninth, with the score 10–7, Candy Maldonado came to the plate with two outs and two runners on base. Maldonado couldn't have "won it with one swing," but he could have tied it. Chris Brown hit only seven homers that year; Maldonado hit eighteen (which was tops on the Giants), so Maldonado would actually have been scarier than Brown.

Of course he didn't tie it. He flied out to right field.

So Herzog got *most* of the details wrong. The game wasn't in 1987. Coleman didn't reach base by taking "a purpose pitch on the arm." Chris Brown didn't make the last out, and the final score was not 10–8. Nevertheless, the *essence* of Herzog's story is still there. The *essence*, his real point, is that you don't stop trying to score when you've got a big lead because the other team won't stop trying to score. And his point is just *slightly* less well-made with the truth.

FRANK CHANCE & JACK HARPER

Frank Chance belies the stereotype. He may look patrician and speak in complete sentences, but he is also as tough as they come. He once got into a brawl with heavyweight James J. Corbett, and he is relentless on the field. In 1906, he coolly destroyed the career of a pitcher he didn't like. The story goes that Chance was angry when Jack Harper of Cincinnati beaned him once too often. Chance was always getting hit in the head—a trait that shortened his career and perhaps his life—but something about this particular incident angered him. So he convinced the Chicago owner, Charles Murphy, to get Harper in a trade. Then Chance had the pitcher's salary cut by two-thirds and benched him. Harper, of course, had no legal right to challenge this treatment. He pitched a single inning for the Cubs that year, and never played again.

—Cait Murphy, *Crazy '08* (2007)

In Jack Harper's first major-league start, in 1899, he beat Washington 5–4 to break the Cleveland Spiders' twenty-four-game losing streak (the Spiders then capped their season with sixteen straight losses).

From 1901 through 1903, pitching for the Cardinals and the Browns and the Reds, Harper was consistently adequate, posting ERAs higher than the league averages (but not so high that his career was in any danger). In 1904, he won twenty-three games with a solid ERA and looked just a little bit like a star.

Harper returned to mere adequacy in 1905. In 1906, still with the Reds, Harper got off to a rough start: 1–4, 4.17 ERA (when a 4.17 ERA was truly awful). On May 7, the Reds traded Harper to the Cubs, apparently completing an earlier deal that sent infielder Hans Lobert to Cincinnati.

The next day in the Chicago *Daily News*, Chance said, "Harper will be a very good man for us. This will make the pitching staff the best in country." Would Chance have said that if his intention was to bury Harper?

And here's where it gets weird. For nearly a month, Harper didn't pitch at all. On June 6 against the Giants, Harper finally pitched. He started and retired all three Giants he faced in the first inning. After which—as Murphy says—he never pitched in the majors again.

Three batters and out forever? Would Frank Chance really have been so bent on revenge? And how would that have worked, exactly? Did the Cubs keep Harper on the roster all season, while racking up their 116 wins? Did they then release him and somehow convince the other fifteen clubs to spurn Harper's modest talents? I'm just wondering *how* a team could bury a useful player, in those days before you could just park somebody in the minors.

As might have been expected, my harshest critic was Earl Weaver. Baseball is Earl's religion and he thought I was being sacrilegious. He saw the ballpark as a beautiful chapel, but when I was around there was a problem with bats in the belfry. I think the incident that finally convinced him I was beyond redemption occurred in Chicago my second year in the league. I was working the plate in the seventh inning of a close game. Tommy John was pitching for the White Sox and Don Buford was the Oriole batter. As John began winding up, the ball squirted out of his hand and dribbled a few feet behind the pitcher's mound. Tommy continued his follow-through because he didn't want to risk straining his arm by stopping abruptly. Naturally I couldn't resist the opportunity. I threw up my right arm. "Strike one!"

The fans went crazy. Buford stepped out of the batter's box and glared at me. "What the hell are you doing?"

"It caught the outside corner," I said.

Ed Herrmann, the White Sox catcher, agreed with me. "It was a good pitch, Don."

Weaver was on me in an instant, screaming about my making a mockery of the game. I told him it was just a joke, and I changed the call.

But Tommy John couldn't stop laughing. He walked Buford. Then he walked the next batter. Then he

So I wondered what really happened on June 6, 1906. Why *did* Harper exit the game after one inning? Surely one of the local writers noticed, right? And why hadn't Harper pitched before then?

Here's what the *Chicago Tribune*'s man noticed: "Jack Harper started the game, but pitched only one inning. Three Giants were retired in a row, but McGann, the last of the three, hit the ball directly at Harper and hurt his hand so severely that he could not continue."

Fortunately, the *Daily News* correspondent offered more details and went some way toward explaining Harper's previous absence from the mound.

New York, June 7.—The Chicago National League men are looked upon in New York now as the real thing in baseball. In spite of the fact that the Cubs beat the Giants 11 to 3 in the second encounter, Manager Chance would almost have given New York the victory if he could have avoided the misfortune that came with the victory. Jack Harper will be out of the game for two or three weeks more now. He had the same thumb that has kept him out of the game for over two weeks split open in just the same way, only worse this time. He will lose the nail and if he is ready to get into the game in three weeks Manager Chance thinks he will be lucky.

Harper was in fine condition yesterday when he stepped to the rubber to start the second annihilation of the champions. He showed it when he retired the first three men up, but McGann, before he went out, shot the ball in a line to Harper, and Jack caught it in his hands, but somehow or another that tender thumb got in the way and Jack had to give up the idea of pitching the rest of the game.

"I think they might have let me alone for one game," said Harper last night as he held his sore hand in his good one. "In all my experience as a professional player for the last nine years I have never had any such an experience as this before."[1]

But of course he was out for a lot longer than three weeks. Harper didn't appear in the pages of the *Tribune* again until September 9: "Pitcher Jack Harper has notified President Murphy he is thoroughly rested, and will join the Spuds in Boston Sept. 19. Jack evidently wants to cut in on the world's series receipts now by helping win the pennant after it is clinched."

There's a passing mention of Harper in October, but the next real update in the *Tribune* was published on April Fools' Day, 1907:

Columbus, O., March 31.—[Special.]—Presidents Murphy and Bryce closed a deal tonight by which the Columbus club gets Jack Harper, one of the Cubs' pitching possibilities, and in return Chicago will get one of Columbus' pitchers next fall if Harper decides to return to the game to make a living out of baseball. If, however, Harper decides to make a living out of his shoe store the deal is off. In that case neither club will lose anything, as Chance has no place for Harper with the present material.

Now we're getting somewhere. We know that Harper was injured in 1906, though we don't know exactly how serious the injury was. We also know the Cubs—and, yes, the *Tribune* called them Spuds—weren't exactly hurting for pitching. In '06, six Cubs pitched at least 144 innings; the *highest* ERA posted by one of them was 2.21 (Carl Lundgren). Only three other pitchers saw any action at all. Harper, with his single inning, was one of them. The other two pitched roughly seventy innings apiece, and both posted sub-3.00 ERAs.

And 1907? Same thing, only better. Eight Cubs pitched. Five guys pitched more than 138 innings, and the highest ERA among the five was 1.69. The worst pitcher on the staff was Jack Taylor, whose 3.29 ERA was lower than Harper's career mark.

These last two paragraphs are what we call "piling up facts," all of which point to this one: Jack Harper simply wasn't good enough to pitch for Frank Chance's Cubs. It's not clear why the Cubs wanted him in the first place, but there's little doubt about why he pitched just one inning for them: he wasn't healthy enough or good enough to do more than that. No reliable evidence supports the notion that Harper's career was destroyed by a vindictive Frank Chance.

Cait Murphy wrote a good book. I know she did. I read it. And in *The New York Times*, George Will applauded Murphy's "astonishing details." Details are even more astonishing when they're actually, you know, true. These days, there's really no excuse for not checking to see if they are. Particularly when the story is being told not about what a player *did*—which is really just a detail—but about what he *was*.

gave up a double, a single and another walk. Then he took a walk himself. But as he was leaving the field, he cocked his head a bit and looked at me. And winked.

—*Ron Luciano & David Fisher,*
The Umpire Strikes Back (1982)

In Luciano's second year in the league, 1970, he worked only two Orioles-White Sox games, and Tommy John didn't pitch in either of them. In 1971, Luciano didn't work a single Orioles–White Sox game. In 1972, Tommy John was pitching in the National League, and he didn't return to the American until 1979, Luciano's last season as an umpire.

So what about Luciano's first year? He umpired two Orioles–White Sox games. He was behind the plate in one of them. Tommy John didn't pitch in either game.

Which leaves only Luciano's last year, 1979, when Tommy John pitched for the Yankees and Earl Weaver still managed the Orioles. Luciano umpired only two Orioles games all season—perhaps because of the enmity between him and Weaver—and neither of them were against John, or the Yankees. In his umpiring career, Luciano never worked a regular-season game in which John pitched and Weaver managed.

JOHNNY BENCH & GERRY ARRIGO

I knew I had to get my way with pitchers. . . . So I would call pitches for a reason. If a pitcher kept fighting me, sometimes I'd let him throw what he wanted just to show him. Mostly, though, I'd run out and chew his ass. Maloney used to say I treated him like a two-year-old. Other guys started calling me "the Little General." That was music to my ears, if I was playing the position the way it was meant to be played.

I kind of proved that one day against the Dodgers. I was catching Gerry Arrigo, a big left-hander who had been spot-starting for us for a few years, and he was throwing a fastball that I thought was just as soft as an orange. He had a good curveball and he could get a hitter out with it, but then he'd let up on the fastball and not help himself at all. I did almost everything I could to get him to throw the damn thing, but each time he came in with it just as limp and soft as ever. I was so frustrated, so impatient with a guy who just wasn't giving what he could that when he threw the thing again I just reached out with my bare hand and caught it like a tennis ball.

The Dodgers and almost everybody else in the ball park saw it, and I guess nobody could really believe it. Least of all Arrigo. We had a saying at the time— "raisin heart"—which meant that if you weren't doing the job, just not facing the pressure and everybody knew it, your heart dried up like a grape to a raisin. That's what happened to Arrigo, and he just stood out there on the mound staring at me, his heart shrinking by the second. The Dodgers doubled up, they were laughing so hard, and Arrigo, trying to get his composure back, stayed out there, shaking me off and shaking me off. He was pretty flustered. But his fastball suddenly returned.

The story traveled around the league like good news.

—Johnny Bench in *Catch You Later* (Bench and William Brashler, 1979)

Bench debuted with the Reds in late August of 1967, when he was only nineteen, and took over almost immediately as the No. 1 catcher. He caught 154 games in '68 and 147 games in '69, after which Arrigo was gone, so if this happened, it happened in one of those three seasons. And we'll start with 1969 because 1) Arrigo was just a spot starter that season, starting sixteen games, and 2) this anecdote is told in the book just after Bench recounts his 1969 hitting stats.

So we're looking for games against the Dodgers in 1969 in which Bench caught Arrigo. Considering that Arrigo pitched in only twenty games that season, due to an arm injury, we should be able to make that list fairly quickly.

In '69, Arrigo pitched against the Dodgers only twice. Both games were in September, as he started the second games of doubleheaders on the 16th and the 23rd. In the first of those games, he was yanked in the third inning despite having given up only two hits and two walks. In the second, he pitched into the seventh inning and earned the win, allowing nine hits and three walks.

First thing: I'll check *The Sporting News* for any mention of Bench's bare-handed catch. . . . Nothing. Not in September of '69. Nothing in the *Los Angeles Times*, either.

So, going back to '67 . . . Bench came up in late August, but Arrigo pitched just one inning that month against the Dodgers, and Bench was on the bench. For what it's worth, Arrigo did start the game, on the 28th of August, in which Bench made his major league debut (that was against the Phillies, and Arrigo got knocked out in the sixth inning, having issued six walks).

Which leaves only 1968. In '68, Arrigo pitched against the Dodgers five times, all of them starts. On the 4th of May, he pitched a two-hit shutout (the third and last shutout of his career). On the 30th, he got knocked out in the fifth inning. On the 7th of July, he got kayoed in the third inning. On the 6th of September in the first game of a doubleheader, he lasted six innings. And on the 18th in Los Angeles, Arrigo pitched $8\frac{1}{3}$ scoreless innings and beat Don Sutton, 2–0. In each of those games, Bench was behind the plate.

Again, I scoured *The Sporting News*, which in both seasons contained many references to Arrigo and Bench . . . but never together. And you'd think if "the story traveled around the league like good news," the story would eventually have landed in the "Bible of Baseball." But it didn't, leastways not that I could find. Which doesn't mean it didn't happen, in a game against the Dodgers, or some other team, or perhaps even during spring training. I've searched far and wide, though, and the earliest version of this story I can find is the one in Bench's book.

Which contains, by the way, this odd finale: "I don't think Gerry held it against me. He is a house painter in Cincinnati now, and just the other day he painted my condominium. He did a heck of a nice job, so he can't harbor any vengeance. But I can still hear that grape of a heart losing juice."

SONNY SIEBERT & DANNY CATER

And then there was the time I had to knock down Danny Cater, who used to be my best friend. Danny and I had gotten close playing winter ball together in Puerto Rico. Back in the States he started hitting me pretty good. It seems like he was always going two-for-three or three-for-four against me. My wife, who was baseball smart, asked me about it. "Why does he hit you so well? Is it because he's your friend and you don't want to pitch him tight and risk hitting him?" That woke me up, and I realized she was exactly right.

Now, Cater was the kind of guy who liked to be on the field early, and he liked to socialize. He was always talking to you. The next time we played against each other and I was scheduled to pitch, he did his usual thing: "How's Carol? How are the kids?" I didn't answer him, so he asked me what was wrong. "Hey Danny, be alive tonight," I said.

"What? You gonna hit me? What are you talking about?" he said.

"Just be loose in there tonight," I said.

The first time he came up I threw the first pitch under his chin. But he was ready for it, and he got out of the way without any trouble. I thought, "That really didn't serve my purpose," so I threw another knockdown on the very next pitch. It was the best knockdown I've ever seen. It scared him to death, and he pitched himself backward and down on the ground as if his life literally depended on it.

Danny has never spoken to me since. I lost a friend, but I gained an edge over a hitter who used to own me. In fact, I don't think Cater ever got a hit off me again. It taught me that it's tough for a pitcher to be friends with a hitter, because to be successful you simply must use both sides of the plate.

—Sonny Siebert in *Tales from the Ballpark: More of the Greatest True Baseball Stories Ever Told* (Mike Shannon, 1999)

Siebert and Cater faced each other for a lot of years. Siebert debuted in 1964, with the Indians, and he later pitched for the Red Sox and (briefly) the Rangers before moving to the National League in 1974. Cater debuted in 1964 with the Phillies, but joined the White Sox in '65, and also played for the A's, the Yankees, and the Red Sox before going to the National League in '75.

The two didn't cross paths in '75 because Siebert's stint in the NL lasted just one season; in '75, he was back in the AL for his last major-league season. However, their paths certainly *did* cross in Boston.

They were Red Sox teammates in 1972, and in 1973 until May 4, when Siebert was traded to Texas. Did they really go through all of 1972, and (including spring training) more than two months in '73 without speaking to one another, at all?

That's probably not something we can know.

We can, on the other hand, look at their statistical history together and see if there's some clear (or even hazy) demarcation between Cater hitting Siebert and Cater not hitting Siebert. This time line runs from 1965 through 1971, and picks up again for those five months in 1973.

Remember what Siebert says: "It seems like he was always going two-for-three or three-for-four against me."

In seven seasons, Cater never got three hits against Siebert. He never went 3 for 3 or 3 for 4 or 3 for anything else. Their first meeting in a major-league game was in 1965. Not until more than three years later did Cater got as many as *two* hits in a game against Siebert; on August 4, 1968, Cater went 2 for 3 with a double. And in their next meeting, Cater went 2 for 2. So maybe those two games are what Siebert remembers. Except those two games came nearly a year apart; Cater's 2 for 2 happened on June 15, 1969. They met again seven weeks later, on August 3, and Cater was 0 for 4. In fact, after that 2 for 2, Cater went just 3 for 16 in their remaining battles.

So if Siebert really did knock down Cater, if there really was a turning point in their history, he apparently knocked him down on August 3, 1969. If it really made a difference, Siebert might have saved himself two or three hits, maybe four. Personally, I'm not sure if three or four hits are worth a friendship. But then, that's just one of the many reasons I write about the game instead of playing it.

Late Note of Humility: It's possible that I was too quick to dismiss the story in question. Before Harper joined the Cubs in 1906 he started five games for Cincinnati . . . and three of those starts came against the Cubs. In two of those starts, he plunked one Chicago batter. Chance's day-by-day logs don't have a column for HBP, and the *Chicago Tribune* didn't mention any hit batters. But I cannot say with any confidence that Harper didn't nail Chance once or even twice early that season. And thus I can't say with any confidence what Chance had in mind for Harper when he got him.

GEORGE UHLE & BABE RUTH

The Indians Walked Koenig to Pitch to Ruth

Tris Speaker, Cleveland Indians manager of the 1920's, asked if the writer ever heard of passing anyone intentionally to get at Babe Ruth?

"Certainly not," was the answer. "Speaking of things that never happened."

"Don't be so sure," laughed Spoke. "Maybe it only happened once, but it sure happened. We were in the ninth inning one day, leading the Yankees by one run, but they had the tying run on second base.

"Mark Koenig was the batter and George Uhle the pitcher. Ruth was on deck. Out in center field, I didn't think anything unusual was going on when Uhle's first pitch was a low curve for a ball. But when the second was two feet outside, I decided it was time to have a talk with George.

" 'Are you nuts,' I asked him. 'Make this fellow hit the ball. Don't you know the gentleman who will be up next if you walk Koenig?'

"Uhle said: 'Tris, I'd rather pitch to Ruth than to Koenig any time. I thought I'd try to get Mark out on a bad pitch, but if I walk him I'll still be all right. I can take care of the big fellow.'

" 'Okay,' I told him, 'but if that's the way you feel about it let's tell Ruth.' I walked toward the plate and motioned O'Neill out of the catcher's box. 'We're putting him on, Steve,' I said. 'George would rather pitch to Ruth.'

"The big fellow's neck turned purple and he really was cutting when he stepped to the plate. George gave him two curves on the inside and he fouled them over the stands in right. Then he worked the count to three and two. George broke off a beautiful curve. The Babe started to lunge at it, then tried to hold his swing, but it didn't make any difference. The umpire yelled strike three.

"In the clubhouse, everyone was slapping Uhle on the back and some of the boys even thought I must be a great manager for figuring out strategy like that. But when the room quieted down, I called Uhle over to my locker.

" 'George,' I said, 'that was terrific. But please do me a favor. Never try it again. I don't want to have a heart attack in center field. And I'll never come closer than I did while you were pitching to that big guy'."

—Ed McAuley in the Cleveland *News* (reprinted in *Baseball Digest,* August 1950)

Babe Ruth joined the Yankees in 1920. Tris Speaker managed the Indians from the middle of the 1919 season through the end of 1926, after which he joined the Washington club. Mark Koenig debuted with the Yankees on September 8, 1925, and was the Yanks' regular shortstop in 1926. So essentially we've got a small window here: one season plus one month. It's hard to understand why Uhle would be so confident about getting Ruth out, especially considering that Uhle was a right-hander and of course Ruth batted lefty. But, hey, that's what makes it such a good story.

And Uhle might have felt invincible, at least in '26. That season he went 27-11 and finished tops in the American League in wins and winning percentage (and second in ERA, shutouts, and strikeouts). What's more, if this happened late in '25 or early in '26—assuming, of course, that it happened at all—Uhle might have thought Ruth was vulnerable, as the Babe had struggled in '25, at least relative to his own lofty standards.

Before tracking down Uhle's appearances against the Yankees during this period, I should mention one question that comes to mind: Why would Babe Ruth have been batting behind Mark Koenig? Ruth was Ruth, and Koenig was . . . well, Koenig wasn't a bad hitter for a shortstop.

But the Yankees played in the 1926 World Series, and a quick check of the box scores reveals that my skepticism is unfounded. In all seven games, Earle Combs was in the leadoff slot, Ruth batted third as usual, and between them was Koenig.

We'll start with September 1925 . . . and we'll quickly dispense with September 1925, because according to Uhle's daily sheets he pitched only three times in September, and none of those games was against the Yankees.

Which leaves 1926. Uhle started against the Yankees six times, and he owned them. He completed five of those games, winning all five, and finishing the season with a 5-1 record and a 1.93 ERA against the best team in the league. Here are the dates and scores of those five wins:

June 7	5–2
July 8	6–1
Aug. 4	4–2
Aug. 25	6–0
Sept. 18	3–1

So there's at least one hole in Speaker's story. Remember, he says it was the ninth inning, the Indians "leading the Yankees by one run." But Uhle never beat the Yankees by one run. And if this happened in the ninth, the Indians couldn't have extended their lead beyond one run.

But this is a minor quibble. One-run lead or two-run lead, with a runner on base you'd certainly rather pitch to Mark Koenig than Babe Ruth. Or even—actually, *especially*—with a three-run lead. We don't have play-by-play accounts for 1926 games, which means our first plan of attack is checking the game stories in the *Times*. And I'll start with the three closest games. Babe Ruth was the most famous man in the country; if he struck out to end the game, it would presumably have been mentioned in the papers.

On June 7, Uhle did strike out Ruth in dramatic fashion. As the *Times'* James R. Harrison reported, "Uhle showed that Ruth can be pitched to by fanning the Big Boy in the seventh with the bases full and only one out. Only two innings before he had walked G. Herman, but in this instance different strategy had to be used, and the strategy consisted of three swooping curves which Babe failed to touch."[1]

Wrong inning, and anyway Uhle hadn't just walked Koenig (intentionally or otherwise). With one out, Koenig and Earle Combs both singled, bringing up Lou Gehrig. It's true that Gehrig did

Most of the good Babe Ruth stories have been told a million times. This one, though, seems to have generally escaped the attention of the Babe's many biographers.

Babe Ruth's story, "as told to Bob Considine," presented no such foreign and domestic complications. Babe cut out only one scene. Speaking of his wastrel years, before Christy Walsh put a damper on his reckless spending, Babe recalled that on an excursion to a Havana race track he was approached by a pack of Cuban operators who assured him that they'd be happy to fix the next race for him as a gesture of inter-American amity.

Babe was delighted to join the conspiracy. The sharpies had a heart-to-heart talk with the jockeys, then returned and gave Babe the name of the next winner. Babe said fine, he'd bet thirty thousand dollars. To win. The startling size of the bet so impressed the hoods that they re-fixed the race, and all got away with parts of Babe's money.

"No good for the kids," Babe said, scratching the item out of the script.

walk to load the bases, but I've found no indication that it was intentional, or that Speaker baited Ruth.

On August 4 in Cleveland, Uhle got the Babe again. Struck him out twice, actually. In the second inning with the bases loaded, "G. Herman worried Uhle along to the three and two count, then let a good strike float through. 'Batter out.' George glared at Nallin and was still beefing when he came to bat three innings later."

Uhle did *not* walk Koenig to get to Ruth. Koenig was batting second that afternoon, followed by Gehrig, and then Ruth. Uhle had walked Koenig and Gehrig, but there's no indication that he walked either of them on purpose. Neither is there any indication that the Yankees mounted any sort of threat in the ninth.

So it turns out that September 18 is our game. Sort of. With the Indians nipping at the first-place Yankees' heels in the standings:

> The second largest crowd in Cleveland baseball history went into violent convulsions as the harassed New Yorkers faded away before the fiery attack of the home boys. The crowd numbered about 27,000, several thousand of whom overflowed onto the field. Ropes were stretched along the left and right field sides of the park, leaving a small opening in deep centre.
>
> In their eagerness to rake in the golden shekels, the Cleveland management allowed spectators to stand along the right field side, already the shortest in either league. The result was an absurd condition of play, which resulted in measly pop flies becoming two-baggers.
>
> Fortunately, this laughable setting for an important game did not have any effect on the outcome. What beat the Yankees was their own failures and hitting frailties, and the Indians undoubtedly would have won on the biggest field in the world.[3]

It's no surprise that this game stuck in Speaker's head. In the seventh, the Indians had runners on second and third, and Yankees manager Miller Huggins ordered Urban Shocker to load the bases with an intentional walk to Speaker, who "began to kid Shocker and other Yankee players." Huggins shot out of the dugout toward Speaker, and the two had to be separated by two umpires. The Indians did not score, and heading to the eighth they still had a 3–1 lead. Which brings us back to our story. Sort of:

> The Yanks' best chance to overcome Uhle's 3–1 lead came in the eighth inning when Combs singled and Koenig walked with one out. Both moved up on a wild pitch. With Ruth up Speaker ran in to comfort his pitcher, but at three and two the Babe lifted an easy fly to Summa. Meusel then flied to Speaker.

Ruth didn't bat in the game again. With the win, the Indians pulled to just 2½ games behind the Yankees in the standings.

Many of the details don't match up, obviously. But it's clear that this is the incident Speaker was recalling. In just a few minutes, there was an intentional walk (though the walk-ee was Speaker himself), a walk to Koenig with the Babe on deck, and Ruth making an out with the game on the line.

What we can't know is if his memory was really so faulty, or if he just wanted to tell a more entertaining story.

WHEN THE BABE DID . . . SOMETHING

If baseball has its own *Rashomon* moment, it's Babe Ruth's "Called Shot" in the third game of the 1932 World Series. You know the story, I'm sure: Ruth, facing the Cubs' Charlie Root, got engaged in a verbal back-and-forth with the players in the Chicago dugout. "Then, Ruth waved his arm," John Chancellor intones in the *Baseball* documentary. "Whether he was merely gesturing toward the Cub dugout, or pointing toward the center-field stands, no one will ever know for sure."

Then, Ruth hit the ball into Wrigley Field's center-field bleachers.

It's true, I suppose: we'll never know for sure what Ruth intended with those gestures. But that's true of most things, isn't it? With most things, we're perfectly content with *almost* sure.

Ruth's biographers have written many pages about the Called Shot, of course, but I've found that they tend to focus on what the newspapers published, which is natural enough because the newspa-

pers are easy to look at, and anyway writers tend to trust other writers. According to Robert W. Creamer in *Babe: The Legend Comes to Life*, the story written by Joe Williams, and syndicated by Scripps-Howard around the country, "was the only one I found of those written on the day of the game that interpreted Ruth's gestures as pointing toward center."[1]

Other writers picked up on the story, of course, and it quickly became a big part of Ruth's legend. He would hem and haw when asked directly about his actions that afternoon, but in his 1947 autobiography Ruth explicitly claimed that he'd pointed to the bleachers just before hitting the homer. As Creamer wrote, "This version is the one that was substantially followed by Hollywood in the movie of Ruth's life that starred William Bendix, and as bad as the movie was it gave the legend the permanence of concrete."

That filmed version is preposterous, of course. But the *actual* version was *actually* filmed, with hand-held 16-mm cameras, by two fans in the lower stands. Both reels have been tightly held by their owners, and I wasn't able to look at either while writing this article. The first that surfaced was shot by Matt Kandle, from the grandstand on the third-base side. A Canadian writer was allowed to view the film in 1989—later it aired on television—and here's the key passage from his write-up in a SABR journal, *The National Pastime*:

> Now watch closely. The film is slowed down. Slow, slow . . . Charlie Root is starting his wind-up.
>
> And then Ruth points!
>
> Very quickly—his right hand off the bat for just an instant. But he *points!*
>
> And then he points *again*, just before Root pitches, not as he pointed after the first pitch, not an extended, arm-sweeping motion.
>
> Rather, he points like he's cocking a gun, like he *means* it, a killer gesture; his arm levered, then a staccato wrist movement, like a marksman aiming a pistol, or a duelist! The arm up in the air, then down. Then pumped up and down once more, blindingly fast, the instant before Root releases the ball. *Bang, bang*, bye-bye . . .
>
> A split second later—this is all part of the majestic arithmetic of the moment—the pitch is made and the Babe lifts up his leg and pounds the pitch with every drop of juice he has, twisting around after he connects. Oh, what a sublime, consummate swing! He just remains there for an instant in baseball heaven, corkscrewed up and frozen, and Charlie Root too is still, paralyzed, shoulders slumped (yup, he should have brushed him back). And then the Bambino is off and running toward first base . . .[2]

In 1999, another roll of film surfaced, which ESPN aired in 2000. According to Glenn Stout in his book *Yankees Century*, "the film clearly demonstrates that Ruth didn't point to center and he never called his shot."[3]

Funny thing about those films, though: different people will watch them and see different things. I would not suggest the films don't constitute evidence; they're probably the best evidence, one way or the other, that we'll ever have. But that doesn't mean they're conclusive, in part because the angles from which they were shot just don't allow for precision regarding Ruth's exact movements. He certainly did *something* with his right hand, and more than once. But what, exactly, it's still not easy to say. The Babe's biographers often have relied on the accounts in the newspapers—that of Williams, along with those who followed him—but it's clear that if all of them had seen something notable with their own eyes, they'd have written about it for the next day's editions. But few of them did.

As far as I know, there's something quite elemental that nobody's ever done: collect all the eyewitness accounts in one place. I'm afraid I'm not prepared to do that now. What I will do is collect all the eyewitness accounts in my library, and offer them for your consideration . . .

Joe Sewell was the Yankees' third baseman in 1932, and throughout the World Series. Sewell:

> The third game was in Chicago. By now the Cubs were yelling back, and the language was getting brutal. Mrs. Sewell told me they could hear it in the stands, and it was embarrassing.
>
> The big inning was the fifth. I led off with a fly ball to Hack Wilson in center field and came back to the bench to get me a drink of water just like I always did. Ruth batted after me and the ball park was jumping. Everybody in the place was screaming at the Babe. Burleigh Grimes was sitting there on the Cub bench with a towel on his head, and he and Ruth were cussing each other—I'm talking about *cussing* each other. The Babe took a strike and the yelling got louder. He took

Photo courtesy of TSN Archives/Icon SMI

Babe Ruth and Johnny Sylvester

another strike and the yelling got even louder than before. He backed out of the box, and he had his bat in his left hand, and with two fingers on his right hand, he pointed to center field. Didn't say a word to the pitcher, Charlie Root. Next pitch—crack! I've still got a clear mental picture of that ball going out of that ball park. You ever seen a golf ball hit? That's exactly how it went. There was a tree full of boys beyond the fence in center field, and they all dropped out of it and chased that ball.

Someone on our bench said, "Look at old Burleigh." He was waving that white towel, asking for a truce.[4]

In 1921, Ruth took a shine to a three-year-old boy named Ray Kelly. With the approval of Kelly's father, Little Ray—as the Babe called him—became Ruth's personal mascot, and in later years would occasionally accompany the Yankees on road trips. Kelly did eventually grow up, and "left" Ruth in 1931. But in '32, Ruth invited Kelly and his father to Yankee Stadium for the first two games of the World Series. And afterward, Ruth asked Kelly's father, "Can I take Little Ray to Chicago? I have a feeling we're gonna take these guys in four straight."

That's how Little Ray came to be in Wrigley Field for Game 3. It's not clear where he was sitting, but considering that the Babe usually got what he wanted, Kelly might have been sitting in the dugout when everything happened . . .

So I went out to Chicago with them and in the third game—it was sometime in the middle innings, I think the fifth or sixth inning—that's when this business with the "Called Shot" developed. Charlie Root was the pitcher for the Cubs and he threw the first pitch and Babe missed that one, so it was one strike. That's when he put up one finger and I always assumed what he was saying was, "That's one strike."

The next pitch was a ball and the third pitch was a ball and then came a called strike and that's when the Babe put up two fingers, indicating, "Okay, that's two strikes."

That's four pitches: two balls and two strikes. The Cubs were all yelling at him and before the next pitch, the Babe stuck up his hand— elevated his arm with his palm up, pointing over Root's head out to the center field bleachers. The next pitch came in and he creamed it! He hit the longest home run that was ever hit in that stadium up to that point.[5]

Like Burleigh Grimes, Cubs pitcher Guy Bush was on the bench, having started Game 1 and been knocked out in the sixth inning. Here's what he told interviewer Paul Green . . .

☙ *I only wish I could publish
the picture that goes with this
story . . .*

The Red Sox were losing to the St.
Louis Browns, 9–7, in the bottom
of the ninth inning when Boston
catcher Sammy White walloped a
grand slam to win the game.

Thrilled beyond belief, White
happily trotted around the bases
as the Fenway Park faithful cheered
their lungs out. Then White capped
off his four-bagger with a flourish.

About 10 feet from home, he
dropped to his hands and knees
and slowly crept up to the plate.
And when he finally got there, the
crazy catcher leaned over and
kissed home!

—The Baseball Hall of
Shame's Warped Record Book
*(Bruce Nash and Allan Zullo,
1991)*

*White is said to own the (warped)
record for "Wackiest finish to a
home-run trot," and this is said to
have happened in 1952, White's
rookie season. White did hit a walk-
off grand slam in 1952, on the 11th
of June. And here's an interesting
detail that Nash and Zullo don't
mention: White's homer, just the
fourth of his career, came against
Satchel Paige, who apparently was
badly rattled by the antics of Jimmy
Piersall. As the* Herald's *Will Cloney
wrote afterward, "The brash rookie
beat out a bunt to open the inning
and then practically went into
hysterics on the base path with
a series of pantomimes that
bewitched even an old-timer
like Satch."*

Green: In Game 3, Ruth supposedly pointed before hitting a home run.

Bush: Well, I'll tell you, he was talking to me. He was actually answer-
ing a few things I was saying to him. There's been a lot of publicity
about that, a lot of "yes," "no," and just a lot of questions about it over
the years about Ruth calling a home run.

He was left-handed, you see, and our dugout was on the third base
side and he was looking right into the dugout. He came to the plate
and he stood there about a minute and stepped out. Charlie Root was
pitching. Ruth had the bat in his left hand and I thought—now, I'm
going to be honest with you—I thought he pointed to the right-center
or centerfield bleachers. Charlie Root pitched the ball just as soon as
Ruth stepped back into the box and when he did, Ruth hit the ball
clear out of the ballpark.

It came out in the newspapers and everything that he pointed to the
bleachers, which he might have or he might not. Charlie Root, before
he died, said Ruth never called the home run. I kind of disagreed with
him because I believe that Ruth meant to call the home run. He was so
mad, see, I believe that he pointed and I'll always believe that he
pointed but I have no way to prove it.[6]

*So that's three witnesses saying, more or less, that Ruth did call his home run by pointing to
the outfield bleachers. Here's the aforementioned Burleigh Grimes . . .*

I never said nothing to Ruth. Guy Bush and Bob Smith were the guys
who were riding him, calling him a "big ape" and a lot worse, and he
was hollering back at them. I was always supposed to be the bad guy,
so they were always faulting me, but Bush was the ringleader.

Ruth held up his finger to say that he had one strike left, and the
next thing you know everybody's saying he called his shot. Sure, Ruth
played along with it. Why not?[7]

*Charlie Grimm was Chicago's player-manager and presumably would have been pay-
ing as much attention as anybody to the proceedings, though considering he was playing first base, it seems unlikely that he actually heard Ruth saying anything, as he claims
here . . .*

All this time a noisy battle of words was mounting from the rival
dugouts. This brings us up to Ruth's famous visit to the plate with one
out in the fifth inning. Bush, leading the tirade from our bench, turned
a blast on the Babe. One of the nicknames he didn't like was "Big Monkey," and I'm sure Guy included it. Even before Root got his first of two
pitches for strikes, Babe pointed straight away and turned toward our
dugout—no doubt for Bush's benefit. Those who saw Ruth pointing his

finger chose to believe, when he drove the ball over the center-field bleachers, that he was calling his shot.

I hesitate to spoil a good story, one that has been built up to such proportions down the years that millions of people have insisted they saw the gesture, but the Babe actually was pointing to the mound. As he pointed, I heard Ruth growl: "You'll be out there tomorrow—so we'll see what you can do with me, you so-and-so tightwad."

. . . Root never squawked as the legend grew that Ruth had called his shot for baseball's most celebrated home run. But he did balk when he was offered a chunk of money to recreate the scene in the Babe Ruth movie made later in Hollywood . . . [8]

Second baseman Billy Herman was at his infield position, like Grimm, so he probably was keeping a close eye on Ruth . . .

That was the Series in which Ruth supposedly called his shot. I say "supposedly." He didn't really do it, you know. I hate to explode one of baseball's great legends, but I was there and saw what happened. Sure, he made a gesture, he pointed—but it wasn't to call his shot. Listen, he was a great hitter and a great character, but do you think he would have put himself on the spot like that? I can tell you what happened and why it happened . . .

I think it was around the fifth inning when Ruth came up. Of course, it was always an occasion when that guy stepped up to the plate, but this time it seemed even more so. He'd already hit a home run, in the first inning with two on, and the Chicago fans were letting him have it, and so was our bench. I was standing out at second base, and I could hear it pouring out of the bench. Charlie Root was pitching. He threw the first one over, and Ruth took it for a strike. The noise got louder. Then Root threw another one across, and Ruth took that, for strike two. The bench came even more alive with that. What Ruth did then was hold up his hand, telling them that was only two strikes, that he still had another one coming and that he wasn't out yet. When he held up his hand, that's where the pointing came in. But he was pointing out toward Charlie Root when he did that, not toward the center-field bleachers. And then, of course, he hit the next pitch out of the ball park. Then the legend started that he had called his shot, and Babe went along with it. Why not?

But he didn't point. Don't kid yourself. I can tell you just what would have happened if Ruth had tried that—he would never have got a pitch to hit. Root would have had him with his feet up in the air. I told you, Charlie Root was a mean man out on that mound.[9]

The front page of the next day's Boston Post *featured a photo of White, spread-eagled on the ground at the plate, "as he puts his lips to the pentagon."*

One of my favorite games was against the Boston Red Sox in Cleveland in 1958 or 1959, and every time I see Bill Monboquette he reminds me about it. He pitched against me that day. We were ahead, 1–0, going into the ninth inning, and up to then I'd struck out Ted Williams three times in a row. Pete Runnels was the leadoff hitter in the ninth, and while he was up at the plate getting ready to hit, Williams was stalking around down in the dugout and looking out at me kind of weird. It scared the hell out of me.

Runnels got a hit to bring up Williams, and as he dug in at the plate, he was still glaring at me. I was thinking that I'd just blow his big ass away again.

But this time he hit a ball that made it to the upper deck of the old Stadium, which was a helluva long way, and the Red Sox won, 2–1. Somebody said I should have chased him around the bases. I didn't . . . I respected him too much.

Besides, I was afraid he'd come after me and hit me—not the ball—again.

    —*Russell Schneider*, Tales from the Tribe Dugout *(2002)*

Ted Williams didn't strike out often, and rarely struck out twice in one game, let alone three times. . . . In fact, Williams never struck out three times in one game in 1958, or in 1959, or for that matter in 1960 (his last season). We could check 1957, but that would be sort of

Gabby Hartnett was the catcher and thus had a better view on the proceedings than anybody else, assuming of course that he wasn't looking elsewhere:

I don't want to take anything away at any time from Babe Ruth, for I know that if it weren't for Ruth, we wouldn't have collected those nice salaries.

We had been riding him all during the World's Series, and he was coming back at us strong, too. The Mark Koenig incident was Ruth's ammunition. The Cubs had voted the ex-Yankee shortstop only a one-half share of the World Series jackpot after he had helped hit them into the pennant.

Ruth shut up our bench one day in New York. "When you guys can make $80,000 a year," shouted the Babe, "that's the time to pop off." He was also peeved because our trainer, Andy Lotshaw, was riding him. The Bambino didn't mind the players, but he didn't take kindly to Lotshaw's joining in the jockeying.

There are a lot of versions about that home run Ruth hit, but I was as much to blame as Charley Root for what happened. After all, I called the pitch. But to be exact about it, when the Babe put up the index finger on his left hand and pointed into center field, this is what he said:

"It only takes one to hit it." . . . And he was yelling that to the entire Cub bench.[10]

Ford Frick would one day become most famous as baseball's Commissioner, a post he held from 1951 through '65, and before that he was National League President for many years. In 1932, though, he was still a sportswriter, and later he would serve—while N.L. prexy—as Babe Ruth's ghostwriter . . .

The situation was dramatic. Root's first pitch was a ball. The second was a called strike. On the third pitch the Babe swung at a low outside fast ball—and missed. Strike two! At that point, Ruth stepped from the box, dusted his hands, and then raised his right arm, with one finger extended, in the now famous gesture.

Root pitched. There was a crack of the bat, a white blur as the ball took off, and a moment later the Babe was pigeon-toeing around the bases, grinning broadly as he doffed his cap to the roaring crowd. On the strength of that gesture, another Ruth legend had been born.

At the moment, there was no doubt in my mind, or in the minds of any of the writers who were covering the Yankees. The Big Guy had done it again. He had called his shot, and in the most spotlighted arena imaginable. A World Series game! That's what we wrote. That's what we believed.

Later that night Charley Root questioned the gesture. That Babe had raised one finger was evident. But, Root insisted, he did not point toward the stands. The one-finger gesture was the Babe's way of saying that he still had one big swing left. Knowing Charley Root as I did, I had to believe his sincerity. He was a great competitor and a tough loser, but he was honest, too, and fully prepared to give the Babe full credit as the greatest home run hitter of all time. Furthermore, Charley's version was backed by Gabby Hartnett, Cubs catcher, who quoted Ruth as remarking, as he made the gesture, that he still had one big one left.

Nor did Babe ever seem willing to make any claim. Some days later when I was doing a bit of "ghosting," I had occasion to bring up the subject with Babe. "Tell me, Jedgie," I asked him, "did you really point to the stands and call that shot?" The Babe grinned. "Jeez, kid," he replied, "you can read the papers can't you? You know what the writers said." [11]

Cubs third baseman Woody English knew what the writers said. Many years later he said of the "Called Shot" story, "That came from a reporter's imagination. The pressbox at Wrigley Field is way up on the third deck behind home plate; it's a long distance from home plate. This reporter looks down, sees Babe at bat holding up his hand and maybe pointing out to the fence." So what really happened?

I was playing third base at that moment, and I saw exactly what happened. I was looking at Ruth and saw what he did. We were all yelling to beat the band at him and he held up those two fingers. He may have been pointing out to right center field, but he was calling out, "That's only two strikes, only two strikes." He wasn't calling his shot, he was just holding up the two fingers, suggesting that he had one strike left. [12]

Rookie Frankie Crosetti played shortstop for the Yankees in 1932, and almost seventy years later he was still talking about Ruth and all his old Yankee teammates . . .

So when he thought the Cubs stiffed his friend, he got on them. Babe would really razz them good. Called them cheapskates, penny-pinchers, tightwads. The Cubs, they razzed him back, making fun of his big belly and calling him Fatso. Someone in their dugout offered to hitch a wagon to him. And they said a lot of stuff to each other you can't print in this book.

In that game you're talking about, Root got a strike on Babe and, boy, did the Cubs let him have it. Then Root got another strike past Babe—I think that made it 2 and 2—and now they really ripped into him. Babe stepped out of the box. He put up his hand but *he did not point to center field!* What Babe did was turn slightly toward the Cubs dugout and hold one finger in front of his face, meaning he had one more strike left. I was watching and he didn't point to center field like every-

pointless since Gary Bell didn't reach the majors until '58.

So we know this didn't happen—at least not in a game that counted—as Bell says it did. But did Bell give up a homer to Williams? Perhaps after two strikeouts?

Yes and no.

Bell's first major-league start was against the Red Sox. The Splinter didn't strike out or hit a homer.

Bell next faced the Red Sox on June 24, and this time he struck out Williams twice. Boston's starter was Frank Sullivan, not Bill Monboquette.

The next time they faced off, on the 3rd of August, Williams didn't strike out . . . but in the ninth he hit a two-run shot to beat Bell, 3 to 2. Boston's starter in that game was Ike Delock.

The two met one more time that season, in mid-September, and again Bell struck out Williams twice (aside from Bell, only Jack Harshman and Dick Donovan managed to strike out Williams more than once in a game in '58).

In 1959, Bell faced Williams in five games, but didn't strike him out once (Williams did hit a third-inning homer).

In 1960, they matched up for only two plate appearances, one of which ended in a strikeout. No home runs that season, though.

It looks like Bell has conflated his two strikeouts in his second meeting with Williams, with Williams's big homer in their third meeting. Bill Monboquette, though? He didn't pitch in any of Bell's games against the Red Sox in '58.

one says. It just so happened he hit a home run on the next pitch! Boy, that shut the Cubs up. Babe was like a little kid running around the bases . . .

Naturally, the next day, after a couple of writers wrote that he called the shot, everyone wanted to know whether or not he pointed. But I was with Babe, sitting next to him in the dugout, and, no matter how many questions the reporters asked, he never said that directly. He also didn't exactly deny it. He just went along with whatever they said, let them fill in the details. That's why the story spread. After they left, and I remember this like it happened yesterday, I asked him what that was all about and he told me, "You and I both know I didn't point, but if those writers want to think that I pointed to that spot, let them. I don't care."[13]

Well, I don't know if Crosetti really remembered that conversation as if it were yesterday, but when a Yankee who apparently liked Ruth debunks a story, you have to consider him a pretty credible witness, right? Also, Crosetti, unlike many who have told the story over the years, gets the count right: two balls and two strikes (many accounts have the count being 0 and 2 when Ruth homers).

What follows is a bit strange, as Yankee catcher Bill Dickey claims to have been in the on-deck circle while Ruth batted, though Dickey was still three batters away; the lineup went Ruth, Gehrig, Lazzeri, then Dickey. But the rules regarding such things were a bit more relaxed in those days, and it's quite possible that Dickey and even Lazzeri were on the field with Gehrig . . .

I know the true story—I was in the on-deck circle with Gehrig at the time—but I'm gonna hold my tongue.

I used to get into arguments with Gabby Hartnett. He'd say, "Ruth did *not* point." And I'd say, "Oh, yes he did, Gabby. Oh, yes he did." And he'd get so mad at me he couldn't see.

Let's just leave it at that.[14]

Joe McCarthy managed the Yankees, of course, but just two years earlier he'd managed the Cubs and was quite familiar with most of the players on not only his team, but the other as well . . .

I won my first pennant with the Yankees in 1932. We played my old team in the Series that year, the Cubs. Beat them four straight. It wasn't a very friendly World Series. There were some pretty rough bench jockeys on both sides. The Cubs were on Ruth an awful lot. Babe had a knack for stirring things up, you know. That's the Series where they say he called his home run. That's a good story, isn't it? A lot of people still believe today that he really did that. Did he? No. You see, the Cubs were riding him from the bench every time he came to the plate, and finally he pointed over at them. Then he hit the next pitch out. After he hit the ball, somebody said, "Did you see where he pointed?" Well, a lot of them did see his hand go up and they said, "Maybe he did point that way." That's how the story began. Tell you the truth, I didn't see him point anywhere at all, but I might have turned my head for a moment.[15]

So that's twelve eyewitness accounts. Finally we'll turn the floor over to Joe Williams, who wrote the story that got everybody jazzed in the first place. He would revisit the story many times over the years, and quoted many witnesses . . .

Lou Gehrig: The gestures were meant for Bush. Ruth was going to foul one into the dugout, but when the pitch came up, big and fat, he belted it.

Art Fletcher: There was no talk about it in the dugout at the time.

Charlie Root: The Babe didn't point to center field; he pointed to our dugout, specifically to Claude Passeau. We were giving him a rough time from the bench and Claude was the jeer-leader.

Further, Williams wrote,

Some years later I was in Hollywood and the Babe's life story (or what passed for it) was in production, and I was having lunch with Bill Bendix, who was playing the lead and Joe E. Brown's son, who was doing the ballyhoo. A problem in casting had developed that day. To give the picture a touch of authenticity—and no sports biography ever needed one more—Root had been asked to play himself in the film, for which contribution to realism and the higher arts he would be suitably rewarded. "But Root wouldn't do it," said young Brown. "Says it's a damn lie and never happened."

This was realistic evidence that there was more fable than fact in the called shot, for Root was known to have no small respect for the dollar, and the opportunity to appear in a Hollywood epic must have been tempting.

I think I was as close to the Babe as any sportswriter of the era. Possibly closer. I was often a houseguest. I sensed early that it was fruitless to try to draw him out on matters of controversy or personal conflict.

I've always thought it significant that he never once stated in my presence that he had called THAT home run off Charles Root of the Cubs in the 1932 World Series—except possibly by inference.[16]

In the midst of a discussion about the Called Shot on a website, someone credibly representing herself as Charlie Root's granddaughter weighed in with this . . .

Charlie Root, the pitcher who supposedly served up the "Called Shot," was my grandfather. To his dying day, he vehemently debunked the legend. The Babe himself, when interviewed by sportswriter Hal Totten, said, "Of course I didn't point. Only a fool would do that with Root pitching."

Grandpa was never opposed to throwing a "brushback" pitch, and he always said that if Babe had had the "nerve" (not Grandpa's choice of words) to predict a homerun while hitting against him, he would have knocked him on his "backside" (also not Grandpa's choice of words) . . .

It is a pity that Charlie Root is known more for this infamous event than for his outstanding record. Many of his pitching records with the Cubs still stand and will probably never be broken. He had a distinguished career, he was a true gentleman, and it is a pity that he has never been inducted into the baseball Hall of Fame.

—*Kathy Root Hart*

Charlie Root was one hell of a good pitcher. But he's no Hall of Famer. While he wouldn't be the worst pitcher in the Hall of Fame, if elected—he was better than Rube Marquard, and just as good as Jesse Haines—many, many pitchers not in the Hall of Fame were as good as, or better than, Root. He did win 201 games, but he won more than nineteen in a season only once, and in four World Series with the Cubs—the Cubs lost all four of them—Root went 0 and 3 with a 6.75 ERA. Yes, it's a pity that Root's remembered only for giving up a home run. But if not for that home run, I'm afraid, he would be remembered hardly at all.

If anybody wanted to believe the story about the Called Shot, it must have been the guy who wrote the story in the first place. But it's clear that he didn't believe it, either. What's also clear—or mostly clear—is that Ruth held up his hand, with one or two fingers extended, and said something like, "It only takes one pitch." That's audacious enough, and in a sense the Babe was calling his shot. But it seems highly unlikely that he was pointing toward the center-field bleachers and predicting that he'd hit a homer on the next pitch. Though maybe he would have, if only he'd thought of it.

BOBO NEWSOM & LEFTY GROVE

People will probably think I'm lying when I say this, but Lefty Grove never beat me and I guess we hooked up 18 or 20 times. Sometimes Lefty or myself left early and neither of us got the win or loss, but he never beat me. Look it up.

—Bobo Newsom in *Baseball Digest* (May 1957)

When Newsom said this, it wasn't so easy to look up. Today it is.

Grove spent his entire career in the American League, 1925 through 1941. Newsom didn't. He debuted with the Dodgers in September of '29, pitched briefly for them again in 1930, spent '31 in the minors, pitched one inning for the Cubs in '32, spent '33 in the minors, and finally began in earnest his long, peripatetic (mostly) American League career in 1934 with the Browns.*

So that's a range of eight seasons, 1934 through '41, and Grove pitched for the Red Sox in all of them. For each of those seasons, Retrosheet lists the starting pitchers in each game—in the Red Sox game logs—and the winner. For some reason they don't list the loser, so once I've got the list of games they both started and Grove won, I'll have to consult box scores elsewhere to determine whether Newsom lost one (or more) of them. Exactly the sort of slog that I actually enjoy.

First off, they didn't hook up eighteen or twenty times. Due to the vagaries of the baseball schedule and Grove's injuries—he missed most of 1934 and was never completely healthy after 1937—they started only nine regular-season games against one another. It is true, however, that Grove never did beat Newsom.

Newsom did lose one of those nine games, but he didn't lose to Grove, who'd been lifted for a pinch hitter in the seventh. Similarly, Grove lost one game other than to Newsom, who'd been lifted for a pinch hitter in the eighth. There were two games—both

---

* Newsom was forty-six when he pitched his last game in the majors. In addition to the Dodgers, the Cubs, and the Browns, he pitched for (in order) the Senators, the Red Sox, the Browns, the Tigers, the Senators, the Dodgers, the Browns (in '34), the Senators, the Athletics, the Senators, the Yankees, the Giants, the Senators, and the Athletics (and in case you weren't counting, that was five different stints with Washington).

of them Red Sox losses—in which neither pitcher figured in the decision. Among the nine, Grove won just one: in 1940, he beat Newsom's Tigers 6–5 in thirteen innings, Newsom having given way to a pinch hitter in the twelfth.

Which leaves four games that Newsom won and Grove lost. Oddly, those four were their first three matchups and their last.

On the 11th of August in 1935, Newsom beat Grove, 4–2.

A few weeks later, on the 1st of September, both pitchers went the distance in a marathon. In the bottom of the fourteenth, Newsom drove home the winning run to beat Grove, 2–1.

On May 10, 1936, Newsom beat Grove, 4–0, allowing only six hits.

It was another five years before both pitchers got a decision in the same game. On the 11th of July in 1941, Grove faced off against Newsom, who was by then pitching for the Tigers. It was a big game for Grove; eight days earlier he'd recorded his 299th win. And while numbers weren't fetishized then as they are now, 300 wins was big news. Grove had won only seven games in 1940 and didn't get off to a great start in '41; his 299th career win on July 3rd was just his sixth of the season.

Bobo Newsom

Photo courtesy of Transcendental Graphics

He pitched well on the 11th, but not well enough. As the Associated Press reported, "Lefty Bob Grove gave only six hits today in trying for his 300th major league triumph, the same number as Buck Newsom allowed, but the 41-year-old veteran got little help at the plate and the Red Sox suffered a 2-to-0 shut-out by the Tigers."

Grove started a week later against the White Sox and took the loss. Another week later, on the 25th of July at Fenway Park, Grove started against the Indians. He did get No. 300, but it wasn't easy. After three innings the Red Sox trailed 4–0. After seven innings the score was 6–6. In the bottom of the eighth, though, the Red Sox scored four runs on Jimmie Foxx's two-run triple and Jim Tabor's two-run homer (his second of the game). Grove finished off the Indians in the ninth, with centerfielder Dom DiMaggio squeezing Lou Boudreau's fly ball for the final out.

Afterward in the clubhouse, somebody asked Grove if he was going to quit. "Quit now?" he said. "They'll have to cut the uniform off me. I'm going out for another 300. They couldn't be any harder to get than the first 300." [1]

Grove started five times in August but didn't win. In his start on the 27th he pulled a muscle in the first inning and didn't start another game until September 28, the last day of the season. He lasted just one inning against the Athletics, his original team, and never pitched again.

And Bobo Newsom? Sure, he exaggerated a bit. But that's what Newsom did. He was a storyteller, and storytellers exaggerate without even thinking about it. One thing he didn't have to exaggerate, though: Lefty Grove won 300 games, but he never beat ol' Bobo.

Here's another Bobo story, from Arthur Daley's book *Inside Baseball:*

> He's had some truly incredible experiences. The Showboat was pitching for Washington on opening day of 1936 against the Yankees when the swift Ben Chapman dumped a bunt toward Ossie Bluege at third. It had to be one of those lightning-fast, blind-throwing plays. The infielder pounced on the ball, unaware of the fact that Bobo was standing near by, dreamily contemplating the impression he must be making on President Roosevelt and the other spectators by his pitching artistry.
>
> Bluege never looked. He just threw. The ball crashed sickeningly behind Newsom's right ear and the Great Man ran around in circles like a pain-crazed elephant. That was in the third inning, mind you. But Bobo continued the game and finally beat Lefty Gomez in the ninth, 1–0.
>
> "When the President of the United States comes out to see Ol' Bobo pitch," he announced dramatically afterward, "Ol' Bobo ain't a-gonna let him down." He had pitched those last six innings with a fractured jaw.

More on the Great Man from Daley's book . . .

But he could blow down regularly such power hitters as Jimmy Foxx, Al Simmons, Charlie Gehringer and Hank Greenberg. When Hammering Hennery was approaching Babe Ruth's home run record and had fifty-eight, he squared off against Newsom. As Bobo described it, "Ol' Bobo whuffed him three times on ten pitches." On the fourth trip to the plate Newsom deliberately fed him three balls, cockily strolled up from the mound and remarked: "Hankus, me lad, this is it."

And he "whuffed" him again.

In Detroit's pennant year of 1940 Bobo had won nineteen games in late September and needed a twentieth victory for a handsome bonus. Although scheduled to start the second game of a double-header, he was in the bullpen during the first fray. When Manager Del Baker signaled for a relief pitcher, in lumbered Bobo—on his own. Baker screamed in dismay.

"If Bobo ain't worryin' none," said Bobo, "you shouldn't neither."

So he won the first game—and the second one, too.

Yes and no.

Or rather, no and yes. In 1938, Greenberg did have fifty-eight homers when he faced Newsom— pitching for the Browns that season—on the 28th of September. And Newsom did keep Greenberg in the ballpark that afternoon. But he hardly "whuffed" him four times. While getting beat 6–2, Newsom gave up a single to Greenberg,

More extraordinary than that, even, was the time he was hurling against Cleveland. Earl Averill rocketed a line drive which caromed off Bobo's knee. He howled like a stricken bull moose, but hobbled over to pick up the ball and throw out the Indian at first. Bench jockeys taunted him for rubbing the knee and grimacing in pain. Eventually Newsom lost, 5 to 3 and dragged himself back to the clubhouse.

"Mike," he drawled to Trainer Mike Martin, "Bobo thinks his laig's broke."

It was—the kneecap splintered from end to end.[2]

The story about Opening Day in 1936 certainly is true. Well, most of it is true. It all happened on the 14th of April. Roosevelt was there and tossed out the first pitch, "then sat back and for more than two hours watched as tense, keen and dramatic a ball game as he ever will see." In the fifth inning (not the third, as Daley wrote), Newsom was struck behind the right ear by Bluege's errant throw. The game was stopped for seven minutes, though it's not at all clear that Newsom's jaw was broken; the newspapers reported a "bad bruise" and Newsom took his turn in the rotation just four days later. He did wind up pitching a complete game, with the Senators scoring the game's only run in the bottom of the ninth when Carl Reynolds doubled to plate Cecil Travis.[3]

And the supposedly splintered kneecap, courtesy of Earl Averill? Newsom's and Averill's career intersected for seven seasons, 1934 through 1940. According to *Baseball: The Biographical Encyclopedia*, this happened in 1935, and in typically (for Newsom) colorful fashion . . .

> The next year Newsom was traded midseason to Washington. In one game he got two strikes on the Indians' Earl Averill and shouted, "Now, Bobo, I'm gonna whiff you with an outside pitch!" Averill lined the pitch off Newsom's knee. Newsom managed to throw him out at first, however, and then proceeded to shake off the pain and pitch a complete game. "I got a piece of news for you," he informed the Senators' trainer after the contest. "Bobo thinks his leg is broke." It was, and Newsom was out for five weeks.[4]

In 1935 the Browns actually sold (not traded) Newsom to the Senators for $40,000 on the 21st of May. One week later, on the 28th in Washington, Newsom started against the Indians. He limited the Tribe just two runs until the eighth, when they scored three more for a 5–4 lead, which was how the game ended. In the first inning, Cleveland's Joe Vosmik tripled, then scored on what the Associated Press described simply as "Averill's grounder," with no mention of any ricochet off the pitcher.[5]

So was that it? According to *The Sporting News*, Newsom was actually injured in the third inning. And, yes, it was Averill.

Whether Griffith will get $40,000 worth of pitching out of Newsom now is a matter of conjecture, but it certainly was worth something to the Washington prexy to see the interest and gameness exhibited by his new purchase. Newsom seemed well on his way to a second straight victory for his new club and a clean sweep over the Indians when Averill's liner struck him on the knee in the third inning and bounced halfway to the Senators' dugout. Buck was after the ball like a flash, not knowing the extent of his injury.

Nor were the Griffmen aware of a fracture, for Newsom waved them away and continued to pitch in spite of an excruciating pain which he veiled with grins and taunts to the Indians. He went the route, although weakening in the eighth to lose a 5 to 4 decision. Not until he was removed to a hospital that night, when X-rays revealed a fracture of the lower pole of the kneecap, were Harris and Griffith aware of the loss of their new moundsman. Buck spent three painful days and nights while waiting for the swelling to go down so that a cast might be placed on the knee.[6]

At the time, the prognosis was that Newsom would miss five weeks, and that was almost exactly right, as he next started on July 7 against the Yankees. He pitched a complete game . . . and lost 11–1 (the only consolation being his own RBI single that kept Johnny Broaca from pitching a shutout).

In 1967, in the fourth inning of a game against the Pirates, Bob Gibson was struck on the leg by a line drive off the bat of Roberto Clemente. Gibson faced three more batters, walked two of them, then exited the contest with a broken leg. He didn't pitch again for seven weeks. Ever since, Gibson has been lionized for his toughness, and rightfully so. Newsom, while nowhere near the pitcher Gibson was, *was* the greater showman. And you know, he might have been just as *tough* as Gibson.

along with a couple of pop-ups and a fly ball to center field. At least according to the Associated Press.

Greenberg did later tell interviewer Mike Ross, "When I was going for the home run title in 1938 and he was with the Browns, I couldn't hit him. He kept pitching me outside, low and away, and it was hard for me to pull a ball and hit a home run off him. When I look back at it I maybe didn't hit one or two home runs off him in my whole career.'" (Actually, Greenberg hit four home runs off Newsom in his career, including two in one game in 1939.)

And in the closing stages of the pennant race in 1940, Newsom did indeed win both ends of a doubleheader. It happened on the 25th of September, but I cannot say that he came, unbidden, out of the bullpen to win the first.

WALTER MAILS & JIM POOLE

Jim Poole was a Portland slugger who hit Walter (The Great) Mails as if he owned him. But there came a day years ago when the Oakland-Portland game depended on one pitch. The count was three and two.

Mails stopped the game, walked to home plate, took off his cap and addressed the crowd as follows:

"Ladies and gentlemen—and Mr. Poole," he began, "the moment in our lives has arrived when either you will be the Great Poole and I will be the Ordinary Mails or I will be the Great Mails and you will be the Ordinary Poole. After looking into the crystal ball, I have determined that any man who rides over the mountains from Tennessee on a mule to report as you once did, can't possibly be smart enough to outluck the Great Mails. I will now return to the mound and will throw you a fast ball which you will take. Ladies and gentlemen, we will then go home, leaving Mr. Poole in disgrace."

Mails went back to the mound, threw the fast ball for a strike. Poole took it.

"Why did you take it?" Mails asked him, a moment later.

"I thought you were going to cross me up and throw me a curve," Poole replied.

—James K. McGee in the *San Francisco Call-Bulletin*
(reprinted in *Baseball Digest*, September 1950)

In checking this story, the first thing I did was the first thing I always do when checking a story from the minor leagues: I consulted the Professional Baseball Player Database, a CD-ROM produced by Old Time Data Inc.

There wasn't a match. The Database shows that Mails did pitch for Oakland, in 1930 and '31, but that Poole never played in the Pacific Coast League. After chasing my tail for a while, I finally noticed that both players' records started in 1927, and then I remembered that the Database (or at least the version I was using) *begins* with 1927. What's more, 1) I knew that Mails had pitched professionally at least as far back as 1920, with the Indians, and 2) when I

Googled Jim Poole I found this: "An active player for 34 seasons, until he was 51 in 1946, Poole spent only three years in the majors. In the minors, he played for 30 teams, often as a player-manager . . . He once hit 50 home runs at Nashville of the Southern Association."

So we know Poole really was a slugger, and we also know we're missing some minor-league seasons for both players, pre-1927. But were they ever in the Pacific Coast League at the same time?

I found Poole's career in *Minor League Baseball Stars* (SABR, 1984) and I found Mails's complete Pacific Coast League record in Dennis Snelling's book *The Pacific Coast League: A Statistical History, 1903–1957*

(McFarland & Co., 1995). From there, it was easy to discover that Mails's and Poole's Coast League careers matched up in two seasons: 1923 and 1924, and in both seasons Mails did pitch for Oakland and Poole did hit for Portland.

Both players were among the best in the league. Over those two seasons, Mails pitched a huge number of innings and won forty-seven games, and Poole batted .346 with sixty-five homers and 295 runs batted in.

In 1923 and '24 the Pacific Coast League scheduled 202 games per team (which sounds like a lot, but in 1904 and '05 a couple of PCL teams played 225 games). In those days the schedule ran from early April through the middle of October, and most series were scheduled for seven games, beginning on Tuesday and finishing with a twin bill on Sunday.

The annual baseball guides listed the schedule for the coming season, and the next edition would list how many times each team played another. So I've got the schedules as listed before the seasons—pending weather and travel issues, of course—and I also know that Oakland was supposed to play Portland twenty-eight times in 1923, thirty times in 1924.

So that's fifty-eight games to find (and check). And with that, I've gone nearly as far as my computer and my library can take me. Nobody's yet posted old PCL results, let alone box scores, on the InterWebs. Fortunately, I live in Portland, so now it's just a matter of going to the library and slogging through the microfilm (which is, believe it or not, how we used to do almost everything).

In 1923, Mails pitched against Portland eight times. Poole played in seven of those games. In none of those seven did the writers covering the Beavers for the two Portland newspapers mention anything about Mails striking out Poole with the game on the line.

In 1924, Mails pitched against Portland six times. In one of those games—Mails went all sixteen innings of a 2–2 tie—Poole didn't appear (that tie, by the way, meant the two clubs actually faced off thirty-one times, because the tie was later replayed). Poole did play in the other five. Again reading through the coverage in the Portland papers—the *Daily Journal* and the *Oregonian*—we find just one incident that resembles our story: on August 27, Mails beat the Beavers 6 to 3, and in the fifth inning he struck out Poole with the bases loaded.

Unfortunately, if Mails did announce to everybody within earshot that he would strike out Poole with a fastball, the writers in attendance didn't bother mentioning it in the next day's editions. Which certainly doesn't mean it didn't happen, as Mails was perhaps the greatest showman the game has ever known, at least this side of Satchel Paige. Mail called himself the

---

Earl "Oil" Smith was, in his time, quite the famous figure in baseball, though of course today he's almost completely forgotten . . .

A World Series produces all sorts of strange things. During a crucial spot in the tense and exciting classic of 1925 Earl Smith of the Pirates, one of the talkingest catchers to ever wear pads, had been giving Goose Goslin of the Senators a verbal lacing all the way. Suddenly he changed tactics and grew downright sympathetic as the Goose brought his big bat to the plate with runners aboard at a critical moment in the deciding game.

"Too bad, Goose," he said dolefully, "that they voted Peckinpaugh ahead of you as the most valuable player. I really think you deserved it."

The hard-boiled Smitty was almost in tears as he commiserated with Goslin at the injustice of his losing out to Peck. The Goose, listening eagerly, fouled off seven successive slow balls. When the cagey Smith ordered a fast one, the distracted Goslin fanned ignominiously.

"I dunno, though," Smith snapped merrily as the furious Goslin headed for the dugout, "maybe they were right after all."
—Inside Baseball: A Half Century of the National Pastime (Arthur Daley, 1950)

If something like this happened, it didn't happen exactly like this. In the seventh game, Smith did catch

---

for the Pirates, and Goslin did
strike out. In fact, Goslin made
the last out of the World Series,
whiffing to end the top of the ninth
inning. But the bases were empty.
And I would guess that when Goslin
took that third strike, Smith had
better things to do afterward than
taunt the Goose.

Great Mails, but he wasn't the only one who called him that. He really *was* great.

Examples are legion, but perhaps the best I can offer—because I found it while looking for something else, which means there probably are many more like it—occurred in 1935, on the 22nd of September. Mails was pitching for San Francisco against Seattle, and here's how Ed. R. Hughes opened his story in the next day's *San Francisco Chronicle*:

> The 1935 season of the Coast League wound up yesterday in proper manner, when the Great Mails called in all his outfielders as he pitched to Moran with two men out in the seventh inning. It was the last inning of the second game of a double header, with the Seals leading 10 to 1.
>
> Dramatically Mails called all the outfielders in. Quickly he got two strikes on Moran, and as he let go his third pitch all the Seals' infielders were walking off the field. Had Moran hit the ball at all there would have been no one but Mails to field it, but he swung and missed. It was probably a frame act, but it was a good one.

Mails was nearing the end of his long career, and this would be the last win of his professional career. He probably didn't say or do half the things he was later said to have said and done. But the other half must have been pretty amazing.

DIZZY DEAN & CINCINNATI

"Wild" Celebration

On Sunday, Sept. 30, 1934, Dizzy Dean was pitching against the Cincinnati Reds in the last game of the season in St. Louis. The game was about half over when the news arrived that Brooklyn's Johnny Babich, opposed by three fairly reputable workmen named Fred Fitzsimmons, Hal Schumacher and Carl Hubbell, had whipped the Giants, 8–5, in their final game. That meant that the Cardinals couldn't lose the pennant, and Mr. Dean celebrated in characteristic fashion. With the Reds shut out in the ninth, 8–0, he deliberately filled the bases with walks and then struck out the last batsman.

—H. G. Salsinger in the *New York Herald Tribune*
(reprinted in *Baseball Digest*, March 1951)

The last game of the Cardinals' 1934 season *was* on September 30, and Dizzy Dean *did* pitch against the Reds. Entering play that afternoon, the first-place Cardinals did hold a one-game lead over the second-place Giants—the third-place Cubs were far behind—which meant that if the Giants lost, the Cardinals didn't have to win. The Dodgers did beat the Giants, 8–5, and the Cardinals did beat the Reds, 9–0 (not 8–0 as reported, but in the context of the story that's hardly even a trifle).

One small problem: the story implies that Johnny Babich started for the Dodgers, but he did not. He did get the win but was actually the Dodgers' fourth pitcher of the game, following Ray Benge, Dutch Leonard, and Tom Zachary. Babich came on in the ninth and pitched two scoreless innings. Salsinger does have the Giants' pitchers correctly named, though: Fitzsimmons started,

Schumacher relieved in the eighth, and Hubbell came on in the tenth.

In that inning, the Dodgers scored three times for an 8–5 lead, and Babich cruised in the bottom of the inning to eliminate the Giants from contention. It had been a stunning collapse. Defending World Champs, the Giants held a seven-game lead as late as September 7. But while they were losing thirteen of their last twenty-one games—including their last five straight—the Cardinals were winning eighteen of their last twenty-three, one of the great stretch runs in major league history.

That leaves two questions unanswered: 1) did the Giants' game end before the Cardinals' game, and 2) did Dean really walk the bases loaded in the ninth?

We would expect the former to have been the case, as the Giants' game was in New York, the Car-

Billy Herman, longtime Cubs second baseman and Hall of Famer, told this story about Dizzy Dean.

But I always had very good luck with him, better luck than I had with his brother Paul, even though Dizzy was a lot better pitcher. I always used to kid Diz about how well I hit him. I'll tell you a story about that. In 1960 Billy Jurges was managing the Red Sox, and I signed on as one of his coaches. We were training out in Arizona, and Diz was living nearby in Phoenix.

Dean invited us out to his house one night. He showed us around, and then took us into the den. The walls were decorated with pictures and trophies and all the mementos of his career. He also had a lot of box scores framed and hung up there. We got to kidding him about the year he won 30 games. He was proud as hell of that, and with good reason. But he always had a hard time beating the Cubs, and we let him know about that. So Diz pointed to one of the box scores.

"There," he said. "There's one I beat you."

Well, for some reason I went over and looked at the box score.

"No wonder," I said.

"What do you mean?" he asked.

"There's a reason you won that game, Diz," I said.

"What are you talking about?" he asked.

"I didn't play that day," I said.

Diz gave me an indignant look and squinted at the box score. Sure enough, I wasn't in the lineup that game. It was the first time I ever

The great Dizzy Dean

dinals' game in St. Louis, one time zone away (i.e., later). And according to Salsinger, the Cardinals' game "was about half over" when word arrived from New York that the Giants had lost. Is that right? In the *Times*, John Drebinger wrote:

> Out in St. Louis the Cardinals, who had begun the final day of the race one game ahead, pressed relentless on toward their goal as they walloped the last-place Cincinnati Reds for the fourth consecutive day, with one of their invincible Deans again on the firing line.
>
> But a few seconds before this had come about the National League pennant had already been clinched for them by a vengeful band of Dodgers bent on making Bill Terry regret to the last his ill-fated taunt of last Winter when he asked whether Brooklyn was still in the league.

Of course, the story would actually be even better if Dean didn't know about the pennant until late in the game; more drama that way. So let's see what the Associated Press's man in St. Louis had to say. Remember, the Cardinals opened the ninth inning with a nine-run lead.

Photo courtesy of Sporting News/ZUMA Press/Icon SMI

Given his wide lead, Dizzy was pitching his heart out at the start of the ninth for his seventh shutout of the year. As Pool singled, Schulmerich doubled and Comorosky walked, to fill the bases with none out, his dream of becoming the shutout king of the major leagues faded.

Then came the final flash from the Brooklyn-Giant game. The Dodgers had won; the pennant belonged to the Cardinals for sure. Grinning in that cocksure way of his, Dizzy rose to the heights then. He struck out Clyde Manion and Ted Petoskey, a pinch-hitter for Frey, and then pumped a fast one down the middle to little Sparky Adams, who fouled out to Bill DeLancey.

As the ball stuck in DeLancey's glove, Dizzy ran over to his battery-mate, snatched the ball and just barely succeeded in reaching the dugout before the frenzied fans surged over the diamond, cheering him for his thirtieth victory of the season and for the first St. Louis pennant since 1931. The Cardinals' margin over the Giants was two full games.

Those details are confirmed by the St. Louis *Post-Dispatch*:

Dizzy closed the game with a grand flourish of power. Pool opened the ninth inning with a single to left and Schulmerich slashed a double down the left-field line. Comorosky walked on four pitched balls, and it seemed that Dizzy surely would be balked in his quest for his seventh shutout of the season.

About that time the scoreboard flashed the news that the Dodgers had defeated the Giants and with the stands roaring and scrap paper confetti falling in showers from the upper decks of the stands, Dizzy went to work. . . .

There was a mad rush of spectators from the stands, but a flying squadron of coppers surrounded Dizzy and formed a flying wedge to lead him to the dugout and thence to the clubhouse.

So almost everything about this story checks out. Well, everything except the best part, where Dean "deliberately filled the bases with walks and then struck out the last batsman." There was just one walk, and he didn't strike out the last batsman. That said, he did strike out two batsmen after the bases were loaded, and it's *possible*, isn't it, that he passed Comorosky on purpose? Well, no. If the newspaper stories are correct, the walk to Comorosky came *before* Dean knew the Giants had lost. And while he certainly had a flair for the dramatic, I don't think even he would have played around with a pennant like that.

Postscript: Oddly, in *Ol' Diz: A Biography of Dizzy Dean* (1992), author Vince Staten incorrectly lists Cincinnati's final three batters as Jim Bottomley,

saw Dean where he couldn't say a word.

—Billy Herman in Baseball When the Grass Was Real (Donald Honig, 1975)

Dizzy Dean debuted in the majors on the last day of the 1930 season, pitched a complete game to beat the Pirates, then spent all of 1931—Billy Herman's debut season—in the minors. Dizzy was a sensation in 1932, which is when their story together begins.

Herman's exactly right, though: Dizzy did have a hard time beating the Cubs. He started against them thirty-one times in his career, from '32 through '37 (after which the Cards sold him to the Cubs). Of those thirty-one games, Dean—and for that matter the Cardinals as a team—won only thirteen. And his problems were particularly pronounced after his rookie season, when he won three of five against Chicago. After 1932, Dean won only ten of twenty-six starts against the Cubs.

Even in 1934, Dean's thirty-win season, he managed to beat the Cubs only once in five tries (and took a couple of terrible beatings in the meantime). And wouldn't you know it? That single 1934 win was the only game Dean ever started against Chicago in which Herman did not play. In Dizzy's thirty other starts against the Cubs, Herman batted .370 against him.

Ernie Lombardi, and Mark Koenig; neither Bottomley nor Koenig actually batted in the ninth, and Lombardi didn't play in the game at all.

All this happened on Sunday. Dean had also pitched a shutout on Friday. In the *Post-Dispatch*, J. Roy Stockton wrote about Dizzy: "Sending a pitcher into a world series game with only two days' rest after two such brilliant performances would be a risky thing to do. It would be far better to give Dizzy another day or two of rest and have him at his best when he does go to the firing line to show the Tigers and the world series crowd how baseball really should be pitched." Nevertheless, Dizzy did start the first game on Wednesday, with only two days' rest, and he beat the Tigers 8–3.

DIZZY DEAN & JOHN MCGRAW

The Giants led the Cards 3–2 in the eighth. Though it was May and early in the 1932 season, it looked as if the National League pennant rested between these two clubs and every game in which they met was played as if it were the season's last.

Mancuso of the Cardinals had established himself on first when Dizzy Dean, the greatest pitcher of his time, but like most twirlers no great hitter, stepped to the plate. Manager Gabby Street signaled for a bunt, an obvious stratagem to move Mancuso to second and a better position to score and tie the count.

Johnny Vergez, the Giants' third baseman, and Bill Terry from first moved in close to try for a double play. Hughie Critz, the Giant second sacker, moved over to take the play at first if the ball went to Terry. Travis Jackson shifted from short to cover second in case the double-play potential developed.

Dizzy's "bunt" lofted into the air to become a weak pop fly. But it was just beyond the reach of Vergez's fingers, and Eddie Leach, the Giant left fielder, had to come far in to snag it on the bounce.

Dean broke for first and rounded for second as Leach tore in. The heave to Critz at second was way over his head, and Dizzy slid in safely. He was up again and off to third as Mel Ott caught the ball in deep right. He skidded into third with the base coach frantically signaling him to follow Mancuso home.

Up he got and off he went, as Catcher Shanty Hogan stood waiting for the relay. Ott had tossed to Terry, who let go with a quick heave to Shanty. The ball scaled into the stands. Dizzy scored the run with a spectacular and completely unnecessary slide. That run won the game.

John McGraw, the Giants' fabulous and trigger-tempered manager, removed his brand new straw hat in the Giant dugout and smashed it. "Yep," says Dizzy, who is now a baseball broadcaster in Texas, "Mr. McGraw sure must have been awful mad. Maybe I was the one who made him resign as manager. All I know is he quit a few days later and turned the job over to Terry."

—Lawrence Robinson in *Baseball Yearbook*
(1952 edition, published by *True: The Man's Magazine*)

Without doing much research, it's easy to pinpoint the date on which McGraw resigned as manager of the Giants, because McGraw's resignation became famous for making something else nonfamous.

On June 3, 1932, Lou Gehrig hit four home runs

in a 20–13 Yankee win in Philadelphia. But what might have been the biggest baseball story of the season wasn't even the biggest story of the day. At the time, John McGraw was the second-most famous figure in the game (behind the Babe). Of course, that's since been reversed: even non-fans know who Lou Gehrig was, while only geeks like me and you know anything about John McGraw. But when McGraw announced his retirement on June 3, Gehrig's feat was relegated to second class in the headlines department.

What we're looking for, then, is a Giants-Cardinals game prior to June 3, started by Dizzy Dean. Which is easily narrowed down. Though the two clubs faced off twenty-two times that season, only four of those games came before June 3: on May 5, May 6, and May 8 (doubleheader). And the same Retrosheet page reveals that Dean started for St. Louis in the second May 8 game.

Did Dean score the game-winning run? Perhaps he did; the Cardinals won that one, 6–5. From John Drebinger's gamer in the *Times*:

> Dizzy Dean, eccentric recruit hurler of the Cardinals, put on a rare performance in the nightcap, first by figuring in four of his team's six runs, and then staggering through to the finish by fanning Jackson in the ninth with the tying run on second, after the Giant captain had previous pelted him for two doubles and a single.
>
> Opposed by the left-handed Jim Mooney, Dean got away to a two-run lead in the first on a homer by Collins with one on, and in the second round took matters into his own hands by driving two more runs across with a double, which also finished Mooney.
>
> Dean's crowning stroke, however, came in the fourth, when, with Gelbert on first, he tapped the ball over the bewildered Vergez, who was tearing in to field an expected bunt. This so confounded the Giants that Koenecke's wild return got away from the infielders and not only Gelbert, but Dean had scored as well.

That run did win the game, though in a roundabout sort of way. It was only the fourth inning, and made the score 6–2, but the Giants scored three more runs and the Cardinals didn't score any more at all, so Dean's run was decisive, sort of.

All that fooling around in the infield might well have made McGraw "awful mad," as Dean related. McGraw was never the most tolerant of managers anyway. And as Giants catcher Bob O'Farrell would later tell Lawrence Ritter, "Maybe it was because he was getting old and was a sick man, but he was never any fun to play for. He was always so grouchy."

But McGraw didn't quit "a few days later," unless we apply the most liberal of definitions to *few*.

The Giants were in bad shape, losing ten of their first fifteen games (and according to one source, making fifty-eight errors in those games). That series in St. Louis—the loss to Dean notwithstanding—was actually a highlight of the spring, as the Giants took three of four games from the defending World Champions.

McGraw was in worse shape than his time. He suffered from sinusitis, and from prostate problems, and was absent from the dugout during much of May. Finally, in early June McGraw had to make a decision. As one biographer has written:

> Soon the Giants would leave on another road trip; he would either have to send them off in Bancroft's care or endure another two weeks of train rides, hotel stays, watching what his players ate and what they did at night, concentrating as much energy as he could, for two hours plus in the afternoons, on winning another ballgame. No, he'd finally had enough—enough self-doubt, enough of being a part-time manager, enough of a life that was designed for healthy young athletes, not a fat and sickly man nearing sixty.[1]

Photo courtesy of Transcendental Graphics

McGraw in action

Nash and Zullo tell this typical story about Ol' Diz.

Whatever else he might have been, flamboyant pitcher Dizzy Dean was a man of his word.

Shortly before a game against the Boston Braves in 1934, the future Hall of Famer loudly announced to the opposing players and everyone else within hearing distance that he wasn't going to toss a curveball the whole game.

"I ain't throwin' nothin' but fastballs," Dean declared.

Sure enough, he didn't bend a ball all afternoon. And ol' Diz still shut out the Braves, 3–0—giving up only three hits the whole game.

—Bruce Nash and Allan Zullo,
The Baseball Hall of Shame's
Warped Record Book *(1991)*

Oddly, Dean pitched only once against the Braves in 1934. He did not beat them 3–0. He beat them 4–2 on July 19 and gave up seven hits. In his career, Dean pitched four shutouts against the Braves. In the first two, in '35 and '37, he beat them 7–0 and 1–0, giving up ten hits and five hits. After '37 he pitched for the Cubs and whitewashed Boston only once more in his career. In 1939 on the 21st of May, Dean made his first start of the season and shut out the Braves on three hits. So it's actually that game that comes closest to matching our story, albeit with the considerable discrepancy of five years. What's more, by all accounts Dean's fastball in 1939 just wasn't what it had been during his prime. Of course, it's highly possible that

this—or something like it—did
happen against some other team,
as this is exactly the sort of thing
that Dean would have enjoyed.

McGraw handed the managerial reins to first baseman Bill Terry. A year later, McGraw would be healthy enough to manage the National Leaguers in the first All-Star Game. But that fall it was clear that McGraw's prostate cancer had spread to his kidneys and stomach. He would not live to see Opening Day in 1934.

LOU BOUDREAU & RON SANTO

One of the first moves I made was to recall Ron Santo. He'd been a catcher in the minors, but I moved him to third base. Don Zimmer, who was nearing the end of his playing career, had been playing that position and helped Santo make the switch—and in effect, helped Santo take Zim's job.

—Lou Boudreau in *Covering All the Bases* (Boudreau with Russell Schneider, 1993)

At this writing, Ron Santo is not in the Hall of Fame. But he certainly deserves to be, and I believe that one day he will. It's not likely that Santo would have been a Hall of Fame catcher, or a Hall of Fame first baseman. If Ron Santo is a Hall of Famer, it's because he combined power and patience at the plate with solid defense at third base. So by extension, Boudreau is essentially taking credit for turning Santo into a Hall of Fame (or Hall of Famish) player.

But did he? Boudreau makes six distinct assertions in the above passage, and all of them are subject to verification.

- Boudreau was managing the Cubs when Santo reached the majors.
- Boudreau was responsible for bringing Santo to the majors.
- Santo was a catcher in the minor leagues.
- Boudreau shifted Santo from behind the plate to third base.
- Zimmer had been playing third base before Santo's arrival.

- Zimmer helped Santo learn to play third base.

Let's take those one at a time . . .

1. Was Boudreau managing the Cubs when Santo joined the big club? Yes, he was. Santo debuted on June 26, 1960 (and he debuted with a bang, driving in five runs in a doubleheader in Pittsburgh). Boudreau, who opened the season in the Cubs' broadcast booth, had switched places with manager Charlie Grimm on May 5, and he managed the club for the rest of the season.

2. Was Boudreau responsible for bringing Santo to the majors? Actually, this one's not really verifiable. However, managers in the 1960s were not generally responsible for deciding which minor leaguers should be called up. What's more, if this was "one of the first" moves Boudreau made, he sure took his time making moves, because Santo spent more than seven weeks in the minors—specifically, with Hous-

A bit of revisionist history, courtesy of Larry Bowa, who played with Mike Schmidt in the early '70s and with Ryne Sandberg in the early '80s . . .

Sandberg's first year with the Cubs started out like a nightmare. The youngster had just one hit in his first 32 at-bats. He hung in there, however, and finished at .271.

Throughout Sandberg's ordeal, Bowa never lost faith in his infield partner. The veteran kept telling the other Cubs that Sandberg would be able to do everything that Mike Schmidt could do, except hit with Schmidt's awesome power.

Sandberg's toughness in the face of his early-season adversity really impressed Bowa.

"No knock on Schmitty," Bowa said, "but he might have panicked if he'd gone through anything like that as a rookie. Ryne Sandberg never came close to panicking."

—Pete Cava, Tales from the Cubs Dugout (2002)

If Schmitty had ever gone through anything like that as a rookie?

Sandberg did get off to a 1-for-32 start in his first season (1982) with the Cubs. It was a rough couple of weeks. But Schmidt? He didn't get off to a terrible start, but otherwise it was a rough year. As a rookie in '73 with the Phillies, Schmidt batted .196 and struck out 136 times in 132 games. In those days, you weren't supposed to strike out that often unless you were Bobby Bonds. Did Schmitty panic? In '74 his average jumped to .282, he hit thirty-six home runs, and was one of the best players in the league.

---

ton in the American Association—*after* Boudreau took over from Grimm. Boudreau did not take the job and immediately tell management, "Get me that Santo kid, and get him now!" (Or if he did, management didn't listen.)

3. Was Santo a catcher with Houston? No, he was not. According to the 1961 edition of the *Official Baseball Guide*, Santo played in seventy-one games with Houston in 1960 . . . all seventy-one at third base. In 1959, Santo's first professional season, he played in 136 games with San Antonio in the Texas League . . . 134 at third base. He was a third baseman.

That said, we can guess the source of Boudreau's confusion. When Santo played high-school baseball in Seattle, he was mostly a third baseman by his senior season, but he also caught some, and (according to Santo) the Cubs' head scout told him, "There's no way you're ever going to be a third baseman in the major leagues, son. Maybe you can make it as a catcher. But that's about it." When the Cubs signed Santo, they signed him as a catcher.[1]

That didn't last long. According to Santo, he got moved to third base in his first professional spring training, "because of the plethora of catchers." As we've seen, Santo played third base, exclusively, in 1959 and '60.

4. Did Boudreau move Santo from behind the plate to third base? Obviously, Boudreau did not move Santo in 1960. But Boudreau, who did work for the Cubs in 1959 and probably did have owner Phil Wrigley's ear, *might* have helped convince management to turn Santo into an ex-catcher. It's not *likely*. But it's possible and would go a long way toward explaining Boudreau's confusion.*

Santo does have something to say about Boudreau in his autobiography: "He later told me that had he been the manager in the spring, I would have never gone down to Houston and I would have been the starting third baseman ahead of Zimmer." (Of course, that's exactly what a manager might tell a rookie, in hopes of building the kid's confidence.)

5. Had Zimmer been playing third base before Santo showed up? Yes. Prior to Santo's arrival, the Cubs played sixty games, and Zimmer played third base in forty-one of them (he also played some second base). He'd started at third in the four games immediately prior to Santo's promotion.

---

* Speaking of confusion, Santo's got plenty of his own. On pages 7 and 8 of his autobiography, Santo writes about playing a high school all-star game at the Polo Grounds and, shortly afterward, trying out for the Yankees at Yankee Stadium, then trying out for the Indians at Municipal Stadium. A few pages later, Santo claims that when he played in his first game for the Cubs . . . he had *never set foot in a major league ballpark in his life*.

6. Did Zimmer do everything he could to help Santo? In Santo's book, all he says is "Zimmer, for his part, didn't fully comprehend the switch. He thought he was just being moved to second base for a time to replace Jerry Kindall and he might be back at third at some future time. Well, he would have had to wait until he was 44 before I would leave the Cubs and their third base spot."[2]

Zimmer, in *his* autobiography, relates the story with a bit more color:

> In the middle of the 1960 season, we were in Pittsburgh when Boudreau summoned me to tell me they were bringing Santo up. I had been playing third, but I assumed I'd be moving over to second where Jerry Kindall wasn't hitting a lick. There was no manager's office in the visiting clubhouse in Pittsburgh and Boudreau was sitting on a stool in the corner of the room.
>
> "Santo's coming up," he said to me. "He'll be playing third."
>
> "I figured that," I said. "So I'll be moving over to second?"
>
> "Well, not now anyway," Boudreau said. "We're going to leave Kindall there."
>
> "You mean to tell me I'm not at second either?"
>
> "We just feel right now we want to go with the younger guys," Boudreau replied.
>
> Younger guys? I said to myself. Kindall was like two or three years younger than I was and I was out-hitting him by nearly 100 points.
>
> "What's wrong," Boudreau said. "Don't you want to be a Chicago Cub?"
>
> "Screw the Chicago Cubs if I can't play here hitting .270 when the other guy's hitting .180!"[3]

Actually, Kindall was four years and four months younger than Zimmer. And while Zimmer *was* hitting .270—or, to be precise, .272—when he got benched, Kindall was batting .273. Yes, Zimmer was drawing more walks and hitting with more power. But the difference between them, at that time, wasn't anything like what Zimmer remembers. Which I suppose throws that entire conversation into question, doesn't it?

Again, though, while it's *possible* that Zimmer tutored Santo in the finer points of playing third base, it's telling that neither man mentioned anything of the sort in their memoirs.

Conclusion: Most of what Boudreau remembered—and perhaps all of it, except Santo replacing Zimmer at third base—didn't actually happen.

Larry Bowa established, during his two managerial stints, that he's not a world-class psychologist or performance analyst. Solid third-base coach, though.

ALVIN DARK & THE GIANTS

Name some names . . . sure . . . Alvin Dark. I saw him and heard him get on a Giant pitcher while the team was coming down the stretch for the 1954 pennant. It shook up the whole ball club. This pitcher had just given up a three-run homer to the opposing pitcher. He came to the bench and said he didn't want to throw the pitch the catcher had called for. Alvin Dark heard him and let him have it. He didn't wait for Manager Durocher or any of Leo's coaches. "We're trying to win a pennant, and if you don't want to throw a pitch, don't throw it. If you don't want to pitch, get out. But don't alibi, just bear down." The pitcher came back with shutout innings and a victory. Alvin Dark isn't the spitfire type, and that wasn't a display of temper, but of competitive fire.

—Joe Garagiola in *Baseball Is a Funny Game* (Garagiola & Martin Quigley, 1960)

This story comes in the middle of a discussion of "spitfire-type players," also described as "take-charge guys" and "holler guys."

If we take Garagiola literally and believe that he not only saw and heard this happen but that the pitcher "came" to the bench—rather than *went* to the bench—then there is just a brief stretch in 1954 when this might have happened. Garagiola spent most of that season (his last in the majors) with the Cubs, but on September 8 the Giants claimed him off waivers.

The Giants did not play on the 8th, but on the 9th they met the Cubs in a doubleheader at the Polo Grounds, and we may presume that's when Garagiola joined his new club. From the 9th through the close of their season on the 26th, the Giants played eighteen games. And while there wasn't a *great* pennant race in the National League, there certainly was *a* pennant race: on the morning of the 9th, first-place New York led second-place Milwaukee by four games, with the Dodgers two behind the Braves.

So we have eighteen games to check. Retrosheet has box scores for every Giants game that season, and play-by-play accounts for most of them, which makes the search fairly simple. In those eighteen games the Giants gave up only nine home runs (and none at all in their last seven games). Three of those homers were hit by catchers, and three by third basemen. First baseman Ted Kluszewski hit one, and so did rightfielder Stan Musial. That's eight home runs.

And the ninth? It came on September 11 in Harlem, home of the Polo Grounds and New York's baseball Giants. Ruben Gomez was pitching for the Giants in the top of the second, and he retired the first two Cincinnati hitters. But Johnny Temple singled and scooted to third base when Hobie Landrith sent a base hit to right field. That brought up left-handed pitcher Jackie Collum, who shocked everybody in the ballpark by hitting a home run.

Why might Dark have been particularly upset by this turn of events? Yes, Collum was just a pitcher, and even in those days pitchers rarely hit home runs. But there might have been another reason: at 5'7" and 160 pounds, Collum was one of the smallest pitchers of his era. He had never hit a home run before, and he would never hit another.*

So maybe Gomez did complain about his catcher's call—and by the way, the catcher was Ray Katt, not Garagiola—and maybe Dark did handle the situation before Durocher had the chance. The other details do check out, sort of. Gomez shut out the Reds in the third, fourth, and fifth innings. In the sixth, though, Kluszewski hit a 400-foot bomb into the right-field stands, and in the seventh third baseman Chuck Harmon hit a solo homer of his own. Heading to the bottom of that inning, the Giants trailed 5–3. But then, "In the last of the seventh the Polo Grounders really put on a show." [1]

Dark led off with a single against Collum, who was immediately relieved by right-hander Howie Judson. Pinch hitter Dusty Rhodes—destined for glory in a few weeks—popped out. Mays hit an easy fly to center field, which turned into a double when Gus Bell was perplexed by the lights. Pinch hitter Hank Thompson popped out, but Don Mueller walked to load the bases. Next up: Whitey Lockman, Durocher's third pinch hitter of the inning. And a few pitches later, Lockman hit a long homer "against the front of the upper right-field deck." [2]

That made the score 7–5 and that's how it ended, thanks to a fine relief appearance—just his second of the season—by Giants ace Johnny Antonelli. And as the *Times* noted, "With the Dodgers again tripping the Braves, the Polo Grounders once again have placed themselves in a commanding position for the final two weeks to the wire." The Giants finished the season with a fairly comfortable five-game lead, but of course on September 11 nobody knew about that. Every game seemed important.

So this story, as far as we can check, did happen essentially as Garagiola wrote in his book.

Alvin Dark wrote a book, too: *When in Doubt, Fire the Manager* (Dutton, 1980). He doesn't mention this incident, but he does offer another example of his leadership that season. The Giants won the pennant in 1951 (I'll bet you knew that), but they finished behind the Dodgers in '52 and dropped all the way to fifth place in '53. According to Dark, when the Giants got off to an unimpressive start in 1954, owner Horace Stoneham was considering firing manager Leo Durocher . . .

---

* In fairness to Collum, he was actually a pretty good hitter, finishing his career with a solid .321 on-base percentage.

Another story from *Baseball Is a Funny Game* . . .

Front office interference is a phrase that upsets more fans than any other phrase in baseball. The general manager ought to leave the field manager alone, say the baseball fans. But it is not, and it cannot be, that way. The manager and general manager may not always be in agreement, but they must be working it out together. The manager is usually hand picked by the general manager for qualities that the general manager thinks will get the best out of the material he gives his man to work with. They must be together. Game strategy is up to the manager, but there are times when he cannot see the forest for the trees.

Frank Lane's pet example involves the Cardinals of 1956 and an outfielder. "Do you figure on using _____ next year?" he asked Fred Hutchinson.

"No, get rid of him."

"How can I if you don't play him? You got him on the bench, playing Sauer (forty years old) in his place. If the other club feels you think Sauer is better than _____, how can I trade him?"

Hutch saw the point, played _____ the last month, and the following winter Lane traded him. There's the case for "front office interference."

I enjoy baseball stories with redacted names. As sort of a sideline, I'd love to locate every story with unidentified players and try to identify them. Anyway, three

St. Louis outfielders played down the stretch in 1956 and were traded prior to Opening Day in 1957: Rip Repulski, Whitey Lockman, and Bobby Del Greco.

So who (if anybody) was sitting on the bench while Sauer played? Well, Sauer hardly played. He served mostly as a pinch hitter during that season, with just a month of regular duty in left field, beginning in late May. However, Sauer did start five games in left field in August, the first of them on the 19th, the last of them on the 28th. In each of those five games, Del Greco was in center field. So he's not our mystery outfielder.

We still can't quite name our man, though, because both Repulski and Lockman were on the bench in those games. Which brings us to September. Sauer was back on the bench and started just one game all month: on the 26th, back in Chicago (the site of his greatest glories), he enjoyed the last four-hit game of his career. Lockman started only thirteen games in September. And Repulski apparently started twenty-six games that month, all of them in left field (Sauer's position, however briefly, in August). So it was Repulski who was being showcased, and in November the Cardinals traded him and Bobby Morgan to the Phillies for Del Ennis . . . who drove in 105 runs with St. Louis in 1957 (then fell off a cliff in 1958).

In June of '54, Joe Reichler, then with the Associated Press and now in the commissioner's office, called me aside in the Polo Grounds and said, "Alvin, do you like Leo?"

I said, "Yeah, I like him. He's a great manager. He gets more out of his players than anybody."

"Well, you better do something, because Stoneham says if you're not on top by the All-Star game Durocher's through."

We held a meeting that very afternoon. No coaches allowed. I told the players what Reichler had told me: "From now on, we have to praise Leo every chance we get." I said, "Whitey, you know Leo's been on you many times, even though you're having a great year." Lockman was shaking his head. "He's been on me, he's been on all of us. He's always on you in the clubhouse. But publicly he's for you, and it's time we started telling everybody what a great manager he is, how we wouldn't be the team we are without him."

After that, every time one of us went on the radio with Russ Hodges or Laraine Day, or on television, we'd always mention what a great job Leo was doing. Which he was. We beat the Dodgers six straight after that: three at the Polo Grounds, three at Ebbets Field. By the All-Star break we were six games in the lead. The Dodgers closed to within a game in September, but we surged again and won going away.

It's not as if the Giants were playing poorly. At the end of May, they were just a game and a half out of first place. They did play exceptionally well in June and moved into a first-place tie on the 9th. On the 15th they grabbed first place for themselves and never trailed again. They did take three straight from the Dodgers in late June, then again a week later. At the All-Star break, the Giants had a five-and-a-half-game lead—so Dark was off by a whole half-game—and the Dodgers never got closer than three games in September.

YOGI BERRA

Dickey was always telling me to be heads-up behind the plate. On July 4, 1949, I made a play that made him proud of me. I was pretty proud myself. It happened in the first game of a doubleheader against the Red Sox. In the top of the ninth inning, the Red Sox loaded the bases against Vic Raschi. Then Al Zarilla lined a single in front of Cliff Mapes in right field. Johnny Pesky, who was on third, thought Cliff was going to catch the ball, so he held up. When the ball dropped, Pesky broke for the plate; but Mapes, who had a powerful arm, threw a bullet to me. It sailed so I had to catch it like a first baseman, but I grabbed it before Pesky's foot hit the plate. There were 63,000 people in Yankee Stadium that day, but it seemed like I was the only one who knew it was a force play. "He's out!" I screamed at home plate umpire Joe Paparella. "It's a force play. I don't have to tag him. The throw beat him. He's out."

Paparella seemed confused. He hesitated. Finally he said, "By God, you're right. He is out." Raschi then got Bobby Doerr to fly out to Mapes to end the game.

Until that day I was known as a good-hitting catcher. But after that play I gradually began to get the reputation as a good defensive catcher, too. Dickey reminded the reporters after the game, "I've been telling you that Yogi's going to be the best defensive catcher in the game. He might be right now."

—Yogi Berra in *The Men of Autumn: An Oral History of the 1949–53 World Champion New York Yankees* (Dom Forker, 1989)

Bill Dickey's careful tutelage began in 1949. As Arthur Daley would later write in *Kings of the Home Run,*

That was an important year for Berra in many respects. It was Casey Stengel's first year as Yankee manager, and Ol' Case hired Bill Dickey, the Yankee and Hall of Fame catching immortal, for one specific purpose.

"He's all yours," said Casey, nodding in Yogi's direction. "It's up to you to make a catcher out of him."

Dickey made the swift discovery that Yogi's troubles had come from his feet. He caught as if he had two left feet. He was always out of position and off balance. Yet Dickey never had a more apt pupil.

This led to one of Yogi's classic lines: "Bill is learnin' me his experience."

Photo courtesy of Louis Requena/The Sporting News/ZUMA Press/Icon SMI

Yogi Berra and Bill Dickey

In 1952, *Complete Baseball* said of Yogi Berra, who'd recently become the second catcher in American League history to be named Most Valuable Player, "Berra . . . has become a fine receiver after careful tutelage and an unpromising beginning."

In 1955, not long before Berra would pick up his third MVP, the magazine *Baseball Stars* said of Berra, "He had trouble throwing far back in 1947, and Dickey taught him how to disentangle his feet. He's alert and swift in handling balls hit in front of the plate, and has the proper instincts for directing his pitchers, and with a calm, chatty approach he steadies them in moments of stress. The shifting of the game's No. 1 technician"—already there was talk about moving Yogi to the outfield to save his knees—"does not evoke any loud hurrahs from the Yankee pitching staff."[1]

In 1962, Mickey Mantle wrote—or rather, some ghostwriter wrote—"Nobody doubts Yogi's brilliance as a field general and handler of pitchers anymore. It would be a waste of time to write about it."[2]

Berra never won a Gold Glove. They didn't exist before 1957, and by then he was catching only four or five times per week. He probably wouldn't have won the award earlier, either, as he'd have been competing for honors with Cleveland's Jim Hegan, who was generally considered the best defensive catcher of his generation. Imaginary Gold Gloves notwithstanding, though, it's quite possible that no player in history was able to move his defensive reputation from Grade F to Grade A so quickly or famously as Lawrence Peter Berra. Which is what makes his story about the 4th of July in 1949 not only interesting but also—at least in the minds of both Berra and his observers—pivotal.

The Yankees did host the Red Sox in a doubleheader on July 4, 1949, before a huge crowd listed in the newspapers as 63,876. The Bombers took the first game, 3–2, and the second, 6–4. Raschi pitched in the first game, and the second didn't even include a ninth inning, as the contest was stopped in the middle of the seventh because of darkness (lights had been installed in the Stadium three years earlier, but in '49 a strange rule said you couldn't turn on lights in the middle of a game).

For the rest of the story let's turn to the *Times*, as things got a little crazy in the ninth. With the Yankees leading 3–2 after eight innings, Raschi slipped a called third strike past Boston's leadoff man, Dominic DiMaggio. But Pesky singled, so did Ted Williams, and Vern Stephens walked to fill the bases. That (as Berra so precisely recalled) brought up Al Zarilla.

First, though, a delay, as "over the field hung wind-tossed dust which almost obliterated a view of Joe DiMaggio in center and caused a brief pause."

Afterward, things unfolded essentially as Berra recalled. What Berra might *not* have recalled is that before that unlikely force play in the ninth, he wasn't exactly making Dickey proud. As the *Times*' J. P. Dawson noted, "In the unparalleled ninth inning of the opener, a legitimate single was converted into a prosaic force-out at the plate which averted what would have been the tying run for the Sox. That helped Vic Raschi ride above the dust storm and eccentricities of Yogi Berra to bag his thirteenth triumph."

What's this? Eccentricities?

"In the opener, Berra erred, missing Tebbetts' easy foul pop in the fifth, messed up Billy Hitchcock's following pinch pop in front of the plate until Raschi finally speared the ball himself, and caused apprehension in the eighth overtaking a missed third strike on pinch hitter Matt Batts as Doerr thundered over the plate with what would have been the tying run. However, the kid from the hill in St. Louis had the presence of mind just to stand on the plate for that curious force play in the ninth."[3]

Is there just a hint of sarcasm there? The *Times*' man, James P. Dawson, seems to have taken a particular interest in Yogi, as neither the *Herald Tribune* nor the *Daily News* had much to say about Berra either way. In the three papers, I did not find any quotes from Bill Dickey about Berra's defense.

Which doesn't prove anything, as there were a lot more than three papers in those days.

That said, while Berra's reputation with the glove obviously improved quite a bit between 1947 and 1952, I'm skeptical about the 4th of July in 1949 as some sort of obvious dividing line.

BOB GIBSON & TOMMY DAVIS

Kareem Abdul-Jabbar: I had a talk with Sandy Koufax, and he said he loves Tommy Davis, because Tommy Davis won two games for him where he went head-to-head with Bob Gibson.

Tim McCarver: On inside fastballs.

Abdul-Jabbar: Inside fastballs, that he hit out for home runs.

McCarver: That's correct.

Abdul-Jabbar: And there were not more than three or four hits, for both teams, in the whole game.

McCarver: That's right. Sandy told me the same thing. And Bob, after that, it changed Bob's style of pitching. In the late innings, from the seventh inning on, he never came inside to hitters, because of what Tommy Davis did. Back-to-back games, in a week, both game-winners, both inside fastballs.

I'll be back with more. This is great stuff, guys.

—*The Tim McCarver Show* (syndicated, aired July 14–20, 2007)

First thing I'm wondering . . . did Gibson give up two home runs to Tommy Davis in his entire *career*?

Yes, he did. Gibson generally handled Davis quite adroitly. In sixty career at-bats against Gibson, Davis managed only ten hits. But four of them were homers.

Okay. But did Gibson ever give up two homers to Davis in the same season?

Davis first reached the majors in 1959, but he batted just once (and not against Gibson). Their story together begins in 1960, when Davis played in 110 games and Gibson pitched eighty-seven innings. That season, Gibson gave up seven homers, but none of those were hit by Tommy Davis or any other Dodger.

In 1961, Gibson gave up thirteen homers, including two against the Dodgers. And Tommy Davis got one of them, on May 25 in the seventh inning. That was the only run of the game, with eight hits total between the teams. The winning pitcher? Sandy Koufax.

So this would seem to fit perfectly into Koufax's story—as relayed through Abdul-Jabbar and McCarver—except for one tiny detail: the other Dodger homer that season was hit not by Davis, but by Duke Snider, more than a month earlier. In the third inning.

In '62, Gibson gave up just one homer to a Dodger, and it was Tommy Davis. Again it was a 1–0 loss for the Cardinals, and this time Davis's deciding blow came in the bottom of the ninth inning. And again Koufax was the winner.

In his autobiography, Bob Gibson says of manager Solly Hemus, "Hemus's treatment of black players was the result of one of the following, and I won't try to speculate which: Either he disliked us deeply or he genuinely believed that the way to motivate us was with insults."

Gibson was there and I wasn't, and I have absolutely no doubt that some significant number of baseball decisions in the 1950s and '60s were made, subconsciously or otherwise, because of a player's skin color. And when it comes to Hemus, Gibson offers plenty of damning examples. But this eye-catching example simply isn't true:

"Once," Gibson writes, "a black pitcher named Frank Barnes was working on a no-hitter in the fifth when he walked a batter and Hemus relieved him on the spot, never to start him again."

Barnes started three games in his brief major-league career, one each in three different seasons. But only one of those starts, in 1960, came during Hemus's two and a half seasons as manager. This was also the only one of Barnes's starts that Gibson could have seen, as the other two were before he joined the club.

So what Gibson's recalling is Barnes's start against the Cubs on the 14th of May. In the first inning, Barnes gave up a single and walked two batters, but nobody scored. In the second inning, Barnes gave up a single and walked one batter, but nobody scored. In the third, Barnes walked one batter. In the fourth, the leadoff

In '63, Gibson gave up three homers to the Dodgers, and Davis hit one of them, on June 22. But the Cardinals won 2–1, and Koufax didn't pitch.

So we've accounted for three of Davis's four homers off Gibson, and without going any farther we know he didn't hit two game-winners within one week, as McCarver remembers. Still, I'm curious about that fourth homer. Aren't you?

Tommy Davis hit his fourth homer off Bob Gibson on May 19, 1967, at Shea Stadium; by then Davis was playing for the Mets.

So we've got three home runs in three different seasons and are left to wonder.

In Gibson's most recent autobiography, *Stranger to the Game*, he does mention Davis's 1962 walk-off job:

> Koufax missed part of 1962 and won only fourteen games that year, but he was in the first of five consecutive seasons in which he would lead the league in ERA. My first crack at him came late in the season in St. Louis, long after the Cardinals had been eliminated (we would finish in sixth place, six games over .500) but while the Dodgers were involved in a hot race for the pennant with San Francisco. I welcomed the challenge and stayed with Koufax through eight scoreless innings, giving up only two hits. The man on the Dodgers who could beat you—whom you couldn't *let* beat you—was Tommy Davis, who had an incredible 153 RBIs that year for a team that didn't score many runs, and I had to face Davis in the ninth. I had been striking him out all night with sliders low and away, however, and I seemed to have the edge on him. I had noticed that as I continued to pitch him outside, Davis was gradually sneaking up toward the plate. By the ninth inning, he was practically on top of the plate, and so, out of duty, I buzzed him inside with a fastball. I don't know if he was setting me up, but he must have been looking for a fastball on his ribs, because he backed off a step, turned on that thing, and crushed it over the left-field fence. That was all Koufax needed.

As we've seen already, this was not Gibson's "first crack" at Koufax; they'd faced off at least once in 1961, on the 25th of May. And this second crack didn't come "late in the season in St. Louis"; it came in the middle of the season in Los Angeles. Those are relative trifles, though, as Gibson's right about Davis beating him—and making a winner of Koufax—with a homer in the ninth.

McCarver didn't play in either of the games in question and wasn't even with the Cardinals for the first one. On May 25, 1961, he was playing with Charleston in the International League. And on June 18, 1962, he probably was watching from the bench as Gene Oliver handled the catching duties. What seems to have happened here is that Koufax probably remembered the story correctly, or close to correctly. And then McCarver, a professional storyteller, condensed two seasons into two weeks, because it's a better story that way. And it seems to me that if Gibson never threw an inside fast-ball in the ninth inning after Davis hit that home run in 1962, the hitters would eventually have figured that out and done a lot better than they did.

Dusty Baker recently recalled the advice Hank Aaron gave him about facing Bob Gibson . . .

"Don't dig in against Bob Gibson, he'll knock you down. Don't stare at him. He doesn't like it. If you happen to hit a home run, don't run too slow, don't run too fast. If you happen to want to celebrate, get in the tunnel first. And if he hits you, don't charge the mound, because he's a Gold Glove boxer." I'm like, 'Damn, what about my 17-game hitting streak?' That was the night it ended."

—*Nick Cafardo,* Boston Globe, *Aug. 21, 2005*

Indeed it was.

Baker played briefly for the Braves from 1968 through '71, but it wasn't until '72 that he earned his shot at a regular job. And it wasn't until the 12th of July in '72 that he faced Gibson during the regular season. Baker entered the game riding a 17-game hitting streak, his batting average jumping from .295 to .339. But Gibson shut Baker and most of his teammates down, finishing with a six-hit shutout.

---

man reached on an error, after which Barnes gave up a single and walked a batter, loading the bases with nobody out. He'd given up five walks and (more to the point) three hits.

At which point, Hemus pulled him.

It's true that Barnes never started again; in fact, he never pitched in the majors again. I certainly wouldn't dare argue that Frank Barnes got a fair deal. He was an ex–Negro Leaguer, he spent most of the 1950s racking up big numbers in the high minors, and I have a hard time believing he wouldn't have been an adequate major leaguer during that time. But Gibson's specific example just doesn't square with the facts.

DAZZY VANCE & ROGERS HORNSBY

"I'd sure like to be pitching against the free-swingers playing ball today."

Speaking was Dazzy Vance, the former fireballing Dodger great who now runs a hunting and fishing lodge near Clearwater, Fla.

"I had to pitch against guys like Rabbit Maranville who punched at the ball," recalled the big fellow. Even against that kind of batter Dazzy fanned 262 in one season—1924.

"Rogers Hornsby said just the other day that if it hadn't been for me he would have hit .450 in 1924," Vance announced. "He got only one hit off me. I'd get two strikes on him and then throw him one inside belt high. He'd go after it but he couldn't hit it. He'd only go for it if he had two strikes on him.

"One day before a game a writer was talking to him about different pitchers and striking out," Dazzy said with a twinkle. "I asked the writer what Hornsby had said and he told me he said he had never struck out three times in one game.

"I told the fellow not to write that until after our game, then I went out and fanned Hornsby the first three times he came up."

—Charlie Park in the *Los Angeles Mirror-News* (reprinted in *Baseball Digest,* June 1960)

The first time I read this one, I got the impression that Vance struck out Hornsby three times in a game in 1924. Rereading it, though, I see there's no explicit connection between 1924 and those (supposed) three strikeouts. So that one's going to take some work, probably.

But let's begin with 1924, and the claim that Hornsby got only one hit against Vance all season. I've got each player's daily sheets from that season. Vance started only three games against Hornsby's Cardinals. We don't have play-by-play information, but that problem is not a big one, because Vance completed thirty of his thirty-four starts; if Hornsby did something in a game that Vance started, he probably did it when Vance was pitching.

And yes, Vance completed all three games. On May 17 in St. Louis, he pitched thirteen innings and won, 4–3; Hornsby went 1 for 5. On June 14 in Brooklyn, Vance pitched nine innings and won, 5–2; Hornsby went 0 for 4. And on August 10, again in Brooklyn, Vance beat the Cardinals once more, 8–4; Hornsby went 1 for 5.

So Vance was off by just a little. Hornsby got two hits off Vance that season, rather than one; he was 2 for 14. Certainly not good by Rajah's standards, but then a lot of guys couldn't hit Vance. His 262 strikeouts that season represent the top figure between 1912 (Walter Johnson) and 1946 (Bob Feller and Hal Newhouser).

Would Hornsby have batted .450 in 1924 if not for Vance? Obviously not.

Hornsby finished at .424: 227 for 536.

If we simply remove Hornsby's at bats against Vance, he bats .431. Awesome, but not quite .450. To get Hornsby *close* to .450, we have to make him 14 for 14 against Vance: .446. Tack on a couple more hits during the season—since we're just having fun, how about off Eppa Rixey?—and Hornsby's sitting at .450 (well, .4496 really, but for some reason baseball people like to round everything up).

I do think it's fair to suggest that if Dazzy Vance had never been born, Rogers Hornsby would have hit roughly .430 in 1924, giving him the highest batting average in the majors since the nineteenth century. But he's almost got that anyway, as Nap Lajoie's .427 is the only figure higher than Hornsby's .424.

So rather than quibble any further over six point of batting average, let's turn to the other part of the story. Did Vance ever strike out Hornsby three times in one game? And if he did, was he really the first to do it?

We'll begin in 1924, because that's where this whole thing started. On May 17, Hornsby struck out once. On June 14, Vance struck out eleven Cardinals. Hornsby was three of them. So, yeah, it happened.

Photo courtesy of Transcendental Graphics

Dazzy Vance and Walter Johnson

Was that the first time it happened? Nineteen twenty-four was Hornsby's tenth season in the majors. Granted, he was a great hitter. But had he really gone the previous nine seasons without striking out three times in one game?

Almost. It had happened just once before, and nearly eight years earlier. On August 26, 1916—this was Hornsby's first full season in the majors, and he was still only twenty—Hornsby's Cardinals faced the Phillies and starter Erskine Mayer. Mayer, a sidearming right-hander, struck out only four Cardinals. But Hornsby was three of them, which rated a mention in the *Times'* short gamer: "Mayer struck out Hornsby three times with none on bases."

DENNY RIDDLEBERGER
& BOOG POWELL

It always surprised Ted when players who had been around awhile didn't think about hitting the way he did, when they didn't learn to pay attention to what a pitcher was throwing and how the ball moved. He told a story about watching a game on television and seeing Boog Powell, Baltimore's big left-handed-hitting first baseman, being fooled again and again by a slow looping curve ball. Powell had a big stride and a big swing; he'd swing himself almost into the ground. Ted said that as he watched the game, he thought for sure Powell would start looking for that curve ball but he never seemed to, and it had made Ted laugh to see Powell keep making that big swing of his and keep missing the ball. I don't know who the pitcher was in the game that Ted saw on TV, but in '70 and '71 we had a young left-handed pitcher named Denny Riddleburger who also had a big slow curve ball. When we played Baltimore, Ted would bring Riddleburger in to pitch to Powell. Denny would serve up that big slow curve and Powell would stand there and cock and cock and cock the bat, and then swish, he'd swing and miss it entirely. Every time Denny pitched to Boog, Ted would be hiding in the corner of the dugout where the fans couldn't see him, laughing, with tears running down his face. Riddleburger would throw another one and Ted would throw up his arms and his legs and laugh and laugh. Once in a while Powell would foul one off. I don't know how many times Powell faced Riddleburger but I doubt he ever did hit a fair ball off of him.

—Wayne Terwilliger in *Terwilliger Bunts One*
(Terwilliger with Nancy Peterson and Peter Boehm, 2006)

The point of this story, I guess, is that Boog Powell wasn't real sharp. If only he'd guessed that the left-handed pitchers with the slow curves would try to retire him with slow curves, well, then of course he would have fared better against them. And there was nothing Ted Williams enjoyed more than pointing out the stupidity of hitters who weren't Ted Williams. Especially big left-handed power hitters who had problems with left-handed pitchers with big curveballs.

Did Boog Powell have problems with left-handed curveballers? I'll be honest with you, just this once . . . I don't *quite* care enough to do the many, many hours of work it would take to answer that question with any sort of precision. Doesn't seem far-fetched, though. After all, the platoon split is mostly because of the breaking ball. Seems reasonable to think a left-handed hitter with a big swing—and John Wesley Powell had one of the biggest—would struggle against a southpaw with a big breaker.

Did Riddleberger have a big curveball? "I was a sidearm pitcher, and my best pitches were my sinker ball and changeup," he told me. "But I did throw a sidearm curve, like a Little League curveball, that broke about three and a half feet."

Did Powell struggle against left-handed pitchers, generally? Riddleberger joined the Senators in 1970, Williams's (and Terwilliger's) second year with the club. Let's look at Powell's platoon splits over the previous three seasons, 1967 through 1969.

Vs	PA	Avg	R	RBI	BB	SO	OBP	Slug
RHP	1222	.270	52	174	153	167	.360	.466
LHP	504	.252	20	87	47	100	.324	.415

Powell's splits, at least over these three seasons, were nothing out of the ordinary. And he actually did quite well against lefties in 1969. That was Williams's first season as Senators manager, after he'd spent most of the previous eight years away from the game. And of course Powell played for the Orioles, right up the road from the District of Columbia, home of the Senators.

So how many times did Williams "bring Riddleberger in to pitch to Powell"? And what happened when he did?

In 1970, Riddleberger faced Powell twice. On September 15, in his major-league debut, Riddleberger got Don Buford on a grounder, Mark Belanger, and Boog Powell on (yes!) a strikeout. On October 1, Riddleberger retired Powell on a fly ball to center field.

In 1971, Riddleberger faced Powell four times. Those four plate appearances included one single, one double, one pop-up, one walk . . . and exactly zero strikeouts.

Remember what Terwilliger wrote: "I don't know how many times Powell faced Riddleburger but I doubt he ever did hit a fair ball off of him." Well, while Riddleberger was a Senator, Powell faced him six times and hit four fair balls off of him.*

---

* In 1972, then pitching for Cleveland, Riddleberger faced Powell twice more (on consecutive days) and retired him both times, on a grounder and a strikeout. In his short career, then, Riddleberger faced Powell eight times, and the only strikeouts were the first time and the last.

STEVE DALKOWSKI & TED WILLIAMS

On May 7, 1966, shortly after his release from baseball, *The Sporting News* carried a blurred, seven-year-old photograph of Dalkowski, along with a brief story head-lined LIVING LEGEND RELEASED. The first sentence of that story read as fol-lows: "Steve Dalkowski, a baseball legend in his own time, apparently has thrown his last professional pitch." The story was not considered particularly dramatic at the time since few people even on the periphery of organized baseball had not heard of Steve Dalkowski.

To understand how Dalkowski, a chunky little man with thick glasses and a perpetually dazed expression, became a "legend in his own time," it is necessary to go back 10 years to a hot spring day in Miami, Fla. Dalkowski is pitching batting practice for the Baltimore Orioles while Ted Williams watches curiously from be-hind the batting cage. After a few minutes Williams picks up a bat and steps into the cage. Reporters and players, who had been watching with only casual interest, move quickly around the cage to watch this classic confrontation. Williams takes three level, disciplined practice swings, cocks his bat and then motions with his head for Dalkowski to deliver the ball. Dalkowski goes into his spare pump. His right leg rises a few inches off the ground. His left arm pulls back and then flicks out from the side of his body like an attacking cobra. There is a sharp crack as his wrist snaps the ball toward the plate. Then silence. The ball does not rip through the air like most fastballs, but seems to just reappear silently in the catcher's glove as if it had somehow decomposed and then recomposed itself without anyone having followed its progress.

The catcher holds the ball for a few seconds. It is just a few inches under Williams' chin. Williams looks back at the ball, then out at Dalkowski, who is squinting at him. Then he drops the bat and steps out of the cage.

The writers immediately ask Williams how fast Steve Dalkowski really is. Williams, whose eyes were said to be so sharp that he could count the stitches on a baseball as it rotated toward the plate, says that he did not see the pitch, and that Steve Dalkowski is the fastest pitcher he ever faced and probably who ever lived, and that he would be damned, if he would ever face him again if he could help it.

—*The Suitors of Spring* (Pat Jordan, 1973)

Well, it wouldn't have been necessary to go back ten years, to that hot spring day in Miami. Not quite. Ten years before 1966—when the item appeared in *The Sporting News*—was 1956, and in 1956 Steve Dalkowski hadn't yet thrown his first pitch as a professional. According to a 2003 "Where Are They Now?" piece in *Sports Illustrated*, in the spring of '57 he was still pitching for New Britain High School and set a (still-standing) state record when he struck out twenty-four batters in one game.[1] That summer, he made his professional debut with the Kingsport Orioles in the Class D Appalachian League. So the *earliest* Dalkowski could have faced Williams would have been spring training in 1958.

There's just one problem with 1958, though: it doesn't seem that Williams and Dalkowski would have been within two thousand miles of one another. From 1956 through 1958, the Orioles—Dalkowski's team—trained in Scottsdale, Arizona. During those years the Red Sox did train in Florida; Sarasota, to be precise. In 1959, the Orioles did switch their operations to Miami . . . but that same spring the Red Sox moved to Scottsdale! And would remain there through 1965, by which point Williams had long become a professional fisherman.

So if this happened, it almost certainly did not happen in 1958, because there would have been no reason for Dalkowski to have been in Miami, throwing pitches to Ted Williams. But what about later? Beginning in the early 1950s (and perhaps earlier), Williams spent his winters in Florida: first in Miami, and later in the Keys. So it's certainly possible that in 1959, Williams, before flying off to spring training in Arizona, stopped off in Miami and tried out the hard-throwing Oriole prospect. Or in 1960, Williams's last season as a player. Or later on. Dalkowski's last spring training with the Orioles was in 1965, and for most (maybe all) of those years, Williams traveled to Scottsdale each spring, more for appearance's sake than anything else (the Red

Sox were still paying him, but he didn't have any real responsibilities).

Possible, but unlikely. As much has been written about Williams as any other player in the last half century, with the probable exception of Mickey Mantle, but none of the books about Williams mention Dalkowski in passing. Williams didn't mention Dalkowski in his autobiography at all.[2] Dalkowski doesn't appear in Michael Seidel's *Ted Williams: A Baseball Life* (Contemporary Books, 1991) or Leigh Montville's *Ted Williams: The Biography of an American Hero* (Doubleday, 2004).

So where did this story come from? Well, again, it might actually have happened as Jordan recounted the story in 1973. But while researching this chapter, I found something else that Jordan wrote, in 1995 for *The Sporting News*, that included this paragraph:

> Steve's speed and wildness were legendary. Stories sprang up about him, some of which were true, some not. Ted Williams faced him once in batting practice in spring training. The Thumper watched a fastball buzz by his eyes, stepped out of the box, and said Dalkowski was the fastest pitcher he ever faced, and he'd be damned if he'd face him again unless he had to (not true).[3]

Not true? I'd love to know what Jordan learned between 1973 and 1995 that changed his mind about the Dalkowski-Thumper Incident. I did find one clue, though. In John Eisenberg's outstanding oral history of the Orioles, longtime Baltimore scout Walter Youse relates *this* story:

> [Orioles manager Paul] Richards said he'd never seen anyone else throw a ball that started down at the shins and moved up into the strike zone. They brought him up to Baltimore and let him throw batting practice before a game against the Red Sox, and

everything just stopped. All those big-leaguers came over to watch. Ted Williams included. No one had ever seen anything like it.[1]

There's something about this story that bothers me. Considering his dangerous wildness, would the Orioles really have let Dalkowski throw batting practice, full speed? And if he wasn't throwing full speed, the Red Sox (Ted Williams included) wouldn't have been impressed, would they? What seems more likely—again, if something like this really happened—is that Dalkowski was simply allowed to visit the major leaguers and throw a few pitches; this often happens, even today, with young players who have just signed a professional contract.

Unfortunately, we can't check with Youse, who passed in 2002.

There's another impressive story told about Dalkowski, and this one's true. In that 2003 *Sports Illustrated* article—which says the Williams incident happened in 1958, by the way—author Peter McEntegart relates this story: "In an exhibition game that spring against the Cincinnati Reds in Baltimore's Memorial Stadium, with his parents watching, Dalkowski fanned the side in the ninth on just 12 pitches. He would never again pitch in a big league ballpark."

This did happen. From the April 28 issue of *The Sporting News:*

Southpaw Dalkowski Whiffs Three Redlegs on 12 Pitches

BALTIMORE, Md.—Baltimore spectators won't soon be forgetting a blazeballing young Oriole lefty named Steve Dalkowski—and neither will the Cincinnati Redlegs.

Stout Stevie, a lad who either walks 'em or strikes 'em out, brought down the house in Memorial Stadium here when he pitched the ninth inning of an April 13 exhibition finale by (a) firing his first warm-up offering miles over Catcher Joe Ginsberg's head, then (b) fanning all three Redlegs he faced, on 12 pitches.

His three victims were Don Hoak, Dee Fondy and Alex Grammas.

To that list might also be added Birdie Tebbetts, Reds' pilot, who confessed, after watching Dalkowski's "radio pitch" (it can be heard, but not seen), that "I told Grammas to stand back in the batter's box and not take a chance on getting hurt."

JOE TEPSIC & THE DODGERS

In 1946, the Dodgers couldn't wait to triumphantly announce the signing of Penn State phenom Joe Tepsic. By the end of the season, they couldn't wait to get rid of him.

In addition to receiving a $17,000 bonus, Tepsic had a contract clause requiring Brooklyn to carry him on its major league roster for the entire year. He played sparingly, going hitless in five at-bats.

In the heat of the pennant race between the Dodgers and Cardinals, Tepsic was too green to be of any help. On behalf of the players, veteran outfielder Dixie Walker asked Tepsic to go to the minors voluntarily so the Dodgers could call up a badly needed pinch-hitter. But with total disregard for his team's welfare, Tepsic refused. The Dodgers eventually lost to the Cardinals in a postseason play-off. Understandably, Brooklyn dumped Tepsic. He never played in the majors again.

—*The Baseball Hall of Shame* 2 (Bruce Nash and Allan Zullo, 1986)

First off, hats off to Nash and Zullo for digging up this story. So many things happened to the Dodgers over the next decade or so that Tepsic has been almost entirely forgotten.

He was a big story in the fall of '46, though. In the middle of September, with the Dodgers in the middle of that hot pennant race, the players met to decide how to apportion their World Series money. At that time, most of the Series money that went to the players went to the winners and the losers, but teams in second through fourth place got small cuts, too.

Pepsic, who was twenty-two when he joined the Dodgers, did bat only five times that season, just as Nash and Zullo write, and he did go hitless. He played in fifteen games, mostly as a pinch runner. Apparently his teammates were not impressed. Under the headline "Tepsic Snubbed in Melon Cut," the following item appeared in the September 25 issue of *The Sporting News*:

BROOKLYN, N.Y.—Dodger players apparently believed Joe Tepsic, former Penn State star, did well enough for 1946 when he drew a $15,000 bonus for signing earlier this season, and when they cut up their World's Series melon (or slice of melon) on September 17, gave him one-eighth of a share. Tepsic, who was signed with the proviso that he would not be sent to the minors without his consent, had refused to go down to the lower leagues when requested to do so to make room on the roster for a more experienced player.

The Dodgers voted 36 full shares, with half shares going to Tom Brown, shortstop now in the Army, and Mike Sandlock, a catcher who wound up in St. Paul after chores with the Dodgers and Mobile. A quarter share went to Pitcher Juan Pierre Roy, who jumped to Mexico and back in one long hop.

Included among those voted full shares

are Harold Parrott, road secretary; Danny Cornerford, property custodian, and Trainer Doc Wendler. Five-eighths of a share was divided among Babe Hamberger, jack-of-all-trades; the batboy and clubhouse attendants.

A week later in *The Sporting News*, Dan Daniel had more details. According to Daniel, the players initially didn't give Tepsic anything at all. "The dope is that when the meeting closed, Tepsic was out in the cold. Durocher knew that Joe would appeal to Commissioner A. B. Chandler for redress, and induced a reconsideration which resulted in the allotment of the one-eighth share."

Further, according to Daniel, the "more experienced player" who'd have replaced Tepsic on the roster was Chet Ross, a veteran outfielder then playing in Montreal.[1]

There remains some confusion over exactly *why* Tepsic was never sent to the minors that season. The Dodgers announced on July 8 that they'd signed Tepsic. Branch Rickey was then running the franchise, and he said, "Tepsic has all the physical capabilities that a boy needs to make good in the majors. Unless he shows signs of needing minor-league schooling, he will remain with the Dodgers all season."[2]

Apparently, no rule precluded Tepsic from being sent to the minors. *After*

Photo courtesy of George Brace

Joe Tepsic, 1946

that season, the owners passed a new rule stipulating that any player given a signing bonus of $6,000 or more would be considered a major-league "bonus player" and could not be sent to the minors without passing through waivers first.[3]

Not in '46, though. But due to some wrinkle in the rules, or in his contract, apparently Tepsic didn't have to go to the minors if he didn't want to. And he didn't want to, even when Rickey supposedly offered him a $1,500 bonus to go down. Granted, Durocher could occasionally have used Tepsic, who at one point supposedly told Durocher, "I am better than fifteen players on this club." But Tepsic almost certainly was not better than fifteen of his teammates, and Durocher hardly used him at all.

On the other hand, there's little evidence that Chet Ross would have helped the Dodgers much. In *TSN*, Dan Daniel described Ross as a "good right-handed hitter," but that hadn't been true for some time.

In September of 1939, Ross broke into the majors with Casey Stengel's Boston Bees (as the Braves were called for a few seasons) and batted .323 in eleven games. He took over in left field the next season and led the club in triples, homers, and RBIs. At twenty-three, he was one of the more valuable young players in the league.

That changed on March 8, 1941. In the ninth inning of the Braves' first exhibition game of spring training, Ross broke his left ankle sliding into second.[4] He spent a week in the hospital and returned to the team in May.

The ankle still weak, Ross didn't play much, and when he did play he didn't hit. On the morning of July 18, he was batting .085: four hits in forty-seven at-bats. The 18th was a nice afternoon for Ross, though; the Braves got only four hits off Pittsburgh's Ken Heintzelman, but Ross got two of those, lifting his average into three digits (.120).

Or rather, it was a nice afternoon until the ninth inning (again), when Ross slid into second base (again) and tore ankle ligaments (again), and this time he tossed in a fractured fibula just for fun.[5] Which of course ended his season.

Not his career, though. Ross came back in '42 and would play for the Braves through the '44 season. Not that he was healthy enough to take advantage of the wartime pitching. In '42 he batted .195, and in '43 and '44 combined—the draft really depleted baseball's ranks beginning in '43—Ross batted .221 with twelve homers in 439 at bats. He struck out a lot and didn't walk much. That wasn't good enough, even during the war, and in August of '44 the Braves traded Ross to Indianapolis. He refused to report and before the '45 season was drafted into the navy (at the time of the trade, Ross had already passed his pre-induction physical and perhaps just didn't want to bother going to Indianapolis when he figured he'd be shipping out soon to basic training).[6]

Which brings us to 1946. The war is over, Chet Ross is playing baseball again, and the Dodgers are looking for a bench player. Is Ross really going to help them? After being discharged from the service in the spring, he reported to the Braves, who sent him to Indianapolis. He played in just five games, was dispatched to Montreal, and wound up batting .243 with some power in 111 at-bats.* Consider those stats, along with what he'd done for the Braves from '42 through '44, and it's hard to imagine him making a real difference in the pennant race. And here's something else: if Ross was so desirable, why didn't the Dodgers bring him to the majors in September, when the rosters were essentially unlimited?

Nevertheless, the fact remains that Durocher wouldn't use Tepsic, which meant for nearly two months the Dodgers were playing a man short, and that may well have cost them the pennant, as they finished the schedule tied with the Cardinals—it was the first tie in major-league history—and lost a best-of-three playoff for the championship.

So, yes, it's easy to blame Joe Tepsic. But before we wonder about his selfishness, let's not forget about Branch Rickey. It was Rickey who wanted Tepsic so badly. And something else about that season is so obvious that I'm upset with myself for not including it among the blunders that I listed in my last book.

On the 15th of June, Rickey traded third baseman (and future Hall of Famer) Billy Herman to the Braves for a catcher named Stew Hofferth, who was thirty-three and would never play another game in the majors. At the time, Herman was doing well enough for the Dodgers, but he was about to turn thirty-seven and Rickey was famous for trading a player "a year too early rather than a year too late."

That credo usually worked to Rickey's advantage, but in this case it cost him the pennant. While Herman would play in only fifteen games the next season before retiring, in '46 he still had plenty left in the tank. After joining the Braves, he batted 306/409/440 in seventy-five games. Meanwhile, his successors—Cookie Lavagetto, mostly—were a collective near-disaster, batting 238/343/318 the rest of the way.

So why did Rickey trade Herman? Depends on whom you ask.

---

* Ross finished the season with the International League champion Royals, and in the team photo he's standing in the back row, right next to Jackie Robinson. His career ended in 1947 after brief, ineffective stints with minor-league teams in Milwaukee and Baltimore.

Johnny Vander Meer pitched two straight no-hitters in 1938, but had a surprising answer when asked to name his greatest game.

What's the greatest game I ever pitched? That was in Brooklyn. No, it wasn't the second no-hitter. It was in September of '46. The Dodgers were deadlocked at the time with the Cardinals, fighting for the pennant. The game meant an awful lot to them. It went nineteen innings and ended in a 0–0 tie. They finally had to call it because of darkness because at that time you weren't allowed to turn the lights on to complete a game.

I went the first fifteen innings and gave up only seven hits. I struck out fifteen and walked only two. I was still going strong, too, and probably could have kept pitching, but I was thrown out at the plate trying to score in the top of the fifteenth and McKechnie was afraid I might have tired myself out. Harry Gumbert came in and finished it. I don't think I made a bad pitch that whole game. Branch Rickey said later it was the greatest game he ever saw pitched. I thought it was pretty fine myself, but I wish I could have won it.

—*Vander Meer in Donald Honig's* Baseball Between the Lines *(1976)*

Vander Meer's memory is good. Not perfect. But close. This game was on the 11th of September in Brooklyn, and he did pitch fifteen shutout innings, he did allow seven hits, and he did issue two walks. He didn't strike out fifteen Dodgers; he

Some of the newspaper writers killed Rickey over the deal. Jimmy Powers said it was because Rickey was so cheap that he just couldn't tolerate Herman's $20,000 salary. Joe Williams said it was because Rickey actually preferred to lose; that he didn't want to win until 1947, with Jackie Robinson installed in the lineup.

In longtime Dodger employee Harold Parrott's book, he wrote that Herman was dealt after refusing to pay for the damages to his hotel room after a wild party. "Once on the books of the Brooklyn club," Parrott wrote, "the brawl, and the damages, soon came to light. Incidentally, it must have been a pretty good party; they had to get a plasterer to dislodge the whiskey glasses that were imbedded in the ceiling.

"When he learned of Herman's caper, Rickey acted fast. He had a young Dodger team and didn't want any night crawlers around to teach his kids bad habits. Within a week, Billy Herman was on his way to the Boston Braves."[7]

Herman told a somewhat different story to Peter Golenbock:

> I got the blame for it, but I didn't do it. I wasn't even in my room that night. It was my room all right, but I had traded rooms with another player. I won't tell you his name. But I switched rooms with him so he and his buddy, my roommate, could party. I just went up to the other room and slept, and I didn't know anything about it until I checked out the next morning. I wasn't even there.
>
> Still, it might well have been the reason Rickey traded me, because Rickey was an idiot about those kinds of things anyway. It was also true that I was making too much money for Rickey to pay. He was a tight, cheap, old bastard. It was all right that he traded me. I didn't care. I got more money with Boston. I just wasn't going to complain and get someone else in trouble.[8]

That was a long time ago, and we'll never know exactly why Rickey dumped Herman. I will note, though, that some (including Parrott) have argued that Rickey was really just making room for young Eddie Stanky at second base, Herman's usual position. But this ignores that Herman actually played mostly at third base in '46, and that the Dodgers, as events transpired, desperately needed a decent third baseman.

If Rickey hadn't traded Herman, the Dodgers would have won the pennant. If Joe Tepsic had agreed to a demotion, the Dodgers would probably have won the pennant. So why wouldn't he? Here's one clue, an item from the October 12, 1945, edition of *The Washington Post*:

MARINE HERO TO SPARK LIONS AGAINST NAVY

State College, Pa., Oct. 11 (AP).—Guadalcanal hero Joe Tepsic will be Penn State's main threat when the Nittany Lions oppose the mighty Navy eleven at Annapolis Saturday.

A Jap bayonet ripped Tepsic's arm and shoulder two years ago, but a year of hospitalization, followed by a year of rest and recreation, has enabled the former Marine to stage a brilliant sports comeback.

Last spring, less than a month after his admission to college under the GI Bill of Rights, Tepsic reported for baseball. He showed good form and his .500 batting average attracted the attention of a dozen major league scouts.

This fall he turned to football, where his exploits on the gridiron already have won him recognition as one of the better backs in the East. His running, kicking and passing have been outstanding, and in two games he has rolled up a total of 24 points.

If you want some idea of what Tepsic might have experienced on Guadalcanal, watch Terrence Malick's movie *The Thin Red Line*. And if you *really* want to know what it was like fighting on the islands in the Pacific, read E. B. Sledge's book *With the Old Breed* (Oxford University Press, 1990).

Granted, many future major leaguers saw combat during the war and could have been killed. My guess, though, is that few of them saw combat quite like Joe Tepsic saw combat or came quite so close to being killed. My guess is that after surviving the best efforts of the Japanese army and navy, and spending two years recovering, and vaulting from the Penn State gridiron to the middle of the National League pennant race, Tepsic simply decided that he'd paid his dues and wasn't going down if he didn't have to. Sure, it's easy to consider him selfish, because he was. But then, few of us—and few if any of Tepsic's teammates—have experienced what he did on Guadalcanal. So I'm inclined to cut him some slack and blame Branch Rickey for the Dodgers' second-place finish.

Tepsic never did play in the majors again. He did play professionally until 1951, finishing his career with a good season in the Gulf Coast League.

struck out fourteen. He did get on base in the sixteenth, via his first hit in six at-bats. He did not get thrown out at the plate in that inning; the Reds did have a runner cut down at the plate in the nineteenth inning, and perhaps that somehow got misplaced in Vander Meer's memory of the game. He apparently was removed after fifteen innings simply because he'd pitched fifteen innings.

Interestingly, what Vander Meer perhaps does not recall is that this game had little apparent impact on the Dodgers' pennant chances. Yes, they wound up in a play-off with the Cardinals, which they lost. But nine days after the nineteen-inning tie, the Dodgers and Reds played a makeup game, and the Dodgers won, 5–3.

The loser of that game? Johnny Vander Meer, of course.

PIE TRAYNOR & CY BLANTON

They've always said that Pie Traynor was a failure as a manager. Yet he had the 1938 pennant all but won. Then in the gathering darkness of a historic September afternoon Gabby Hartnett hit a home run off a pitch he never saw to snatch away the championship from the Pirates and give it to his own Cubs.

That broke every Pittsburgh heart. However, expectations were high for 1939. It's quite possible—fate performs odd tricks—that Traynor lost the job as the result of an exhibition game in spring training. Cy Blanton, one of his more solid pitchers, was supposed to pitch six innings at most against the Indians.

At the end of six innings, Blanton had a no-hitter. So Traynor, the soft-hearted sentimental gentleman, let him pitch the seventh, eighth, and ninth. Blanton got his no-hitter, but the strain on an arm not ready for such extensive use was too much. Blanton won only two games that year. In that same exhibition, a homer was hit off the hot-tempered Johnny Allen of the Cleveland Indians. So Allen lowered the boom on the next batter, Lee Handley. Handley went to the hospital with a creased skull and was of little value for a third of the year. Traynor resigned at the season's end.

Now he's back with the Pirates in an official capacity once more. Pie teems with so much class that some of it might rub off. The Pittsburghers will be the better for being near him.

—Arthur Daley, *The New York Times* (January 10, 1957)

F irst, the facts we can easily find.

It's not precisely true that the Pirates essentially had the '38 pennant "all but won." Hartnett hit his famous Homer in the Gloamin' on September 28; entering that game, the Cubs were a half game behind the Pirates. The game was tied 5–5 before Hartnett's home run, and without it the game would probably have been called on account of darkness. He did hit the home run, and the Cubs went ahead of the Pirates by a half-game. The Cubs beat the Pirates again the next day, then finished the season with one win and two losses (and a tie) against the Cardinals. Meanwhile, the Pirates finished in Cincinnati with three losses and a win. Hartnett's homer certainly was the most dramatic moment of the pennant race. It was not decisive. The Pirates might well have lost the pennant even without it.

And what about Blanton and Handley in '39?

Blanton did pitch a no-hitter that spring against the Indians, in New Orleans on April 9, eight days before the Pirates opened the "championship season" (what we now call the "regular" season) in Cincinnati. In Traynor's defense, it should be said that Blanton probably didn't throw many pitches, as the Indians had just one baserunner.

Johnny Allen did bean Lee Handley in the eighth, shortly after a home run. Afterward he was contrite: "It was a sidearm flip. I'm thankful I didn't put much on the ball. As for suspicion that I threw at him deliberately, that's foolish."[1]

So that part checks out. And did their injuries cost the Pirates the pennant? In 1938, Blanton had gone 11–7 with a league-average ERA; in '39, he pitched only 42 innings. The Pirates undoubtedly missed him. Handley, meanwhile, was a subpar hitter and so-so third baseman who played 139 games in 1938, then only 101 in '39. It's safe to say that the injuries to Blanton and Handley couldn't have cost the Pirates more than a few games, and those few games couldn't have cost the Pirates the pennant. Not close. Here are the final 1939 National League standings:

	W	L	GB
Cincinnati	97	57	—
St. Louis	92	61	4½
Brooklyn	84	69	12½
Chicago	84	70	13
New York	77	74	18½
Pittsburgh	68	85	28½
Boston	63	88	32½
Philadelphia	45	106	50½

The Pirates were a lot closer to last place than first and wouldn't have been within hailing distance of first place if they'd traded their two best players for the Reds' two best. Then again, they probably didn't need to finish first for Traynor to keep his job. In those days, it was important to finish in the top half of the league, in the "first division," which brought with it a financial reward. A modest financial reward, to be sure. But every little bit helped. And as Fred Lieb would write a few years later, "Few managers can survive a one-year plunge from a close second to sixth."[2]

Considering the Pirates finished ten games out of fifth place, though, we must return to the conclusion that that game in New Orleans, while certainly not any fun for Handley and perhaps damaging to Blanton, meant practically nothing to Traynor's career as a manager. More than anything else, impatience was the undoing of Traynor. In five full seasons as a manager, four of his teams finished well above .500. When one didn't, he got canned. And the future Hall of Famer never got another shot.

HAWK HARRELSON & THE ORIOLES

In my twenty-one or twenty-two games with the Red Sox in the last weeks of the 1967 season, I drove in thirteen runs, almost all of them in big games. Against the White Sox one night, I came up with the bases loaded and cleaned them with a triple off Gary Peters. Later in the same game I drove in a run with a double and hit a home run.

And I won a game against Baltimore with a base hit off Eddie Watt. That was a big one, because, although the Orioles were out of the race by then, they were just murdering us in September. To beat them at that point was important to all of us. We were beginning to get a complex about Baltimore. We played the Orioles a lot in those last few weeks and they nearly knocked us right out of business.

—Ken Harrelson in *Hawk* (Harrelson with Al Hirshberg, 1969)

I met Ken Harrelson some years ago, in the visitors' broadcast booth at the Kingdome in Seattle. He was wonderful, seemed as if he didn't have anything better to do than tell stories about the old days to a tongue-tied stranger. I asked him to sign my copy of his autobiography, and he wrote:

*To Rob,
My Best to my Pal,
Ken Harrelson
'Hawk'*

So I've got a soft spot in my heart for the ol' Hawkeroo. Always will, I guess. And considering that his book was published less than two years after the story at the top of the page, I don't expect to find much amiss. But then, if we only check the stories we're sure about, we'll miss quite a bit, won't we?

I've told the story about Harrelson joining the Red Sox in another book, so let me be brief here. On August 25, 1967, Kansas City A's owner Charlie Finley, in a typical fit of petulance, simply released Harrelson, who at that point had posted outstanding numbers in his sixty-one games. Suddenly a free agent—then perhaps the most attractive veteran free agent ever—Harrelson signed a hefty contract with the Red Sox on August 28. At the close of play that evening, the Red Sox were tied atop the American League standings with the Twins, and the Tigers and White Sox both were within two games of first place. The Red Sox had recently lost right fielder Tony Conigliaro to a terrible beaning, and Harrelson was exactly what they needed.

Which is how Harrelson remembered it.

Superficially, his memory wasn't too far off. He didn't play "twenty-one or twenty-two games with the Red Sox"; he played in twenty-three (and started twenty-two). He didn't drive in "thirteen runs"; he drove in fourteen. And since the pennant race went down to the last day of the season—the Red Sox taking the flag when the Tigers lost—by definition every game in which Harrelson played was a big game. But did he really make a difference? Remember, he's quite specific about his contributions:

> Against the White Sox one night, I came up with the bases loaded and cleaned them with a triple off Gary Peters. Later in the same game I drove in a run with a double and hit a home run.

This was September 1, Harrelson's fourth game with Boston, and he's not precisely right about the details. His first-inning triple came with runners on first and third, not with the bases loaded. He did homer and double later and finished the game with four runs batted in. The final score was 10–2, and the Red Sox would have won with *Woody* Harrelson in right field that evening. Next:

> And I won a game against Baltimore with a base hit off Eddie Watt. That was a big one, because, although the Orioles were out of the race by then, they were just murdering us in September. To beat them at that point was important to all of us. We were beginning to get a complex about Baltimore. We played the Orioles a lot in those last few weeks and they nearly knocked us right out of business.

In September, the Red Sox played the Orioles seven times. They lost the first three games, a sweep at Fenway. Beginning on the 22nd, the Sox and O's met in Baltimore for a four-game set. Boston lost the first game, 10–0, and the third game, 7–5. They won the second game, 10–3, and the fourth game, 11–7. Now, let me ask you . . . how on earth could Harrelson have "won a game against Baltimore with a base hit off Eddie Watt"?

Answer: he didn't. Not really. In the 11–7 game, neither Harrelson nor Watt—Baltimore's relief ace—played at all. Which leaves the 10–3 game. In the top of the fifth, with the Red Sox already ahead 5–2 and Watt pitching, Harrelson knocked a run-scoring single into right field.

And that's it. Harrelson's mind, barely one year later—published in 1969, his memoirs presumably were dictated in 1968—was already playing tricks on him. He got an awful lot of money from the Red Sox and they did win the pennant, so his mind told him he must have played an important part. But he did not. Of his fourteen runs batted in with Boston, five came in Red Sox losses. Eight came in Red Sox blowouts, in which the Sox outscored their opponents 29–6. And one came in a 5–3 win against the Twins on the last day of the season. The Sox scored all five of their runs in the bottom of the sixth, the third run coming on Harrelson's fielder's-choice grounder.

In his day, Harrelson was famous for a variety of things; oddly enough, something nobody even really noticed will probably be his lasting legacy as we move ever farther from the 1960s . . .

The arrival of the golf glove in baseball came in 1963 and was credited to Ken "Hawk" Harrelson, then a rookie with the Kansas City Athletics. After playing 27 holes of golf one afternoon with teammates Ted Bowsfield, Gino Cimoli and Sammy Esposito, Harrelson found himself in that night's starting lineup after the New York Yankees had made a pitching change to left-hander Whitey Ford.

"I was taking BP and had a blister on my left hand from all that golf," recalled Harrelson, now a broadcaster for the Chicago White Sox. "I remembered I had my golf glove up in my pants, so I ran upstairs and got it just before the game started. I put it on. The first time I go to the plate, Whitey hung me a curve ball, and I hit it over the left-center-field wall about 450 [feet]. I hit another one later on in the game. I was really getting some catcalls from the Yankee dugout. Back in those days, they had bench jockeys. You can't believe some of the names they were calling me."
—Jack O'Connell, MLB.com
(August 21, 2007)

Well, no. Not in 1963. In 1963, his rookie season, Harrelson didn't hit any homers against the Yankees. The game he's remembering? September 4, 1964, Harrelson's twenty-third birthday. He homered

☛

off Ford in the third inning, giving the A's a 2–0 lead. Then, with two outs in the ninth and nobody on base, he homered off reliever Pete Mikkelsen to send the game to extra innings. But the Yankees scored four in the tenth to put the game away.

Oddly, there seems to have been little comment about Harrelson's golf/batting glove in the press the next day.

The Red Sox won that game and the pennant, and Harrelson's grounder did play a part. But that represents the *sum total* of his contribution to the pennant run. At least in terms of his hitting. Maybe he made a key throw or was a great guy in the clubhouse. I don't know. I just know he didn't make a lick of difference with the bat.*

From Maury Wills's On the Run . . .

I remember a game that Warren Spahn pitched against us in the twilight of his career. He was old but he was still winning ballgames throwing what we call slop—a screwball here, take a little off there, bust a fastball in on your fists. It wasn't a real good fastball like he had early in his career, but it was fast enough when he had us leaning out over the plate looking for the slow stuff.

Spahn had us down, I think it was 1–0, and was throwing about a one-hitter in about the seventh inning. I went up and down the bench yelling, "C'mon guys! We're letting this old man beat us. He can't even move and here we are swinging from our heels because the ball looks big coming in. And we're walking back to the bench talking to ourselves.

"We got to bunt this guy," I said. "He can't field his position anymore. Let's bunt!"

I led off the inning with a bunt for a hit. Wes Parker came up. He laid down a bunt for another hit. Somebody else came up and laid down another bunt. Then somebody got a base hit and the next guy squeaked one through the infield somewhere. Before you knew it, we had about four runs, Spahn was out of there and we won the game.

Wes Parker first played for the Dodgers in 1964, and prior to Spahn's last appearance in 1965, there is only one game that remotely resembles Wills's recounting. I mean, really remotely. On the 16th of June in 1964, Spahn had a three-hitter after six innings but was losing 2–1. The Dodgers put him away with three runs in the seventh. The big hits were Roseboro's leadoff double and Willie Davis's two-run triple. Wills followed with a single, which might have been a bunt, then was caught trying to steal second. Parker did not bat in the inning.

---

* Harrelson did play brilliantly for the Red Sox in 1968, leading the American League with 109 RBIs and finishing third in the MVP balloting despite Boston's fourth-place finish.

AL SIMMONS

Simmons was very much of a clutch hitter. When the Athletics and Senators played a crucial series in 1930, Washington led in the ninth, 6 to 3. Up stepped Big Al with a three-run homer to tie the score. The A's won eventually in the fifteenth, but not before Simmons had ruptured a blood-vessel in his leg with a slide into third.

They carted him off and the doctor ruled that he could sit on the bench but not play in the second game of the double-header. "Mr. Mack," said the sad medico, "you can use him only as a pinch-hitter. However, he'll have to hit the ball into the stands because he can't run."

The Senators were ahead, 7 to 3, in the ninth. The bases were full when Connie beckoned Al with a long, bony finger. "Let's see if that doctor knows what he's talking about, Al," he said, brightly. "Go up there and hit."

Did he hit? He slammed the first pitch into the stands for a grand-slam homer, hobbling happily around the bases. Connie beamed. "By golly, Al," he chirped, "that was a nice one." Oh, yes. The Athletics hammered across another run in that frame to win the game and plant their feet firmly on Pennant Road.

—Arthur Daley in *Inside Baseball* (1950)

For the record, I do not believe this story upon first reading. Too many details, and too improbable a conclusion to the day's events. But Simmons did hit thirty-six home runs in 1930. And according to the SABR Home Run Log, he did hit homers against Washington in both ends of a twin bill on the 30th of May that season. So with that solid start in mind, let's run through the whole story, detail by detail.

Was it a crucial series? Well, I suppose you might consider it a crucial series, if you think there's such a thing as a crucial May series. That said, when the series opened the Athletics were in second place,

three games behind the Senators. So it might have seemed moderately crucial at the time, even if the Senators finished the season eight games behind the first-place A's.

In the first game, did Simmons hit a three-run homer in the ninth inning, tying the score? Yes, he did. And there were two outs at the time, too.

Did the A's win that game in the fifteenth inning? No. They won in the thirteenth.

Did Simmons suffer a ruptured blood vessel while sliding into third base? It's not clear, but "ruptured a blood-vessel" sounds pretty serious, doesn't it? According to the AP story in the *Times*, Simmons "hurt his knee in the opener," but he also "scored the winning run by doubling and tallying on a single by McNair in the thirteenth inning." So how bad could it have been, really?

In the second game, did Simmons pinch-hit in the ninth inning with the A's trailing 7 to 3? No, he did not. He pinch-hit in the fourth inning with the A's trailing 7 to 4 (or 7 to 5; I can't be certain which it was).

Did Simmons hit a grand slam? Yes, he did.

Did the A's wind up winning the game? Yes, they did, 15 to 11, and despite the absence from the lineup of not only Simmons, but also of regulars Mickey Cochrane, Jimmy Dykes, and Joe Boley, all of whom were injured in the opener.

So was Simmons hurt, or wasn't he? It's clear that he really was hurt. After hitting that grand slam on the 30th of May, he didn't appear in another box score for more than a week. On the 3rd of June, the *Times* reported that Simmons "is in the Graduate Hospital of the University of Pennsylvania 'resting up,' he says. Simmons ruptured a blood vessel near the right kneecap sliding into third base on Memorial Day. A physician punctured the knee to reduce the swelling and on Saturday it was again opened."

He got back into a box score on the 7th, when he pinch-hit in the ninth (and flied out to end the game). The next day, Simmons returned to the starting lineup.

LUKE APPLING & RED RUFFING

No one could deliberately foul off pitches as deftly as Chicago White Sox short-stop and Hall of Famer Luke Appling.

He once fouled off an incredible 24 pitches in one at-bat. It happened in 1940 when the New York Yankees were whipping the Sox, 8–2. "I figured since we weren't going to win anyway, I'd have me a little fun and see if I couldn't wear out Red Ruffing," Appling recalled.

"So I started fouling off his pitches. I took a pitch every now and then. Pretty soon, after 24 fouls, old Red could hardly lift his arm and I walked. That's when they took him out of the game and he cussed me all the way to the dugout."

In a game with the Detroit Tigers three years later, Appling pulled off a similar foul feat. Batting against Dizzy Trout, Appling fouled off 14 consecutive pitches. Trout was so ticked off at Appling that on his next pitch, he threw his glove in-stead of the ball.

Recalled Appling, "I fouled off that one, too."

—*The Baseball Hall of Shame's Warped Record Book* (Bruce Nash and Allan Zullo, 1991)

In 1940, Red Ruffing started against the White Sox four times. In none of those four games was the score ever 8–2. Ruffing lost to the White Sox twice, 3–7 (June 4) and 0–1 (August 25), and he beat them twice, 4–0 (July 14) and 10–1 (September 19). Leaving aside the losses for a moment, we'll start with the big win.

In the 10–1 game, Ruffing went the distance, and John Drebinger's game story in the *Times* didn't in-clude a single mention of Appling.

In the 4–0 game, Ruffing also went the distance. Appling did draw a couple of walks, but otherwise didn't earn any mention in the gamer.

In the 7–3 loss, Ruffing didn't walk anybody, and Appling, almost alone among his teammates, didn't do anything worth mentioning in the newspapers.

In the 1–0 loss, Ruffing pitched a complete game.

Appling scored the only run in the ninth, moments after singling. No mention of foul balls.

So that's four starts and three complete games, and in the other Ruffing didn't walk any White Sox at all. This does seem like a tall tale, and later in his life Appling was an accomplished teller of tall tales. Which doesn't mean there's not some grain of truth in this one. While it's difficult to pin down any of the stories about Appling's ability to foul off pitch after pitch, the sheer volume of the stories suggests that the ability existed in some form. As Bill James wrote (with a little help from yours truly) in *The Baseball Book 1991*:

> Any number of stories relate to this uncanny skill; perhaps the best known describes the time Lou Comiskey fined Appling twenty-

The literature includes at least a few wildly improbable stories about foul balls, and this is one of the best of them . . .

It would take a heap of digging to find a player more adept of fouling off pitches than Richie Ashburn. The Phillies' center fielder could slap foul balls with the best of them.

Ashburn was known to have fouled off 14 pitches in a single at-bat. His most famous foul balls were hit during a game in 1957.

As he often did until he got a pitch he liked, Ashburn smacked a foul liner into the third base stands. There, it struck a spectator square in the nose. Her name was Alice Roth, and she was the wife of Earl Roth, then the sports editor of the *Philadelphia Evening Bulletin*.

The unfortunate Mrs. Roth received emergency treatment for a broken nose and then was carried out of the stands on a stretcher. As she was being carried to an emergency room, Ashburn fouled another ball into the stands.

Who did it hit? Mrs. Roth, of course.

—*Rich Westcott*, Tales from the Phillies Dugout *(2006)*

five dollars for some minor offense. An angry Appling proceeded to foul twenty-five bucks worth of balls into or near the owner's box. Other versions of this story have Appling avenging himself on the White Sox because they denied him free passes to the game, or because he asked for a dozen free baseballs to distribute at a father/son banquet and was turned down.

Apart from getting even with ornery executives, the real purpose of the skill was to wear down the pitcher, forcing him to throw Appling's pitch from fatigue and frustration, and many other stories tell of Appling doing this to Ruffing, or Gomez, or Bridges, or Newhouser. . . . Take the ability to spoil pitches away from him, and he'd have been a .260 hitter with fifty walks a year—in other words, he'd have been Don Gutteridge rather than Luke Appling.

Well, I'm not sure about *that*. But while all those stories probably are apocryphal—he probably never fouled off twenty-four pitches in one plate appearance—it's clear that he was doing *something* worth remembering. We simply don't have pitch-by-pitch accounts of regular-season games from Appling's era, but my guess is that the newspaper writers did occasionally keep an approximate tally of Appling's foul balls, when it seemed that something strange was happening. I would guess, too, that the tallies occasionally were mentioned in the next day's newspapers. I just haven't seen them for myself yet.

BABE PHELPS & VAN LINGLE MUNGO

"One game I'll never forget," confides Babe Phelps in the Brooklyn dugout, "is the one in '36 against the Cubs when I first broke my thumb. We scored two runs in the first inning. Chicago came back with two. Then we scored seven runs. I counted with a homer and a single in the same inning. Then Gabby Hartnett fouled one into my thumb and I had to quit."

"A game YOU'LL never forget?" interrupts Van Lingle Mungo, the only pre-Grimes man (with Phelps) on the roster. "I'M the one who'll never forget it. The Cubs hacked at that 9–2 lead. I couldn't stand it, I was sitting in the dugout with my hand in a big bandage. I took the splint off the 'sprained' third finger of my right hand and marched to the bullpen. I pitched three balls and took the mound in the eight inning. I stuck it out until the 13th inning when we won, 14–13. One week later my 'sprained' finger hurt so badly they took an X-ray. Yep, you guessed it. I had pitched that ball game with a broken finger!"

—Jimmy Powers in the New York *Daily News* (September 6, 1940)

Is this one even worth checking? After all, it's being recounted only four years after it supposedly happened, and by two players who were there.

It's easy to check the score, though: Dodgers 14, Cubs 13. So what about it? Was there a game like that in 1936?

The Dodgers and Cubs met twenty-two times that season. The Dodgers won only seven of those games, and none of those games was remotely like 14–13. Not in 1936.

Next step is to check other seasons. My natural inclination is to work from below, but Phelps didn't play much in '35 so we'll check '37 first. They played twenty-two times that season, too—from 1920 through 1961, each National League team was scheduled to play each of the other seven teams twenty-two times per season—and the Dodgers

won only eight of them. The scores of those games: 12–1, 6–5, 2–1, 8–3, 6–3, 10–2, 6–4, and 4–3.

Again, nothing resembling 14–13. So let's check 1935, which was Phelps's first season with the Dodgers. Again, twenty-two games, and this time Brooklyn won only five of them (the Cubs won the pennant that season). And the second of those wins? On the 22nd of July, Dodgers 14, Cubs 13. Here's the line score:

```
Bro  1 0 6  0 2 1  0 2 0  1 1 -  14 22 2
Chi  0 2 2  1 1 0  3 2 1  1 0 -  13 20 3
```

So the year's wrong, but the score's right. The other details, though? The easily checkable details are all a bit off. Phelps says both teams scored twice in the first inning, but they didn't. Phelps implies and Mungo asserts that the Dodgers at one point had a 9–2 lead. They didn't. They were up 7–2, 9–5, 10–6, 12–9. And they didn't win in the thirteenth, as Mungo says. They won in the eleventh.

Of course, the real point of the story isn't the year, or the score, or the magnitude of the Cubs' comeback, or how many innings were played. The point of the story is that Van Mungo was a real man. And for more about that, we'll have to dig a little deeper, which in this case means the archives of *The New York Times*, where we learn that Mungo, while he did wind up with the victory, was not exactly the Dodgers' savior, either.

In the bottom of the eighth, Brooklyn held a 12–9 lead, but the Cubs scored twice before Mungo entered to record the third out, thus preserving a one-run lead. The Dodgers failed to score in the top of the ninth. In the bottom of the ninth, Mungo retired Chicago shortstop Billy Jurges and pinch hitter Tuck Stainback, but with two outs leadoff man Augie Galan hit a dramatic homer to tie the game.

In the top of the tenth, the Dodgers went ahead 13–12. But in the bottom of the tenth, with Mungo still pitching, Phil Cavaretta—who'd turned nineteen just three days earlier—led off with a game-tying homer. Mungo did escape further damage, and after the Dodgers scored a single run in the eleventh, Mungo preserved the lead.

The *Times* does confirm Phelps's injury: "In the fourth Phelps was forced to retire when a sharp foul off pinch hitter Hartnett's bat struck his right thumb. . . . Indications tonight were that Phelps sustained a fractured right thumb when struck by the foul tip off Hartnett's bat. The extent of his injury will not be known until X-ray plates are developed, however."

Mungo didn't pitch again until August 17, nearly four weeks later. And one more note about his injury . . . he first came up lame on July 3, exiting a start against the Braves after six innings. His next outing was *not* on the 22nd (the date of our game in question); twenty-four hours earlier, he'd pitched two relief innings against the Cardinals and given up five runs.

JUAN PIZARRO & FRED HANEY

I don't think our managers and front office ever understood Pizarro. He was always in shape and ready to pitch, but he was moody . . . it was hard to blame him for acting the way he did. One time, he pitched a one-hitter in Pittsburgh, but when his turn came up at Philadelphia in the next series, he didn't pitch because I was playing second base. A lot of teams had an unwritten rule that you could have five white guys and four black guys on the field, but you crossed the line when you had five black and four white guys. . . . Fred Haney wouldn't put five black players on the field unless it was an emergency and there was nothing else he could do. If somebody was hurt and I had to fill in at shortstop or second base, that gave us four black guys, and Pizarro wouldn't pitch. That was what happened in Philadelphia.

—Felix Mantilla in *I Had a Hammer* (Hank Aaron with Lonnie Wheeler, 1991)

A touchy subject, obviously, which means we must define our parameters as precisely as possible.

This story, which appears in Hank Aaron's autobiography, is essentially about Fred Haney and the currents of racism that ran just beneath and often above the surface of professional baseball in the 1950s. Mantilla's story obviously is about Haney's tenure in Milwaukee, which ran from 1956 through '59. Mantilla reached the majors with the Braves in 1956, Pizarro a year later; specifically, Pizarro debuted on May 4, 1957, starting against the Pirates in Pittsburgh.

So if this happened, it happened at some point between May 4, 1957, and the last day of the 1959 season (which ended with a best-of-three playoff series between the Braves and the Dodgers).

For the moment, let's hold off on counting blacks and whites in the lineup (because it's a distasteful exercise). Instead let's check the other stuff. Let's look for one-hitters in Pittsburgh, or against Pittsburgh, or excellent games in general, ideally followed by a series in (or against) Philadelphia shortly afterward (thanks to Retrosheet, this information is not hard to find).

In 1957, Pizarro's best game was a five-hitter in Philadelphia on June 16; he started against the Giants four days later.

In 1958, Pizarro opened the season with Wichita, but got back to the big club in late July. He pitched complete games in each of his first three starts, and on September 10 he pitched a three-hit shutout— his best game of the season—against Cincinnati. Oddly, after that game he started just once more that season, on September 23. Or perhaps not so oddly. While Pizarro did pitch a gem against the Reds, the first-place Braves had plenty of capable starting pitchers, and by the middle of September they were essentially get-ting ready for the World Series. Also, if Pizarro *had* taken his next "turn" in the rotation—and there really wasn't a set rotation we would recognize—it wouldn't have been in Philadelphia, or against Philadelphia.

In 1959, again Pizarro didn't pitch a one-hitter . . . but he did pitch a two-hitter, on July 3. In Pittsburgh. And the Braves' next series? In Philadel-phia. Just as Mantilla remembered.

Only one problem. Pizarro pitched in Pittsburgh on Friday, July 3. The Braves played in Philadelphia on July 4, and again on July 5 . . . at which point the season stopped for the All-Star break. So there wasn't any chance for Pizarro to start in Philadelphia. On the other hand, Pizarro didn't start again until July 14, which does seem odd, doesn't it?

I've been putting this off . . . but let's get to the heart of Mantilla's story. Let's figure out if Haney really was averse to "putting five black players on the field unless it was an emergency."

To do that, first we have to define *black*. This is not something I'm com-fortable with, because of course race is an arbitrary social construct more than anything else and thus defies rigorous analysis. When I talk about *black* in the context of baseball, though, my test is this: "If this player had debuted in the major leagues before Jackie Robinson, would he have been consid-ered the first Negro in the majors since the color line was drawn in the nine-teenth century?" If the answer is yes, then in this context he's *black*.

But how do we find the answer? Frankly, there's little question about most guys—Hank Aaron, for instance, qualifies—but I'd like to be as systematic as possible. I think the best I can do is simply look at photos of every player, and I've got photos of them—at least the ones immortalized on bubble-gum cards—in *Topps Baseball Cards: A 35 Year History* (which was published in 1986 and includes a small reproduction of every Topps card printed from 1951 through 1985).

Thirty-six men played for the Braves in 1959. To the question posed above, for six we might answer yes: Aaron, Bill Bruton, Wes Covington, Felix Mantilla, Lee Maye, and Juan Pizarro. Aaron, Bruton, Covington, and Maye were all outfielders, exclusively. Aaron usually started in right field, Bruton usually started in center field, and Covington and Maye combined for 130 starts in the outfield. In the great majority of games, the Braves were starting an all-black outfield.*

---

* The Braves were probably the first team to regularly feature an all-black outfield. Ac-cording to Aaron, Warren Spahn enjoyed telling this joke: "What's black and catches flies? The Braves outfield."

With all that in mind, let's look at that stretch of games after Pizarro pitched his two-hitter in Pittsburgh on July 3. Mantilla was wrong: Pizarro was not available to pitch in Philadelphia. He certainly was available to pitch after the All-Star break, but didn't start another game until July 14. So let's look at those games between the break and July 14:

	Opponent	Brave Starter	#Blacks
July 9	Dodgers	Joey Jay	3
July 11	Dodgers	Carlton Willey	1
July 12	Giants	Lou Burdette	3
July 13	Giants	Warren Spahn	3
July 14	Cubs	Juan Pizarro	4

Certainly, we might wonder why Pizarro didn't start any of those games, after having thrown so well on the 3rd. Especially considering that Joey Jay had struggled for most of the season. But Carl Willey had pitched a shutout on July 5, and Burdette and Spahn were Burdette and Spahn. One fact: Haney *never* settled on a regular rotation. Burdette and Spahn both started a ton, of course. Bob Buhl started twenty-five games, and the other guys— Jay, Willey, Pizarro, and Bob Rush—were in and out all season, depending on Haney's whims.

More to the point, even when Pizarro didn't start, there weren't four black players in the starting lineup; that is, Pizarro could have started any of those games and the Braves would *still* have been under the alleged limit of five. Which sort of refutes Mantilla's central point, at least in this particular instance.

(Interestingly enough, in the July 11 game the Braves did have five blacks on the field for nearly three full innings. Pizarro came out of the bullpen in the top of the fourth, and Covington, Bruton, and Mantilla all entered during the bottom of the fourth. Aaron had started, so for the entire fifth and sixth innings, and partway through the seventh—when Pizarro was lifted, with the bases loaded—five blacks were on the field. Maybe this was one of the "emergencies" Mantilla mentioned?)

This story, which ostensibly is about Fred Haney and Juan Pizarro, is really about Fred Haney and Felix Mantilla. In 1958, none of Pizarro's starts featured five black players (Pizarro plus four). But six of his starts did feature four black players, and in five of those games the black Brave left on the bench—in addition to the fourth outfielder—was Mantilla. In Pizarro's first two starts in 1959, there again were four black players on the field . . . and again the potential fifth on the bench was Mantilla. Finally, in Pizarro's third start, on June 28, for the first time there were five blacks in Milwaukee's starting lineup: Pizarro, three outfielders, and Mantilla at second base. And five days later—the two-hitter in Pittsburgh—the same five were in the lineup (with Mantilla playing shortstop this time).

Pizzaro would start ten more games after July 3, and only on September 10 were four other blacks in the lineup. In five of those games, three other blacks were in the lineup, and in three of those games Mantilla was on the bench. But then, Mantilla generally *deserved* his spot on the bench. In 1958, he'd played in 85 games and batted .221; in '59 he would play in 103 games—starting 71 of them—and bat .215. Not until 1962 did Mantilla establish himself as a decent hitter.

Mantilla was there. I was not. Mantilla undoubtedly had to cope with any number of racist assholes over the years. I have not. But this story seems to me like the manifestation of a long-held grudge, held by a player who thought he should have been playing more, but shouldn't have been. Sometimes it's easier to blame an old white guy who might, it should be said, have harbored an odd prejudice or two, than to acknowledge that you just weren't good enough to play.

DWIGHT GOODEN & GEORGE FOSTER

> In my rookie year, the only black players were me, Straw, Hubie Brooks, George Foster, and Mookie. The club traded Hubie in 1985, then got rid of Foster, who was leading the teams in home runs in 1986, because he said the Mets made certain decisions based on race. The statements caused such a commotion, everyone got hurt. George was out of a job, and we lost our most productive hitter at the time.
>
> Was Foster right? I didn't think Mets executives were racists, but there were little things that caught my attention over the years. Like, Lenny Dykstra, who is white, and not Terry Blocker, who is black, being called up to replace Mookie after a spring-training injury in 1985. And first baseman Randy Milligan lingering in the minors, even after he'd won the International League's Triple Crown award, because Keith Hernandez didn't need a backup.
>
> —Dwight Gooden in *Heat: My Life On and Off the Diamond*
> (Gooden with Bob Klapisch, 1999)

Here's a question, Dwight: if you didn't think Mets executives were racists, then what exactly *did* you think they were?

Yes, that was a rhetorical question. For the moment let's focus on Gooden's testable assertions.

Gooden's rookie year was 1984. In addition to the "black players" he mentions, there was also Rafael Santana, along with (albeit briefly) Kevin Mitchell and Herm Winningham (and I have not conducted an exhaustive search). The Mets did trade Hubie Brooks in 1985, but Santana replaced Brooks as the everyday shortstop.

Mookie Wilson did have a sore shoulder in the spring of '85, but he opened the season on the active roster and was in the lineup just about every day until early July, when he went on the disabled list because of the shoulder injury. Maybe that's what Gooden was thinking of. It's true that Blocker—who actually debuted with the Mets in April, a few weeks *before* Dykstra—didn't get a chance to play in Wilson's absence . . . but then, when Blocker had played, earlier that summer, he'd batted .067, with one single in fifteen at-bats. Dykstra did take over in center field when Wilson went down . . . but wouldn't even Dwight Gooden have to admit that Dykstra would eventually leave little doubt about who was the better player, him or Terry Blocker?

Randy Milligan did *not* linger in the minors after winning the International League's Triple Crown. Which, by the way, he didn't win. Milligan did, in 1987, lead the IL in both batting average (.326) and runs batted in (103), but with twenty-nine homers he fell just short of Jay Buhner's thirty-one and Sam Horn's thirty. So Gooden missed by a couple of home runs. Problem is, he missed on the rest of it, too. Upon the completion of Milligan's season with Tidewater—the Tides were swept in the play-offs by the Yankees' Columbus affiliate—he did get the call

Mel Stottlemyre was Gooden's pitching coach during Gooden's first ten seasons with the Mets, 1984 through '93 . . .

From the start we were careful not to overload Doc. We put him at the back end of the rotation, so that his first start would be in Houston, rather than New York, and we were careful to limit his innings.
—Mel Stottlemyre in Pride and Pinstripes (2007)

Well, this is a lovely bit of revisionist history. First of all, while it's true that Gooden opened his rookie season near the back end of the rotation—he started the Mets' fourth game of the season, in Houston—it didn't have anything to do with not making his first start in New York, because the Mets opened their season in Cincinnati. My guess is that Gooden opened the season as the No. 4 starter because he was nineteen freaking years old.

As for limiting Gooden's innings . . . well, okay. As a rookie, Gooden started thirty-one games and pitched 218 innings, which sounds like a lot but was just thirteenth in the league that season. So I suppose one might defend Stottlemyre's claim about Gooden's workload as a rookie.

But what about Gooden's second season? In 1985, when Gooden won twenty-four games and the Cy Young Award, he also led the league with 277 innings. He was twenty freaking years old.

Gooden's two best seasons were his first two seasons. Like a

from the big club and debuted with a pinch-hitting appearance on September 12. Milligan certainly wasn't going to supplant Keith Hernandez, not with the Mets in the middle of a tight pennant race. I would argue that Milligan could have been used more than he was—he batted just once more down the stretch—but the Mets' bench included Lee Mazzilli, who did a fantastic job as a pinch hitter that season. If Davey Johnson really thought Milligan could help, he'd have used him.

And after the season the Mets did not bury Milligan in the minors; they traded him to Pittsburgh. Milligan struggled with the Pirates, who traded him to the Orioles. Milligan did enjoy a few big seasons as a part-timer, but finished his career with seventy home runs.

When the Mets traded Hubie Brooks to the Expos, they traded a shortstop who couldn't really play shortstop and got a Hall of Fame catcher (Gary Carter) who was, it's true, white. Still, I think most of us would make that deal, knowing what we now know.

Of course the key figure in this passage is George Foster. In 1986, Foster was in the fifth year of a five-year deal that paid him $2 million per season (at the time, that was a huge salary). He wasn't playing well that summer. In late July, carrying a sub-.300 on-base percentage, Foster lost his job as the Mets' everyday left fielder. A couple of weeks later he was quoted in a Westchester newspaper about his demotion:

> I'm not saying it's a racial thing. But that seems to be the case in sports these days. When a ball club can, they replace a George Foster or a Mookie Wilson with a more popular white player.
>
> I think the Mets would rather promote a Gary Carter or a Keith Hernandez to the fans so parents who want to can point to them as role models for their children, rather than a Darryl Strawberry or a Dwight Gooden or a George Foster.

That was it for Foster. He hadn't played well as a part-timer, which must have made the decision to release him fairly painless for management. Davey Johnson made his case with the intelligence that characterized his career:

> Normally, I wouldn't comment on something a player is quoted as saying. But this is an affront to me. He was alluding to my integrity as a baseball manager. I cannot have anybody on the club who questions my motives.
>
> George is a fine man, a good man, and he's been a great ballplayer. But it hurts me. He put me into a corner. The only thing I can think of

is he's had a great career and I've had the unfortunate task of sitting him down near the end of his career.

In the four years he's been here, he's been streaky. This year, with the emergence of Kevin Mitchell, I couldn't afford the luxury of waiting for George. My job is to put the best nine players out there.

Remember what Gooden said in his book? When the Mets released Foster, according to Gooden, they lost their "most productive hitter at the time." But when the Mets released Foster, he was not leading the team in home runs (as Gooden recalled); he had thirteen, fewer than Gary Carter and Darryl Strawberry. When the Mets released Foster, he was among ten Mets with at least 200 plate appearances. Among those ten, his 718 OPS ranked ninth. When the Mets released Foster, they owed him nearly $700,000 for the rest of the season, plus another million for the buyout clause that covered the next two seasons. When the Mets released Foster, they released him because when he lost his job because of poor performance, he cast about looking for reasons other than his performance. Which would have been okay, except he shared his unfounded allegations with the newspapers. At which point he became more trouble than he was worth. After drawing his release from the Mets, Foster did sign with the White Sox for the rest of the season. He batted .216 in fifteen games and hasn't been seen since.

It would be one thing, I suppose, if Gooden noticed evidence of bias while ignoring evidence of non-bias. But it seems that he was *imagining* evidence of bias wherever he looked (or recalled, years later while working on his book). Which isn't to say he hasn't faced all sorts of repellent behavior over his career, and his life. I'm sure that he has. But his Mets-related examples just don't pass even the most casual of tests.

lot of people, Stottlemyre blames this on Gooden's personal problems, writing, "It was only years later, after repeated incidents, that I started to think his use of drugs had a significant effect on his pitching. I still can't say for sure where and when that effect showed up, but Doc never did regain that explosiveness in his fastball, at least not on a consistent basis."

Gee. I wonder if Stottlemyre ever considered the possibility that throwing 751 innings before his twenty-first birthday—257 innings in the minors, 494 in the majors—might have had a significant effect on his pitching.

PAUL WANER & PAT MALONE

Paul Waner had his nights out even when he was Pittsburgh's and the National League's best hitter.

Waner showed up for a game with the Chicago Cubs after one of those nights, a bit wobbly and with a big head. Pat Malone, who was scheduled to pitch that day, strolled behind the batting cage, watching the Pirates at their hitting practice. He had a habit of throwing the high, hard one under Waner's chin in an effort to "loosen" him up at the plate.

Paul turned to Malone and said, "If you want to knock me down, this is the day. I couldn't possibly get out of the way of a duster."

Result: Waner hit two home runs that day.

It must be remembered, however, that Paul Waner was one of those extremely rare exceptions in baseball.

—Sec Taylor in the Des Moines *Register* (reprinted in *Baseball Digest*, August 1952)

Waner was famous among his contemporaries for his drinking. I mean, he was famous for other things, too. Though now mostly forgotten, Paul Waner was the third-best hitter in the National League between World Wars I and II (behind only Rogers Hornsby and Mel Ott, and well ahead of everyone else). But it's the drinking that's survived the decades. Years later, all of Waner's colleagues had their favorite stories, and this one, recounted by Billy Werber, is one of my favorites.

> Paul was a friendly sort of guy. On a hot sunny day at Forbes Field in Pittsburgh he'd leg out a triple to the gap and slide into third covered with dust and sweat. While he was dusting himself off, he talked about this or that and I had to move away from him, so strong was the smell of whiskey through his perspiration. I am told that one year Paul an-

nounced he was going on the wagon. His batting average was soon hovering around the .250 mark, when, with the aid and consent of his manager, he began imbibing again. Soon his average was back over .300. It was said that he had the sharpest bloodshot eyes in baseball.[1]

Here's shortstop Dick Bartell, who joined Waner's Pirates at the tail end of the '27 season, when he was only nineteen, and spent the next three seasons with Pittsburgh.

> And then there was Paul Waner. He and Lloyd had been raised on corn liquor down in Oklahoma. Lloyd didn't drink much when he was playing, but Paul was another story. There were plenty of times he showed up at the ball park and he wasn't sober.

In the dugout we had an ice chest. He'd stick a pint of whisky in there and take a swig between innings, before he'd go up to bat. Sometimes the trainer would bring him a Coke during the game. If he wasn't going to hit that inning, he'd sit out in the bullpen and pour out half the soda and replace it with a small bottle of booze.

It affected his fielding sometimes. He'd play some balls on the hop because he couldn't get under them. But it never affected his hitting. Maybe it relaxed him or gave him sharper vision or something.

People said, "Imagine what he could have done if he didn't drink."

I don't know. Probably would have hit .212 and lasted two years.

I heard that the Pittsburgh front office offered him a $5,000 bonus if he'd quit drinking. So he quit, and went into a slump. Couldn't buy a base hit.

They asked him what happened. He said, "When I was drinking, that ball looked as big as a grapefruit and had hair all over it."[2]

And here's another version, told by Elden Auker in his recent autobiography. Granted, Auker never actually played in the same league as Waner, but they both wintered in Florida during their careers, and they often hit the links together.

When Waner golfed, he carried a pint of whiskey in his bag and would sip from it all the way around the course. One story that made the rounds about him was that, after leading the league in hitting one year, the owner called him and told him that he didn't appreciate that he had been drinking throughout the season. The owner said he wanted Waner to sign a contract that forbade him from drinking, for which he would get a bonus. He signed the contract. When the new season started, Waner couldn't *buy* a hit for the first two or three weeks, so the owner called him back in and told him to forget about that clause. He started drinking again, and the hits soon followed.[3]

Waner won three batting titles: in 1927, 1934, and 1936. So if we're looking to confirm this story, we could start there. Ah, but here's another telling, and more specific:

Okay, so maybe there's an exaggeration along the way in the delightful saga of this free-style elbow-bender of incredible capacity, but Pie Traynor, the Hall of Fame third baseman with whom—and for whom—he played, insists this one is true:

Taking over as manager at Pittsburgh, Traynor expressed the thought that maybe his .370-hitting right fielder would bat .400 if he gave up the raw stuff in favor of a little beer.

Pirates first baseman Elbie
Fletcher told this story about Paul
Waner:

It was a pity we didn't do better in
those years because we had some
good ballplayers. We had Arky
Vaughan, Johnny Rizzo, Bob Elliott,
and of course the Waners. Paul was
kind of along in years when I joined
the club, but he could still hit. He
was a master. You know how some
players have their favorite bat, how
they rub it and hone it and baby it
along? Well, Paul maintained that
the bat had nothing to do with it.
One day, just to prove his point, he
told us to pick out any bat we
wanted and he'd use it in the
game. Each time he went up to the
plate we'd toss him a different bat.
Well, he went four for five.

"It's not the bat that counts,"
he said after the game. "It's the
guy who's wielding it."
— *Donald Honig*, Baseball
When the Grass Was Real
(1975)

*Fletcher and Waner were
teammates for only two seasons,
1939 and '40 with Pittsburgh. The
latter season was not a good one
for Waner, as he played in only
eighty-nine games and batted just
.290 (well below his career
average). More to the point, in '40
Waner never collected more than
three hits in a single game.
Nineteen thirty-nine was a different
story, though. On the 26th of May,
Waner went 4 for 5 against the
Cubs. Ah, but Fletcher wasn't a
teammate yet; he would be traded
from the Braves to the Pirates on
June 15. But Waner did go 4 for 5*

"For you, Pie, I'd do anything," said Waner, always a good
team man.

The first time around the league that year, P.G. was batting a tepid
.240. When the Pirates pulled into New York and checked into their
hotel one evening, Waner took a walk and Traynor tagged along.

They passed a bar, and Pie suggested that they stop in. The bar-
tender inquired, "What'll you have, gents?"

Traynor said he'd have a beer.

"Me, too," said Waner.

"He will like hell. Give him a shot of whiskey," said Traynor,
who swore that the Waner of old then began to rip National League
pitching.[4]

Waner hit .370 in 1928 and .368 in 1930 and didn't win the batting title
in either season. But he also hit .380, .362, and .373 and did win the batting
titles in those seasons. So if we're using .370 seasons and batting titles as
clues, we've got a lot of seasons to check. Fortunately, the addition of Pie
Traynor gives us a real starting point. He took over as manager in 1934,
which would be *really* convenient if Waner had batted .370 (ish) in 1933.

He didn't. In '33 he batted only .309. Still, isn't it possible that Traynor
blamed Waner's low-for-him batting average on the sauce? And that he got
off to a particularly slow start in '34? Possible, yes. True, no. He got off to a
great start that season, hitting safely in twenty-six of his first twenty-nine
games, batting .355. Waner would finish the season at .362, good for the
National League batting championship and second in the MVP balloting.

Which brings us to 1935, when Waner did get off to a slow start. At the
close of play on the 12th of May, Waner was batting just .231 over twenty-
two games. The Pirates had not gone once around the league—they hadn't
played the Phillies yet—but they'd played six of the other seven teams. Beginning on the 13th, Waner went on a real tear, batting .376 over the nineteen remaining games in May. He couldn't maintain that pace, but, overall,
Waner did bat .335 after those first twenty-two games.

So had he gotten back on the sauce in the middle of May? Obviously, we
can only guess. Traynor managed the Pirates from 1934 through 1939, and
'35 wasn't the only season in which Waner got off to a crummy start. In
1938, he *really* struggled. Coming off a .354 average in '37, Waner was batting just .187 at the end of May. He batted .303 the rest of the way and finished at .280, but it was easily the worst season of his career to that point.

As popular as this story is among Waner's contemporaries, it seems more
apocryphal than not, don't you think? But if it's true, or if there's a *grain* of
truth in it, the spring of 1935 appears to be the most likely origin.

Wow. Long digression. Getting back to our *original* story, though, *did* Paul Waner ever hit two homers off Pat Malone? Waner reached the majors in 1926 and spent most of the next nineteen seasons in the National League (fifteen of them with the Pirates). Malone lasted just half as long, and his NL career overlapped with Waner's for only seven seasons: 1928–1934. Malone didn't give up many homers, and Waner didn't hit many; playing his home games at cavernous Forbes Field, Waner was more of a doubles and triples guy. So if Waner ever hit two home runs in one game against Malone, that fact should really *pop*.

And so it does. At Wrigley Field on June 4, 1933, Waner hit solo homers off Malone in the second inning, and then again in the seventh. Oddly, those were the only two runs the Pirates scored in a 9–2 loss.

Two more things I'd like to mention, while thinking about Waner's well-documented affection for the spirits.

Waner was exceptionally durable. From 1926 (Waner's rookie season) through 1938, only Lou Gehrig played more games than Waner . . . and Gehrig wasn't far ahead. Waner died relatively young, due to pulmonary emphysema and pneumonia. He was only sixty-two. Not long before, Lawrence Ritter interviewed Waner in his home for some hours. Ritter's teenage son was there, too. "With the youngster present, the Waners served no alcoholic beverages, and Paul avoided the subject of drinking during the course of the interview."[5]

one more time that season: in the second game of a doubleheader—again he victimized the Cubs—on the 4th of September. That was an evenful day for both Waner and Fletcher. In the first game, Waner doubled in the ninth to drive in the decisive run against Dizzy Dean. And in the second game, the key blow was Fletcher's grand slam in the eighth.

🖎 *Dick Allen tells this story about another famous tippler:*

We're playing the Yankees in spring training, '65. Mantle's on first, I'm playing third. One of the Yankees hits a rope to right center. Now here comes Mantle, he's heading for third, right for me. I can see it's going to be close. There's a huge swirl of dust. The umpire's right in there with us. When the dust finally settles, the ump looks down at both of us sprawled on the ground and shakes his head. "I've never smelled so much booze in my life," he tells me and Mantle. "Get off your asses before you set each other on fire."

—Dick Allen in Crash: The Life and Times of Dick Allen *(Dick Allen and Tim Whitaker, 1989)*

JIMMY WYNN & WILLIE STARGELL

Here's a typical Jimmy Wynn story: Whenever we were in Pittsburgh, we'd all go out with Willie Stargell . . .

We were in Pittsburgh during 1966 for a day game on July 3rd with a July 4th doubleheader scheduled to begin the next morning at ten. After we'd finished the single day game, Jim and I, along with Jesse Gonder of the Pirates, went over to Willie's house. . . . About nine o'clock we decided to go out to a club and have a drink. Then after we were at that place for a while, we went on to another, and it was clear that there would be many more stops to follow.

I went along for a while but this type of evening was just not for me. When the time came to move on to the third bar, around midnight, I said, "Man, we gotta doubleheader beginning at ten in the morning, we gotta get some rest." Stargell, Jimmy, Jesse, and whoever else was there just laughed. Willie put a big arm around me and said, "No, no, no, man, we're going to just a few more places and it won't kill you, you can come along."

So we hailed a cab, packed ourselves in, and set out for the next nightclub. When we got to the next joint, I told the guys I'd pay the cabfare. After they all climbed out, I ordered the driver to take me on to the hotel. . . .

In the first game of the doubleheader, Jimmy went 5 for 5 with two home runs; in the second game he got two more hits—a total of seven hits for the afternoon! And that was not even the half of it. That whole sleepless, mile-high crew stole the afternoon. Jesse Gonder got three hits in the first game, didn't play the second; Willie Stargell, well never mind. All Willie did was go 4 for 4 in the first game (with two home runs), and 5 for 5 in the second while I, playing both games on lots of rest and a full tank of natural energy, scratched out one bunt single.

Between games, Willie sent a note to me from the Pirate clubhouse. All it said was, "You should have stayed with us last night." Jimmy, meanwhile, needled me for seven hours and then, just to rub it in, asked me if I might not want to go out that night.

—Joe Morgan in *Joe Morgan: A Life in Baseball* (Morgan and David Falkner, 1993)

Jesse Gonder played for the Pirates in only two seasons: 1966 and '67. So if Morgan's remembering those details correctly, it's easy to pinpoint the season in which this must have happened. And in '67, Gonder's last season in the majors, he collected only five hits, and never more than one in a single game. So if Gonder's involved, then 1966 is the season (as Morgan says). So let's start there.

Did Morgan's Astros play a doubleheader in Pittsburgh on July 4, 1966?

No, they did not. On July 4 the Astros lost to the Braves, 3–2, in Atlanta. Did Morgan's Astros play any doubleheader in Pittsburgh in 1966?

No, they did not. They played three games in Pittsburgh beginning on June 3, four in Pittsburgh beginning on June 27, and two in Pittsburgh beginning on August 29. All of those games were singletons. The Astros did play seventeen doubleheaders that season. But none against the Pirates.

Before moving to other details of Morgan's story, let's assume that Gonder doesn't belong in the story and see if we can find this July 4 doubleheader in another season. Morgan and Wynn both established themselves as Houston regulars in 1965, and Morgan was traded to Cincinnati after the '71 season. So that gives us six more Independence Days to check. Did Morgan's Astros *ever* play a doubleheader in Pittsburgh on July 4?

No, they did not.

Did Morgan's Astros *ever* play a doubleheader in Pittsburgh?

Yes! They did! From 1965 through '71 the Astros played six doubleheaders in Pittsburgh. Finally, maybe, we're getting somewhere. But before we check those twin bills, let's check a few other specifics.

We already know that Jesse Gonder didn't collect three hits in a 1967 game. Did he ever get three hits in a game in 1966, his only other season as a Pirate? He did. On August 21 against the Cubs he got four hits, and the next day against the Phillies he got three more. But in his few games against Morgan's Astros, Gonder never collected more than one hit. So whatever else Jesse Gonder might have done in his career, in this particular movie he's an extra, or at best a bit player.

Did Jimmy Wynn ever go "5 for 5 with two home runs" in one game?

No, he did not. Among its many other wonders, Retrosheet lists "Top Performances" for every player, and we can quickly discover that Wynn never did get five hits in one game; however, on two occasions while playing for Houston, he did go 4 for 4 with two homers (we'll cross-reference those games in a bit).

Did Willie Stargell ever go *9 for 9* (with two home runs) *in a doubleheader*? Or "4 for 4 (with two home runs)" or "5 for 5"?

No, he did not get nine hits in a doubleheader. But between 1965 and '71 he did enjoy four games that included at least four hits and two home runs (we'll check those later, too).

Let's look at those five doubleheaders the Astros played in Pittsburgh.

April 18, 1965: Wynn and Stargell played in both games, but neither homered.

Little Joe told this one last summer and probably was a bit surprised when somebody bothered to check those devilish details.

You know, Jon, you're talking about '64. I got called up in '64. I got my first major-league hit against the Phillies during that stretch when they lost ten in a row. My first at bat in the big leagues, I got a base hit, and it was a game-winning hit, walk-off base hit. Mauch went into the locker room, threw stuff all around, he was mad because they'd lost like eight in a row by then, and he said, "You guys got beat by a guy that looks like a Little Leaguer."

That was my introduction to Gene Mauch.

—Joe Morgan during ESPN broadcast, July 15, 2007

Jon Miller asked Morgan, "Was he right?"

Morgan responded, "Well, I was five-five and 140 pounds, so I don't know. Maybe so. That was my first major-league hit, and it caused quite a stir."

Morgan's first major-league hit was a game-winner, and it was against Gene Mauch's Phillies. But it didn't come during the Phillies' ten-game losing streak that cost them the '64 pennant. It came on September 22, 1963, and it came in the middle of a fine run for the Phillies, who won nine of their last twelve games.

By the way, Morgan was listed then and is listed now as having been 5'7". But baseball has long included players shaving years and

☞

*adding inches, and if "Little Joe"
says he was 5'5", I'm inclined
to believe him. Should the
encyclopedias be changed?*

*There's a postscript here:
Morgan's story sent a legion of
viewers scurrying to Retrosheet—
just as I did—and some of them
brought Morgan's poor memory to
the attention of the New York Post's
Phil Mushnick, who used the
inaccuracies as Prime Exhibit No. 1
in a bizarre general indictment of
ESPN. He concluded, "Morgan
seems to be just one symptom of
what ESPN has become, that no
matter what you watch, listen to
and read that carries the ESPN
brand, ESPN should just tear it up
and start over."*

*Umm, okay, Phil. Funny thing,
though: I thought old baseball
players are supposed to spin the
occasional tall tales. Don't we love
them for doing exactly that?*

*Anyway, when Mushnick
contacted ESPN, a spokesman
acknowledged the errors and said
Morgan would issue a correction the
next chance he got. In the fourth
inning of his next broadcast, he did.
I'm wondering, though, where that
line is drawn. Does Mushnick expect
every professional athlete who's
ever told a tall tale—at a banquet,
or in a book, or while calling a game
on the radio—to issue a retraction?
I think it's perfectly fair to check
the veracity of stories for our own
edification. But I'm not sure that
we should hold ex-athletes to a
higher standard than we do our
elected officials. As Mudcat Grant
says, "There ain't no fun telling
a boring story."*

May 30, 1967: In the first game, a 3–2 Astros victory, Wynn and Stargell combined for zero hits in eight at-bats. In the second game, Wynn was held hitless again and Stargell didn't play.

July 23, 1967: In the first game, Wynn went 3 for 4 and homered twice. But he took the collar in the nightcap. Stargell didn't play at all.

June 16, 1968: In the doubleheader, Wynn was 2 for 8 with a homer, and Stargell skipped the opener and was 0 for 3 in game two.

September 2, 1968: Wynn went 2 for 9 in the two games; Stargell skipped the first game, went 0 for 2 in the second.

May 30, 1969: Both Wynn and Stargell did reasonably well, but no bushel of hits and no home runs at all.

So the doubleheader angle just isn't working. But we're not quite through. Remember, I said we'd cross-reference those top performances. Well, when I was scanning the list something caught my eye: June 5, 1966. I saw that date twice, once for each player. And, yes, it was the same game:

June 5	ab	r	h	2b	3b	hr	rbi
Wynn	4	3	4	1	0	2	3
Stargell	5	3	5	1	0	2	4
Morgan	4	0	1	0	0	0	0

Jesse Gonder didn't play, this wasn't the first game of a doubleheader, and it wasn't on July 4. This *was* a day game, but they certainly wouldn't have begun at ten in the morning; it was a typical Sunday-afternoon contest.

This clearly is what Morgan was remembering, though. It was in Pittsburgh. The two teams played the day before—leaving plenty of time for nighttime revelry—and in that game Stargell did go 4 for 5, which means he did get nine hits in two games, exactly as Morgan remembered. It was a big story, as Stargell's nine hits came in consecutive at-bats, leaving him just one short of the National League record (in his next at-bat, two nights later, he grounded into a fielder's choice against Bob Gibson).

The Jesse Gonder stuff? I don't know where that comes from, but Gonder presumably was more active as a socializer than as a hitter that weekend. But this is really a Wynn/Stargell story, and Wynn and Stargell both did enjoy huge games just a few hours after they were out all night having a good time. If you believe the part of the story that we can't check.

NOTES

1903   Rube Waddell & Beans

1. Bill Nowlin, "Consider Your Sources: Baseball and Baked Beans in Boston," *Baseball Research Journal* 34 (Society for American Baseball Research, 2005).
2. Tom Nawrocki, "The Chicago School of Baseball Writing," *National Pastime* 13 (Society for American Baseball Research, 1993).

1914   Bill Brennan & Grover Land

1. "Tinker's Protest Upheld," *New York Times*, May 23, 1914.
2. "Tinker's Odd Protest of Game," *New York Times*, May 19, 1914.

1960   Tommy Lasorda & God

1. Associated Press, "Royals, Wings Divide; Altobelli Grand Slams," *Montreal Gazette*, July 5, 1960.

Shoulders of Giants

1. Charles C. Alexander, *Ty Cobb* (Oxford University Press, 1984).
2. Al Stump, *Cobb: A Biography* (Algonquin Books, 1994).
3. Ron Shelton, *Cobb* (Internet Movie Script Database, July 1993 draft).
4. Norman Macht, "Cobb *Never* Supported Cochrane," *National Pastime Number* 15 (Society for American Baseball Research, 1995).

5. Charles Bevis, *Mickey Cochrane: The Life of a Baseball Hall of Fame Catcher* (McFarland, 1998).
6. Arthur Daley, "Sports of the Times," *New York Times*, February 10, 1958.
7. Bill Veeck and Ed Linn, *Veeck—As in Wreck* (G. P. Putnam's Sons, 1962).
8. David Jordan, Larry Gerlach, and John Rossi, "A Baseball Myth Exploded," *National Pastime* 18 (Society for American Baseball Research, 1998).
9. Jules Tygiel, "Revisiting Bill Veeck and the 1943 Phillies," *Baseball Research Journal* 35 (Society for American Baseball Research, 2007).
10. A. S. "Doc" Young, *Great Negro Baseball Stars and How They Made the Major Leagues* (A. S. Barnes, 1953).
11. Dick Thompson, "Where Matty Learned His Fadeaway," *Baseball Research Journal* 25 (Society for American Baseball Research, 1996).
12. Jim O'Connor, Ken Burns, and Geoffrey C. Ward, *Shadow Ball: The History of the Negro Leagues* (Knopf Books for Young Readers, 1994).

1952   Johnny Sain & Satchel Paige

1. Louis Effrat, "Bomber Lead Is Cut to 2½ Games With 10–9 Loss in Wild Contest," *New York Times*, June 26, 1952.
2. Danny Peary, *We Played the Game: 65 Players Remember Baseball's Greatest Era* (Hyperion, 1994).

1953   Browns Finish . . . Barely

1. Bill Veeck and Ed Linn, *Veeck—As in Wreck* (G. P. Putnam's Sons, 1962).
2. Robert Morrison, "Marion Predicts Big Rebuilding Job; Browns Wind Up with 100 Losses," *St. Louis Post-Dispatch*, September 28, 1953.
3. J. G. Taylor Spink, *Baseball Guide and Record Book 1954* (Sporting News, 1954).
4. Harry Mitauer, "Browns Go Down Fighting in 11th, 2 to 1," *St. Louis Globe-Democrat*, September 28, 1953.

1922–1927   Fred Haney & Babe Ruth

1. "Yankees Take Two From Tigers," *New York Times*, August 12, 1923.

1918   Babe Ruth & Lee Fohl

1. "Lee Fohl Resigns as Indians' Boss," *New York Times*, July 20, 1919.
2. Franklin A. Lewis, *The Cleveland Indians* (G. P. Putnam's Sons, 1949).
3. Fred Stein, *Mel Ott: The Little Giant of Baseball* (McFarland & Co., 1999).
4. Joseph M. Sheehan, "Giant Homer in 9th Defeats Cards, 3–1," *New York Times*, July 25, 1946.

1962   John Felske & Hal Jeffcoat

1. "Walker New Palatka Manager," *Sporting News*, August 4, 1962.
2. Bill Brown, "Phils' Felske in Agreement with His Own Firing," *Sporting News*, June 29, 1987.

1986   Steve Boros & Steve Garvey

1. UPI, "Manager Out at the Plate," *New York Times*, June 7, 1986.
2. Mark Kreidler, "Garvey Ejected for First Time in Career," *San Diego Tribune*, June 6, 1986.

1944–1948   Harry Reid & Bud Beazley (sp?)

1. Dennis Snelling, *The Pacific Coast League: A Statistical History, 1903–1957* (McFarland, 1995).

1977–1986   Dave Kingman & Steve Palermo

1. Bruce Jenkins, "Kingman Out—Knee Injury," *San Francisco Chronicle*, May 31, 1984.

1977   Reggie Jackson & Billy Martin

1. Billy Martin and Peter Golenbock, *Number 1* (Delacorte Press, 1980).

1965   Maury Wills & 150 Steals

1. Maury Wills and Mike Celizic, *On the Run: The Never Dull and Often Shocking Life of Maury Wills* (Carroll & Graf, 1991).
2. Buzzie Bavasi with John Strege, *Off the Record* (Contemporary, 1987).

1952–1956   Billy Martin & Jackie Robinson

1. David Falkner, *The Last Yankee: The Turbulent Life of Billy Martin* (Simon & Schuster, 1992).
2. Associated Press, "Series Chances Slim," *New York Times*, August 30, 1955.

1977–1979   Thurman Munson & Carlton Fisk

1. Daniel Okrent and Steve Wulf, *Baseball Anecdotes* (Oxford University Press, 1989).
2. Marty Appel, *Now Pitching for the Yankees* (Total Sports Publishing, 2001).

1936   Dick Bartell & Cy Pfirman

1. Dick Bartell and Norman Macht, *Rowdy Richard* (North Atlantic Books, 1987).

2. Robin Harris, "Bartell in Brawl as Jints Lose, 8–3," *New York Daily News*, September 28, 1936 (3rd ed.).

3. Arthur E. Patterson, "Mates Prevent Bartell from Striking Pfirman," *New York Herald Tribune*, September 28, 1936.

1985 Ron Oester & .300

1. Mark Vancil, "Anderson Takes ERA Title Sitting Down for Twins' Finale," *Minneapolis Star Tribune*, October 2, 1988.

1918 Edd Roush & Zack Wheat

1. "Dodgers Lose Weird Game," *New York Times*, June 4, 1918.

2. John B. Foster, ed., *Spalding's Official Base Ball Record* (American Sports Publishing Co., 1919).

3. Susan Dellinger, *Red Legs and Black Sox: Edd Roush and the Untold Story of the 1919 World Series* (Emmis Books, 2006).

4. "Wheat Will Leave Before Labor Day," *Brooklyn Daily Eagle*, August 29, 1918.

1952 Harvey Haddix & Hank Sauer

1. Danny Peary, *We Played the Game. 65 Players Remember Baseball's Greatest Era, 1947–1964* (Hyperion, 1994).

2. Ralph Kiner with Danny Peary, *Baseball Forever: Reflections on 60 Years in the Game* (Triumph Books, 2004).

3. Ralph Kiner with Joe Gergen, *Kiner's Korner: At Bat and on the Air—My 40 Years in Baseball* (Arbor House, 1987).

1958 Feller's Lost His Fastball

1. John Sickels, *Bob Feller: Ace of the Greatest Generation* (Brassey's, 2004).

2. Bob Feller, *Strikeout Story* (A. S. Barnes & Co., 1947).

3. Bob Feller with Bill Gilbert, *Now Pitching, Bob Feller* (Carol, 1990).

4. Tom Meany, *The Sporting News*, Sept. 2, 1937.

5. John Drebinger, "Melton Pitch Hits Leiber on Head as Giants Win at Chicago, 3 to 1," *New York Times*, June 25, 1941.

6. John Drebinger, "Leiber, Fit, Reaches Giants' Miami Camp," *New York Times*, February 25, 1942.

1947 The Death of Bob Feller's Fastball

1. Ed McCauley, "Critical Shafts Spur Feller to 30-Win Aim," *Sporting News*, June 25, 1947.

2. "Here's the Pitch," *Baseball Yearbook*, 1952.

1940 Bob Feller & Birdie Tebbetts

1. Bob Feller, *Strikeout Story* (A. S. Barnes & Co., 1947).

2. Birdie Tebbetts with James Morrison, *Birdie: Confessions of a Baseball Nomad* (Triumph Books, 2002).

1956–1957 Ted Williams & Tommy Byrne

1. John Drebinger, "Bombers' Larsen Drops 1–0 Contest," *New York Times*, August 8, 1956.

2. Ted Williams and John Underwood, *My Turn at Bat: The Story of My Life* (Simon and Schuster, 1969).

3. Leigh Montville, *Ted Williams: The Biography of an American Hero* (Doubleday, 2004).

4. Williams and Underwood, *My Turn*.

5. Ibid.

6. Montville, *Ted Williams*.

1956–1957 Willie Mays & Sal Maglie

1. Joseph M. Sheehan, "Gomez Subdues Brooklyn, 2 to 1," *New York Times*, May 11, 1957.

1970–1972 Willie McCovey & Willie Mays

1. Bob Stevens, "7 Hours of Frustration—Giants Lose," *San Francisco Chronicle*, May 4, 1970.

The Hidden Genius of Lawrence S. Ritter

1. David Lawrence Reed, "Lawrence S. Ritter, the Last New York Giant," *Baseball Research Journal* 33 (Society for American Baseball Research, 2004).

1906–1933 Cy Rigler & John McGraw

1. "Rigler and Dahlen Fight in Ball Park," *New York Times*, April 21, 1912.
2. "Dahlen and Rigler Fined," *New York Times*, April 24, 1912.
3. "Tender Suspends Herzog," *New York Times*, May 5, 1915.
4. "Rigler Could Take It," *Sporting News*, December 26, 1935.

1916–1918 Hal Chase Tries to Throw One . . .

1. Martin Donell Kohout, *Hal Chase: The Defiant Life and Turbulent Times of Baseball's Biggest Crook* (McFarland, 2001).
2. "Magee and Neale Put on Fist Fight," *New York Times*, August 6, 1918.

1928 John McGraw & "Buck Lai"

1. "Giants Sign Chinese Player; To Get Test at Spring Camp," *New York Times*, Jan. 10, 1928.
2. William T. "Buck" Lai, *Championship Baseball: From Little League to Big League* (Prentice-Hall, 1954).
3. Keoni Everington, "Remembering Buck Lai, APA Baseball Pioneer," *AsianWeek*, Nov. 28, 2001.

1930–1932 Jimmie Reese & Jewish Yankees

1. Peter S. Horvitz and Joachim Horvitz, *The Big Book of Jewish Baseball: An Illustrated Encyclopedia & Anecdotal History* (S.P.I. Books, 2001).

1965 Don Drysdale & Walt Alston

1. Jane Leavy, *Sandy Koufax: A Lefty's Legacy* (HarperCollins, 2002).
2. Don Drysdale with Bob Verdi, *Once a Bum, Always a Dodger* (St. Martin's Press, 1990).
3. Walter Alston and Si Burick, *Alston and the Dodgers* (Doubleday, 1966).
4. Walter Alston with Jack Tobin, *A Year at a Time* (Word, 1976).

5. John Roseboro with Bill Libby, *Glory Days with the Dodgers, and Other Days with Others* (Atheneum, 1978).
6. Ira Berkow, "Sports of the Times," *New York Times*, July 5, 1993.
7. Jim Murray, "He Makes the Most of His Run," *Los Angeles Times*, July 6, 1993.

1959 Joe Taylor & Charlie Metro

1. Charlie Metro with Tom Altherr, *Safe by a Mile* (University of Nebraska, 2002).
2. James A. Riley, *The Biographical Encyclopedia of the Negro Baseball Leagues* (Carroll & Graf, 1994).
3. Larry Moffi and Jonathan Kronstadt, *Crossing the Line: Black Major Leaguers, 1947–1959* (Iowa Press, 1994).

1970 Joe Foy & Gil Hodges

1. Jack Lang, "Foy's Flop Is an Old Story for Mets," *Sporting News*, November 7, 1970.

1947–1948 Rex Barney & Burt Shotton

1. Rex Barney with Norman L. Macht, *Rex Barney's Thank Youuuu for 50 Years in Baseball from Brooklyn to Baltimore* (Tidewater, 1993).

1939 Leo Durocher & Red Evans

1. James P. Dawson, "Giants Down Dodgers With 13 Hits in Brooklyn," *New York Times*, April 19, 1939.
2. Roscoe McGowen, "Phils Top Dodgers on Balk by Evans," *New York Times*, April 23, 1939.
3. Roscoe McGowen, "Cubs, After Gaining 6–2 Decision, Bow to Tamulis, 3–1, Before 19,836," *New York Times*, September 2, 1939.

1930 Leo Durocher & Ed Barrow (& Babe Ruth's Watch?)

1. Edward Grant Barrow and James M. Kahn, *My Fifty Years in Baseball* (Coward-McCann, 1951).
2. Leo Durocher and Ed Linn, *Nice Guys Finish Last* (Simon and Schuster, 1975).
3. Elden Auker and Tom Keegan, *Sleeper Cars and Flannel Uniforms* (Triumph, 2001).
4. Robert W. Creamer, *Babe: The Legend Comes to Life* (Simon and Schuster, 1974).

1926 Pete Alexander & Joe McCarthy

1. Harry Cross, "Giants' Bats Fail to Dent Alexander," *New York Times*, May 9, 1926.
2. Jack Kavanaugh, *Ol' Pete: The Grover Cleveland Alexander Story* (Diamond, 1996).
3. Alan H. Levy, *Joe McCarthy: Architect of the Yankee Dynasty* (McFarland, 2005).
4. Donald Honig, *The Man in the Dugout* (Follett, 1977).

1932–1941 Joe McCarthy & Rookies

1. "Rebuilding the Yankees," *New York Times*, May 31, 1941.
2. Jack Smith, "Yanks Nip Tribe, 6–4, Trail 1st by Game," *New York Daily News*, June 17, 1941.

1940 Johnny Babich & the Yankees

1. Al Silverman, *Joe DiMaggio: The Golden Year 1941* (Prentice-Hall, 1971).

1947 Vic Raschi & Jim Turner

1. James P. Dawson, "Drastic Shake-Up Hits Yanks Today," *New York Times*, May 8, 1947.
2. James P. Dawson, "Page's Homer With 2 Out in 9th Brings 4–3 Triumph to Yankees," *New York Times*, July 11, 1947.
3. L. H. Gregory, "Greg's Gossip," *Oregonian*, May 11, 1947.

1985–1990 Whitey Herzog & Roger Craig

1. Rick Hummel, "The Hits Kept Coming," *St. Louis Post-Dispatch*, July 23, 1986.
2. Rob Rains, "Herr's Insurance Claim Settled," *St. Louis Globe-Democrat*, July 23, 1986.

1906 Frank Chance & Jack Harper

1. " 'Looks Good' to Gotham Fans," *Chicago Daily News*, June 7, 1906.

1932 World Series When the Babe Did . . . Something

1. Robert W. Creamer, *Babe: The Legend Comes to Life* (Simon and Schuster, 1974).
2. Don Bell, "Did He Really 'Call his Shot'?" *National Pastime* 10 (Society for American Baseball Research, 1990).
3. Glenn Stout and Richard A. Johnson, *Yankees Century: 100 Years of New York Yankees Baseball* (Houghton Mifflin, 2002).
4. Anthony J. O'Connor, *Voices from Cooperstown: Baseball's Hall of Famers Tell It Like It Was* (Galahad Books, 1998).
5. Brent P. Kelley, *They Too Wore Pinstripes* (McFarland & Co., 1998).
6. Paul Green, *Forgotten Fields* (Parker Publications, 1984).
7. O'Connor, *Voices*.
8. Charlie Grimm with Ed Prell, *Jolly Cholly's Story: Baseball, I Love You!* (Henry Regnery, 1968).
9. Donald Honig, *Baseball When the Grass Was Real: Baseball from the Twenties to the Forties Told by the Men Who Played It* (Coward, McCann & Geoghegan, 1975).
10. J. G. Taylor Spink, "Looping the Loops," *The Sporting News*, November 27, 1946.
11. Ford Frick, *Games, Asterisks, and People: Memoirs of a Lucky Fan* (Crown, 1973).
12. Eugene C. Murdock, *Baseball Players and Their Times: Oral Histories of the Game, 1920–1940* (Meckler, 1991).
13. Richard Lally, *Bombers: An Oral History of the New York Yankees* (Crown, 2002).

14. O'Connor, *Voices*.

15. Donald Honig, *The Man in the Dugout* (Follett, 1977).

16. Peter Williams, *The Joe Williams Baseball Reader* (Algonquin Books of Chapel Hill, 1989).

1934–1941   Bobo Newsom & Lefty Grove

1. Associated Press, "Grove Registers 300th Victory as Red Sox Check Indians, 10–6," *New York Times*, July 26, 1941.

2. Arthur Daley, *Inside Baseball: A Half Century of the National Pastime* (Grosset & Dunlap, 1950).

3. James P. Dawson, "Roosevelt Watches Yanks Lose to Senators, 1 to 0," *New York Times*, April 15, 1936.

4. David Pietrusza, Michael Silverman, and Michael Gershman, eds., *Baseball: The Biographical Encyclopedia* (Total/Sports Illustrated, 2000).

5. Associated Press, "Indians Conquer the Senators," *New York Times*, May 29, 1935.

6. Denman Thompson, "Left-Handed Luck Waylays Senators," *Sporting News*, June 6, 1935.

7. Mike Ross, "Hank Greenberg and Bobo," *National Pastime* 22 (Society for American Baseball Research, 2002).

1932   Dizzy Dean & John McGraw

1. Charles C. Alexander, *John McGraw* (Viking, 1988).

1960   Lou Boudreau & Ron Santo

1. Ron Santo with Randy Minkoff, *Ron Santo: For Love of Ivy* (Bonus Books, 1993).

2. Ibid.

3. Don Zimmer with Bill Madden, *Zim: A Baseball Life* (Total Sports Publishing, 2001).

1954   Alvin Dark & the Giants

1. John Drebinger, "Lockman Is Hero," *New York Times*, September 12, 1954.

2. Ibid.

1949   Yogi Berra

1. "Yogi Berra: 'Most Valuable Player' Is Putting It Mildly!" *Baseball Stars*, November 6, 1955.

2. Mickey Mantle, "The Unknown Yogi Berra," *Inside Sports*, August 1962.

3. James P. Dawson, "63,876 See Bombers Triumph by 3–2, 6–4," *New York Times*, July 5, 1949.

1957–1965   Steve Dalkowski & Ted Williams

1. Pete McEntegart, "Where Are They Now? Steve Dalkowski," *Sports Illustrated*, June 30, 2003.

2. Ted Williams with John Underwood, *My Turn at Bat: The Story of My Life* (Simon and Schuster, 1969).

3. Pat Jordan, "The Wild and the Innocent," *Sporting News*, June 5, 1995.

4. John Eisenberg, *From 33rd Street to Camden Yards: An Oral History of the Baltimore Orioles* (Contemporary Books, 2001).

1946   Joe Tepsic & the Dodgers

1. Dan Daniel, "Bums Give Tepsic a Thin Slice After He Refuses to 'Move Over,' " *Sporting News*, October 2, 1946.

2. "$17,000 for Dodger Star," *New York Times*, July 9, 1946.

3. *Official Baseball Guide—1947* (Charles C. Spink & Son, 1947).

4. Howell Stevens, "Injury Jinx Stings Bees Right Off Bat," *Sporting News*, March 13, 1941.

5. Associated Press, "Pirates Lose, 4–3, After 5–1 Victory," *New York Times*, July 19, 1941.

6. "Major League Flashes," *Sporting News*, August 17, 1944.

7. Harold Parrott, *The Lords of Baseball* (Longstreet, 2002).

8. Peter Golenbock, *Bums: An Oral History of the Brooklyn Dodgers* (G. P. Putnam's Sons, 1984).

1939   Pie Traynor & Cy Blanton

1. Associated Press, "Blanton, Pirates, Hurls No-Hitter to Check Indians, 6–0, Over Route," *New York Times*, April 10, 1939.

2. Frederick G. Lieb, *The Pittsburgh Pirates: An Informal History* (G. P. Putnam's Sons, 1948).

1928–1934 Paul Waner & Pat Malone

1. Bill Werber and C. Paul Rogers III, *Memories of a Ballplayer: Bill Werber and Baseball in the 1930s* (Society for American Baseball Research, 2001).
2. Dick Bartell and Norman Macht, *Rowdy Richard: A First-hand Account of the National League Baseball Wars of the 1930s*

and the Men Who Fought Them (North Atlantic Books, 1987).
3. Elden Auker with Tom Keegan, *Sleeper Cars and Flannel Uniforms: A Lifetime of Memories from Striking Out the Babe to Teeing It Up with the President* (Triumph Books, 2001).
4. Bob Broeg, *Super Stars of Baseball* (The Sporting News, 1971).
5. Clifton Blue Parker, *Big and Little Poison: Paul and Lloyd Waner, Baseball Brothers* (McFarland, 2003).

THANK YOU THANK YOU THANK YOU

In the 1970s, when Steve Martin was still doing his comedy act in nightclubs, at the end of his show he would say, "Before I go I'd like to thank each and every one of you: thank you thank you thank you thank you thank you . . ." And he would literally thank everyone in the audience, which might number a few hundred prescient souls.

Boy, I wish I could get away with that, because I know I'm going to forget someone. (If you're that someone, you have my all-time humblest apology. And if you let me know, I'll send you a book, apologetically signed. Honestly.)

Fortunately, I haven't yet forgotten Bill James, to whom I owe both my career generally and this book specifically. When I worked for Bill, all those years ago, one of my favorite things about the job was spending hours in musty old Watson Library, trying to track down these stories that Bill called "tracers." I'm grateful to Bill for a lot of things, but for the moment let's stick to this book, which obviously wouldn't exist without him.

I haven't forgotten Don Zminda or Geoff Reiss. They know why.

I haven't forgotten Marty Bernoski, David Kull, Eric Ortiz, Matt Szefc, or Patrick Stiegman, my main men in Bristol, Connecticut.

I haven't forgotten Calvin Bohn, Jason Brannon, Gray Claytor, Pete Fornatale, or Mike Kopf, all of whom did a great deal of research for this book. I haven't forgotten Alain Userau, Bob Timmermann, David Lipman, Bill Deaner, Gabriel Schechter, Mike Lynch, John Bennett, or Tom Nahigian, who also contributed to these pages, and I'm sure I'll never forget Mary K. Mannix and the Frederick County Public Libraries. I haven't forgotten Dave Smith or Tom Ruane, who make Retrosheet even more useful than you'd think it could be.

I haven't forgotten Mary Brace, Jaime Calsyn, Andrew Newman, Mark Rucker, or (especially) David Eskenazi. They responded to my photo requests with good cheer and better haste (which is particularly useful when you—or rather, me—wait until the last minute to even *think* about anything except the words).

I haven't forgotten the helpful people at the Hall of Fame library.

I haven't forgotten Rich Burk, Bob Valvano, Jason Smith, Bob Haynie, Max Kellerman, Larry Krueger, Chuck Swirsky, Todd Wright, Chuck Wilson, Anita Marks, Norm Wamer, Ian Furness and Elise Woodward, Isaac Ropp and Jason Scukanec, Kevin Kugler, Eric Loy, Mike Curto, or Kevin Cremin. How could I forget these gullible souls who let me talk about men in tights on the radio nearly every day of the week for eight months?

I haven't forgotten Mark Armour, Allen Barra, Larry Blakely, Jeff Bower, Maury Brown, Craig Calcaterra, Eddie Epstein, Dwight Jaynes, Rany

Jazayerli, Jonah Keri, Richard Lally, Rich Lederer, Michael Lewis, Mike McClary, Eric Neel, David Pinto, Joshua Prager, Keith Scherer, David Schoenfield, Alan Schwarz, Dan Shanoff, John Sickels, Joe Sheehan, or Royce Webb. Fellow Travelers all, and without them my little world would seem an awful lonely place.

I haven't forgotten Jim Baker. BFF.

I haven't forgotten David Fine, Dave Mlodinoff, or Rob Nelson (we had a great couple of years, guys).

I haven't forgotten Joe Posnanski's various talents (which are equal measures inspirational and terrifying).

I haven't forgotten, nor will I forget, Jay Mandel (who's been my agent through six non-bestsellers and will, if I'm lucky, be on my side for another six).

I haven't forgotten Brant Rumble, my editor at Fireside (who's allowed me to write *exactly* the books that I've wanted to write).

I haven't forgotten Brant's colleagues, including (but not limited to) Anna deVries, Mark Gompertz, Trish Todd, Chris Lloreda, Megan Clancy, Sarah Bellgraph, Allison Brennan, Kevin McCahill, Jessica Chin, Joy O'Meara, Marcia Burch, or publicist Jessica Roth, all of whom have played key roles in getting this book into your hands. I haven't forgotten copy editor Steve Boldt, who cheerfully offered a few hundred reminders that I'm not nearly as smart as I think I am.

I haven't forgotten my mom. I haven't forgotten my dad. I haven't forgotten my brother or his wife or my nephews. I haven't forgotten my wife or my son or my faithful black mutt.

Not yet, anyway. I've got a pretty good memory for those who have treated me better than I've deserved. But I'll know I'm in trouble when I forget you. Each and every one of you.

Rob Neyer
Portland, Oregon
January 2, 2008

INDEX

Page numbers in **bold** refer to illustrations.

Aaron, Henry "Hank," xv–xvi, 13, 105, 269, 295, 296, 297
Abdul-Jabbar, Kareem, 267
Aber, Al, 212
Adams, Karl, 155
Adams, Sparky, 251
Addie, Bob, 16
Alexander, Charles C., 25
Alexander, Grover Cleveland "Pete," 155, 195–97
Allen, Dick, 305
Allen, Johnny, 284, 285
Allen, Lee, 223
Alou, Felipe, 67
Alston, Walter, 77, 131, 173–74
Altobelli, Joe, 10
Anderson, Allan, 93–94
Anson, Cap, 156, 157
Antonelli, Johnny, 261
Appel, Marty, 86–87, 88
Appling, Luke, 291–92
Armas, Tony, 63
Arnovich, Morrie, 172
Arrigo, Gerry, 222–23
Ashburn, Richie, 127, 292
Aspromonte, Ken, 214
Auker, Elden, 191–92, 193, 303
Averill, Earl, 244–45

Babich, Johnny, 204–7, **205,** 249
Bagwell, Jeff, 14–15
Bailey, Bob, 54
Bailey, Ed, 97
Baird, Doug, 100

Baker, Bill, 137, 159
Baker, Del, 129
Baker, Dusty, 269
Balboni, Steve, 12
Ballew, Bill, 79
Bancroft, Dave, 255
Barnes, Clarke, 165
Barnes, Frank, 268–69
Barney, Rex, 181–84, **183**
Barra, Allen, 24
Barrow, Ed, 118, 189–91
Bartell, Dick, 89–91, 202, 302–3
Bates, Del, 87–88
Batts, Matt, 265
Bauer, Hank, 83, 84
Baumgartner, Stan, 45, 49
Baumholtz, Frankie, 95
Bavasi, Buzzie, 78, 132
Beamon, Charlie, 175
Bearden, Gene, 33
Beasley, Bud, 55–57, **56,** 58
Beazley, Dan, 55
Beazley, Johnny, 49, 55
Beckley, Jake, 147, 148
Bee, Clair, 167
Beesley, Earl, 55
Belanger, Mark, 274
Bell, Gary, 236, 237
Bell, Gus, 261
Bench, Johnny, 54, 222–23
Bendix, William, 230, 239
Benge, Ray, 249
Benson, Gene, 113, 114–15
Berardino, Johnny, 113–17

Berenguer, Juan, 217
Berg, Moe, 170
Berkow, Ira, 174
Berra, Yogi, 74, 84, 128, 263–66
Berres, Ray, 32
Berry, Charley, 73
Betts, Huck, 187
Bevens, Floyd, 45
Bevis, Charlie, 27
Bird, Doug, 70
Bird, John T., 143
Blair, Paul, 70, 71, 115–17
Blanton, Cy, 284–85
Blasingame, Don, 132
Blass, Steve, 184
Blethen, Clarence "Climax," 7–8
Blocker, Terry, 299
Blomberg, Ron, 170, 171, 172
Bluege, Ossie, 243, 244
Blyleven, Bert, 94, 142
Boehm, Peter, 273
Bogart, Humphrey, 120
Boggess, Dusty, 131–34
Bohn, Calvin, 176
Boley, Joe, 290
Bonds, Bobby, 94, 140, 258
Bonham, Tiny, 204n
Bonura, Zeke, 185, 186
Boone, Bob, 80
Bordick, Mike, 93
Borgmann, Glenn, 61
Boros, Steve, 52, 54, 57
Boswell, Ken, 179
Bottomley, Jim, 251
Boudreau, Lou, 121, 243, 257–59
Bouton, Jim, 70
Bowa, Larry, 51, 52, 258–59
Bowsfield, Ted, 287
Bragan, Bobby, 159, 181, 182, 183–84
Brandt, Ed, 16–18
Brannon, Jason, 162
Brashler, William, 222
Brennan, Bill, 4–5
Bresnahan, Roger, 106, 156
Bressler, Rube, 150–51, **150**

Brett, George, 12, 92, 216
Brideweser, Jim, 213
Bridges, Tommy, 292
Bridwell, Al, 106–7
Brietz, Eddie, 164
Briles, Nellie, 143–45
Bristol, Dave, 57
Broaca, Johnny, 245
Brock, Lou, 77
Broeg, Bob, 105
Brooks, Hubie, 299, 300
Brosius, Scott, 93
Brown, Chris, 215, 217–18
Brown, Joe E., 239
Brown, Tom, 95, 278
Brown, Warren, 56
Browning, Tom, 92
Brucker, Earle, 32
Bruton, Bill, 296, 297
Bryant, Clay, 9, 10
Bryce, Thomas J., 220
Buford, Don, 220, 274
Buhl, Bob, 297
Buhner, Jay, 299
Burdette, Lew, 297
Burns, Ed, 56, 57
Burns, Ken, 30
Busby, Jim, 213
Busch, Gussie, 36
Bush, George W., 55
Bush, Guy, 233–34, 239
Butcher, Max, 89, 90
Butler, Art, 5
Byrne, Tommy, 126–29, 212–14
Byron, Bill, 5

Cafardo, Nick, 269
Callison, Johnny, 67–68, 179–80
Campanella, Roy, 28, 168, 183
Campaneris, Bert, xvi
Cannizzaro, Chris, 145
Canseco, Jose, xvi–xvii
Cardenal, Jose, xvi
Carew, Rod, 59, 61
Carey, Max, 10

Carnarius, Maxwell G., 10
Carter, Gary, 300, 301
Cater, Danny, 224–25
Cava, Pete, 97, 258
Cavaretta, Phil, 294
Cecil, Rex, 209, 210
Chance, Frank, 219, 220, 221
Chancellor, John, 30, 230
Chandler, A. B., 279
Chapman, Ben, 243
Chapman, Ray, 21–22, 24, 108, 142
Chase, Hal, 161–63
Chill, Ollie, 39, 41
Cimoli, Gino, 287
Clark, Jack, 216
Clark, Will, 215
Clarke, Nig, 30
Clarkin, Jim, 189
Clemens, Roger, 14, 24
Clemente, Roberto, xvii, 143–45, 245
Cloney, Will, 234
Cobb, Charlie, 23, 24
Cobb, Ty, 7, 19–22, 23–28, **26,** 30, 76, 78, 106, 107, 120
Cobb, William R., 19, 153, 154
Cochrane, Gordon, 27
Cochrane, Mickey, 25–28, 108, 171, 290
Cochrane, Sara, 26–27
Cohen, Andy, 172
Coleman, Vince, 77, 215, 216, 217, 218
Collins, Joe, 83
Collins, Pat, 39, 41
Collins, Phil, 49
Collins, Ripper, 254
Collum, Jackie, 260–61
Combs, Earle, 202–3, 227, 228
Comiskey, Lou, 291–92
Comorosky, Adam, 251
Compton, Mike, 87–88
Conger, Pat, 195
Conigliaro, Tony, 111, 286
Conlan, Jocko, 158, 168–69
Connors, Billy, 50
Considine, Bob, 228
Consolo, Billy, 129

Coombs, Jack, 168
Cooney, Jim, 196
Cooney, Phil, 171
Corbett, James J., 219
Corcoran, Jimmy, 56–57
Cornerford, Danny, 279
Cottrell, Robert Charles, 31*n*
Coumbe, Fred, 45, 46, 47, 48
Coveleski, Stan, 152
Covington, Wes, 296, 297
Craig, Roger, 97, 132, 215, 216, 217
Cramer, Doc, 95–98
Crawford, Sam, 147, 148
Creamer, Robert W., 158, 192–93, 213, 230
Critz, Hughie, 253
Crosetti, Frank, 200, 201, 202, 203, 237–38
Crowder, Enoch, 101–2
Cuellar, Mike, 59–61
Cullenbine, Roy, 124

Dahlen, Bill, 159
Daley, Arthur, 161, 162, 207, 243–44, 247, 263, 284, 289
Daley, Bud, 73
Dalkowski, Steve, 184, 275–77
Daniel, Dan, 279, 280
Danning, Harry, 172
Danning, Ike, 170, 171
Dark, Alvin, 260–62
Dascoli, Frank, 137, 168–69
Davidson, Bob, 217
Davis, Harry, 1, 2
Davis, Tommy, 267–69
Dawson, James P., 166–67, 208–9, 265
Day, Laraine, 262
Dean, Dizzy, 124, 249–52, **250,** 253–56, 305
Dean, Paul, 250
Deininger, Pep, 154
DeJesus, Ivan, 51
DeLancey, Bill, 251
Del Greco, Bobby, 262
Delock, Ike, 237
Demaree, Al, 197
Devaney, John, 78
Devereaux, Mike, 58

Devine, Christopher, 85, 86
Dickey, Bill, 238, 263–64, **264,** 265
Dickson, Murry, 211
Dierker, Larry, 140
Dietz, Dick, 141
Dillinger, Bob, 133–34
DiMaggio, Dominic, 243, 265
DiMaggio, Joe, 17, 18, 144–45, 201, 202, 206, 207n, 265
Ditmar, Art, 127
Dobbins, Dick, 56–57
Doerr, Bobby, 263, 265
Donahue, Red, 148, 149
Donnelly, Frank, 166
Donovan, Dick, 237
Drebinger, John, 111, 128, 250, 254, 291
Dressen, Charlie, 78
Dryden, Charles, 1–3
Drysdale, Don, 131–34, 173–74
Duren, Ryne, 213
Durham, Joe, 175
Durocher, Leo, 131, 182, 185–88, 189–94, **191,** 260, 261–62, 279, 280
Dyck, Jim, 37
Dykes, Jimmy, 171, 290
Dykstra, Lenny, 299

Easter, Luke, 28
Edwards, Bruce, 183
Edwards, Doc, 87, 88
Ehmke, Howard, 8
Eisenberg, John, 117, 276–77
Eisenstat, Harry, 171, 172
Ellberbe, Frank, 40
Elliott, Bob, 304
English, Woody, 237
Ennis, Del, 262
Enright, Jim, 135
Ermer, Cal, 73, 74
Erwin, Tex, 159
Esposito, Sammy, 287
Evans, Billy, 142
Evans, Jimmy, 5
Evans, Red, 185–88
Everington, Keoni, 167–68

Falkner, David, 306
Farmer, Ed, 51
Farrell, Turk, 176–77
Fehler, Gene, 37
Feller, Bob, 27, 108–10, **109,** 111, 113, 114, 115, 121–22, 123–25, 270
Felske, John, 50, 51
Ferriss, Dave, 115
Fewster, Chick, 150
Fingers, Rollie, 51
Finley, Charlie, 286
Fishel, Bob, 37
Fisher, David, 9, 60, 62, 84, 116, 221
Fisher, Jack, 77
Fisk, Carlton, 85, 86, 87, 88
Fitzgerald, Dick, 175, 176
Fitzsimmons, Fred, 249
Fletcher, Art, 158, 239
Fletcher, Elbie, 304–5
Fohl, Lee, 39, 40–41, 45–48
Fondy, Dee, 277
Ford, Russ, 212
Ford, Whitey, 37, 211–14, 287, 288
Forker, Dom, 211, 212, 263
Foster, George, 299, 300–301
Foster, Rube, 30–31
Fournier, Jacques, 117
Fox, Nellie, 201
Fox, Pete, 145
Foxx, Jimmie, 243, 244
Foy, Joe, 178–80
Francona, Tito, 213
Frederico, Freddy, 116
Freeman, Don, 76
Frey, Benny, 251
Frick, Ford, 236–37
Frisch, Frank, 65, 91, 159, 160
Froelich, Ben, 154–55
Fullerton, Curt, 7
Furillo, Carl, 183

Galan, Augie, 294
Gammon, Wirt, 73
Garagiola, Joe, 65–66, 260
Garagiola, Joe, Jr., 87

Garrett, Wayne, 179
Garvey, Steve, 52–53, 54
Gehrig, Lou, 8, 87, 118–20, 168, 207, 228, 238, 239, 253–54, 305
Gehringer, Charlie, 244
Gelbert, Charlie, 254
Gelman, Steve, 133
Gerlach, Larry, 28, 29
Gershman, Michael, 2
Gettel, Allen, 116
Gibson, Bob, xii, 110–11, 245, 267–69, 308
Giles, Bill, 53–54, 88, 176–77
Giles, Warren, 95, 132, 133, 134
Gilmore, James A., 4, 5
Ginsberg, Joe, 277
Goeckel, Ed, 5
Goldstein, Izzy, 170
Goldwyn, Sam, 223
Golenbock, Peter, 70, 72, 82, 178, 282
Gomez, Lefty, 144–45, 173–74, 292
Gomez, Ruben, 260, 261
Gonder, Jesse, 306, 307, 308
Gooden, Dwight, 299, 300–301
Gordon, Joe, 201, 202, 204, 206, **207**
Gordon, Sid, 181
Gordon, Walter, 82
Gorman, Tom, 135–38, 217
Goslin, Goose, 152, 247–48
Gossage, Rich, 51
Gowdy, Curt, 87
Graham, Frank, 43
Grammas, Alex, 277
Grant, Mudcat, 173, 308
Green, Dallas, 58
Green, Lenny, 175
Green, Paul, 99, 103–4, 233–34
Greenberg, Hank, 17–18, 145, 171, 172, 244–45
Gregory, L. H., 209
Grieve, Tom, 142
Griffith, Calvin, 72
Griffith, Clark, 161, 245
Grim, Bob, 211, 213, 214
Grimes, Burleigh, 104, 232, 233, 234, 293
Grimm, Charlie, 56–58, 65, 234–35, 257, 258
Grimsley, Ross, 61

Groat, Dick, 106
Groh, Heinie, 101, 102, 159
Gross, Milton, 144
Grove, Lefty, 11, 241–43
Guidry, Ron, 12–13, 85–86
Guinn, Jeff, 159
Gumbert, Harry, 282
Gumpert, Randy, 197n
Gutman, Bill, 169
Gutteridge, Don, 113–14, 292
Gwynn, Tony, 53

Haddix, Harvey, 95, 105, 107
Hadley, Bump, 108
Hagen, Paul, 52
Haines, Jesse, 239
Halberstam, David, 208, 209, 210
Hamberger, Babe, 279
Handley, Lee, 284, 285
Haney, Fred, 43–44, 295, 296, 297–98
Harder, Mel, 32
Hargrove, Mike, 142
Harmon, Chuck, 261
Harper, Jack, 219–21
Harrelson, Ken "Hawk," 286–88
Harris, Bucky, 45, 49, 245
Harris, Gail, 137
Harrison, James R., 44, 227
Harshman, Jack, 237
Hart, Kathy Root, 239
Hartnett, Gabby, 236, 237, 238, 284, 293, 294
Hatten, Joe, 64
Hatton, Grady, 65
Hayes, Von, 51
Haynes, Joe, 121
Hearn, Charles Bunn, 156–57
Heath, Mike, 217
Hebner, Richie, 145
Heffner, Jeep, 119
Hegan, Jim, 264–65
Hegan, Mike, 68
Heilmann, Harry, 19–20
Heiman, Lee, 169
Heintzelman, Ken, 280
Helm, Ernie, 131

Hemsley, Rollie, 123
Hemus, Solly, 95, 268, 269
Henderson, Rickey, 77, 92
Henderson, Steve, 141
Hendricks, Jack, 100
Henrich, Tommy, 17, 18, 201, 202
Herman, Babe, 150
Herman, Billy, 235, 250–51, 281–82
Hermann, Ed, 220
Hernandez, Keith, 299, 300
Herr, Tom, 216–17
Herzog, Buck, 160
Herzog, Whitey, 33–34, 70, 71, 215–18
Heydler, John, 100, 163
Higgins, Pinky, 123, 125
Higuera, Teddy, 93–94
Hirshberg, Al, 286
Hitchcock, Billy, 73, 74, 265
Hitler, Adolf, 171
Hoak, Don, 277
Hodges, Gil, 178, 179, 182, 183
Hodges, Russ, 262
Hofferth, Stew, 281
Hogan, Shanty, 253
Holmes, Tommy, 65
Holway, John, 30, 113
Honig, Donald, 126, 181, 197, 282, 304
Hooper, Harry, 152
Horn, Sam, 299
Horner, Bob, 53
Hornsby, Rogers, 49, 270–72, 302
Horrigan, Kevin, 34
Horton, Rick, 217
Houk, Ralph, 67–68, 73, 74, 142
Hubbard, Glenn, 53
Hubbell, Carl, 110, 249
Huggins, Miller, 8n, 21, 41, 153, 154, 156, 189, 228
Hughes, Ed R., 248
Hummel, Rick, 216–17
Hunt, Ron, 140
Hunter, Catfish, 69, 70
Hurst, Tim, 147, 148
Hurwitz, Hy, 127–28
Hutchinson, Fred, 131, 132, 261
Hutto, Jim, 87

Irvin, Monte, 28

Jablonski, Ray, 138
Jackson, Reggie, 69–71, 93
Jackson, Travis, 196, 253
Jacobson, Bill, 39, 41
Jaeckel, Jake, 50–51
James, Bill, xi–xiv, 43, 80, 97, 120, 135, 291–92
Jasper, Hi, 46
Jay, Joey, 297
Jeffcoat, George, 89, 90
Jeffcoat, Hal, 50–51
Jenkins, Bruce, 63
Jennings, Hughie, 120
Jensen, Jackie, 213
Jessel, George, 118–19, 120
Jeter, Derek, 209
John, Tommy, 220–21
Johnson, Alex, 92
Johnson, Ban, 35
Johnson, Billy, 201
Johnson, Bob, 142
Johnson, Cliff, 70
Johnson, Connie, 175
Johnson, Darrell, 211
Johnson, Davey, 300–301
Johnson, Earl, 176
Johnson, Richard A., 173
Johnson, Vince, 204
Johnson, Walter, 27, 142, 207, 270, **271**
Johnston, Jimmy, 104
Jones, Davy, 148–49
Jones, Harry, 123
Jones, Sam, 39, 41–42
Jones, Tommy Lee, 24
Jordan, David, 28–29
Jordan, Pat, 275, 276
Judson, Howie, 261
Jurges, Billy, 250, 294

Kabbes, Ron, 10
Kahn, Roger, 13, 50, 51
Kaiser, Ken, 60, 62
Kandle, Matt, 231
Karpel, Herb "Lefty," 172

Katt, Ray, 137, 261
Kavanaugh, Jack, 196
Kay, Michael, 12, 209
Kaye, Danny, 118–19
Kell, George, 217
Keller, Charlie, 201, 202
Kelly, George, 195–96
Kelly, Ray, 233
Kennedy, Bob, 97
Keough, Marty, 128
Killebrew, Harmon, 59, 61
Killefer, Red, 161–62
Kindall, Jerry, 259
Kiner, Ralph, 65, 105–7
King, Clyde, 78
Kingman, Dave, 62–63
Kittle, Hub, 141
Klapisch, Bob, 299
Klein, Chuck, 49
Klem, Bill, 91, 159
Klieman, Ed, 122
Klinger, Bob, 159
Kluszewski, Ted, 260, 261
Knetzer, Elmer, 155
Koenecke, Len, 254
Koenig, Mark, 226, 227, 228, 229, 236,
    252
Kohout, Martin Donell, 162
Konetchy, Ed, 162
Koosman, Jerry, 178
Kopf, Mike, 213
Koufax, Sandy, 27, 132, 134, 173, 174, 267, 268,
    269
Kreidler, Mark, 54
Krichell, Paul, 189
Kronstadt, Jonathan, 176, 177
Kruk, John, 52, 53
Krukow, Mike, 217
Kucks, Johnny, 211, 213, 214
Kuhn, Bowie, xv
Kurtzer, Bob, 13
Kutcher, Randy, 217

Labine, Clem, 13, 137
Lai, William "Buck", Jr., 167, 168

Lai, William Tin "Buck," 164–69
Lajoie, Nap, 48, 271
Land, Grover, 4–5
Landes, Stan, 137
Landis, Kenesaw Mountain, 30
Landrith, Hobie, 260
Lane, Frank, 261
Lang, Jack, 179
Lanier, Hal, 141
Lardner, Ring, 3
Larsen, Don, 128, 129
La Russa, Tony, 93
Lasorda, Tommy, 9–11
Lavagetto, Cookie, 168, 281
LaValliere, Mike, 216
Lazzeri, Tony, 197, 238
Leach, Eddie, 253
Leavy, Jane, 173
Lebovitz, Hal, 121
Lee, Bill, xiii
Leiber, Hank, 108–12
Leonard, Dutch, 113, 114, 115, 249
Leonard, Jeffrey, 215, 217
Lewin, Josh, 142
Lewis, Bob, 57
Lewis, Franklin, 46–48
Lieb, Frederick G., 35, 39, 40, 42, 116, 285
Linn, Ed, 28
Litwhiler, Danny, 64–66
Lobert, Hans, 219
Lockman, Whitey, 137, 261, 262
Lolich, Mickey, xi, 98
Lombardi, Ernie, 223, 252
Lopez, Al, 159, 201, 223
Lotshaw, Andy, 236
Lowell, Mike, 93
Lowry, Philip J., 40, 139
Luciano, Ron, 84, 115–16, 220–21
Lundgren, Carl, 221
Lupica, Mike, 69
Luque, Adolfo, 89, 91
Lynch, Thomas J., 159
Lynn, Fred, 79–81, 88
Lyons, Al, 204
Lyons, Leonard, 108

Maas, Duke, 211
McAuley, Ed, 226
McCarthy, Joe, 195, 196–97, 198–99, 200–203, 204, 206–7, **207,** 238–39
McCarver, Tim, 87, 88, 267, 268–69
McCosky, Barney, 122, 124
McCovey, Willie, 87, 139–40
McDaniel, Lindy, 97–98
McDonough, Ed, 154–55
McEntegart, Peter, 277
MacFayden, Danny, 159
McGarigle, Bob, 20
McGee, James K., 246
McGowan, Lloyd, 10
McGraner, Howard, 156
McGraw, Frank "Tug," 53–54
McGraw, John J., 30, 158, 159, 164, 165, 166, 167, 169, 172, 253–56, **255**
Macht, Norman, 26, 27, 202
Mack, Connie, 48–49, 182, 204, 206, 289
McKechnie, Bill, 111, 282
McManus, Marty, 41
McNair, Eric, 290
McNally, Dave, 61
McNally, Mike, 8
MacPhail, Lee, 67
McReynolds, Kevin, 53
McSherry, John, 217
Maddux, Greg, 14–15
Magee, Lee, 162–63
Magerkurth, George, 187
Maglie, Sal, 127, 133, 135–38, **136,** 211
Mails, Walter, 246–48
Maldonado, Candy, 218
Malick, Terrence, 283
Malone, Pat, 302, 305
Maloney, Jim, 222
Mancuso, Gus, 253
Manion, Clyde, 251
Mansch, Larry, 150
Mantilla, Felix, 295, 296, 297–98
Mantle, Merlyn, 70
Mantle, Mickey, xii, 70, 128, 213, 264, 276, 305
Mapes, Cliff, 263
Maranville, Rabbit, 270

Marcucci, Lilio, 57
Marion, Marty, 33, 37
Maris, Roger, 73–74, 179, 201, 211n
Marquard, Rube, 104, 150–52, 239
Martin, Billy, 69, 70, 71, 72–75, 82–84, **83**
Martin, Hershel, 187
Martin, Lois, 70
Martin, Mike, 244
Martin, Pepper, 185, 186
Masi, Phil, 64–65
Mathewson, Christy, 30–31, 155n, 163, 207
Mauch, Gene, 307
Mauney, Dick, 64
Maxwell, Charlie, 212
May, Lee, 13
Maye, Lee, 296
Mayer, Erskine, 272
Mays, Carl, 19–22, 48, 142
Mays, Willie, 84, 87, 97, 135–38, 139–40, 141–42, 261
Mazeroski, Bill, xvii, 143–45
Mazzilli, Lee, 300
Medwick, Joe, 160
Mele, Sam, 72
Melton, Cliff, 111
Mendoza, Minnie, 60
Metro, Charlie, 175, 176
Meusel, Bob, 39, 40, 228
Meyers, Chief, 152, 158
Mikkelsen, Pete, 288
Miller, Bob, 77–78
Miller, Eddie, 204
Miller, Jon, 139, 140, 307
Millies, Walter, 27
Milligan, Randy, 299–301
Millstein, Gilbert, 91
Mitauer, Harry, 37–38
Mitchell, Jerry, 25
Mitchell, Kevin, 299, 301
Mitterwald, George, 60
Mize, Johnny, 49, 84, 91, 182–83, 184
Moffi, Larry, 176, 177
Monboquette, Bill, 236, 237
Montville, Leigh, 130, 276
Mooney, Jim, 254
Moran, Charles, 187

Moran, Pat, 196
Morgan, Bobby, 262
Morgan, Joe, 306–8
Morong, Cyril, 125
Morris, Jack, 142
Moss, Les, 33–34
Mueller, Dick, 261
Mueller, Don, 137
Muncrief, Bob, 65–66
Mungo, Van Lingle, 90, 293–94
Munson, Thurman, 13, 70, 85–88
Murphy, Cait, 219, 221
Murphy, Charles, 219, 220
Murphy, Johnny, 17–18
Murray, Billy, 154
Murray, Eddie, 63
Murray, Jim, 174
Mushnick, Phil, 308
Musial, Stan, 13, 35, 95, 260
Myer, Buddy, 94
Myers, Doug, 53, 176
Myers, Elmer, 46
Myers, Hi, 104

Nallin, Richard F., 228
Nash, Bruce, 5, 8, 129, 160, 234, 255, 278, 291
Neal, Charlie, 98
Neale, Greasy, 163
Newhouser, Hal, 270, 292
Newkirk, W. G., 82
Newsom, Bobo, 241–45, **242**
Nicholson, Bill "Swish," 48
Nolan, Gary, 142
Norris, Mike, 110–11
Nowlin, Bill, 2–3
Nugent, Gerry, 28

O'Connell, Jack, 287
O'Doul, Lefty, 177
Oester, Ron, 92
O'Farrell, Bob, 254
Ogden, Jim "Curly," 11
Okrent, Dan, 30, 86, 142
Oliva, Tony, 59, 61
Oliver, Al, 143

Oliver, Gene, 269
Olson, Ivy, 160
O'Neill, Steve, 45, 47, 226
Ortiz, Roberto, 27
Ostler, Scott, 110
Otis, Amos, 12, 178
Ott, Mel, 16–18, **17,** 48, 49, 253, 302
Owens, Brick, 39, 41
Owens, Jim, 176

Paige, Satchel, 28, 32–34, **33,** 37, 113, 114, 115, 234, 247
Palermo, Steve, 62, 63
Palmer, Jim, 59–61
Paparella, Joe, 263
Park, Charlie, 270
Parker, Wes, 288
Parnham, Jim "Rube," 11
Parrott, Harold, 278, 282
Passarella, Art, 35
Passeau, Claude, 239
Patek, Freddie, 70
Peary, Danny, 32, 105, 116
Peckinpaugh, Roger, 247
Pelzman, J. P., 59
Pepe, Phil, 67
Perez, Tony, xvi, 53, 54
Perini, Lou, 64
Perry, Gerald, 93
Perryman, Emmett "Parson," 10
Pesky, Johnny, 263, 265
Peters, Gary, 286, 287
Peterson, Nancy, 273
Petoskey, Ted, 251
Pfeffer, Jeff, 155
Pfiel, Bob, 51
Pfirman, Cy, 89–91
Phelps, Babe, 89, 90, 293–94
Pierce, Billy, 97
Piersall, Jimmy, 234
Pillette, Duane, 37
Piniella, Lou, 62, 70
Pinson, Vada, 81, 132
Pipp, Wallie, 39, 41
Pitts, Jonathan, 215, 216
Pizarro, Juan, 295–98

Plimpton, George, 156
Podres, Johnny, 134
Pool, Harlin, 251
Poole, Jim, 246–48
Povich, Shirley, 94, 161
Powell, Boog, 73, 116
Powell, John Wesley "Boog," 273–74
Powers, Jimmy, 89, 91, 282, 293
Pratt, Del, 22
Prell, Ed, 57
Priddy, Jerry, 198–99, 201, 202, 203

Quigley, Martin, 65, 260
Quisenberry, Dan, 51

Rader, Doug, 58
Raffensberger, Ken, 106, 107
Ramos, Pedro, 127–30
Randolph, Willie, 70
Raschi, Vic, 208–10, 263, 265
Rawlings, Johnny, 162
Reagan, Ronald, 56–58
Reese, Jimmie, 170–72
Reese, Pee Wee, 78, 183, 188
Reichler, Joe, 262
Reid, Harry, 55, 56, 58
Reiser, Pete, 45, 49, 50, 51
Repoz, Roger, xii
Repulski, Rip, 262
Reynold, Carl, 244
Reynolds, Isabel, 167
Rhodes, Dusty, 261
Rice, Grantland, 30
Rice, Hal, 95
Richard, J. R., 141–42
Richards, Paul, 276
Richman, Milt, 37
Rickey, Branch, 28, 182, 279, 280, 281–82, 283
Riddleberger, Denny, 273–74
Rigler, Charles "Cy," 100, 158–60
Riley, Jim, 175–76
Ripken, Cal, Jr., 120
Ripple, Jimmy, 89, 90, 91
Risley, George, 9, 10
Ritter, Lawrence S., 146–52, 254, 305

Rixey, Eppa, 155, 271
Rizzo, Johnny, 304
Rizzuto, Phil, 84, 172, 200, 201, 202, 203
Roarke, Mike, 217
Roberts, Bip, 52, 53–54
Roberts, Doug, 24
Roberts, Robin, 65–66, 73–74
Robertson, Billy, 72
Robertson, Sherry, 72
Robinson, Frank, 117, 131–33
Robinson, Jackie, 29, 82, 83–84, 282, 296
Robinson, Lawrence, 253
Robinson, Wilbert, 100, 104, 223
Rojas, Cookie, 71
Roosevelt, Franklin D., 243, 244
Roosevelt, Teddy, xii
Root, Charlie, 230, 231, 233, 234, 235, 236–37, 239–40
Rose, Pete, 92
Roseboro, John, 173, 174
Ross, Chet, 279, 280–81
Ross, Mike, 245
Rossi, John, 28, 29
Roth, Alice, 292
Roth, Earl, 292
Roush, Edd J, 99–104, **103,** 162, 165
Roush, Will, 102
Roy, Juan Pierre, 278
Ruby, Harry, 170–71
Ruffing, Red, 291, 292
Runnels, Pete, 236
Rush, Bob, 297
Rusie, Amos, 142
Russell, Jack, 18
Ruth, Babe, xv, xvi, 8, 19, 22, 39, 40, 43–44, **44,** 45–49, 100–101, 106, 107, 129, 135, 168, 170, 171*n*, 172, 191–94, 207, 226–29, 230–40, **232,** 244, 254
Ryan, Mike, 87, 88
Ryan, Nolan, 27

Saigh, Fred, 35–36
Sain, Johnny, 32–34, 74
Salsinger, H. G., 249, 250
Saltzgaver, Jack, 118, 119
Sandberg, Ryne, 51, 258
Sanders, Ray, 65

Sandlock, Mike, 278
Sanguillen, Manny, 145
Santana, Rafael, 299
Santo, Ron, 257–59
Saperstein, Abe, 28
Sargent, Jim, 64
Sauer, Hank, 65, 105–7, 261–62
Schacht, Al, 133, 170
Schlossberg, Dan, 170
Schmidt, Mike, 51, 258
Schmidt, Willard, 156–57
Schmit, Frederick M., 156–57
Schneider, Russell, 181, 236
Schuld, Fred, 151
Schulmerich, Wes, 251
Schultz, Barney, 97
Schumacher, Hal, 91, 249
Schwarz, Alan, 101n
Secory, Frank, 137
Seeley, Blossomm, 152
Seidel, Michael, 276
Seitzer, Kevin, 12
Selkirk, George, 201, 202
Sentell, Paul, 154
Severeid, Hank, 40
Sewell, Joe, 232–33
Shaefer, Germany, 148–49
Shannon, Mike, 175, 179, 224
Sharman, Bill, 168, 169
Shawkey, Bob, 43–44
Shea, Steve, 51
Sheehan, Joseph, 137
Sheehy, Pete, 118
Sheffield, Gary, xv–xvi, xvii
Shelton, Ron, 24, 25, 26
Sherry, Henry, 96
Shocker, Urban, 39, 41, 228
Shor, Toots, 212
Shorten, Chick, 39, 41
Shotton, Burt, 49, 181–82, 184
Showalter, Buck, 49
Sickels, John, 109–10
Siebert, Sonny, 130, 224–25
Sifakis, Carl, 4, 7
Silverman, Al, 200, 206

Silvers, Phil, 120
Simmons, Al, 244, 289–90
Simpson, Suitcase, 211
Singleton, Ken, 12, 13
Slaughter, Enos, 213
Sledge, E. B., 283
Smith, Bob, 234
Smith, Earl "Oil," 247–48
Smith, H. Allen, 10, 154, 156
Smith, Ira L., 2, 10, 154, 156
Smith, Lonnie, 12
Smith, Ozzie, 216
Smith, Red, 29–30, 170
Smith, Reggie, 57
Smith, Roy, 94
Smith, Zane, 53
Snelling, Dennis, 55–56, 246
Snider, Duke, 267
Snyder, Frank "Pancho," 89, 91
Snyder, Jerry, 9, 10
Soderholm, Eric, 93
Spahn, Warren, 15, 288, 296n, 297
Speaker, Tris, 27, 45, 46–47, 48, 144, 207, 226–27, 228–29
Spencer, Jim, 111
Spiers, Bill, xvi
Splittorff, Paul, 69–71
Stainback, Tuck, 294
Stallard, Tracy, 179–80
Stanky, Eddie, 282
Stargell, Willie, 306, 307 8
Staten, Vince, 251–52
Steinbrenner, George, 67–68
Stengel, Casey, 25, 32, 84, 128, 179, 180, 211, 212, 213–14, 263, 280
Stephens, Vern, 265
Stern, Bill, 189
Stevens, Bob, 141
Stewart, Walter, 16, 18
Stockton, J. Roy, 252
Stoneham, Horace, 261–62
Stottlemyre, Mel, 300–301
Stout, Glenn, 173, 231
Strawberry, Daryl, 299, 300, 301
Street, Gabby, 253

Stump, Al, 23–25, 26
Stupp, Don, 92
Sturm, Johnny, 202–3
Sukeforth, Clyde, 181–82
Sullivan, Frank, 237
Sutton, Don, 223
Swift, Bob, 129
Sylvester, Johnny, **232**

Tabor, Jim, 243
Tango, Tom "Tangotiger," 60
Tanner, Joe, 10
Tasby, Willie, 128
Tate, Scribbly, 119–20
Tatum, Ken, 115, 116, 117
Taylor, Jack, 221
Taylor, Joe, 175–77
Taylor, Sec, 302
Taylor, Tony, 140
Tebbetts, George "Birdie," 123–25, 265, 277
Temple, Johnny, 74, 260
Tener, John K., 158, 159, 160
Tepsic, Joe, 278–80, **279,** 281, 282–83
Terkel, Studs, 146
Terry, Bill, 89, 90, 91, 250, 253, 256
Terwilliger, Wayne, 169, 273
Thomas, Frank, 107
Thompson, Danny, 59, 61
Thompson, Dick, 30–31
Thompson, Hank, 261
Thorn, John, 27, 201
Tiant, Luis, xvi, 13
Timmermann, Bob, 167
Tinker, Joe, 4, 5
Tobin, Johnny, 39, 41
Torre, Joe, 209
Totten, Hal, 239
Tovar, Cesar, 60
Travis, Cecil, 244
Traynor, Pie, 284–85, 303–4
Trillo, Manny, 51
Trosky, Hal, 203
Trout, Dizzy, 129, 291
Trucks, Virgil, 211–13
Tudor, John, 216

Turley, Bob, 127, 212
Turner, Jim, 208–10
Tygiel, Jules, 29, 30

Uhle, George, 226–29

Valentine, Bobby, 115
Vance, Dazzy, 125, 150, 151, 270–72, **271**
Vander Meer, Johnny, 124, 282–83
Vaughan, Arky, 304
Veach, Bobby, 19
Veeck, Bill, 28–30, 33, 35–38, 114
Veeck, William, Sr., 163, 196–97
Vergez, Johnny, 253, 254
Vernon, Mickey, 126, 127, 129
Versailles, Zoilo, 173
Vidmer, Richards, 165
Vincent, Fay, 15, 17
Virgil, Ozzie, Jr., 53
Vosmik, Joe, 94, 95–98, 244

Waddell, Rube, 1, **2,** 3
Wagner, Honus, 153–57, **155,** 207
Walker, Dixie, 201, 278
Walsh, Christy, 228
Waner, Lloyd, 302
Waner, Paul, 302–5
Ward, Aaron, 39, 40
Ward, Arch, 198
Watson, Emmett, 97
Watt, Eddie, 286, 287
Wayman, Joseph M., 100*n*
Weaver, Earl, 13, 58, 59, 60, 220, 221
Wendler, Doc, 279
Werber, Billy, 302
West, Joe, 58
Westcott, Rich, 87, 117, 127, 187, 196, 292
Wheat, Zachary D., 99–104
Wheeler, Lonnie, 295
Whitaker, Tim, 305
White, Charlie, 175
White, Doc, 149
White, Sammy, 127, 234–35
Wiggen, Henry, xv
Wilborn, Ted, 93

Wiles, Tim, 2
Will, George, 14, 221
Willey, Carl, 297
Williams, Bernie, 80
Williams, Billy, 9, 10
Williams, Charlie, 52–54, 57
Williams, Dave, 31
Williams, Dick, 52, 73, 74
Williams, Frank, 217
Williams, Joe, 230, 231, 239, 282
Williams, Ted, 126–30, **127,** 180, 213, 236–37, 265, 273, 274, 275–77
Wills, Maury, 76–78, 288
Wilson, Arthur, 159
Wilson, Bill, 35
Wilson, Glenn, 51
Wilson, Hack, 232
Wilson, Mookie, 299, 300
Wilson, Willie, 12–13, 92
Wine, Bobby, 58

Winningham, Herm, 299
Woods, Pinky, 209
Wrigley, Phil, 258
Wulf, Steve, 30, 86, 142
Wynn, Jimmy, 306, 307–8

Yawkey, Tom, 130
York, Rudy, 123, 125, 144–45
Young, A. S. Doc, 28, 30
Young, Cy, 207
Young, Del, 187
Youngblood, Joel, 217
Youse, Walter, 276–77

Zachary, Tom, 249
Zarilla, Al, 263, 265
Zimmer, Don, 257, 258–59
Zinn, Guy, 171
Zook, Jacob, 88
Zullo, Allan, 5, 8, 129, 160, 234, 255, 278, 291